AFRICAN ORACLES

IN 10 MINUTES

Other Avon Books by
R. T. Kaser

I CHING IN 10 MINUTES
RUNES IN 10 MINUTES
TAROT IN 10 MINUTES

AFRICAN ORACLES
IN 10 MINUTES

R.T. KASER

AVON BOOKS ◆ NEW YORK

The font used in this book for shells, bones, and other figures was designed by the author using ALTSYS Fontographer V.4.0 for the Macintosh. Font "Odu" copyright © 1994, 1995 by R. T. Kaser.

The opening and closing quotes by Nigerian Diviner Maranoro Salako are from William Bascom's *16 Cowries,* Indiana University Press, 1980, 1993. Used with permission.

The quotes from Nigerian Diviner Awotunde Aworinde (for the Ifa figure Obara Meji) are from Judith Gleason's *A Recitation of Ifa, Oracle of the Yoruba,* Grossman, 1973. Used with permission.

AFRICAN ORACLES IN 10 MINUTES is an original publication of Avon Books. This work has never before appeared in book form.

AVON BOOKS
A division of
The Hearst Corporation
1350 Avenue of the Américas
New York, New York 10019

Copyright © 1996 by Richard T. Kaser
Published by arrangement with the author
Library of Congress Catalog Card Number: 95-30673
ISBN: 0-380-78132-8

Library of Congress Cataloging in Publication Data:

Kaser, R. T.
  African oracles in 10 minutes / R. T. Kaser.
    p.   cm.
Includes bibliographical references and index.
1. Divination—Nigeria.   2. Fortune-telling by shells.   3. Yoruba (African people)—Religion.   4. Santeria.   5. Cowries—Miscellanea.
I. Title.
BF1773.2.N6K37 1996   95-30673
133.3´248´08996—dc20   CIP

First Avon Books Trade Printing: January 1996

*To the Great Spirit of Philadelphia
and for Tory, Addie, and Turtle,
who sacrificed along with me*

It won't be long, it's not far away
You will see me in an abundance of blessings.

—NIGERIAN DIVINER MARANORO SALAKO,
WILLIAM BASCOM TRANSLATION

PREFACE

This book is based on the sacred traditions of the
Yoruba people of Western Nigeria
. . . systems that are kept alive today
in the religion of Santeria,
practiced by some 5 million African-Americans.

Dear Reader . . . you are about to get a glimpse of an oracle as mighty as the ancient I Ching . . . more mysterious than Viking Runes . . . and cloaked in even greater secrecy than Tarot. You are about to look at your life—and your world—in a whole new way, the way of a people as famous for their skills at commerce as in the arts . . . and notorious for their magic.

No, they were not the Babylonians . . . not the Romans . . . not the Greeks. No, they were not even the Egyptians . . . but you're getting warmer. These divination methods—these means of foretelling—do not come from a sacred place along the Nile, but from much farther to the south and west, on the other side of the River Niger, in what is today the largest state in Africa.

There—a thousand years ago—on a plateau underlaid with crystalline rock, with the Niger River to the north, the Osse to the east, the Ogun to the west, and the lagoons and gulf to the south—the City of Ife lay at the heart . . . of culture, commerce, and Yorubaland itself. It was here the inspired artists did their famous works in bronze. It was here where commerce flourished, and the powerful *Oba* chief lived . . . along with his highly talented diviners—men who could not only read the present and foretell the future, but could communicate directly with the Powers that Be .·. the African "White" Spirits . . . the "Orisha."

When, prior to their birth, these holy diviners had knelt in front of Olodumare, the sky god, to—like all Yoruba—request their destiny, they did not choose to be farmers. They did not choose to be hunters, warriors, or chiefs . . . not even successful merchants in the marketplace. But, rather, they chose the Road of Destiny. . . . They would be diviners. They would be messengers of the gods . . . they would be readers of the signs . . . they would be advisors to the kings . . . they would help everyone who came to them do the right thing . . . to achieve blessings, to avoid curses, and to, thus, fulfill completely their personal destiny.

So, when it came time for the other boys in the City of Ife to be circumcised, those whose souls had made this choice would also shave their heads and begin their arduous initiation into the secrets of Ifa—the art of determining the right thing to do at the right time.

As with most systems of foretelling, the tools these men used were simple—sixteen palm nuts and a tray of chalky, yellowish red camwood dust. To learn the destiny of a newborn child—or the fate of a would-be chief—the diviner would "beat" the 16 nuts by snatching away with one hand as many as he could, leaving only one or two remaining in his other palm.

"If one, two . . . if two, one." That is the rule he used. If <u>one</u> nut remained in his hand, he quickly pressed <u>two</u> fingertips into the dust of his divining board . . . **••** . If two nuts remained in his hand, he pressed a single fingertip . . . **•** . By repeating the process four times, he would wind up with one of 16 figures. . . .

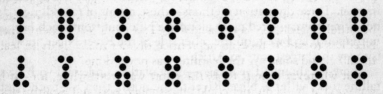

Then he would repeat the whole process again, drawing a second figure to the left of the first. . . .

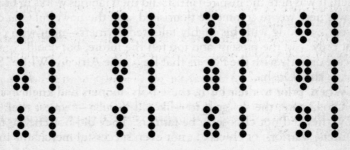

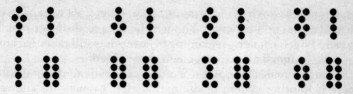

Though for the novice it's difficult to tell them apart at first, to the practiced eye of the diviner each figure was recognizable at a glance . . . and even better, each possible combination of figures (and there are 256) would be known to him immediately. Each of these pairs stood for something slightly different in his eye. And by interpreting these Odu "twins," he was able to divine.[1]

After casting the figure, the diviner's job was to start reciting from the Yoruba "scriptures" the hundreds and hundreds of verses of sheer poetry that are associated with that figure! And for each figure there might be the equivalent of 25 printed pages of text (or more!) for the diviner to recall . . . and then proceed to recite entirely from memory.

These scriptures, mostly in the form of lyrical parables similar to biblical passages, Greek myths, folktales, and Native American legends, number in the hundreds of thousands of lines. Though some have been recorded and painstakingly translated into hauntingly beautiful English, no one has managed to write all of them down. Needless to say, it took an apprentice diviner many years to learn them . . . and some say the learning was never done.

But whatever time it took, the effort was worthwhile, for—if he was good at it—a diviner could amass much personal wealth (since he got to keep the bulk of every sacrifice he prescribed) . . . have many wives . . . wear fine clothes . . . live in a big compound . . . and maybe (since he knew the secrets of avoiding the inevitable) even enjoy a long life.

To his people, the African Diviner was half doctor, half priest. And like any professional, he guarded his secrets closely, spoke in terms dif-

[1] As a brief aside, I would like to point out to readers that this highly sophisticated system has four times as many "answers" as a similar system the ancient Chinese made famous as the "I Ching." Compared to I Ching's tiny set of 64 answers, the methods you will be using here offer 256 possible outcomes to any question you ask!

ficult for the layman to understand, and in other ways wrapped a cloak of mystery around his craft. Though the art has died out rapidly in modern Nigeria, among remaining believers it is still taboo for any but the fully initiated male to dabble in these mysteries.

Though females, like all the Yoruba, can come to Ifa for guidance, there is another system of divination that women are allowed to practice themselves. Very similar to Ifa, it uses seashells in place of palm nuts.

According to Yoruba legend, the spirit of Oshun, the river goddess, stole the secrets of Ifa from her husband one day when he was away. Though he was none too pleased, once she had his secrets, there was no stopping her, and so her system of 16-shell divination became available for general use. Though not as highly regarded as Ifa, her system is more frequently practiced in modern-day Nigeria, Cuba, and the United States.

In her 16-shell divination, each of the Odu figures, from the male tradition, were assigned numbers 1 through 16. The figures themselves (⁞⁞ , ⁞) were dropped and the means of getting an answer was vastly simplified. Instead of the awkward manipulation of palm nuts (perhaps better suited for the size of the male hand), the women simply took a handful of shells (the currency they used in the marketplace) and cast them on a tray. By noting how many of these shells landed "heads" up, they got a quick count—1 through 16.[2] That was all they needed to begin reciting their own verses for the figures.

These verses, though fewer in number than in the male version, are still copious, and share many stories, themes, and motifs with the "original" Ifa scriptures. But—the truth to tell—no one knows which system actually came first.

What is known, however, is that the basic concept for casting the figures was actually not a Yoruba invention. As a form of *geo*mancy— foretelling the future from making marks upon the earth—the basic concept of using 16 figures for fortune-telling was borrowed from a system practiced earlier by the Arabs. With the spread of Islam through Africa about 1,200 years ago, *Raml*—the Arab's "science of sand"—came to West Africa where it was adopted by the Yoruba as an art form.

---

[2] Or, more correctly, 0 through 16. For in this system, it's also possible to "draw a blank."

Preface

Using the 16—some claim there were only 15—Islamic figures as a framework, the Yoruba wove their own traditions, beliefs, and customs around it until it became a monument to their own ideals, values, philosophy, and moral thinking. Even the "stripped-down" and simplified 16-shell divination system should be regarded as an impressive spiritual and intellectual accomplishment.

It was the seashell oracle that came to Cuba in the 1700s, where in order to preserve and hide the tradition from their captors, the descendants of the Yoruba substituted Catholic saints for the African spirits. And thus the ancient Yoruba traditions and rich heritage were preserved for us to appreciate today.

As is true of the traditions it is based upon, *African Oracles in 10 Minutes* offers two paths into these mysteries, a male path and a female path, with separate answers for each. But which road should you take?

To those who developed these systems, the answer was anatomically obvious. It was taboo for any female to practice the method of palm-nut divination used in Part II of this book. And though males could—if they were so inspired—practice the female method of seashell divination demonstrated in Part I of this book, it was considered an effeminate thing for them to do.

All cultural bias aside, I encourage readers, regardless of gender, to explore both parts of the book. By experiencing each method, you will gain insight into the other. So, to decide whether to begin on the male or the female path, turn right now to Reading #0 ("The Starting Point") on page 1, and let the oracle itself steer you in the appropriate direction. But if you'd like to know more about what you can expect, read on. . . .

African Oracles in 10 Minutes has been written to give you a feeling for each of these two marvelous oracles. It has also been carefully written to give you a glimpse into Yoruba spiritualism. It will not make you a high *Babalawo* priest of Santeria, nor will it substitute for a visit to one if Santeria is your religion. But for those who would nonetheless like to experience what these methods feel like, or if you'd like to try putting these systems to work in your life—well, then, this book is for you.

Whether you go down the male or the female path, you will encounter a series of "Readings." Each Reading will show you how to do something new with the divination "shells" or "nuts" that you will be instructed in making. (Nothing's very hard, and for those who love simplicity, a few coins will suffice as divination tools.)

Just as a Yoruba child is taken—soon after its birth—to the diviner to learn its destiny, you will use your shells or nuts to get a hint at yours. Just as a Yoruba woman might go to the oracle to learn what she must do to keep her business going, you will use the book to think about your work and money. Just as a Yoruba man might go to the oracle to learn how he might keep hold of his mate, so you, too, can learn the fate of any relationship and—better yet—how to prevent losing the one you love.

A traditional consultation with the shells or nuts would involve the identification of potential blessings and possible dangers. But the primary intent of these systems is to identify the specific measures that should be taken to assure that things turn out for the best. The Readings will walk you through the various techniques used by the male and female diviners.

<u>For Readers who are familiar with the other books in this series</u>. Unlike *Tarot in 10 Minutes . . . I Ching . . .* and *Runes . . .* you will want to work these Readings in order—beginning to end—and not skip around too much in the book until you have made an initial pass. Another difference you'll note is that all of the answers have been moved out of the Readings and placed at the end. You'll find the answers for Readings #1 through #9 (the female path) at the end of Reading #10. You'll find the answers for Readings #11 through #19 (the male path) at the end of Reading #20. This was not only necessary for space considerations, since both of these oracles have very large answer sets, but it was appropriate given the traditions surrounding these systems.

Every means of foretelling—be it Tarot, I Ching, Runes, or a business spreadsheet—has its own personality; and each of the books in this series has been written to "give you a feel" for each oracle's unique nature. In the case of *African Oracles in 10 Minutes*, the answers are written in a form and style that closely resemble the "verses" that are actually used in the seashell and palm-nut systems in Africa. Portions have also been modeled after the sorts of consultations you might get if you visited a practicing diviner in America.

Sometimes you will get a parable to think about. Sometimes you will get a "to-do" list. And usually—amidst your answer—you will be instructed about the particular figure that you have just cast or the method of divination you are using. Your answers will also—little by little, bit by bit—fill you in on Yoruba mythology and their system of belief, just as the original verses instruct as well as foretell.

In this respect, I must warn you up front the verses here are also as uninhibited as the originals, and you will find occasional references to body parts and bodily functions that are not generally discussed in Western "polite" society, except in a roundabout (or symbolic) way. Well, perhaps it's time we all had our Western sensitivies raised! As all people who are close to the land appreciate, there is something to be learned from everything. And the Yoruba have attached meaning to all aspects of their existence. *African Oracles in 10 Minutes* follows their lead.

One last word about the verses. Mostly I tried to capture the structure, the essence, and particularly the rhythm of the original verses. But I have not hestitated to use modern American figures of speech if the shoe fit.

As for methodology, the divination methods you will use in this book are based on authentic African or Santerian methods, as observed by scholars and reported by actual practitioners of these arts. But, an odd thing is, no two expert sources agree on virtually anything! There are great variations in the names that are used for each Odu figure . . . the sequence of the figures . . . and the methods for casting the nuts or shells to get an answer. Even in Nigeria, these systems vary from city to city, region to region, and diviner to diviner.

When in doubt, I used the systems and methods that are practiced in the City of Ife, which is regarded as the place where the oracles began. I owe a deep debt of appreciation for the highly regarded work of William Bascom, a scholar in African Studies at the University of Indiana, who spent a great deal of his life documenting, translating, and cataloguing the details of various versions of these oracles.

Though I have updated the systems—occasionally making minor adjustments to enhance performance—and though I have introduced some techniques of my own, all the fortune-telling methods presented in the Readings are based on authentic practices and principles. The Readings will not take you very long to do. In general they follow this format. . . .

You'll ask a question about something you want to know about. You'll cast your shells or nuts to get an Odu diagram or two. Then you'll turn to the appropriate Master Answer section—at the end of Reading #10 if you are doing Part I (The Female Path); and at the end of Reading #20 if you are doing Part II (The Male Path). At this point, the oracle will speak to you . . . much like a Yoruba diviner reciting his or her verses.

Your answer will either be in the form of a traditional verse or it will be in the form of condensed advice (more typical of Santeria divination in the United States). In crafting these answers, I have taken my inspiration from the fragments of the original verses published by scholars and practitioners to date. I have done my best to capture the essence, the flavor, and the intent of these marvelous oracles, as well as give you a feeling for the rich traditions surrounding them.

But I have also used my own intuition and experience with other oracles to create a contemporary, workable version of these Yoruba tools that will not only fit between the covers of a single book but will speak to modern readers of all nationalities and roots. As we are part and parcel of the same human race, there is no reason why we should not all share in these cultural riches of the Yoruba People . . . there is no reason why we should not all praise the diviners of Africa for their perception of what makes things tick.

Though no single book could come close to duplicating the thousands of verses of the two divination systems covered here, I can only pray that I have worked long enough, sacrificed hard enough, and opened myself completely enough to these mysteries to have done them poetic justice.

One thing is for sure: *African Oracles in 10 Minutes* will give you a great deal to work with . . . and perhaps as important, play with. For even in Africa, the first step in learning these oracles is to handle them. The young woman being initiated into the shells is given a practice set to experiment with. The young man is given an unconsecrated set of palm nuts to fool around with. I suggest you consider this book to be your practice set . . . and go from there. *Ashe*, my friend. "So be it."[3]

> —R. T. Kaser
> Good Friday, 1995
> Day of the Supreme Sacrifice
> Under the Egg Moon of April
> All we can ever do is plant seeds

---

[3] "*Ashe*," which is regarded as spiritual energy to the Yoruba, is also a word that is used by them at the close of a prayer. As such, it literally means "make it so" or "so be it," which—coincidentally enough—is the same thing that our word "Amen" means.

CONTENTS

Contents

Contents

THE STARTING POINT

Reading #0

WHERE SHALL I BEGIN?
(Which Way Should I Go?)

Consistent with the beliefs of the African peoples who inspired it, this book offers two "routes" for discovering and achieving your personal destiny . . . one way for women, and another way for men.

By tradition, the path this book calls the **White Cotton Road** uses the seashell divination methods practiced by women . . . or men who are attracted to these mysteries.

The path this book calls the **Melon Seed Road** uses palm-nut methods that in Africa are restricted to men, but here are equally open to women who wish to learn these secrets.

In your effort to achieve spiritual balance, each reader (regardless of gender, gender bias, or gender preference) is encouraged to venture down both the "male" and "female" paths, starting on whichever road calls your name at this moment.

If you would like to let the oracle help you decide which way to go, read on. . . .

TOOLS

To consult the oracle, you need nothing more than a coin, medallion, stone—or any small, flat object that can be thought of as having "heads" and "tails" sides.

HOW TO

 Dig out your coin—old British shillings are traditional, but a U.S. quarter will do just fine. (Or make a stone with a single dot on one side and two dots on the reverse).

Ask, **Which road do I follow?** Then toss the coin on the floor and note which way it has landed.

Jot down a single dot (•) if it lands HEADS UP, and jot down a double dot (••), if it lands HEADS DOWN.

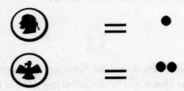

Repeat this procedure three more times, each time noting how your coin has landed. Write each new set of single or double marks <u>below</u> the dots you wrote before.

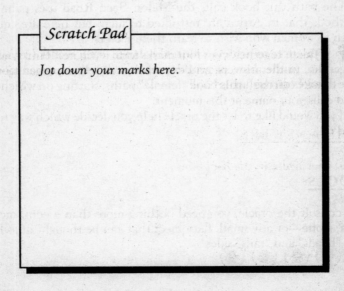

Scratch Pad

Jot down your marks here.

For example, if you throw heads on your first throw and tails on your second, at this point your marks will look like this:

If on the third throw you cast another tails, your marks will now look like this:

And if on the fourth throw you cast heads, your finished "figure" will look like this.

 Taken together, your four marks form a "figure." Find your figure in the answers, and the oracle will tell you what route to take through this book.

THE ANSWERS

Find your figure in the list below:

Four heads

Male

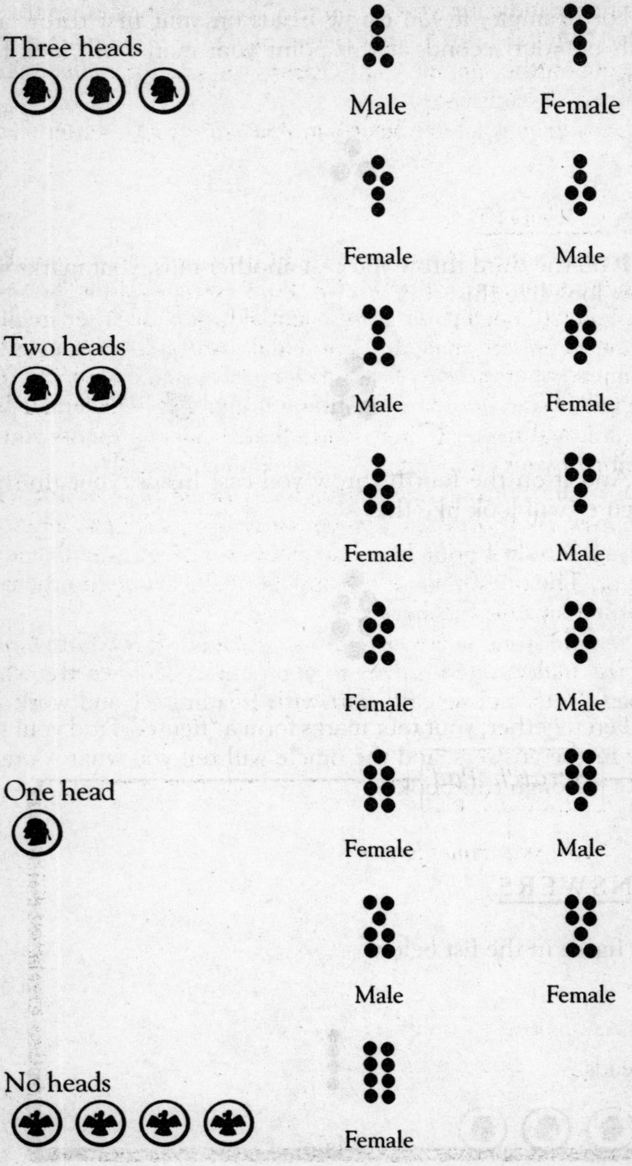

Three heads

Male   Female

Female   Male

Two heads

Male   Female

Female   Male

Female   Male

One head

Female   Male

Male   Female

No heads

Female

If your figure indicates you are on the "male" path, turn to the section called "Melon Seed Road" (Reading #11). If your figure indicates you are on the "female" path, turn to the section called "White Cotton Road" (Reading #1).

Either way, may you go in health and peace. *Ashe*, my friend . . . so be it.

EXTRA CREDIT

Feel it in your bones? Another authentically African way to determine which road to take through this book is to cast your "bones" to find out. You will need three stones, actual bones, or other small objects, one to represent male, one for female, and one for yourself.

Pick objects that are easy symbols for you to remember. By tradition, the male bone would be an oblong stone: ● . The female bone would be an oval stone: ◯ . And the bone that represents you can be anything of your choosing, say a speckled stone: ◉ .

To use your "bones," just gather your three objects into your cupped hands. Blow on them once or twice for good luck. Then ask: **Which way should I go?** Uncup your hands and let the objects fall to the floor. The one (male or female) that falls nearest to the stone that represents you is the answer.

If the female stone is closer to yours, go down the White Cotton Road. If the male stone is closer to your stone, go down the Melon Seed Road. If it's a close call, start with Reading #1 and work your

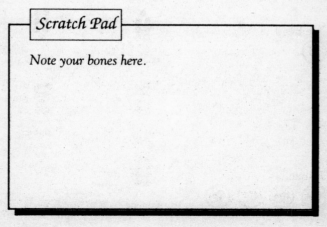

Scratch Pad

Note your bones here.

way down both paths in turn. Or else, toss again. *Ashe*, my friend. The choice is always yours. And so be it.

EXTRA, EXTRA CREDIT!

The scientific method. To select your path in a more "rational" way, review the Contents to see which of the two paths covers the subjects you are most interested in today. Or, to see which method of divination appeals more to you, review Reading #9, which summarizes the seashell casting method and bone oracles used on the White Cotton Road—Part I of this book. Then review Reading #19, which summarizes the palm-nut divination methods used on the Melon Seed Road—Part II of this book. Go down the path that you find more intriguing—shells (Readings #1 through #9) or nuts (Readings #11 to #19). And go in peace.

Go on down your road whenever you are ready to continue.

PART I

The White Cotton Road (The Female Path)

Good fortune out of Eshu's kingdom
walks ponderously northwest to Ijero;
avoiding pestilence,
he takes the slow white-cotton road

— NIGERIAN DIVINER AWOTUNDE AWORINDE
RECITATION ON THE FIGURE OBARA MEJI
JUDITH GLEASON TRANSLATION, 1973

THE READINGS

Reading #1

WHY AM I HERE?
(Who Is My Guardian?)

Welcome to the slow White Cotton Road, the way of the female diviner.... Here we take things little by little, step by step, and nice and easy. In this Reading, you will start at the very beginning of your initiation to the female mysteries.

TOOLS

In West Africa, it is the women who rule the business world, control the marketplace, and know how to count.[1] To fortune-tell like a woman, you must—therefore—first learn to count like one! But not to worry. It's all in the wrist. Count along with me, first on your left hand....

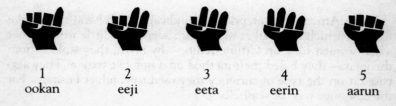

1	2	3	4	5
ookan	eeji	eeta	eerin	aarun

---

[1] **FACT:** "West African market women control much of the transport and trades in textiles, food, and hardware in Ghana and Nigeria." *Africa Counts—Number and Pattern in African Culture,* by Claudia Zaslavsky, Chicago Review Press: Lawrence Hill Books, 1973, p. 224.

9

Now put the left hand away and switch to the right. . . .

6	7	8	9	10
eefa	eeje	eejo	eesan	eewaa

Now with both hands . . .

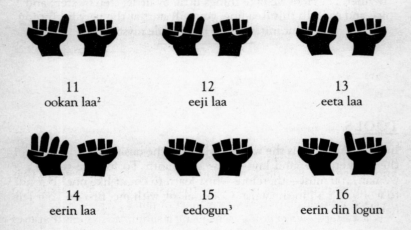

11	12	13
ookan laa[2]	eeji laa	eeta laa

14	15	16
eerin laa	eedogun[3]	eerin din logun

In the African market, prices are indicated with hand signals like these, at which the market women are adept. It is little wonder that when women took up fortune-telling—by myth, they stole it from the men!—they based their method on a number system. They also based it on the type of currency they used to conduct business. For them, money was . . . seashells.

---

[2] *Ookan laa*, literally means "one plus 10". . . .
[3] *Eedogun* means "twenty minus five." It can also be indicated by extending the arm up to the forehead.

BACKGROUND

The method of African fortune-telling you will be learning is called *erindinlogun*, since it involves the throwing and counting of "16"—or in African terms, "eerin din logun"—objects. In the traditional system, seashells are used, specifically the *cowry*, which look like this:

For centuries cowry shells were used as money in the area that is now Nigeria. Since the local word for cowry is *owo*, this method of divination is also known as *owo erindinlogun*[4]—which literally means "twenty minus four cowries"—or, in more familiar terms, "16 shells."

HOW TO

In practice, the fortune-teller throws her 16 shells onto a mat and counts up the number of shells that have landed faceup. By tradition, a number of symbols, ideas, concepts, and myths are associated with each of these numbers. The fortune-teller draws from her personal knowledge of the symbols in reading the meaning of the shells that have fallen upright. But to see how the system works, all you need to do is use a single coin from your pocket or purse.

For starters—we're going to be using a simplified system that uses just one coin or one shell for the consultation. And to get things rolling, let's see if the oracle can tell us why you have come here today. . . .

 Just take your coin in your hand and whisper your question to it. Any of these will work: **Why am I here?** What have I come for? **What is my situation?** What is my problem? **Who will guide me?**

---

[4] Or more properly *owo merindinlogun*, the *m* being inserted to ease pronunciation.

Toss your coin on the ground and note whether it has fallen heads (H) or tails (T). . . .

= Heads   = Tails

If heads, jot down the letter *H* on the Scratch Pad; if tails, jot down a *T*.

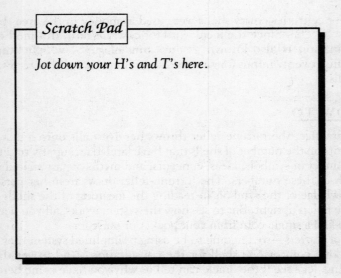

Scratch Pad

Jot down your H's and T's here.

Now, gather up your coin, whisper your question again, and toss your coin on the ground, again noting how it has landed (**H**eads or **T**ails).

If **H**eads, jot down an *H* to the right of the letter you wrote before. If tails, jot down a *T*. For example, *HT* would indicate that on the first throw you got heads and on the second throw you got tails.

Repeat this process twice more, each time noting how your coin has fallen and writing its letter next to the one for the preceding cast of the coin.

　　Your result will be one of 16 possible combinations, each of which can be thought of as a "figure" in this divination system.

 Look up your combination in this Reading's Answer section and follow the instructions for finding your answer.

THE ANSWERS

Using the combination you have just thrown, find your figure in this list. . . .

Your combination . . .		*Your figure . . .*	
HHHH	🔔🔔🔔🔔	Ogbe	8
HHHT	🔔🔔🔔✤	Ogunda	3
HHTH	🔔🔔✤🔔	Irete	16
HTHH	🔔✤🔔🔔	Otura	15
THHH	✤🔔🔔🔔	Osa	9
HHTT	🔔🔔✤✤	Irosun	4
HTHT	🔔✤🔔✤	Oshe	5
HTTH	🔔✤✤🔔	Odi	7
THHT	✤🔔🔔✤	Iwori	12
THTH	✤🔔✤🔔	Ofun	10

13

TTHH	✹✹♠✹	Owonrin	11
HTTT	♠✹✹✹	Obara	6
THTT	✹♠✹✹	Ika	13
TTHT	✹✹♠✹	Oturupon	14
TTTH	✹✹✹♠	Okanran	1
TTTT	✹✹✹✹	Oyeku	2

Now look up your figure (by number or name) in Part I's Master Answer section (starting on page 75). Once you find your figure, read the section of text called "For SPIRITUAL questions."

This portion of the text will not only tell you why you have come here today, but it will tell you which Roman Catholic saint is associated with this figure. You may think of this spiritual entity as your companion, mentor, or guardian as you work your way through the book.

After you have read the Spiritual section of the text, you are welcome to read the Work, Love, Money, and Strategy sections too. In perfect keeping with the way this African oracle works, you may find that one of these other answers particularly clicks with you tonight.

EXTRA CREDIT

To use shells . . . If you would like to conduct this Reading in the most authentic African way, you will need a cowry shell instead of a coin. Just like a coin, your cowry will have two sides (heads and tails). . . .

🐚 = Heads   🐚 = Tails

Tips on locating and preparing cowry shells will come in Reading #2. But to get started, you can use any old shell you have lying around, scallop, cone, or snail. . . .

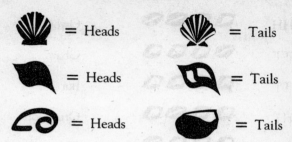

= Heads		= Tails
= Heads		= Tails
= Heads		= Tails

Once you've rounded up a shell and determined which side is heads and which is tails, just follow the instructions in this Reading's How To section, substituting your shell for the coin. Ask your question. Toss your shell four times, noting each time how it lands. Then look up your figure. . . .

Your combination . . .		Your figure . . .	
HHHH		Ogbe	8
HHHT		Ogunda	3
HHTH		Irete	16
HTHH		Otura	15
THHH		Osa	9
HHTT		Irosun	4
HTHT		Oshe	5
HTTH		Odi	7
THHT		Iwori	12
THTH		Ofun	10

15

TTHH	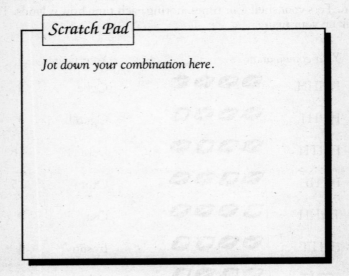	Owonrin	11
HTTT		Obara	6
THTT		Ika	13
TTHT		Oturupon	14
TTTH		Okanran	1
TTTT		Oyeku	2

Scratch Pad

Jot down your combination here.

Consult Part I's Master Answer section for your figure. As before, read the text for Spiritual questions.

EXTRA, EXTRA CREDIT!

To cast all four at once. The method used in this Reading is based on an ancient and revered form of simple divination that uses four shells at once to determine the figure. To try it out, use four coins or four shells, ask your question, and throw them all at once. After you have thrown them, line them up from left to right and read them as heads or tails—all four in a row. The only trick to this is figuring out which shell is first, second, third, fourth, in the combination. If they all fall in a heap, you'll have to go on your instincts to line them up in the right order. I believe you cannot do it wrong. Just line them up using your native intuition.

Go on to the next Reading whenever you are ready to continue.

Reading #2

WHAT IS MY SIGN?
(Where Is My Destiny?)

In this Reading, you will get your African "horoscope." Just as an African child born to this tradition will be taken soon after its birth to the diviner to learn its destiny, so you shall have the chance to learn how you can control yours.

TOOLS

Every fortune-teller requires her tools of the trade. For those who practice *erindinlogun*, a set of 16 shells provides the basic equipment. But any16 *things* will work just as well, provided these *things* are relatively small, flat objects, capable of being thought of as having two sides—like a coin—heads and tails.

Though cowry shells themselves are the most authentic way to consult this oracle, they are not always easy to find.[1] Since cowries are traditionally money in Africa, you can get started with something as simple as 16 coins. Or you could use 16 buttons or beads.[2] (Just mark an X on one side so you will know which side is "heads.")

---

[1] I had luck at African boutiques in large cities (including the Out of Africa chain where cowry belts and bracelets were readily available in all price ranges), boardwalk gift shops (where the cowries were laced into inexpensive plant hangers), and in clothing stores (!) where cowries were sewn into women's swimwear, designer tops, and belts (but it would be relatively expensive to acquire them this way). It's said that they can also be had at special herb shops, often called botanicas, which are generally located in large cities. Why not start with one of the other items suggested and—I'll just bet—you'll come across some cowries fairly soon.

[2] You can find great wooden beads at your local arts and craft store. I also had luck in the jewelry department of thrift stores, or you might have an old set of beads in your jewelry box that would be perfect. If you don't have any beads, buttons also will work, as will plain old dried soup beans. Use a felt-tip marker and place an X on one side of each bead you'll be using.

If you'll be using coins, buttons, or beads, you can skip ahead now to the How To section. But if you'll be using cowries, you may first have to "prepare" them. Here's how. . . .

Most cowries that are strung into bracelets, tied to belts, or sewn into garments are all ready to go. You can tell this because the back-side hump has been removed. The prepared shells look like this. . . .

Topside (heads)
features "lips" with
jagged teeth. This
is known as the "mouth"
of the cowry.

Underside (tails)
reveals an internal
spiral. This is known
as the "stomach"
of the cowry.

If you turn over an "unprepared" shell, you will <u>not</u> be able to see the internal spiral, but rather you will see a rounded hump, which is the way the shell looks in its natural state. For accurate divination, you will have to remove this hump. But not to fear! It's really easy!

To prepare your cowry shells, just place the shell on a cutting board, mouth-side up. Insert an ice pick or the tip of a steak knife between the lips and into the "mouth" of the cowry—close to the corner of the mouth. Gently tap the handle of the pick with your hand so that it pokes a small hole in the underside. Then turn the shell over and insert the blade of your knife into the hole you have made. Wiggle the knife a bit, and the hump will just pop off, revealing the internal spiral that forms the cowry's stomach. It takes a gentle touch, which you should get the hang of quickly. You will need to prepare 16 shells in this way for your initial divination set. In all, you'll need 18 to 20. Buy a few extra, just in case.

BACKGROUND

In a traditional consultation of the shells, the fortune-teller will cast the shells and count up the number that have landed faceup. She will then start reciting what she knows by heart for the particular number of shells—or *figure*—that has turned up.

In the case of the child going to learn its destiny, the figure that turns up can be thought of as one of our Zodiac signs. As such, it may reveal the occupation the child should prepare for, the obstacles that might have to be faced, the things that should be avoided, and the things that should be encouraged. Each sign is also associated with one of the African spirit gods of ancient legend. In this Reading, you will have the opportunity to learn how you fit into this scheme of things.

HOW TO

 Round up your 16 *things* or make your set of divination shells, as described in the Tools section.

 Say a prayer, praising your God or invoking your patron saint (from Reading #1).

 Gather your coins, buttons, beads, or shells into the palms of your hands, blow on them for good luck—and in order to give them the breath they need to "talk" with their mouths.

 Ask your question. **What is my destiny?** Where does this road lead me? **What is my horoscope?** What is my sign? **What do I need to know?** in general? right now? **What is my African spirit?**

If you wish, you may whisper your question to the shells, coins, or beads in your hands, which is the traditional way. Or you can simply state your question silently (which is also traditional).

 With your question in mind, kneel down on the floor, open your hands, and let the coins, beads, or cowries drop to the floor. Once they have fallen, count up the number of shells that have fallen mouth side up, or the number of heads on the coins, or the number of X's that show on your beads or buttons.

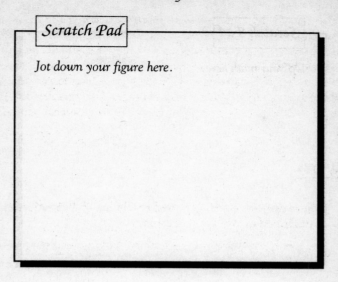

THE ANSWERS

Look up your figure in Part I's Master Answer section. Read the sections of the text called "For DESTINY readings."

EXTRA CREDIT

To conduct this Reading using your birth date. If you don't have your shells yet—or if you regard destiny as too big a thing to determine with one "throw of the dice"—here's an alternative way to arrive at your sign. Just jot down your birthday (month, day, and year) on the Scratch Pad—as if you were going to add them up—like this. . . .

8	Month
29	Day
<u>1952</u>	Year

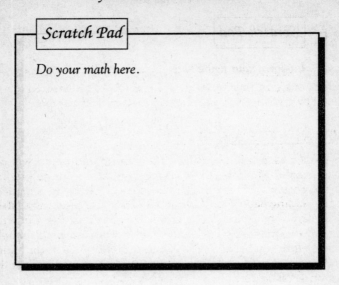

> **Scratch Pad**
>
> *Do your math here.*

Now, add them up. . . .

$$
\begin{array}{r}
+ \quad 8 \\
+ \quad 29 \\
+ \quad \underline{1952} \\
= \quad 1989
\end{array}
$$

Then divide the total by 16. . . .

$$
\begin{array}{r}
124 \\
16)\overline{1989} \\
\underline{16} \\
38 \\
\underline{32} \\
69 \\
\underline{64} \\
5 \quad \leftarrow \textbf{Your Figure}
\end{array}
$$

Your answer is the "remainder" at the end. This is your horoscope sign. Look up this figure (1-15) in Part I's Master Answer section. If you should wind up with a zero at the end (which means that your birth date has been evenly divisible by 16), then 16—not 0—is your figure.

Though this method is not actually practiced in Africa, it uses numbers in a way that is not unlike the very sophisticated math developed by the Nigerian people who invented this oracle.[3]

EXTRA, EXTRA CREDIT!

The money of *erindinlogun*. The authentic divination sets of the Cuban people, who practice a similar form of fortune-telling called *diloggun*, consist of 21 shells. The five "extra" shells are set aside before the reading begins and do not influence the counting of the answer in any way. If you'd like to use the shells in the Cuban way, string five extra shells (beads or buttons) into a little bundle or strand. Before you begin your consultations, just place this bunch in front of you, as a token offering to your spirit guides. African diviners often set aside one or two shells as *erindinlogun's* money.

Go on to the next Reading whenever you are ready to continue.

---

[3] The Yoruba of Nigeria use a counting method that involves addition, subtraction, and multiplication to express sums. The expression *erindinlogun*—the name of the fortune-telling system we are using—literally means "twenty minus four" cowries. Larger numbers are expressed as, for example, "400 times 2 minus 6" for 794. The method used here borrows from the Yoruba's high regard for the number 16 (or as they would say, "20 minus 4") and their sophisticated use of advanced mathematics in the form of division (which involves both multiplication and subtraction) to create this method for "computing" your horoscope. It came to the author in a dream. All comments on its performance are welcome—just write the publisher.

Reading #3

How Is My Love Life?
(Yes, No, or Maybe So-So?)

In this Reading, you'll start to ask the oracle specific and practical questions, starting with your love life. You'll also be able to use this Reading to answer any yes/no question on your mind tonight.

TOOLS

You don't need to learn anything new to ask love questions. This Reading will use the same shells (coins or beads) you rounded up for Reading #2 and the same shell-casting technique you got acquainted with there.

BACKGROUND

When you cast your 16 shells, coins, or beads and count the number of objects that have fallen faceup, the result is a "figure" between 0 and 16. This figure is known as an *Odu*. Each Odu has a number and a name:

The Odu Figures

Name	Number
Okanran	1
Oyeku	2
Ogunda	3
Irosun	4
Oshe	5
Obara	6

Odi	7
Ogbe	8
Osa	9
Ofun	10
Owonrin	11
Iwori	12
Ika	13
Oturupon	14
Otura	15
Irete	16
Opira	0

In this book, you will use the number to look up your figure in the answers. But an African diviner would also call out the figure by its name.

HOW TO

 Get out the 16 shells, coins, or beads you made in Reading #2.

 Say a prayer, praising your God, invoking your patron saint (from Reading #1), or calling up your African spirit guide (from Reading #2).

 Gather your coins, buttons, beads, or shells into the palms of your hands, blow on them for good luck, and . . .

 Whisper your question. **How is my love life?** sex life? married life? celibate life? **How is my relationship going with _____?** How can we make things go better? **Is there any future in this love affair?** If we go through with it, what then? **What is <u>our</u> destiny?** Or looking back, **What was the meaning of my relationship with _____?**

Part your hands and let the shells fall to the ground. Count up the number that have fallen mouth side (head side or X side) up.

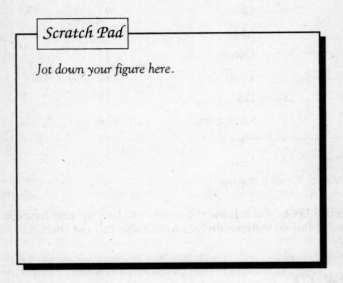

Scratch Pad

Jot down your figure here.

THE ANSWERS

Look up your Odu figure in Part I's Master Answer section, starting on page 75. Read the text in the section called "For LOVE questions." Then, go on and do the Extra Credit section. . . .

EXTRA CREDIT

To find out what you really wanted to know. At this point in the Reading it is absolutely traditional to ask specific yes/no questions to clarify the answer you have just received. The technique involves throwing your shells once or twice more for each yes/no question you want to ask.

Extra Credit Tools. For yes/no questioning, you'll need to know another fact. Not all Odu figures are equal—and this is the key to determining yes/no answers.

Some of the figures are called *Major Odu* and are thought of as being of higher strength, positive (+) or negative (−). Other figures are regarded as *Minor Odu* and are considered to be of lesser strength.

Major Odu	(+)	1, 2, 3, 4, 8, 10, 12
	(−)	13, 14, 15, 16 and 0
Minor Odu		5, 6, 7, 9, and 11

Distinguishing between the Major and Minor Odu is the first step in learning how to get reliable answers to yes/no questions of all kinds.

Extra Credit Background. In a traditional *erindinlogun* consultation, after the initial throw of the shells, the questioner has the opportunity to ask specific yes/no questions. These questions are decided by additional throws of the shells.

The actual technique for interpreting these subsequent throws is quite complex. In this Reading, we'll be using a simplified method. In subsequent Readings you'll learn more advanced techniques.

Extra Credit How To. First, come up with your question. It can be anything that's on your mind or anything related to the figure you have just cast. . . . So, does Jo love me more than anyone else? Will Randy and I make mad, passionate love? Will it be the best sex ever? Will we wake up with a new respect for one another? Will we love each other for a long, long time? Will we share a happy home together? Will there be peace in our family? Will we lead the good life? You get the drift. . . . Whatever you ask, just make sure you express it as favorably as possible. Don't predict your own negative conclusions! Always ask so that a "yes" answer grants the thing you wish to happen.

With your question in mind, gather your shells, blow on them, whisper your question, and cast them onto the floor.

Scratch Pad

Jot down your Odu figures here.

Extra Credit Answers. Based on the number of shells that have fallen mouth up (the number of coins heads up; or the number of beads X up), here's how to read your results. . . .

1, 2, 3, 4, 8, 10, or 12	**YES**
13, 14, 15, 16, or 0	**NO**[1]
5, 6, 7, 9, or 11	**CAST AGAIN**

If you have to "cast again," here's how to interpret your second toss of the shells:

1, 2, 3, 4, 8, 10, or 12	**NO**
13, 14, 15, 16, or 0	**NO COMMENT**
5, 6, 7, 9, or 11	**YES**

---

[1] To add an additional African touch here, substitute "NO COMMENT" for "NO." The oracle will then speak in the more indirect way of the Yoruba. Instead of answering you with a direct "NO," the oracle will be inclined to say "NO COMMENT," unless—of course—the answer is actually "YES."

EXTRA, EXTRA CREDIT!

Yes/No questions with an African-American twist. A similar method of asking yes/no questions is practiced by African descendants in North America as part of their "worship of the saints," a religion known as Santeria. To put a Santerian twist on this simplified yes/no method, here's how to interpret your answers. . . .

Just gather up the shells between the palms of your hands, tell them that you are going to use the Santerian method now,[2] whisper your yes/no question, and let your shells tumble to the ground. Count up the number of mouths, and consult this table. . . .

1, 2, 3, 4, 8, 10, or 12	**NO**
13, 14, 15, 16, or 0	**YES**
5, 6, 7, 9, or 11	**CAST AGAIN**

If you need to cast again, do so now. Count up your shells for the second throw and consult this table. . . .

1, 2, 3, 4, 8, 10, or 12	**YES**
13, 14, 15, 16, or 0	**NO**
5, 6, 7, 9, or 11	**YES** *(if the second number is lower than or equal to the first)*
5, 6, 7, 9, or 11	**NO** *(if the second number is higher than the first)*

[2] You will note that the answers in this Santerian-based system are almost exactly opposite the African method described in the Extra Credit section—which is why you will want to tell your shells which system you are planning to use before you ask a question.

For example, if you cast a 6 on the first throw and a 7 on the second throw, the answer will be NO. If you cast a 6 on the first throw and a 5 on the second, the answer will be YES. If you cast a 6 on both throws, the answer will also be YES.

Go on to the next Reading whenever you are ready to continue.

Reading #4

How Can I Get Ahead?
(Do the Signs Look Good or Bad?)

In this Reading, you will continue to ask the oracle specific
questions, this time about your financial or employment situation.
The Reading will also enhance your skills as an African diviner by
showing you a special trick this oracle performs in helping you
decide between any two things.

TOOLS

To find out about your financial prospects, all you need are your 16
shells (from Readings #2 and #3). Just as before, you'll ask your question, cast your shells, and count up the number of shells (coins or
beads) that have landed mouth side up (or heads). This number is
the Odu figure you have cast.

Once you have looked up your figure in the "back of the book,"
you can go on to get additional information by working the Extra
Credit section.

HOW TO

 Get out your 16 shells, coins, or beads (see Reading #2).

 Say a prayer, praising your God, invoking your patron saint, or
calling upon your African spirit guide.

 Gather your coins, buttons, beads, or shells into the palms of
your hands, and blow on them to give them life.

 Whisper your question: **How can I get ahead?** financially?
job-wise? **How will my money go this year?** (And will I get
to hang on to some of it?) **How can I get myself out of the**

red? into a better financial situation? a better job? **What will happen if I take this offer?** position? risk? investment opportunity? **Did I make the right financial decision?**

 Open your hands and let the shells fall to the ground. Count up the number that have fallen mouth side up (or the number of coins heads up, or the number of beads X side up).

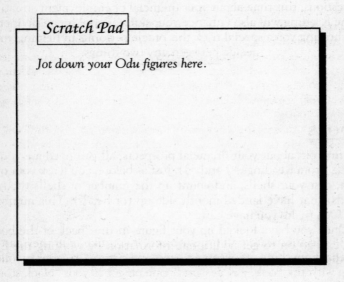

Scratch Pad

Jot down your Odu figures here.

THE ANSWERS

Look up your figure in Part I's Master Answer section, starting on page 75. If your question was more about money than work, consult the section of the text called "For MONEY questions." If it was more about work than money, consult "For WORK questions."

Your answer will speak to you in a parable that you must think about. Look for the line that tugs at your heart. To learn whether the things your answer discussed will come easily or only with help, work the Extra Credit section next.

EXTRA CREDIT

To let your bones do the choosing . . . In Reading #3's Extra Credit section you learned how to get the oracle to choose between "yes" and "no" responses by using your 16 shells and a simplified casting method. Now it's time to learn how it's really done . . . with the aid of divination "bones." The method you will use here can help you decide between any two choices, be they as simple as "yes" or "no" . . . or as specific and complex as you want to define them. To try it out, we'll be using a traditional line of questioning.

Extra Credit Tools. In addition to her 16 cowry shells, the African fortune-teller (as well as her Santerian counterpart in North America) uses other objects to amplify and interpret the message. A variety of ordinary objects are used, including wishbones, additional shells, pebbles, bark, and other purely organic and natural objects. Collectively these are known as Igbo, but for simplicity's sake, we'll call them "bones."

For our purposes, the most important of these Igbo "bones" will be a black pebble (to symbolize the vast, dark, and unknowable universe) and a white shell (to represent the endless sound of the sea and the eternal voice of the gods). . . .

You can substitute two other objects if you like, and they can be just about anything—how about a nut and a stick? In order to follow along with the book, just designate one object as your "black stone" and the other as your "white shell."

Extra Credit Background. Once the African diviner has finished casting the 16 cowries and has noted the outcome (one to 16 shells with their mouths up), she needs to determine whether the outcome will come easily or only with help. For this she uses two of her Igbo bones.

In a traditional consultation, the African diviner hands these two objects to the questioner, who puts one (at his or her discretion and without letting the fortune-teller see) into the left hand and the other into the right hand. (When reading for yourself, you'd just place one object to your left side, one object to your right.) The diviner then casts her 16 cowries again and notes whether the shells indicate that the correct answer is revealed by the object in the questioner's left hand or right hand.

It is only when the questioner reveals the contents of that hand that the outcome is known. If the black stone turns out to be in the designated hand, the situation is said to involve an obstacle that, with some difficulty, can be overcome. However, if the white shell turns out to be in the hand the oracle has revealed, the situation is said to come with a blessing—or easily. In some cases, the oracle declines to answer, in which case the signs are said to be indefinite or mixed, and the result will come only with help.

Let's try it out. . . .

Extra Credit How To. To learn how easily your answer will be attained, you will need your 16 cowries, plus an additional white shell and a black stone. Pick up the black stone, breathe on it, and place it to one side or the other (your left or your right—it's your choice). Then pick up the white shell, breathe on it, and place it on the other side.

Now gather up your shells, breathe on them, and whisper your question: **Are these signs positive or negative?** easy or hard to achieve? **What is the emphasis on?** the problem or the solution? the pro or the con? **Do I need some help on this one?**

Cast your shells and count up the number that have fallen mouth up.

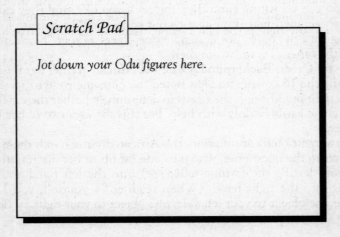

Scratch Pad

Jot down your Odu figures here.

Extra Credit Answers. What you need to do at this point is determine which object the oracle has chosen for you. Using a tradition shared by the Nigerian ancestors as well as their American descendants, here's how to read your results. . . .

Major (+)	Major (-)	Minor
1	13	5
2	14	6
3	15	7
4	16	9
8	0	11
10		
12		
Right Hand	**Left Hand[1]**	**Throw Again**

If you cast a 1, 2, 3, 4, 8, 10, or 12, the object on the <u>right</u>-hand side is indicated. If the object you placed on the right is the shell, the auspices are quite positive—the going will be easy. If the object you placed to the right is the black stone, there are some negative influences to challenge you—the going will be difficult.

If you cast a 13, 14, 15, 16, or 0, the object on the <u>left</u>-hand side is indicated. If that object is the shell, the auspices are positive—the going will be easy. If the object on the left is the black stone, there are things to overcome—the going will be difficult.

---

[1] The numbers **13, 14, 15, 16, 0 = Left Hand.** Some authorities on African divination believe that casting a 13, 14, 15, 16, or 0 at this point should actually be interpreted as "No Comment." You are welcome to try it that way—but I must warn you the odds are that the left hand will hardly ever be chosen. The adjustment I have made at this point results in a system that retains much of the original charm but chooses more evenly between the left and right hands. For more detail on how the two methods perform, see Appendix A.

If you cast a 5, 6, 7, 9, or 11, you need to throw again. Here's what your answer will be, based on the number that comes up in your next throw of the shells:

1	13	5
2	14	6
3	15	7
4	16	9
8	0	11
10		
12		
Left Hand	**No Comment**	**Right Hand**

If the left or the right hand is indicated at this point, your answer will be revealed by the "meaning" of the object that you placed on that side of you. If it is the black stone, the auspices are not favorable at this time—things will progress only with difficulty. If it is the white shell, your prospects are good—things should come easily.

If "no comment" is indicated, it means that things are still undecided. They could go either way, and you'll need some help with this.

EXTRA, EXTRA CREDIT!

Advanced Yes/No questioning. In Reading #3's Extra Credit section you learned how to ask yes/no questions in a simplified way. But at this point, you now have everything you need to ask yes/no questions in the traditional way. Here's how it works. . . .

Place your black stone in front of you to one side or the other (left or right). Place your white shell on the other side. Then gather your 16 cowries (16 coins or 16 beads) into your hands, and whisper your question. Any yes/no question is okay. Try to phrase it as positively as you can. (**Will I marry this year? Will I find work this week? Will we get the money in time?**)

Open your palms and let your shells fall to the floor. Count up the number of shells (heads, or X's) that have landed mouth up. Then consult the charts in this Reading's Extra Credit section. If the oracle indicates that the answer is the side where you have placed the black shell, the answer is no. If the oracle indicates the side with the white shell, the answer is yes. Or you may have to throw again, as the oracle instructs. It's also possible that things are not determined yet, in which case the oracle could answer "no comment."

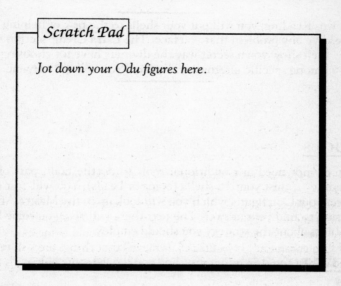

Scratch Pad

Jot down your Odu figures here.

For a Santeria experience. When this custom came to North America, an interesting twist occurred in the way the answers are read. If you would like to use a more authentically American version of this method, just switch hands. That's right. Whenever the charts in this Reading tell you to choose the object on the left-hand side, take the right. And when they tell you to choose the right hand, take the left. (Go figure!) Also, choose the right hand if "NO COMMENT" is indicated.[2]

Go on to the next Reading whenever you are ready to continue.

---

[2] To be even more correctly Santerian—if 5, 6, 7, 9, or 11 falls on the second throw, choose the left hand if the second number is lower than or equal to the first, and choose the right hand if the second number is higher than the first.

Reading #5

WHAT SHOULD I DO?
(How Can I Choose?)

In this Reading, you will put your shells to the task of helping you
resolve any problem that you face. The Extra Credit section will
then show you a secret way the diviners have for choosing
among specific alternatives—which you will get to name.

TOOLS

You do not need any additional tools to do the main part of this
Reading . . . just your 16 shells (coins or beads). You will cast them
to get your Odu figure, which you will look up in the Master Answer
section to find your answer. The text there will give you some help-
ful hints about the strategy you should employ.

HOW TO

 Get out the 16 shells, coins, or beads you made in Reading #2.

 Say a prayer, praising your God, invoking your patron saint,
or calling upon your African spirit guide.

 Gather your coins, buttons, beads, or shells into the palms of
your hands, blow on them for good luck, and ask your question.

 Whisper it or say it silently: **What should I do?** about such-
and-such? or so-and-so? **How can I get what I want?** out of
life? in this lifetime? **What will make things work out for me?**
at home? at work? at play? **What should my plan be?** my strategy? **How can I resolve this problem that I face?** (you name
it).

38

Open your hands and let the shells fall to the ground. Count the number that have landed mouth side up (or the number of coins that have fallen heads up, or the number of beads that have landed X up). Jot down your figure on the scratch pad.

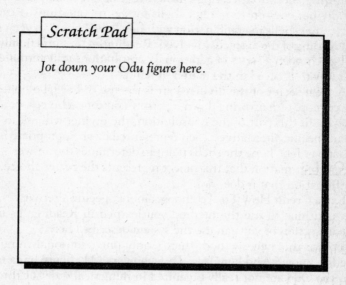

| Scratch Pad |

Jot down your Odu figure here.

THE ANSWERS

Look up your Odu figure in Part I's Master Answer section. Read the text called "For STRATEGY questions." Then go on to the Extra Credit section to learn which of the specific alternatives you are considering will get your job done.

EXTRA CREDIT

To choose among alternatives. One of the great things about this oracle is that it provides many ways for you to receive additional information. Better still . . . you can be as specific in these requests as you like! In this Reading, we'll be asking how best to proceed at this point. But the skills you are learning here can also be applied to many other lines of specific questioning.

Extra Credit Tools. You will need your 16 shells plus your "Igbo bones" from Reading #4's Extra Credit section.

Extra Credit Background. In Nigeria, a complete *erindinlogun* consultation involves many steps in addition to casting the 16 shells. Following the initial casting—which reveals the "main answer"—the diviner goes on to use her shells for yes/no questions (Reading #3) . . . her shells in combination with her "Igbo bones" to get a general reading of the auspices involved (Reading #4) . . . and finally she will go through a series of additional consultations to determine the best way to proceed in the matter at hand.

A great secret of the diviner's art is the use of her Igbo bones for the purpose of narrowing down a person's options, choices, or alternatives. In this part of the consultation, the diviner will ask in turn about specific alternatives, each represented by an appropriate bone. Whatever Igbo bone the shells point to determines the answer . . . either a confirmation that this object represents the better choice, or a confirmation that it does not.

Extra Credit How To. To choose among specific alternatives, you can continue to use the method you learned in Reading 4's Extra Credit section or you can use the system described here.[1]

To use this new method, there's only one additional thing you need to know. And here it is: Though every Odu figure has a number, the Odu are not really organized in numerical order (1 through 16). Each figure has a <u>secret</u> rank. And once you know this secret, a whole new dimension to the oracle will be open to you.

According to one African tradition, the highest-ranking Odu of them all is found when eight shells fall faceup. Next comes 10—which by legend used to be in first place—then 4, 3, 2, and 1 . . . and so on in this order. . . .

---

[1] The method I am introducing here uses an Odu's "secret number" as the key for selecting among specific alternatives. Based on a variety of African divination techniques—but a product of my own trial-and-error experiments—it's a very workable system that has been designed to remove any statistical bias against either the left or the right hand. For more details on the results you can expect, see Appendix A. All comments on the performance of this system are welcome. Please address correspondence to the author c/o Avon Books.

The Odu Figures
By Rank

⠿⠿	Ogbe	8
⠿⠿	Ofun	10
⠿	Irosun	4
⠿	Ogunda	3
⠿	Oyeku	2
⠂	Okanran	1
⠿⠿⠿	Iwori	12
⠿⠿⠿	Owonrin	11
⠿⠿	Osa	9
⠿⠿	Odi	7
⠿⠿	Obara	6
⠿⠿	Oshe	5
⠿⠿⠿	Ika	13
⠿⠿⠿	Oturupon	14
⠿⠿⠿	Otura	15
⠿⠿⠿	Irete	16
	Opira	0

We'll be using this rank-and-file order of the Odu to choose among specific options. The first thing you will want to do is list a couple of the choices that are open to you. Just jot down a couple of things you have been thinking of doing. . . .

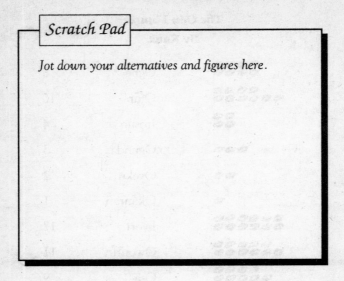

Scratch Pad

Jot down your alternatives and figures here.

Now, take your Igbo bones—your white shell and your black stone—and assign a strategy or option to each. Let's say, I want to know whether I should sit tight for a while or hurry up and act right now. I say, okay, the white shell in this case will stand for taking action, and the black stone will stand for waiting in place. Put one bone to your left. Put the other to your right.

Cast your shells twice, noting each time the figure that has resulted (the number of shells that have fallen mouth side up).

Extra Credit Answers. To interpret your answers you'll need to remember how the Odu figures are ranked, from highest to lowest: 8, 10, 4, 3, 2, 1, 12, 11, 9, 7, 6, 5, 13, 14, 15, 16, 0.

If the second number you cast is "greater" (which is to say of higher rank) than the first number you cast, the oracle has pointed to the object on your left. The option represented by this object has been chosen.

If the second number is "less" (which is to say of lower rank) than the first number, the option represented by the object on your right has been chosen.

If you receive the same figure on both casts, go with the object to your left if the combination is 8/8, 10/10, 4/4, 3/3, 2/2, 1/1, 12/12, or 11/11; and otherwise go with the object to your right.

If all 16 shells turn up tails on either cast (producing the figure 0—Opira), neither hand has been chosen. Try asking again, using two different alternatives this time.

Once an option has been chosen, you can go on to test this option against the others on your list, taking two in turn and repeating the procedure until you find the best option for your current situation.

Here's a table that will help you remember the rules for choosing between your left and right hands. In general, if the second number you cast is to the left of the first in the rank-order listing, you will choose the left hand; if to the right, the right.

SUMMARY TABLE
for Choosing Between Alternatives
(African)

←——————— **Left / Right** ——————→

8, 10, 4, 3, 2, 1, 12, 11, 9, 7, 6, 5, 13, 14, 15, 16

8/8, 10/10, 4/4, 3/3	9/9, 7/7, 6/6, 5/5
2/2, 1/1, 12/12	13/13, 14/14
11/11	15/15, 16/16

If a 0 occurs on either the first or second casting of the shells—neither hand is chosen.

EXTRA, EXTRA CREDIT!

To do it in a Santeria way. In the Santeria tradition, a different system of ranking the Odu figures is sometimes employed. To conduct the Extra Credit portion of this Reading with a Santeria flare, first whisper to your shells that you are going to use the Santeria way this time. Then ask your question, cast your shells twice, and interpret your answers using this ranking of the Odu, from highest to lowest: 1, 2, 3, 4, 8, 10, 12, 13, 14, 15, 16, 11, 9, 7, 6, 5, 0.

If the second number you cast is of higher rank than the first, choose the right hand.[2] If the second number is of lower rank, choose the left hand. If both numbers are the same, choose the right hand for these combinations: 1/1, 2/2, 3/3, 4/4, 8/8, 10/10, 12/12, and

---

[2] Exactly opposite the African method, as is so often true of Santeria's divination methods.

13/13. Otherwise choose the left hand. If 0 shells shows up on either throw, there is no answer. In general, if the second number you cast is to the left of the first in the rank-order list, you will choose the right hand; if to the right, the left.

SUMMARY TABLE
for Choosing Between Alternatives
(Santeria)

←——————— **Right / Left** ———————→

1, 2, 3, 4, 8, 10, 12, 13, 14, 15, 16, 11, 9, 7, 6, 5

1/2, 2/2, 3/3, 4/4	14/14, 15/15
8/8, 10/10, 12/12	16/16, 11/11, 9/9
13/13	7/7, 6/6, 5/5

If a 0 occurs on either the first or second casting of the shells—neither hand is chosen.

Go on to the next Reading whenever you are ready to continue.

Reading #6

HOW AM I BLESSED?
(What Is My Curse?)

Congratulations! You are now over halfway through your initiation
into the mysteries of *erindinlogun*. In this Reading, you'll greatly
expand your skills as a diviner, as you start to cast your shells twice
in order to get a "double" Odu figure. To test the technique, you'll
be asking the oracle to predict the good things that are in store
for you . . . and at the same time to point out the things
you will want to avoid.

TOOLS

The only tools you need to conduct the first part of this Reading are the
16 shells you have been using since Reading #2. But instead of casting
them just once to get an answer, you'll be casting them twice. There
are 289 possible answers now to every question you ask! At the back of
the Master Answer section, you'll find the text that goes with any two
combinations of the 16 primary Odu figures plus Opira (0 shells).

BACKGROUND

In addition to all of the other steps that an African fortune-teller
goes through to conduct her consultation with the shell oracle
(Readings #2 through #5), she is very concerned about accurately
forecasting the good things to come, the problems to avoid, and—especially—the right thing to do or not do.

By directing the course of the questioning now, she tries to determine which blessing is involved and what the potential is for a curse,
as well.

You can think of these "curses" as your personal stumbling block if
you will—your tragic flaws, your pet peeves, or some of the needless
pains you somehow have to bear. But in Africa five types of "curses"
are usually considered at this point—namely: death, disease, fights,
poverty, and loss.

Likewise, five blessings are typically asked about: long life, money, marriage, children, and a house.

In this Reading's Extra Credit section you'll get to tailor the specific things you ask about to match your perception of the blessings and curses at work in your life. But before we get into that, let's just cast our shells. . . .

HOW TO

 Get out your 16 shells, coins, or beads. Say a prayer, praising your God, invoking your patron saint, or calling upon your African spirit guide.

 Gather your coins, buttons, beads, or shells into the palms of your hands, blow on them, and voice your question.

 Ask something like: **What are my blessings?** How will I be blessed? **What blessing can I look forward to?** at work? at home? **What blessing is coming my way?** next week? this month? next year? Or, **What do I need to watch out for?** in love? in general? **How am I cursed?** What's my problem?

 Open your hands and let the shells fall to the ground. Count the number that have landed mouth side up (or the number of coins that have fallen heads up, or the number of beads that have landed X up). Jot down your figure on the scratch pad.

Scratch Pad

Jot down your Odu figures here.

Now, gather up your shells, ask your question again, and cast your shells one more time. Jot down the resulting figure to the right of the one you got on your first cast.

THE ANSWERS

Your answer will be one of the 289 possible combinations of the Odu figures. The answers for these <u>combinations</u> are found at the back of the Master Answer section for this part of the book, starting on page 113.

To find your answer, look up the number of shells (coins or beads) that landed faceup on your first throw. Then find the second number you have cast (to the right of the first and after the "+" sign). Read the complete text.

EXTRA CREDIT

To inquire about specific blessings. If you'd like to try the authentic method of inquiring about <u>specific</u> blessings, as described in the Background section, be my guest. You'll need your black stone and white shell for this.

Extra Credit How To. First, shift your black stone and white shell around in your clasped palms until one lands in the right hand and one goes to the left. Place the object in your left hand down on your left side. Place the object in your right hand to the right.

Now ask about the first blessing you want to consider. You can select from the traditional list of blessings in the Background section or use this modified list:

Blessings

Friends	Not friends
Peace	Not peace
Gain	Not gain
Health	Not health
Love	Not love

What the heck, you can even make up your own list of the things that you regard as blessings.

Now ask about each blessing on your list, in turn. For each blessing you care to ask about, you're going to cast your shells twice. Considered together, the two Odu figures that result from these castings are going to point you to your white shell or your black stone. In all cases, the white shell stands for a "yes"; the blessing you have just named is the one you want to anticipate and plan for. The black stone stands for a simple "no, not this blessing, not now."

To try it out, gather together your 16 shells now, and ask: **Is a blessing of friendship in store for me?** Or, subsequently, Is a blessing of peace coming? Is a blessing of money due me? Will I be blessed with health? Will I be blessed with love in my life?

Cast your shells once, note the number that land mouth side up, and jot down your figure. Then gather your shells up, and cast them again. Jot down your second figure to the right of the first.

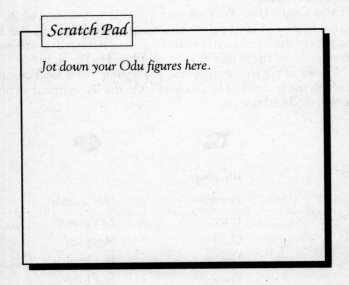

Scratch Pad

Jot down your Odu figures here.

Extra Credit Answers. Look up your pair of figures in the Master Answer section for Part I of this book. The text will tell you whether the left or right hand has been chosen.[1]

If the object that the oracle points to is the white shell, the blessing you have just asked about has been named. (Suspend the questioning at this point.) If the object that the oracle points to is the black stone, no, this is not the blessing. (Go on to ask about the next blessing on your list.) If you should happen to get through your entire list without getting a positive response, go on to the Extra, Extra Credit section.

EXTRA, EXTRA CREDIT!

To inquire about specific curses (if you dare!). Just follow the instructions in this Reading's Extra Credit section, but instead of asking about blessings, ask about curses. . . .

	Curses
Not enemies	Enemies
Not conflict	Conflict
Not loss	Loss
Not sickness	Sickness
Not grief	Grief

[1] If you prefer to figure out for yourself which hand was chosen, use the method described in Reading #5's Extra Credit Section to choose between left and right. (The Master Answer section is using the same method in choosing hands for you.) Or you can use one of the more traditional methods described in Reading #4's Extra Credit section. (In this case, your answers will not always agree with what it says in the Master Answer section.) To check your answers on any two throws, consult the lists in Appendix A.

First place your white stone to one side (left or right) and your black stone to the other. Ask—in turn—**Am I to be cursed with enemies?** with conflict? with loss? **Will illness curse me?** Will grief?

For each possible curse, cast your 16 shells twice and note the figures that result. Look up your combination in the Master Answer section to see which hand has been chosen. If the oracle points to the black stone, the answer is yes, this is the curse you need to watch out for right now. If it points to the white shell, the answer is no, this is nothing for you to worry your head about right now.

Go on to the next Reading whenever you are ready to continue.

Reading #7

WHAT MUST I GIVE?
(How Will I Get?)

In this Reading you will learn what you should do
to keep good luck on your side and bad luck off your back.
The only hitch is, you'll have to make the first move.

TOOLS

In the African tradition, the secret to making the most of any situation is to offer an appropriate sacrifice—or in more Western terms, give up a little something as an offering. In this Reading you'll use your 16 shells to see what the oracle has to say about the things to give up—or the things to avoid.

Then, continuing in the Extra Credit section, you can use your two Igbo bones to help you select among the specific offerings that you are willing to make right now.

BACKGROUND

Once the diviner has finished all of her other duties, she sets about determining what needs to be done to correct a bad situation or assure a good one continues. A sacrifice is usually called for.

At this point in the consultation, the diviner will focus on identifying which of many possible sacrifices will do the trick of seeing that the good things that have been suggested by the consultation come true and the less desirable things are avoided. The sacrifices that are specified usually involve food items, a little money, maybe some items of clothing. These things suffice as the diviner's payment for the consultation. But you won't have to sacrifice any chickens here or pay anything in addition to the cover price (rats!).

If you just want to hear what the oracle has to say, you can do this Reading by merely casting your 16 shells twice and consulting the answers for the Odu combinations at the end of Part I's Master Answer section.

If you choose to go on to the Extra Credit section—and actually consider specific sacrifices you might make—we'll be using a modified system that lets you determine the nature of the sacrifices that you believe would be appropriate based on your cultural traditions, personal beliefs, and present situation. But first, let's just cast the shells.

HOW TO

 Get out your 16 shells, coins, or beads. Say a prayer, praising your God, invoking your patron saint, or calling upon your African spirit guide.

 Gather your coins, buttons, beads, or shells into the palms of your hands, blow on them, and express your question.

 Ask: **What must I give?** to assure success? to gain love? to have more money? to find a house? (You name it, whatever blessing your heart desires.) **What should I give up?** to assure long life? feel personal pride? **What is my sacrifice?** Or, **What must I stay away from?** avoid? resist? **What is my taboo?** what should I never do?

 Open your hands and let the shells fall to the ground. Count the number that have landed mouth side up (or the number of coins that have fallen heads up, or the number of beads that have landed X up). Jot down your figure on the scratch pad.

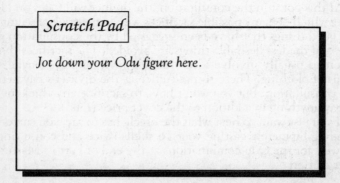

Scratch Pad

Jot down your Odu figure here.

Now, gather up your shells, ask your question again, and cast your shells one more time. Jot down the resulting figure to the right of the one you cast first.

THE ANSWERS

Look up your combination of Odu figures at the back of Part I's Master Answer section. First, look up the number of the first figure you threw. Then look up the second figure (after the "+" sign). Read the complete text. For more specific details, work the Extra Credit section.

EXTRA CREDIT

To consider specific sacrifices. At this point, you can also use your Igbo bones to select a specific sacrifice that would be appropriate in this situation.

    Extra Credit How To. First you need to list the sacrifices you are prepared to make in order to get the results that you desire. You can choose from this list, or note other possibilities on the Scratch Pad.

Spare . . .

A dime
A little time
A bite to eat
A light

Skip . . .

A cigarette
A beer
A cup of coffee
Sex

Lend . . .

A helping hand
A couple of bucks
Your time

Give . . .

Bread to the birds
Food to the homeless
Clothes to the needy

Offer . . .

An apology
Praise
Thanks

Say . . .

A prayer

Scratch Pad

Jot down the five things you are willing to sacrifice at this time. (Be as specific as you like.)

Next, take your two Igbo bones into your hands and roll them back and forth until one object falls into the left hand, and one into the right. Place the object in your right hand (be it the shell or the stone) to your right side. Place the object in your left hand to your left side.

Now, get our your 16 shells (coins or beads), cup them in your hands, blow on them, and say: **Is _____ my sacrifice?** Insert the name of the sacrifice that you will be considering on this throw of the shells.

Cast the shells twice, each time noting the number of shells that have landed mouth side up.

Extra Credit Answers. Look up your pair of figures in the Master Answer section for Part I of this book. The text will tell you whether the left or right hand has been chosen.[1]

If the object your shells point at is the black stone, the answer is no, this is not the sacrifice you should make right now. If your shells point to the white shell, the answer is yes, this is an appropriate of-

---

[1] Or you can also compute for yourself which hand has been chosen, based on the methods you learned in Reading #4 and Reading #5. Consult Appendix A for a quick review of each of these methods and a list for checking your work.

fering—and may it do you well. Cast your shells twice for each sacrifice on your list, until the oracle helps you choose the right offering to make. *Ashe*, my friend. So be it.

EXTRA, EXTRA CREDIT!

A place for your stuff. Now that you are becoming an old hand at African divination, you will need a good place to keep your shells and bones. For the 16 shells, a hollowed-out gourd (a "calabash" in African terms) or a wooden bowl with a lid would be appropriate. You might find a nice wooden, ceramic, or glass container at your favorite flea market, bazaar, or craft show. (And if you want to feel really authentic, don't forget to barter over the price, just as they do in the African markets.) If you're on a shoestring budget, a beloved coffee mug would also work, or even a nice cardboard gift box. And if you're handy with a needle and thread, a bead- or shell-embellished bag would also be great for your shells or bones. Or it would also be fitting to just wrap all your divination tools in some batiked scarf.

Go on to the next Reading whenever you are ready to continue.

Reading #8

WHERE IS THE REMEDY?
(What Is My Cure?)

In this Reading you will learn how to determine what
the "doctor" might order if you were consulting
an authentic African diviner.

TOOLS

At this point, you have all the tools you need. Just keep using your
16 shells and your two Igbo bones.

BACKGROUND

Once the African diviner has determined the blessings (or difficulties) involved and the sacrifices to be made, she will turn her attention to prescribing remedies for the client.

In addition to being very good with numbers, African diviners also
are very good at using medicinal herbs for healing purposes. At this
point in the consultation, the diviner might inquire of her shells
what the correct remedy would be in this particular situation.

In the Extra Credit section, we'll be using a modified system that
lets you select the remedies that you believe in. But you can also just
cast your shells to get the oracle's therapeutic advice. In fact, let's try
that first. . . .

HOW TO

 Get out your 16 shells, coins, or beads. Say a prayer, praising
your God, invoking your patron saint, or calling upon your
African spirit guide.

Gather your coins, buttons, beads, or shells into the palms of your hands, blow on them, and state your question.

 Ask: **What will make me feel better?** about myself? my situation? the one I love? **How can I purify myself?** pamper myself? prepare myself? **What will soothe my spirit?** relieve my tensions? dispel my worries? pain? grief? anguish? anxiety? whatever? **What is the cure for that which ails me?** bugs me? fails me? **What do you prescribe?**

 Open your hands and let the shells fall to the ground. Count the number that have landed mouth side up (or the number of coins that have fallen heads up, or the number of beads that have landed X up). Jot down your figure on the scratch pad.

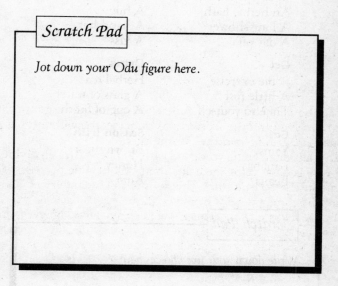

Scratch Pad

Jot down your Odu figure here.

 Now, gather up your shells, ask your question again, and cast your shells one more time. Jot down the resulting figure to the right of the one you cast first.

THE ANSWERS

Look up your combination of Odu figures in the Combinations portion of Part I's Master Answer section. Read the whole text for your combination. Go on to do the Extra Credit section if you'd like to choose among specific remedies that sound good to you tonight.

EXTRA CREDIT

To choose among specific remedies. At this point, it would be appropriate to ask what specific thing would help you feel better. To do this, you'll need your Igbo bones.

Extra Credit How To. First, select five items from this list of remedies (or substitute appropriate choices of your own). . . .

Take . . .
An herbal bath
A long shower
A day off

Have . . .
A hug
A handshake
A kiss

Get . . .
Some exercise
A little rest
Time to yourself

Drink . . .
Herbal tea
A glass of water
A cup of broth

Eat. . .
Yams
Bananas
Beans

Season with . . .
Brown sugar
Honey
Rum

Scratch Pad

Write down your five choices here.

Then get your white shell and your black stone. Place one to your left side and one to your right. Gather your 16 shells (coins or beads) in the palms of your hands, blow on them, and whisper your question: **Is _____ the remedy that will make me feel better?** improve my condition? restore my vigor? Place the name of the remedy you are asking about into the blank.

Toss your shells twice, noting each time the number of shells that have fallen mouth side up.

Extra Credit Answers. Look up your combination of figures in the Master Answer section for Part I of this book. The text will tell you whether the left or right hand has been chosen.[1]

If the object your shells point at is the black stone, the answer is no, this is not the remedy that will help you most right now. If your shells point to the white shell, the answer is yes, this is an appropriate remedy. Cast your shells twice for each remedy on your list, until the oracle helps you choose the right one for this occassion.

EXTRA, EXTRA CREDIT!

A tray for your shells. So far in this book, you have been casting your shells on the floor, but if you'd like to add an authentic touch, it would be fitting to cast your shells onto an oblong or circular basket or tray. Can't find anything to fit the bill? Well then, a woven table mat would be okay . . . or anything made of wicker, natural fibers, or coarse thread.

Go on to the next Reading whenever you are ready to continue.

---

[1] Or use your choice of methods (from Reading #4 and #5) to select the left or right hand for yourself. Check your answers with Appendix A.

Reading #9

LADIES' CHOICE
(Summary, Review, and Full Instructions for Consulting the Cowry Shells)

In this Reading you will combine everything you know about the shell oracle. And with this Reading, your initiation into the secrets of *erindinlogun* is complete. *Ashe*, my friend, so be it.

TOOLS

To review everything we've used in the past eight Readings . . . The basic tools that you need to work with this oracle are 16 coins, 16 beads, or 16 cowry shells that have had their bellies removed. The belly (or rounded underside hump) is removed by inserting a pointed object into the shell's mouth (◖). By poking a hole through to the opposite side and inserting the blade of a knife through this punctured hole and twisting a bit, the belly will pop off, revealing the shell's "stomach" (◗).

If using beads, just take a felt-tip marker and write an X on one side of each, so you will know which side is up. X, in this case, represents the cowry's mouth (◖).

If using coins, you're all set to go. Just remember that the head side of the coin is the same as a cowry's mouth (◖), and tails is the same as the cowry's stomach (◗).

In addition to your 16 coins, beads, or shells, you will need two additional objects: a white shell (◖) and a black pebble (●). These are your Igbo "bones," which play a very important role in the workings of this oracle.

You may add extra cowries, beads, or coins (usually either two or five) as an optional and authentic touch to your reading. This "money of *erindinlogun*" is simply set aside at the start of a consultation and serves no other purpose but to honor the African spirits who are thought to influence the oracle's utterances.

To complete your collection of divination paraphernalia, you can also add a straw mat or shallow oval basket to cast your shells on, as well as appropriate receptacles to hold your shells and Igbo bones when not in use. A wooden, glass, or ceramic jar with a lid would be fine for your shells, and any kind of pouch for your bones. Or you can keep them together if you want.

BACKGROUND

Erindinlogun—or 16-shell divination—is practiced by the Yoruba of Nigeria and their descendants in the Americas, where it is an instrumental part of the religion known as Santeria.

The object of a 16-shell divination is to determine "right action" on the part of the questioner. According to the beliefs of its practitioners, when the shells "speak," they are speaking on behalf of God and God's emissaries (the African "white spirits" known as the Orisha, although it is also appropriate to think of them as Roman Catholic saints).

In this method, the diviner goes through a specific series of specific lines of questioning, with the intent of determining whether, in fact, there is even a problem to be worried about—and if so, what to do about it. Any problem that occurs is regarded as a lack of attunement with the spirits. And almost every resolution involves making some kind of offering to these spiritual forces that are "out of whack" or that need to be fortified. Specific "remedies" are also prescribed for the questioner. And then there are the "verses."

This oracle speaks in two ways. The first way is via the poetry that the diviner has learned for each possible cast of the shells—of which there are 17 possibilities. As part of the consultation the questioner gets to hear the oracle "speak," through these verses. The Master Answer section plays this role in this book.

Secondly, the oracle is also very cooperative in answering yes/no questions and as a result is good at considering specific alternative scenarios. The oracle helps you choose among viable solutions.

HOW TO

 A Reading starts by saying a prayer, praising the divinity. The Lord's Prayer is a good standard. Whatever words you say, speak them from your heart.

 If you choose to use it, set the money of *erindinlogun* (your two or five extra cowries, coins, or beads) aside. These are the things that belong to God and that you cannot understand.

 Take your remaining 16 shells from their container. Cup them in your hands. Breathe on them in order to give them the breath of life and, thereby, the ability to speak. Whisper your question to them.

Your question can be about anything, but some good phrases to start with are:

What should I do about _____**?**

Why do I feel _____**?**

How should I proceed with _____**?**

How will _____ **turn out?**

What prevents me from _____**?**

But the important thing is to ask, in an earnest way, about the matter that is really on your mind. If you bring a real problem or concern to the table, the shells will do a better job for you.

 Whisper your question to the shells. Then open your hands and let them fall onto your mat or—for want of one—the floor. Count up the number of shells that have landed mouth side ( ) up. The result will be a number between 0 and 16. This is your "Odu" figure.

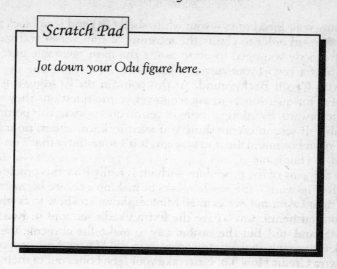

THE ANSWERS

Look up your Odu figure (by number) in the Master Answer section for Part I of this book. This is the portion of the book that imitates the "verses" of *erindinlogun*. It is your job to read the text and find your answer. The text is divided into topic-oriented sections (Work, Love, Money, and so on) to lead you to the right spot. But it may well be that though you have asked a love question, your true answer is in one of the other sections. So, for best results, read the entire text.

To extend your consultation with the oracle . . . Instead of casting your shells just once and consulting the appropriate "verse" in the Master Answer section, you can get additional information by casting your shells again to get two Odu figures in all. Just look up your particular combination of figures in the Master Answer section for Part I of this book. The second cast will put the emphasis on foretelling the things that are in store (both good and bad) and helping you decide what you should do to assure a favorable outcome.

EXTRA CREDIT

To continue your Reading . . . Once you have consulted the verses in the Master Answer section, you should continue your consultation by using your Igbo bones—your white shell (🐚) and your black pebble (⬤)—in order to clarify the meaning of your verses and specify what exactly you need to do to assure the most favorable outcome possible for you in your current situation.

Extra Credit Background. At this point in the Reading it is traditional for questioners to ask whatever yes/no questions they want to put forward. By asking a series of yes/no questions at this point, it's possible to zero in on anything you want to know about, no matter how trivial or mundane it may seem. If it's something that's on your mind, it's fair game.

In this part of the procedure—which is really how this oracle does much of its work—the oracle speaks by making a choice between left and right.[1] *African Oracles in 10 Minutes* shows you how to do this in various authentic ways. (See the Extra Credit sections of Readings #4, #5, and #6.) But the easiest way to make the choice using this book is to simply look up your answers in the Master Answer section.

Extra Credit How To. First, take your Igbo bones out of their container. Place the white shell to one side (left or right), and the black pebble to the other.

Now whisper your yes/no question to your 16 shells, coins, or beads, and then cast them <u>twice</u>, noting each time how many shells have fallen mouth side up.

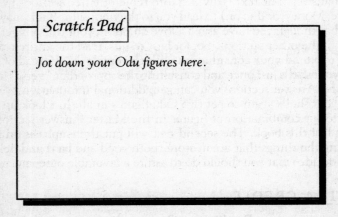

Scratch Pad

Jot down your Odu figures here.

---

[1] Or, for an even easier way to ask yes/no questions, see Reading #3's Extra Credit section.

Extra Credit Answers. Look up your combination of figures in the Master Answer section for Part I of this book. First find the number you cast the first time, then find your second number next to it (after the "+" sign). The text will give you a little something to think about and then it will tell you whether the left or right hand has been chosen.

If the oracle points to your black pebble, the answer is no. If the oracle points to your white shell, the answer is yes. You can ask as many yes/no questions in sequence as you like. Most diviners recommend that you word these questions so that a yes answer will be something positive. Ask, Will I accomplish this with success? But don't ask, Will I fail if I attempt this?

EXTRA, EXTRA CREDIT!

At this point, an African diviner would resume the formal consultation by making a number of determinations about the original Odu figure that was cast (as a result of following the instructions in this Reading's How To section). In turn, she would inquire . . .

Are the auspices of this figure good or bad?

If good, what are the blessings implied?

If bad, what are the things that need to be avoided?

What has caused these blessings or "curses"?

She makes these determinations by using her Igbo bones and 16 shells together, asking a series of yes/no questions for each of these areas of interest. (Consult Readings #4, #5, and #6 for full details.)

But, in general, the easiest way to ask about any of these things is to simply cast your 16 shells twice and note each time how many have landed mouth side up. Look up your combination of figures in the Master Answer section for Part I.

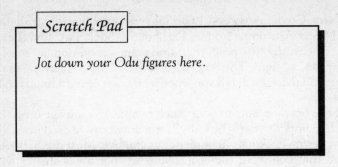

> ### Scratch Pad
>
> *Jot down your Odu figures here.*

Now for the remedy. Finally, the diviner will set about determining what needs to be done to make sure that the promised blessings occur or to avoid the pitfalls that have been foreseen. The first course of action that is generally recommended is to make a small offering (see Reading #7). The second course of action that is often determined at this point is a "remedy"—usually some kind of spiritual cleansing—that the oracle recommends (see Reading #8).

Once again these determinations are made by using the 16 shells in combination with the Igbo bones to ask a series of yes/no questions about the specific alternatives that are possible at this time. The easiest way to conduct this part of the Reading is to simply cast your shells twice and consult the Combinations section of the Master Answer section. Focus on the part of the text that starts, "The best cure for what ails you. . ."

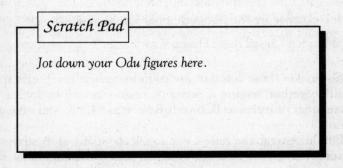

> ### Scratch Pad
>
> *Jot down your Odu figures here.*

Go on to the next Reading whenever you are ready to continue.

Reading #10

To Each Her Own
(Afterword)

In this final Reading for Part I—which is really something more to
"read" than "do"—you will see how the female system of
divination you have just learned compares to the male system
described in Part II of this book. Hopefully you will go on to
complete that Road too.

TOOLS

Whether you have come to this end by first taking the "male" path
down the Melon Seed Road, or by actually starting out on the "female" path up this White Cotton Road—it makes no difference in
the end. For, as it turns out, both paths bring you to the same place
in the end, which is here. Now, the only question remaining is,
Which road—female or male—better suits you?

The two methods of divination demonstrated in this book differ in
the tools they use; the procedures and methods they follow in constructing Odu figures; the type of Odu figures that are generated; the
names for these figures; their sequence; and their rank.

But since the systems are derived from each other, they also share
many features and aspects in common: Both rely on the recitation of
memorized "verses" for the interpretation of the figures. Both utilize
small objects ("bones") to amplify the information contained in the
verses. And both follow the same lines of questioning—and a similar sequence of steps—to arrive at a complete consultation with the oracle.

In the final analysis, it's clear that both oracles are really different
expressions of the same idea. Which one will appeal more to you?
Beats me! But I can tell you this: It probably has little to do with what
gender you are.

My male readers will no doubt find the numerical approach of the "female" system you have just learned to be a straightforward and useful means of consulting the oracle. My female readers will no doubt find the abstract figures from the "male" part of the book equally interesting.

BACKGROUND

As its central feature, the Ifa method of divination presented in Part II uses 16 palm nuts (black in color, oval in shape, and about an inch in diameter). To consult the oracle, these 16 nuts are "beaten" in the hand of the diviner.

Cupped in the palm of one hand, they are "snatched up" with the other—but not completely. They are taken up in such a way that only one or two are left behind. If more than two nuts remain, then the process has to be repeated. The nuts are also "beaten" in the sense that the intent of the system—just like the female approach you have just learned—is to literally "beat" the odds . . . to beat the forces of nature . . . to beat the Powers that Be.

How does the male diviner interpret his results? It's simple really—just backwards from what you might expect. The rule of thumb—as it were—is that if one nut remains in his hand, the diviner makes two marks in the dust of his divining board. If two nuts remain, the diviner makes only one mark.

The marks are pressed into the dust with the diviner's fingertips (using the middle finger to make a single mark, and the middle and index finger to make two), like this • or this ••.

But—unlike Part I's shell-casting system that you now know—nothing can be learned here from a single casting. The diviner will beat his divination nuts at least four times (and more likely eight) in order to get a response.

Each time the nuts are beaten, a new "line" is added to the figure (called an Odu) that the diviner is creating in the dust. On the second toss, he adds a second "line" to the figure, placing it directly below the first mark he made. (It is the very same technique you used in this book's Reading #0 before you had knowledge of any of these secrets.)

If two nuts are left in your hand on the first cast, make one finger mark. If one nut is left on the second cast, make two finger marks together, directly below your first cast mark. At this point your marks will look like this:

If on the third snatch only one nut remains, and on the final snatch, two nuts, your finished Odu figure will look like this one (which, coincidentally enough, is called Odi or Edi). . . .

There are 16 possible figures that can be created by this manipulation of the palm nuts. In the City of Ife, Nigeria, where this method became perfected, this is the order that they are listed in. . . .

Ogbe
1

Oyeku
2

Iwori
3

Odi/Edi
4

Obara
5

Okanran
6

Irosun
7

Owonrin
8

Ogunda
9

Osa
10

Irete
11

Otura
12

Oturupon
13

Ika
14

Oshe
15

Ofun
16

If the names look familiar to you, it's because they are very closely related to the names you used in the seashell-casting method. When women adopted and adapted this system, they kept much of the tradition intact. They changed the methods to feel more natural in their hands, but they kept the names.

As you know, Part I's female way is to just give each of these Odu a number, and forget the intermediate step of constructing an Odu figure out of single and double dots. You just toss 16 shells and count up how many have landed mouth side up. Each possible outcome (0 through 16 shells with their mouths up) is associated with one of the Odu names—or a variation thereof.

Using cowry shells and basing the technique on counting up the number of shells that landed was just an extension of the work Yoruban women did in the marketplace, where cowries were currency. But each cowry shell was not worth very much. Shells needed to be counted up into lots numbering in the thousands, a process that the women rapidly performed by gathering groups of five in each hand and combining four groups into 20 . . . then five groups of 20 into 100 . . . then five groups of 100 into 500 . . . and so on. So it was only natural in adopting this system that women diviners switched to objects that felt comfortable in their hands and used a numerical method that they could relate very well to. In their minds, each Odu figure could be represented by a number, and there was no need to get carried away with generating it by the more time-consuming palm-nut method.

African men, of course, also knew how to count. And each of their figures was associated with a number, too. But, as you will quickly see as you work Part II, the numbering system is different. Using the names as a guide, here's how the female numbering system you have just learned compares to the male way demonstrated in Part II. The numbers in parentheses indicate the order that the Odu figures appear in each system.

Female . . .

1 Shell
Okanran (1)

2 Shells
Oyeku (2)

Male . . .

Okanran (6)

Oyeku (2)

70

3 Shells
Ogunda (3)

Ogunda (9)

4 Shells
Irosun (4)

Irosun (7)

5 Shells
Oshe (5)

Oshe (15)

6 Shells
Obara (6)

Obara (5)

7 Shells
Odi (7)

Odi (4)

8 Shells
Ogbe (8)

Ogbe (1)

9 Shells
Osa (9)

Osa (10)

10 Shells
Ofun (10)

Ofun (16)

11 Shells
Owonrin (11)

Owonrin (8)

12 Shells
Iwori (12)

Iwori (3)

13 Shells
Ika (13)

Ika (14)

14 Shells
Oturupon (14)

Oturupon (13)

Female . . .	Male . . .
15 Shells	
Otura (15)	Otura (12)
16 Shells	
Irete (16)	Irete (11)
No Shells	
Opira (17)	—

It seems the only thing the men and women could agree upon is that Oyeku comes second in the sequence. All other bets are off! But a difference in sequence is really neither here nor there. For despite the external appearances, the inner workings of both the male and female systems are pretty much alike. And even though the sequence is different, the meanings for the male and female Odu are so similar that diviners of each system sometimes even use the same stories to illustrate their point.

Both female and male systems also share the use of "bones" in the divination process. As you know, the women call theirs Igbo. The men call theirs Ibo. The underlying concept is the same. In both cases—male and female—the bones are small objects that are used simply to represent a particular concept.

In both systems, the bones work along with the primary oracular method (shells or nuts) in a very dynamic way. By picking two objects to represent yes and no responses and then tucking them into separate hands, the primary oracle (be it seashell casting or palm-nut beating) will be used to choose the hand where the answer lies.

HOW TO

The men and women use different methods for determining which hand or object has been chosen in this process, but once again, the result is the same. A bone is chosen. And when the bone is chosen, an answer is revealed.

The ability of these oracles to make choices is an integral part of the system—and an integral part of the message that is received from consulting either the shells or the palm nuts. For behind each of these systems is not only a belief in destiny, but a belief that an individual can only achieve his or her destiny by making the right choices.

True to the African culture that these oracles come from, every Odu figure—be it in the male system or in the female system—has a rank. It is this rank that determines which Igbo or Ibo bone will be chosen in a consideration of specific alternatives.

The alternatives that are routinely investigated during a consultation are the same in both systems. After an initial consultation with the seashells or nuts, the shells or nuts are consulted again to learn whether the sign that has just been received should be interpreted as favorable or unfavorable. Then in turn, both methods turn to identifying blessings or curses that are in store.

THE ANSWERS

But the real object of both systems is to determine what needs to be done to assure the good things and ward off the bad. A sacrifice is invariably called for. And a remedy is often prescribed.

In both systems, a portion of the answer comes from listening to the verses that the diviner has learned for each figure. In both systems, these verses include stories, parables, and morals. In both systems, you (the questioner) have to decide what applies to you.

The answer also comes from consulting the bones, which are good at handling specific details, choosing among alternative courses of action, and deciding what specifically needs to be done.

So, with so much in common, which system you decide is your favorite is really a matter of personal preference. Regardless of your gender, it only makes sense to go with the oracle that gives you the better results.

EXTRA CREDIT

Just as with the original oracles, this book provides two separate answer sections. And just to give you something to think about, there's nothing to prevent you from consulting the answers for Part II while you work with the Readings in Part I—and vice versa.

There's nothing to stop you from continuing to use your shells as you work through the Readings in Part II of this book. (There's also nothing to prevent those who did Part II first from bringing the palm-nut method over to Part I and using it to ask any of the questions here.) Once you get the feeling for how each oracle works, there is nothing but the limits of your own imagination to prevent you from using the Readings and the answer sections in this book in an innovative and creative way.

Both of these oracles have been around for a long time, and their present-day practitioners continue to update and modify them to meet the current needs of those seeking help and the current society in which the diviners live.

EXTRA, EXTRA CREDIT!

All that said, the question still remains, which system is the right one for you? I suggest you test-drive both to see which method feels most natural in your hands and which method consistently produces better results for you.

So at this point, and without further ado, I invite you to follow me down the Melon Seed Road to learn the male way of doing these things.

Go on to Part II whenever you are ready to continue.

Master Answer Section
for Part I

THE WHITE COTTON ROAD
(Seashell Divination)

How to Find Your Answers

The primary figures of the *erindinlogun* (16-shell) divination system are listed in this Master Answer section in their traditional numerical order. . . .

Name	Number
Okanran	1
Oyeku	2
Ogunda	3
Irosun	4
Oshe	5
Obara	6
Odi	7
Ogbe	8
Osa	9
Ofun	10
Owonrin	11
Iwori	12
Ika	13
Oturupon	14
Otura	15
Irete	16
Opira	0

To find your answer, just look it up by name or number in the Master Answer section. The answers for each figure include a chart that lists other names used in Africa and America. And—so you can use these answers with the other half of this book if you like—the chart also links each of these figures to the corresponding Odu figures used in Part II. . . .

Part I Figures	Part II Figures
1 Shell Okanran (1)	Okanran (6)
2 Shells Oyeku (2)	Oyeku (2)
3 Shells Ogunda (3)	Ogunda (9)
4 Shells Irosun (4)	Irosun (7)
5 Shells Oshe (5)	Oshe (15)
6 Shells Obara (6)	Obara (5)
7 Shells Odi (7)	Odi (4)
8 Shells Ogbe (8)	Ogbe (1)
9 Shells Osa (9)	Osa (10)
10 Shells Ofun (10)	Ofun (16)

76

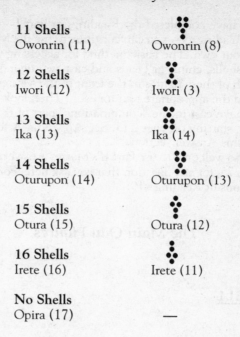

11 Shells
Owonrin (11)   Owonrin (8)

12 Shells
Iwori (12)   Iwori (3)

13 Shells
Ika (13)   Ika (14)

14 Shells
Oturupon (14)   Oturupon (13)

15 Shells
Otura (15)   Otura (12)

16 Shells
Irete (16)   Irete (11)

No Shells
Opira (17)   —

Each answer begins with an "opening verse," which describes the figure you have just cast—in terms of the number of shells that have fallen mouth up and stomach up (heads and tails). You can think of it as a type of "praise song" that the diviner might offer to the figure before beginning to interpret it.

The opening verse is followed immediately with additional "verses" on destiny, spirituality, work, love, money, and strategy. These divisions in the text are meant to guide you to the portion of the answer that is most directly related to the question you asked. But you are welcome to read the entire text for any figure that you cast. As in the original system, it is up to you (as the consultant) to find the part that applies to you today.

The answers for the 16 primary figures are immediately followed by the answers for the 289 combinations (including Opira) that these figures form when you cast two at a time.

After you have completed the Readings in Part I—from Reading #1 through Reading #9—you can continue to use the Master Answer section on your own. The basic method for accessing the answers is to use your shells, coins, or beads and cast two figures side by side. Look up each of these figures in the front of the Master Answer section and read the appropriate text for each. Then look up the pair of figures you have cast in the "combinations" part of the Master Answer section, starting on page 113. See Appendix A for a few other ways to use this Answer section.

You are also welcome to use Part II's Master Answer section, starting on page 275, for any question that you ask here. For complete instructions, consult Reading #19.

The Main Odu Figures

ONE SHELL

owo ookan

African Name (*erindinlogan*)	Okanran
American Names (*Santeria*)	Okana Okanna Sodde
Part II Figure (*Ifa*)	Okanran, 6
African Spirit	Eshu

OPENING VERSE

You have cast one shell mouth side up. You have cast one cowry and one cowry only with the urge to speak tonight—and all the 15 others

78

growling in their 15 bellies pointed up. . . . Thus falls the sign of Owo ookan . . . One Cowry. Do you see why One Cowry—Owo ookan—has come? The shells are hungry for a sacrifice.

For DESTINY readings. Eshu—the spirit who, like Mercury and Hermes, takes messages back and forth to heaven—says you are his child. As such you are linked inextricably to God. Whatever your desire, your prayer is your power. Be careful not to use your connections to play tricks on others. You are the sort of person who should feed the birds, not molest them. Evil can be avoided. Blessings can be assured. Your destiny will be sealed through a series of your own choices. Choose well. And also, give of yourself in order to get what you want.

For SPIRITUAL questions. One-Shell-Okanran went to The-One-Who-Reads-The-Signs-Well, because he wanted to receive the blessings of life, and not just its curses. She said whatever he desired could be had . . . for the right price. *Say a prayer to Saint Anthony—worker of miracles—for whatever your heart desires.*

For WORK questions. One-Shell-Okanran went to The-One-Who-Reads-The-Signs-Well, because he wanted to be successful at his work. She said he must put in plenty of hours and put up with plenty of dung being thrung. One-Shell-Okanran kissed backsides on occasion . . . and that was how he got the power to be great.

For LOVE questions. One-Shell-Okanran went to The-One-Who-Reads-The-Signs-Well, because his wife had left him and he was frustrated and lonely. She said he would surely find a better mate, if only he would quit letting his penis do the looking for him. One-Shell-Okanran relieved himself, gained judgment as a result, and found the one who satisfied his heart.

For MONEY questions. One-Shell-Okanran went to The-One-Who-Reads-The-Signs-Well, because he had no house. She said he would have to pay loan initiation fees and closing costs or else put one month's rent and a security deposit in an escrow account. One-Shell-Okanran hesitated, but obeyed. And now he has a roof over his head (if no money in the bank).

For STRATEGY questions. Let us praise The-One-Who-Reads-The-Signs-Well. One-Shell-Okanran wanted blessings instead of curses. He wanted to be fully employed. He wanted a companion. He wanted a place to call home. By doing what the diviner said, he got all three blessings at once. To get what <u>you</u> want may take a minor sacrifice, along with a humble prayer.

TWO SHELLS

owo eeji

African Names (*erindinlogan*)	Oyeku Eji Oko
American Name (*Santeria*)	Eyioko
Part II Figure (*Ifa*)	⠿ Oyeku, 2
African Spirit	Ibeji

OPENING VERSE

You have cast two shells showing mouths, two shells ready to speak. You have cast 14 showing stomachs . . . 14 with their wombs exposed. Owo eeji. Two Cowries. Do you see why Two Cowries— Owo eeji—has come? These shells are ripe. These days are numbered.

For DESTINY readings. Ibeji—the Guardian Angel of twin children—says you are her child. As such you are directly connected to your spiritual double in heaven. Whatever you desire, your double desires too, and puts in a good word for you. And when you are troubled, your double is troubled too. Thus, everything you do on earth is witnessed in heaven. You are the kind who is not complete without a companion. Your way is intimately bound up with another's. Seek the one who makes your soul sing and your shadow dance; and all will be right with your world. In this pursuit, avoid doing the things that your inner voices warn against.

For SPIRITUAL questions. Oyeku-of-the-Two-Mouths went to the Diviner-of-Secrets, because she wanted to do the right thing with her life. The Diviner-of-Secrets cast the shells and said, TABOO! To do the right thing in life, Oyeku, you must avoid doing the wrong things. *Say a prayer to Saint Peter—the binder and unbinder of entanglements—that all should be unraveled, and everything set right.*

For WORK questions. Oyeku-of-the-Two-Mouths went to the Diviner-of-Secrets, because she didn't like doing her work, and so she did things wrong. The Diviner cast and said, Oyeku! We must wash the shells quick! You are allergic to the place! No joy comes from doing something half-well. And life is too short. Risk a switch. Oyeku-of-the-Two-Mouths quit her job, and found something that made her content.

For LOVE questions. Oyeku-of-the-Two-Mouths went to the Diviner-of-Secrets, because it was the New Moon and she had not had her period yet. Diviner said, Oyeku, have you been doing something you should not? There are so many stomachs to feed already . . . and so many souls dying for rebirth. Take the risk and choose. Oyeku did and picked her own way to happiness.

For MONEY questions. Oyeku-of-the-Two-Mouths went to the Diviner-of-Secrets, because she had spent all her money before payday. Diviner said, Oyeku, is your head hungrier than your stomach? I guess you'll have to owe me for this reading. Avoid buying things on credit, or things will only get worse. Oyeku paid the Diviner back first, and by and by everyone she owed, until—in the end—she was even.

For STRATEGY questions. Oyeku-of-the-Two-Mouths was praising the Diviner-of-Secrets, for the shells had spoken only truth. Things were not going right for her because she was going about it all wrong. You, too, should mark the Diviner's words. To do the right things, avoid doing the wrong things, which in your case is anything that involves depending too little on your own common sense.

THREE SHELLS

owo eeta

African Name (*erindinlogan*)	Ogunda
American Name (*Santeria*)	Oggunda
Part II Figure (*Ifa*)	Ogunda, 9
African Spirit	Ogun

OPENING VERSE

You have cast three shells with their mouths open and ready to speak. You have cast 13 shells with their mouths shut, and their bellies rumbling. It is Three Shells—Owo eeta—that speaks tonight. Three Shells. Do you see why Three Shells—Owo eeta—has come? Blessings in disguise, says Three Shells.

For DESTINY readings. Ogun—the Great Spirit of Iron—says you are his child. As such you will be powerful and hard. Whatever you desire can be as you will. Just remember to use your God-given tools for the purpose God intended. You are deep and penetrating . . . strong and silent. You get what you want by thrusting and hammering, knocking and pounding, building and forging. See that the things you build are good enough to last. See that the rules you make for others are fair. Even the strongest implement wears thinner and thinner with time. One day you will depend upon those who once served you. You will want them to remember you well.

For SPIRITUAL questions. Three-Shells-Ogunda went to the One-Who-Foretells-the-Future, because he wanted to be prepared for whatever was in store—no matter what. Foreteller said, It is pre-ordained. Foreteller said, It is inevitable. Foreteller said, It is in the bag. Good news, she said. Take heed! Take heart! A blessing is in store. *Send a prayer through John the Baptist—the one who forged the way—that you may find your road. Praise be to God.*

For WORK questions. Three-Shells-Ogunda went to the One-Who-Foretells-the-Future, because he was letting his temper show at work and he feared he might lose his job on account of it. Foreteller said, Bite your tongue! Arguing never did anybody any good. Patience, friend. Don't you know a blessing when you see one coming?

For LOVE questions. Three-Shells-Ogunda went to the One-Who-Foretells-the-Future, because he was having sex with too many people and he feared he would get a disease. Foreteller said, Ogunda! Would it be better to keep your penis in your pants? Something is sure to come of this. For one thing, I see a blessing of offspring.

For MONEY questions. Three-Shells-Ogunda went to the One-Who-Foretells-the-Future, because he was making money on the street, and he feared he would get in trouble with the police. Foreteller cast the shells and counted them up. Ogunda, she said, this is not the best way to make a living. Still, I see a blessing of money just the same. Take what comes. And be sure to take care getting there.

For STRATEGY questions. Three-Shells-Ogunda went to the One-Who-Foretells-the-Future, because he wanted to know if his fears were justified. None was. In fact, everything was fine . . . even better than fine. You, too, should keep a lookout for a blessing that you do not recognize as one at first.

FOUR SHELLS

owo eerin

African Name (*erindinlogan*)	Irosun
American Names (*Santeria*)	Eirorosun Eyorosun Iroso
Part II Figure (*Ifa*)	Irosun, 7
African Spirit	Shango

OPENING VERSE

You have cast four shells facing up to the sky . . . 12 shells looking down at the dust. Four shells looking at the future. Twelve shells regarding the past. Owo eerin. Four Shells. Do you see why Four Shells—Owo eerin—has come? These shells put two and two together.

For DESTINY readings. Shango—the Great Spirit of Thunder—says you are his child. As such you are loud! Arrogant! Feisty! Whatever you desire, you can achieve by working in fits and bursts. But your moods—and the fact that your voice carries so far so fast—are inclined to rule you. Watch out you don't intimidate others too much. Watch out you don't start thinking that you are too far above the rest. Promises are as easy and effective as threats. Someday someone may well vie for your power, playing by rules that put you at a disadvantage. Though you may be red-eyed with rage at times, you must remember that you are also pure as white lightning. The gift of inspiration can be yours. Turn your anger into your passion, and everything else will come along.

For SPIRITUAL questions. Four-Eyes-Irosun went to the Seer-of-Truth, because she felt haunted by her past. Seer said, Irosun, it is good to look back. It is good to remember. But no good comes of dwelling on random error. You must let go of what was not. Only then may you change what will be. *Pray to Saint Teresa—barefoot visionary—for 20/20 hindsight and even clearer senses to foresee your destiny.*

For WORK questions. Four-Eyes-Irosun went to the Seer-of-Truth, because she was weary of the job she was doing. Seer said, Irosun, is it the work itself or the hours you are keeping that gets you down? Your vision is blurred from too many evenings of anguish and worry. Get some rest. And then you will be able to put something together with something. Irosun complied. And soon her weariness vanished . . . like dreams in the dawn.

For LOVE questions. Four-Eyes-Irosun went to the Seer-of-Truth, because two suitors were fighting over her and her eyes were red from crying. Seer said, Irosun, I should have such a problem! But until it is resolved, do not let either of them see you naked. Irosun kept her buttocks and breasts covered. And soon she had just the one—true—lover following after her.

For MONEY questions. Four-Eyes-Irosun went to the Seer-of-Truth, because everywhere she went, money was burning a hole through her pocket. Seer said, Irosun, you are running in the red! Perhaps it's time to balance out instead? Irosun was reluctant to do without much of anything. Just the same, she gave up a little something for Lent. And by Easter, she had a little something to spare.

For STRATEGY questions. Four-Eyes-Irosun was praising the Seer-of-Truth, and the Seer was praising God, because all the fortunes had come true. By giving up something she thought she had wanted, Irosun got what she really had needed. She was revitalized. She was more in love than she had ever been before. And she has even stashed away some spare change. You, too, would be well advised to sacrifice something you think you want, but that only gets in the way of the things you really need.

FIVE SHELLS

owo aarun

African Name (*erindinlogan*)	Oshe
American Name (*Santeria*)	Oche
Part II Figure (*Ifa*)	Oshe, 15
African Spirit	Oshun

OPENING VERSE

You have cast five shells with their mouths open to sing . . . 11 shells with their mouths closed to hum. Five shells singing praises. Eleven shells humming along. Owo aarun. Five Shells. Do you see why Five Shells—Owo aarun—has come? These shells are wanting to make beautiful music together.

For DESTINY readings. Oshun—the spirit of the flowing river—says you are her child. As such you are linked inextricably to the tides, the currents, and the cycles of the moon. The rhythm of the Universe is yours. As a result, you are deep, dark, sensuous, and even erotic. Just be careful not to mistake love for sex. Be careful not to confuse sex for love. Use your physical wiles and "woman's intuition" with care, ever mindful of the heart you might break. Though your way is already charted for you—as it is for all rivers—you will get to your destination only by flowing along little by little. Go with the rhythm of the world around you. Let the forces of nature steer you on your true way. Your destiny has its highs and lows, its floods and droughts, but in the end you get to where you were meant to flow.

For SPIRITUAL questions. Five-Shells-Are-Oshun went to the Caster-of-Shells, because she wanted to learn how to divine the will of God. Caster said, Oshun, it will take moons and moons! But for starters, he[1] showed her how to cast things twice and choose between the left and right. Oshun took these teachings to heart. And soon Oshun's voice was praising the will of God in her life—for the secret of the 16 shells had been revealed to her. *Say a prayer to Saint Cecelia—she who sang in her heart—so that you might sing praises from yours.*

For WORK questions. Five-Shells-Are-Oshun went to the Caster-of-Shells, because her job did not stimulate her. Caster said, Oshun, what are your options? Take the time to think about the good—and don't just be dwelling on the bad all the time. Oshun did not have much extra time to spare (for all the time she wasted in complaining). But in the night, as the tide went out, she listed pros as well as cons with her finger in the sand. Then, in her dreams Oshun shifted them around, and placed them according to their rank order of importance. In the morning, as the tide came back to wash away her notes, she knew what to do and how to do it right.

For LOVE questions. Five-Shells-Are-Oshun went to the Caster-of-Shells on the eve of her wedding, because she had cold feet and wanted to be reassured that things would turn out well. Caster said, If you could see how things will be in the out-years, would it tell you what to do tomorrow? Caster said, Risk is your sacrifice. You must ei-

---

[1] By some legends it was the god Orunmila who taught Oshun divination. By other accounts, it was Oshun who stole the art of divination from him while he was away on business. In adopting the "male" system to her own needs, Oshun replaced the men's palm nuts with seashells, developed her own numbering, naming, and ranking system for the answers, and did away with the notion of marking the figures down in dust (or sand).

ther sink or swim. Oshun slept on what the diviner had said. And the next day she risked big, and took her destiny into her own hands.

For MONEY questions. Five-Shells-Are-Oshun went to the Caster-of-Shells, because she wanted to be more successful down at the market. Caster said, Oshun, your accounts are not adding up right, because you are totaling the wrong things. Times your blessings by five. Subtract each negative as one. And be apprised. Oshun took the advice of the diviner and did her homework. In a few days she had a better picture of what the bottom line really was.

For STRATEGY questions. Five-Shells-Are-Oshun was praising the Caster-of-Shells. And the Caster-of-Shells was praising God, because the will of God had been revealed in Oshun's life. Because she had listened to the diviner, Oshun now knew what was important to her, in work, in love, in money, and in all matters of her daily life. It would do you good to determine what is important to you in yours.

SIX SHELLS

owo eefa

African Name (*erindinlogan*)	Obara
American Name (*Santeria*)	Obbara
Part II Figure (*Ifa*)	Obara, 5
African Spirit	Python/Oshumare

OPENING VERSE

You have cast six shells mouths open, and not afraid to speak for the rest. You have cast ten shells mouths shut, in silence voicing their consent. Six shells speaking. Ten shells spoken for. Owo eefa. Six Shells. Do you see why Six Shells—Owo eefa—has come? These shells are seeking strength in numbers.

For DESTINY readings. Python—the spirit of the rainbow—says you are his child. As such you are intimately linked to the sun, the moon, the clouds, the stars, and all things that appear in the sky or fall from it. You can be constant, true, and perpetual. But you can also be wispy, elusive, enigmatic, and changeable. As a result, you can be easily hypnotized. Be careful that you are not taken in by superficial appearances, mirages, or illusions. You are drawn to beautiful but transitory things. But your true happiness comes from appreciating the random moments of joy, which pass all too soon. Your destiny comes from above, at the hand of the Almighty God. Pray and your wishes will be addressed. Sacrifice and your desires will be assured.

For SPIRITUAL questions. Six-Shells-Obara went to the Keeper-of-the-Ways-and-Means, because his prayers were not working anymore. Keeper said, Obara, how can you lose your religion if you have not found it yet? Look to the heavens, and then you will know what it means to believe. *Pray to Saint Francis of Assisi—the one who got back to nature—that you may find your true religion and receive its many blessings.*

For WORK questions. Six-Shells-Obara went to the Keeper-of-the-Ways-and-Means, because his benefits had been reduced by his new bosses, while at the same time he was expected to do more work. Keeper said, Obara, does the one hand not wash the other anymore? Unless you are all of one heart, things will be undone completely. Obara swallowed his pride, kept at it, and by and by his benefits improved, based on performance.

For LOVE questions. Six-Shells-Obara went to the Keeper-of-the-Ways-and-Means, because he was unable to commit. Keeper said, Obara, is love your taboo? To get closer to another, you must be honest. Reveal your secrets. Respect each other's limits. Obara considered the ramifications of spilling his guts and more than once chickened out. But at last he revealed the feelings in his heart, and the relationship that once eluded him became firm and substantial as the stars.

For MONEY questions. Six-Shells-Obara went to the Keeper-of-the-Ways-and Means, because he was borrowing from Peter to pay Paul and didn't know how to get out from under his debt. Keeper said, Obara, I accept all major credit cards! Be generous with one who needs help more than you, and your generosity will be rewarded in mysterious ways. Obara made a tax-deductible contribution on the spot. And pretty soon an unprojected windfall—like manna from heaven—paid his creditors off.

For STRATEGY questions. Six-Shells-Obara was praising the Keeper-of-the-Ways-and-Means who—in turn—was praising God that the truth had been spoken through the shells. Obara had learned that things are not accomplished by ones, but rather twos—not alone but in numbers. You, too, could stand to be a little less dependent on yourself.

SEVEN SHELLS

owo eeje

African Names (*erindinlogan*)	Odi Edi
American Name (*Santeria*)	Oddi
Part II Figure (*Ifa*)	Odi, 4
African Spirit	Obatala

OPENING VERSE

You have cast seven shells mouths open, reciting their verses. You have cast nine shells mouths silent, having forgotten their lines. Seven shells praising the Orisha. Nine shells covering their ears to the voice of the gods. Seven shells. Owo eeje. Do you see why Seven Shells—Owo eeje—has come? These shells are calling your name.

For DESTINY readings. Obatala—the white spirit of creation—says that you are his child. As such, you are intimately and personally connected to the web that binds all things together—past, present, and future—and gives all living things their breath of life, their will, and their meaning. Whatever you desire will come to you via the good use of the energy everyone has at his or her disposal. This energy is called *ashe*. Everything will be fine for you, as long as you do what is right <u>for you</u>. Follow your spirit where it leads . . . give what is appropriate for you to give . . . listen to the oracle. You have a fertile body, a creative mind, and a soul that wishes to express itself. By putting your talents and energies to work, you are destined to become prolific. You will make a mark. You will leave a legacy.

For SPIRITUAL questions. Odi-of-the-Seven-Mouths went to the Voice-of-the-Ancestors, because he did not know which way to turn. He did not know whom he could turn to. Voice said, Odi, take your trust down from the shelf where you have put it up. She said, Suspend your disbelief. And listen to the words of your father's father's father. *Say a prayer to Saint Augustine—who searched far and wide—that you may discover the truth of the elders.*

For WORK questions. Odi-of-the-Seven-Shells went to the Voice-of-the-Ancestors, because down at the marketplace they had put up No Smoking signs. Voice said, Odi, did you not choose your own destiny well? Voice said, There is no way to extend your days. Why subtract from them? Odi did not much care for this advice. But he paid for the office visit and reluctantly complied with the signs. Work was the same old dung day after day. But, unlike his father before him, Odi got to do it until he was old and gray.

For LOVE questions. Odi-of-the-Seven-Shells went to the Voice-of-the-Ancestors, because he felt impotent. For one reason or other, he was simply unable to act. Voice said, Odi, count your blessings. Every penis has a head—yours is just temporarily brain-dead. Voice said, Odi, give it some rest. Let it work itself out. Let it run its own course. Odi slept on his worries and let his dreams do their magic work. And when he woke, it was—miraculously—with an erection.

For MONEY questions. Odi-of-the-Seven-Shells went to the Voice-of-the-Ancestors, because he wanted to find wealth before he died. Voice said, Odi, even the improbable is not impossible. And the Orisha are capable of everything. But if you want to make money, you've got to spend it. And this is going to cost you. Odi reached deep into his lint-filled pockets, found little, but invested what there was. Compounding did the rest. Eventually he was even able to retire on it.

For STRATEGY questions. Odi-of-the-Seven-Shells was praising the Voice-of-the Ancestors, because the shells had spoken the truth. Not only did he smoke less and enjoy it more, but his penis was working again, and he had a little money put away for his old age. He had at last listened to the wisdom of his elders. You should listen to the wisdom of yours.

EIGHT SHELLS

owo eejo

African Names (*erindinlogan*)	Ogbe Eji Ogbe
American Name (*Santeria*)	Eyeunle
Part II Figure (*Ifa*)	Ogbe, 1
African Spirit	Orishala

OPENING VERSE

You have cast eight shells up. You have cast eight shells down. Half of one. Half of the other. Half quiet. Half loud. Eight of each kind. Owo eejo. Eight Cowries. Do you see why Eight Shells—Owo eejo—has come? These shells predict a blessing.

For DESTINY readings. Orishala—the great spirit of the diviner—says you are his child. As such you are not destined to be a farmer, nor a merchant, nor a chief. Your work is with the shells. And it is through you that they will speak. Whatever you desire will come to you, but only if you believe . . . and only if you heed the words of the oracle. Do what the shells tell you to do, and all things will be right . . . all blessings will be yours . . . all curses will be avoided. Whatever problem you confront, the remedy will come. Your life is to the service of the gods and of your fellow human beings. Use your psychic gifts well, my friend, with honesty, and with good intent.

For SPIRITUAL questions. Eight-Shells-Are-Ogbe went to the Dispenser-of-Good-Fortune, because he wanted his destiny to be assured. Dispenser said, Ogbe! Step by step. Inch by inch. Little by little. It all adds up. It all comes together at last. It all makes sense. *Say a prayer to Saint Joseph—who saw angels—that your Guardian will guide both your feet and your head.*

For WORK questions. Eight-Shells-Are-Ogbe went to the Dispenser-of-Good-Fortune, because he was up for a promotion and he wanted a better job. Dispenser cast the shells and said, Ogbe! She said, A lucky name is preceded by a title. She said, Lucky feet put their shoes up on the desk. She said, Lucky buttocks sit on a padded chair. But then she warned, Avoid arrogance. Be patient, and luck will reward you. Ogbe heeded the words of the diviner, and—though it took longer than he had expected for the paperwork to go through—he did, at last, get his promotion.

For LOVE questions. Eight-Shells-Are-Ogbe went to the Dispenser-of-Good-Fortune, because he wanted a new family. Dispenser said, Ogbe! If a child is ugly, his parents do not return him for a handsome child. If a child is sickly, they do not exchange him for a healthy one. If a child needs help, they do not turn him away. She said, Gather around you those who take you as you are. Avoid unfaithfulness and you will have a pleasant life. Ogbe heeded Dispenser's words, and he found joy in the life he shared with his family.

For MONEY questions. Eight-Shells-Are-Ogbe went to the Dispenser-of-Good-Fortune, because he wanted not just a house but a home. Dispenser cast the shells and said, Ogbe! You will live to be healthy, wealthy, and wise. But it will take you three tries to find a home. There will be three people in your life. Three jobs. Three places. All in all, three separate lives. And none can be skipped. Go forth, she said. Ogbe did. And on his third attempt at happiness, he found it.

For STRATEGY questions. Eight-Shells-Are-Ogbe was praising the Dispenser-of-Good-Fortune. And Dispenser was praising the gods, because the shells had spoken truth. Ogbe got the title, the family, and the home he wanted. All it required was time and a little patience. In your present situation, all possibilities are open. All blessings are possible now. Wait and watch for the miracles to unfold in your life.

NINE SHELLS

owo eesan

African Name (erindinlogan)	Osa
American Name (Santeria)	Ossa
Part II Figure (Ifa)	Osa, 10
African Spirit	Oya

<u>OPENING VERSE</u>

*You have cast nine shells with their mouths wide and ready to eat.
You have cast seven shells with their bellies gaping, ready to consume. Nine mouths are gnawing. Seven stomachs are growling.
Owo eesan. Nine shells. Do you see why Nine Shells—Owo
eesan—has come? These shells are howling for a bite to eat.*

For DESTINY readings. Oya—the great spirit of the wind—
says you are her child. As such you are destined to be a force to
reckon with. Be careful that in your efforts to reform the world, you
do not destroy the good as well. You are the sort of person who is inclined to work best by—for the most part—remaining calm, but occasionally gusting. Beware the occasional fit of rage that overwhelms
you with blind anger. Balance work, rest, and play. Your destiny is intimately linked with someone else—a lover, friend, spouse, or
mate—who is equally stormy, hot-blooded, and passionate. Look for
the shared joy that brings out the sparkle in both of you, and you will
accomplish powerful works together.

For SPIRITUAL questions. Osa-of-Nine-Shells went to see
Destiny's Slave, the famous diviner, because she wanted to avoid the
inevitable for as long as she possibly could. Slave said, Osa, nothing
comes to earth that does not fade. Nothing is built that does not
crumble. Not even the rocks are impervious to the effects of wind.
But if you want to live out your allotted span of days, you need but
sacrifice some of the salt of life . . . some of your high . . . and some of
your passion. *Say a prayer to the Virgin Mary—who gave birth to im-
mortality—that the fountain of youth may not elude you.*

For WORK questions. Osa-of-Nine-Shells went to see Destiny's
Slave, because she was planting a garden and she wanted to assure
the harvest would satisfy her hunger. Slave said, Osa, I see many
seeds. I see fruits, roots, and beans. Peppers. Ears of corn. I see many
children of the vine. But if the winds and rains do not come, they will
die before you can eat them in your stew. If the winds do not bring
the rains on time, you will have to haul up water. Osa did as she was

instructed. And when the harvest came, she had enough produce to leave some on the doorsteps of her neighbors.

For LOVE questions. Osa-of-Nine-Shells went to see Destiny's Slave, because there was someone she wanted to see naked. There was someone with whom she wanted to have sex. Slave said, Osa, there is no guarantee that it will last any longer than a summer's breeze. She said, If you want to see this person naked, you must risk your trust. If you have sex with this person, you must risk having your confidence misplaced. Osa took the leap. She saw the other person naked. And it lasted for as long as they both kept their mouths shut.

For MONEY questions. Osa-of-Nine-Shells went to see Destiny's Slave, because she was constipated, bloated, and unable to pass wind. She was willing to pay any price to feel better. Slave said, Osa, you have definitely come to the right place. She said, Incidentally, will this be billed to your insurance or will be you be paying cash before you leave my office today? Osa paid the prices the doctor, the lab technician, and the pharmacist asked, and after an enema or two, she was feeling much better.

For STRATEGY questions. Osa-of-Nine-Shells was praising the diviner, and the diviner was praising the gods, because the shells had spoken truth. By doing what the diviner said, Osa was able to hold back the inevitable, to overcome the impediment, and move the unmovable. Your situation requires you to face up to the things that might, could, and often do go wrong. Avoid what you can. Overcome the rest. And if all precaution fails, seek the appropriate remedy.

TEN SHELLS

owo eewaa

African Name (*erindinlogan*)	Ofun
American Name (*Santeria*)	Ofun mafun
Part II Figure (*Ifa*)	Ofun, 16
African Spirit	Eshu

OPENING VERSE

You have cast ten shells looking up. You have cast six shells facing down. Ten shells, counted with double fists, and ready to speak. Six shells, counted with a single finger pointed up, and having nothing to say for themselves but that. Owo eewaa. Ten Cowries. Do you see why Ten Shells—Owo eewaa—has come? These shells are muttering curses. These shells are ready for a fight.

For DESTINY readings. Eshu—the light spirit of pranks, jokes, and trickery—says you are his child. As such you are inclined to want to have the last laugh. But be careful it is not on you! Since you are well connected to the Powers that Be, you must work at achieving your best behavior. The gods have placed much confidence and trust in you. Through your actions on earth, you do their bidding for them, and they are not ignorant of what you have done in their name. Resist the temptation to take advantage of your status, position, and connections. Use power wisely and without malice or vengeance. In particular avoid sexual misconduct. There is a particular form of deviance that may serve as your undoing if you see it through.

For SPIRITUAL questions. Ofun-of-the-Ten-Shells went to see the Messenger-of-the-Gods, because something had come over him and he was distracted by something he was forbidden to do. Messenger cast the shells and said, Ofun! There is a good reason why you should not be doing certain things. But even if there were no reason, your taboo is your taboo. Get too close and it will burn you. *Say a prayer to any saint you choose—and say it quick!—that you may rise above the temptation of your bugaboo.*

For WORK questions. Ofun-of-the-Ten-Shells went to see the Messenger-of-the-Gods, because he feared he was going to receive a demotion. Messenger said, Ashes and bones. Bones and ashes. Power left untended is ripe for stealing. Ofun, she said, cover your bases. Ofun, she said, erase your tracks. Ofun, she said, protect your buttocks! She did not have to say another word, for Ofun knew what he must do. Silently, swiftly, he made his cunning moves.

For LOVE questions. Ofun-of-the-Ten-Shells went to see the Messenger-of-the-Gods, because the love he felt for another was forbidden to him. Messenger cast the shells and said, Ofun! Mother, father, sister, brother—none of these can have the other. She said, Ofun, when it comes to these, keep your penis in your pants. Or else be willing to know what it means to be ostracized. Ofun did not listen. And that is why he has ended up on the bottom of the heap and his reputation precedes him everywhere he goes.

For MONEY questions. Ofun-of-the-Ten-Shells went to see the Messenger-of-the-Gods, because he was obsessed with money to the point where he could no longer part with any. Messenger said, Ofun, this is serious business. They've got you by the balls. Unless you give them what they want, you will become a falsetto. Messenger said, I know the perfect charity—just make your check out to me. Ofun laughed in a hearty tenor, got up from the diviner's table, and turned to walk away. Years later he died from poverty, a very rich man.

For STRATEGY questions. The diviners were praising the Messenger-of-the-Gods that he had spoken the truth to Ofun-of-the-Ten-Shells. Had he only listened! The message for you is clear. If you want to get out of the situation you are in, you must change your ways. Direct your sights high. In working toward your goals, always do what is right.

ELEVEN SHELLS

owo ookan laa

African Name (*erindinlogan*)	Owonrin
American Name (*Santeria*)	Ogbi Chogbi Ojuani Chober
Part II Figure (*Ifa*)	Owonrin, 8
African Spirit	Babalu Aye

OPENING VERSE

You have cast eleven shells up, their mouths chattering. You have cast five shells down, not able to get a word in edgewise. Eleven shells buzzing. Five shells mute. Owo ookan laa. One-in-addition-to-ten Cowries. Do you see why Eleven Shells—Owo ookan laa—has come? These shells are crying out a warning.

For DESTINY readings. Babalu Aye—the great spirit of change—says you are his child. As such you are destined to adapt to many alterations in your environment. You are destined to evolve as a result of the many experiences you have and the life-altering passages you make. It will do you no good to attempt to hold on to "the good old days." Time passes swiftly . . . and you must let it go its way, heal its wounds, and lighten its scars. Take in everything that goes on around you. Be on the cutting edge if you must—but beware its razor-sharpness. All will be right with you if you deal with the changes that come from without and control the changes that you bring upon your own head.

For SPIRITUAL questions. Ten-Plus-One-Owonrin went to the Guardian-of-Secrets, because she did not agree with a new law that had been passed and so she disobeyed it and got caught. Now she cursed the gods. Secret said, Owonrin, you knew the rule; why did you break it? *Say a prayer to Saint Benedict—the mender of broken things—that the pieces of your life may be fitted together again.*

For WORK questions. Ten-Plus-One-Owonrin went to the Guardian-of-Secrets, because she felt she was being picked on in the marketplace. Secret said, Jobs these days are scarce. Jobs these days are few and far between. Sacrifice your pride or learn the price of honor. Owonrin did not make the sacrifice. And that is how she wound up going door to door.

For LOVE questions. Ten-Plus-One-Owonrin went to the Guardian-of-Secrets, because she felt herself getting involved with someone else. Secret said, Owonrin, a husband cheats on his wife, a wife cheats on her husband . . . and in the end four people are cheated. Stop before you begin. But Owonrin could not resist. And that is why she has moved out of her house . . . and into an apartment.

For MONEY questions. Ten-Plus-One-Owonrin went to the Guardian-of-Secrets, because she had given her friend some money and now she wanted it back. Secret said, Were you taken by your friend? Or taken in? Secret said, Owonrin, a loan is a loan, a gift is a gift. If you dare to reclaim a gift, you risk your friendship. Owonrin did, and that is how she got her new clothes but nowhere to go.

For STRATEGY questions. Ten-Plus-One-Owonrin went to the Guardian-of-Secrets, because she felt cheated. But she did not hear what the diviner said. She thought she knew better. Your situation is the same. Beware the traps you set for yourself. Watch out for pranks pulled on you by others. Try not to be envious. And learn not to be proud.

TWELVE SHELLS

owo eeji laa

African Names (*erindinlogan*)	Iwori Ejila Sebora
American Name (*Santeria*)	Eyila Chebora
Part II Figure (*Ifa*)	Iwori, 3
African Spirit	Aganyu

OPENING VERSE

You have cast twelve shells with their mouths open—a cacophony of voices! You have cast four shells and four shells only with their mouths closed—a void of silence! Twelve shells up. Four shells down. Owo eeji laa. Ten-Plus-Two-Cowries. Do you see why Twelve Shells—Owo eeji laa—has come? These shells are egging you on.

For DESTINY readings. Aganyu—the great spirit of fire—says you are his child. As such you are destined to burn with the fire of your inner passion . . . your secret desire . . . your endless dream. Pursue the thing that calls you—no matter what road it takes you down—and you will not go wrong in achieving your destiny. Look within your heart to identify your mission, your purpose, and the love of your life. Draw from your inner flame the strength and courage to achieve your greatest ambition. But beware: That which makes you glow may just as easily be your undoing in the end. As you go through your daily routines, permit yourself to shine, glow, and rise above the mundane.

For SPIRITUAL questions. Ten-Plus-Two-Iwori went to the Drummer-of-the-Gods, because she felt like she was being pulled in two different directions. Drummer said, Iwori, the way to ecstasy is inclined to involve agony. Drummer said, Iwori, growth is inclined to involve a few growing pains. *Say a prayer to Saint Christopher—who took the weight of the whole world on his back—that he might guide you on this passage that leads to the fulfillment of your dream.*

For WORK questions. Ten-Plus-Two-Iwori went to the Drummer-of-the-Gods, because her dream was to work at a certain place, but she couldn't get through to anyone of importance. Drummer said, Iwori, press "1" if you know your party's extension. Press "2" for a directory of staff. Press "3" and a real human being will be with you shortly. Do not be easily deterred by artificial barriers. Take whatever steps are necessary. Use whatever connections are possible. Go for what you want. Iwori did, and that was how she eventually got the job she wanted.

For LOVE questions. Ten-Plus-Two-Iwori went to the Drummer-of-the-Gods, because she was pregnant but her baby was past due and she felt she could wait no longer for the child to come. Drummer said, Iwori, nine months is only an average. And besides, all things are not known by scientists. Light a candle and wait for the Full Moon. Iwori did. Iwori lit a candle. Iwori waited as patiently as she could. And on the Full Moon the spirit of her unborn child came down from heaven to create its own flame on earth.

For MONEY questions. Ten-Plus-Two-Iwori went to the Drummer-of-the-Gods, because she wanted a house for her family to live in, but interest rates were rising, and she was afraid she would get burnt by the bank. Drummer said, It's a buyer's market, but you'll have to lock in fast. Iwori locked for 90 days and got herself a discounted rate. And that is how she came to live in the place that her family now calls home.

For STRATEGY questions. Ten-Plus-Two-Iwori was praising the Drummer-of-the-Gods, because everything the shells had spoken had come true. She made it past her various obstacles through persistence and inner strength. The situation you are in is much the same. There is a time to hold out for the things you need, to press for the things you desire, and to act on things you want to happen. Go after the things you want . . . and you will get the things you want badly enough.

THIRTEEN SHELLS

owo eeta laa

African Names (*erindinlogan*)	Ika
American Name (*Santeria*)	Metanla
Part II Figure (*Ifa*)	⠶ Ika, 14
African Spirit	Yemoja

OPENING VERSE

You have cast thirteen shells with their mouths open, but saying nothing. You have cast three shells with their mouths shut, revealing everything. Thirteen shells up. Three shells down. Owo eeta laa. Ten-Plus-Three-Shells. Do you see why Thirteen Shells—Owo eeta laa—has come? These shells are icky . . . but bear with me. They can be overcome.

For DESTINY readings. Yemoja—the great spirit of the deep—says you are her child. As such you are destined to be a very mysterious and—therefore—psychically powerful person. Others may revere or dread you for no reason other than the vibrations you send out—and for good reason. Be careful what you think about, for your thoughts have a way of manifesting themselves—for either good or ill. Put your great powers to work for the benefit of others, and you yourself will prosper. Use your powers with malicious intent, and your ill wishes will come back around to visit you. To achieve your full destiny, avoid laying traps for others to stumble into. Avoid falling into pits yourself.

For SPIRITUAL questions. Ika-of-the-Thirteen-Shells went to the Container-of-Bones, because she had been slandered and she wanted revenge. Bones said, Now, Ika! Calm down. Curses have a way of coming round and round . . . and back again to curse the head of the one who made them. *Say a prayer to your favorite saint—Matthew, Mark, Luke, or John—to bless the bed you'll lie upon.*

For WORK questions. Ika-of-the-Thirteen-Shells went to the Container-of-Bones, because she felt that someone at work was out to get her. Bones said, Now, Ika! Avoid being paranoid. But, just the same, if I were you, I'd cover my buttocks. Do your job as best you can, and pray that right will prevail. Otherwise, mind your own business. Ika did. And that was how she was able to keep her position.

For LOVE questions. Ika-of-the-Thirteen-Shells went to the Container-of-Bones, because she felt she was ugly and she wanted a spell to make her beautiful. Bones said, Now, Ika! So what if you never get the centerfold? It doesn't mean you can't make the cover. Bones said, Ika, look beyond your own scars, if you want others to forget them. Ika did. And it was her resulting self-confidence that won her—not only personal success—but a genuine suitor.

For MONEY questions. Ika-of-the-Thirteen-Shells went to the Container-of-Bones, because she was so ill, she felt cursed with a disease and wanted a miracle cure. Bones said, Now, Ika! Yours is a difficult case. I recommend you go to my friend the specialist—but be prepared to pay. Ika was so desperate, she went and paid whatever the doctor demanded. Things got worse before they improved, until finally she was able to live with it.

For STRATEGY questions. Ika-of-the-Thirteen-Shells was praising the Container-of-Bones, because everything Bones had said came true. The things that seemed so bad to her were like hot water that cooled. Your situation is similar. You are up to your buttocks in monkey dirt. You are adrift in the lagoon without a paddle. You are tempted to do something rash, look for a quick fix, or hope for a miracle. But a more lasting remedy comes with time, due diligence, and forthright effort.

FOURTEEN SHELLS

owo eerin laa

African Name (*erindinlogan*)	Oturupon
American Name (*Santeria*)	Merinla
Part II Figure (*Ifa*)	:: :: Oturupon, 13
African Spirit	Oshosi

OPENING VERSE

You have cast fourteen shells with their mouths looking up at you and grinning. You have cast two shells turned away and mooning you with their stomachs. Fourteen up. Two down. Fourteen Cowries.

Owo eerin laa. Ten-Plus-Four-Shells. Do you see why Fourteen Shells—Owo eerin laa—has come? These shells are smiling with many good intentions.

For DESTINY readings. Oshosi—the great spirit of the hunter—says you are his child. As such you are inclined to search your way through life, looking for the things that are destined to cross your path. You are adept at tracking things down . . . at reading the signs around you and using information as well as tools to do your work. It is by persevering that you make your mark. There are many in this world who will depend on the artful execution of your skills. Remain brave in the face of would-be danger. Aim for your mark. Concentrate. Hit your moving target.

For SPIRITUAL questions. Oturupon-the-Fourteenth went to the Worker-of-Miracles, because he had had such a falling out with his best friend that at this moment he could kill him. Miracle worker said, Gongs and drums. Rattles and sticks. Oturupon! You need a remedy. And you need it quick. *Say a prayer to God Almighty—the Holy Arbitrator—that the evil between you may yet turn to peace.*

For WORK questions. Oturupon-the-Fourteenth went to the Worker-of-Miracles, because he had been called away on an urgent matter of business and much trouble lay ahead. Miracle worker said, Oturupon! This is a journey of 380 days at the most, 320 at the least. The best you can do right now is take one step at a time. Oturupon took the words of the diviner to heart. A year later, he got to where he was going. And it was worth the trip.

For LOVE questions. Oturupon-the-Fourteenth went to the Worker-of-Miracles, because he had fallen in love with a smoker and he feared he would die before he got to be a hundred. Miracle worker said, Oturupon! What are you doing in a relationship that's not worth a little sacrifice . . . on both sides? Miracle worker said, If I were you, I'd let someone stronger than a medicine man make my decisions for me. Listen to your heart. Oturupon did. And that was how the two lovers came to common terms.

For MONEY questions. Oturupon-the-Fourteenth went to the Worker-of-Miracles, because he was hungry all the time and his hunger was eating him out of house and home. Miracle worker said, Here, gnaw on this bone: What is your stomach's intention? What is your head's complaint? Oturupon! Sacrifice to your head, forget your gut—and all will be right. Oturupon did. And that is how he quit worrying about spending too much on food.

For STRATEGY questions. Oturupon-the-Fourteenth was praising the Worker-of-Miracles. And the Miracle worker was praising the gods, because the shells had once again spoken the truth. Oturupon had mistaken his blessings for curses, and that is why he felt miserable. Your situation is no better and no worse. There is so much contention in your world. There is so much finger pointing. There is so much guilt and so much blame. Do not contribute to such unseemly behavior. Get on with the real work that needs to be done.

FIFTEEN SHELLS

owo eedogun

African Names (*erindinlogan*)	Otura Ofun Kanran
American Name (*Santeria*)	Manunla
Part II Figure (*Ifa*)	⦂⦂ Otura, 12
African Spirit	Osanyin

OPENING VERSE

You have cast fifteen shells with their mouths open, speaking in an uproar to the world. You have cast but one shell—and one shell only—silent. Fifteen shells upright. One shell reversed. Owo eedogun. Twenty-Minus-Five-Shells. Do you see why Fifteen Shells—Owo eedogun—has come? These shells are telling you what you must do to make your peace.

For DESTINY readings. Osanyin—the great spirit of healing—says you are his child. As such you are destined to minister to others in this life, to sacrifice your own wants for the sake of others, and to devote yourself to the care and nurturing of others. But in your striving to become the saint, be careful you do not become the martyr! In order to do your best, greatest, and most noble work, you will need to devote yourself to your art, science, religion, or other system of beliefs. For it is from out of your devotion that all the rest of your blessings come . . . abundantly and full. It is from your sense of dedication that evil is avoided. It is from the power of your prayer that miracles occur.

For SPIRITUAL questions. Twenty-Minus-Five-Otura went to the One-of-the-Highest-Authority, because her spirit was willing but her flesh was weak. Authority said, Otura! The means are even more important than the ends. Authority said, Otura, I won't take your money this time. Go in peace. *Say a prayer to all the Powers that Be, that you may find the light from out of darkness.*

For WORK questions. Twenty-Minus-Five-Otura went to the One-of-the-Highest-Authority, because the family business was not going well, and she wanted to know how to get it back on track. Authority said, Sales have flown south. Expenses are hitting the roof. And everybody's going in different directions. Authority said, If I were you, I'd recall the dream of the founders. Otura thought that was the dumbest thing she'd ever heard. Still, she followed the diviner's advice. And that was how the family business turned around.

For LOVE questions. Twenty-Minus-Five-Otura went to the One-of-the-Highest-Authority, because her household was turned upside down and she feared things would never be the same again. Authority said, Otura, there is no quick fix for this one. I suggest you get away from it all and take some time to think things through.

Otura did. And absence made her heart grow surer, if not also fonder.

For MONEY questions. Twenty-Minus-Five-Otura went to the One-of-the-Highest-Authority, because her relatives were always asking her for money, and she was running out of cash. Authority said, Otura, what's money for? Authority said, Otura, will they not be there later to help you? Have they not been there in the past? Authority said, I predict a blessing of abundance. Otura went away confused. But she went on helping her relatives and, in the end, they had helped each other through.

For STRATEGY questions. Twenty-Minus-Five-Otura was praising the One-of-the-Highest-Authority. And the One-of-the-Highest-Authority was praising the gods, that the shells had spoken truth. Otura had been anxious and confused, but when she listened to the diviner—when she remembered her family—everything in her head cleared. Your situation is much the same. Sacrifice for your household and all will be right in your life.

SIXTEEN SHELLS

owo eerin din logun

African Names (*erindinlogan*)	Irete
American Name (*Santeria*)	Mediloggun
Part II Figure (*Ifa*)	Irete, 11
African Spirit	Babalu Aye

OPENING VERSE

You have cast sixteen shells, all with their mouths up! You have cast sixteen shells, all trying to talk at once. Sixteen Cowries! Owo eerin din logun! Sixteen blessings. Sixteen evils. Sixteen spirits. Sixteen of everything. Do you see why Sixteen Shells—Owo merindinlogun— has come? These shells are trying to get your full attention.

For DESTINY readings. Babalu Aye—the great spirit of clearing away—says that you are his child. As such, your destiny will be to tear things apart . . . and put them back together again. Try not to look upon the imperfect world with jaded eyes. Though you may well be obsessed, it is not all just about sex and death—and there is no reason to be blue or bitter. Your purpose was set for you before your soul ever left heaven. It is your job to pick up the pieces and leave your world better than you found it. *Ashe,* my friend. God with you, so be it.

For SPIRITUAL questions. Irete-of-the-Twenty-Minus-Four-Shells went to Our-Mother-of-the-Cowries, because she was terribly blue and awfully depressed, and she didn't see how she could go on like this. Our Mother said, Irete! I will add no salt to your wounds. I will put no pepper in your food. Our Mother said, I will offer up smoke for you. I will offer up rum. And for all of this I will not take a dime. *Recite a litany to all the saints that confidence in self will be restored in this case.*

For WORK questions. Twenty-Minus-Four-Irete went to Our-Mother-of-the-Cowries, because everything she did at work turned out wrong. Our Mother said, Irete, oh, what needless pains we bear! Relegate your errors to the shredder. Feed your worries to the trash. Put your self-doubts on the garbage heap. But Irete could not follow the diviner's advice, for lack of trust. And that was how she lost her place.

For LOVE questions. Twenty-Minus-Four-Irete went to Our-Mother-of-the-Cowries, because her relationship had spoiled and she was no longer satisfied with it. Our Mother said, Irete, if you're sure you want to flush it down the toilet, be my guest. Just remember some things refuse to go down the first time. Our Mother said, You must keep your resolve if you want to avoid making the same mistakes again. Irete did not, and that was how she divorced one turd only to marry another.

For MONEY questions. Twenty-Minus-Four-Irete went to Our-Mother-of-the-Cowries, because she had spent all of her money on trinkets and had none left to buy a bigger house to keep it all in, let alone anything in her pocket to pay the diviner. Our Mother said, Irete! Okay, this is a freebie. Take my advice or don't if you like, but I'm afraid you'll have to part with some of your stuff. Irete could not. And that was how she found herself pushing her belongings around in a cart.

For STRATEGY questions. And they were all praising the diviners. And the diviners were praising the gods, that the shells had spoken truth. Irete was her own worst enemy. And it seemed like she could not get out of her rut. Had she only listened to Our-Mother-of-the-Cowries . . . had she only paid the price. Your situation is one that you have brought upon yourself. And only you can undo your own hex.

NO SHELLS

African Names (*erindinlogan*)	Opira
American Name (*Santeria*)	Opira
Part II Figure (*Ifa*)	—none—

OPENING VERSE

Sixteen shells have fallen in front of you. And not a single mouth has come up. Sixteen shells have fallen and not a single voice has spoken. Silence, my friend. This is Opira. Do you see why No Shells has come? These shells are saying nothing tonight.

For DESTINY readings. See the answer for Sixteen Shells.

For SPIRITUAL questions. No-Shells-Opira went to the Diviner-at-the-Roadside on a lark, because there was really nothing on his (or her?) mind and he had no questions to ask. Diviner cast the shells and said . . . nothing, for there was nothing to be said.

For WORK questions. No-Shells-Opira went to the Diviner-at-the-Roadside even though—in her heart of hearts—she doubted the oracle and did not believe in communicating with the gods. Diviner cast the shells, took one look, and whisked them up into her hands again. Perhaps we'd have better luck another day, she said.

For LOVE questions. No-Shells-Opira went to the Diviner-at-the-Roadside because his friends had dared him to do so. Diviner took down the shells to the mat, but simply shook her head and gave him his money back.

For MONEY questions. No-Shells-Opira went to the Diviner-at-the-Roadside because he had nothing better to do with his money. Diviner put the money aside and cast the shells for naught.

For STRATEGY questions. No one was praising the diviners today. But the diviners were still praising the gods, that the shells had spoken truth. Opira did not believe that the shells could talk, and so there was no use in going on. No matter how many times you rinse it, a black cloth cannot be washed white.

The Combinations

ONE SHELL

owo ookan

Okanran is about things that go wrong on account of lack of faith. It is about things that turn right, after requiring a feat of strength, sheer willpower, and the use of one's head. Though tragedy may be involved at first, in the end there will be triumph.

Combinations of Okanran
(Okana Sodde)

1 + 1   *Okanran Meji*

With Okanran falling first and Okanran falling again, we have found Okanran Meji (two Okanrans)—the head of the family. This Odu says a blessing will come from tending to family matters. Watch out for the curse of broken promises. Avoid causing contention. The best cure for what ails you is already known in your own head. *In choosing between alternatives—the left hand is chosen. Okanran Meji has spoken.*

1 + 2   *Okanran Oyeku*

With Okanran falling first and Oyeku falling next, we have found Okanran Oyeku—the head of the household. This Odu says the source of your blessing is a mother figure. Beware she does not pamper you too much, lest you be cursed with overprotection. Avoid turning your back on her later. The best cure for what ails you is respect and due diligence. *In choosing between alternatives—the left hand is chosen. Okanran Oyeku has spoken.*

1 + 3   *Okanran Ogunda*

With Okanran falling first and Ogunda falling next, we have found Okanran Ogunda—the main man. This Odu foretells a blessing that comes as a result of assuming a leadership position. Watch out that you do not grow too arrogant, or your followers may wind up cursing you. Avoid indiscretion and overexposure. The best cure for what ails you is to temper your ambitions with a strong vision. *In choosing between alternatives—the left hand is chosen. Okanran Ogunda has spoken.*

1 + 4   Okanran Irosun

With Okanran falling first and Irosun falling next, we have found Okanran Irosun—the painted head. This Odu foretells of a blessing that comes from wearing the appropriate mask and acting the appropriate part. Do not be so quick to curse luck, lest it turn even worse. Avoid falling into a rut. The best cure for what ails you is to put on a happy face. *In choosing between alternatives—the left hand is chosen. Okanran Irosun has spoken.*

1 + 5   Okanran Oshe

With Okanran falling first and Oshe falling next, we have found Okanran Oshe—the headwaters. This Odu says a blessing will come from someone at a distance. A blessing will come from some secret source. Be aware that things happening elsewhere will eventually catch up to you, lest you curse the fact that they take you by surprise. Avoid myopia. The best cure for what ails you is to look outside your house. *In choosing between alternatives—the right hand is chosen. Okanran Oshe has spoken.*

1 + 6   Okanran Obara

With Okanran falling first and Obara falling next, we have found Okanran Obara—the thundering one. This Odu says a blessing is about to fall down on you from the sky. Your spiritual double in heaven is looking out for you. Beware a lesson learned the hard way. But avoid losing your innocence. The cure for what ails you comes to you as if in a dream. *In choosing between alternatives—the right hand is chosen. Okranran Obara has spoken.*

114

1 + 7   Okanran Odi

With Okanran falling first and Odi falling next, we have found Okanran Odi—the soul's container. This Odu says a blessing will come from the Great Spirit within you. Do not curse the unborn. Do not curse the ancestors. We are all one in the same. And everything is connected. Avoid self-centered behavior. The cure to what ails you involves honoring the living and the dead. *In choosing between alternatives—the right hand is chosen. Okanran Odi has spoken.*

1 + 8   Okanran Ogbe

With Okanran falling first and Ogbe falling next, we have found Okanran Ogbe—the head diviner. This Odu says many a blessing is in store due to the occupation meant for you to have. Beware that you do not work at something else, lest you are cursed with misery and lack of success. Avoid denying the truth about yourself. The cure for what ails you is to accept yourself for who and what you are . . . embrace your destiny. *In choosing between alternatives—the left hand is chosen. Okanran Ogbe has spoken.*

1 + 9   Okanran Osa

With Okanran falling first and Osa falling next, we have found Okanran Osa—the leading lady. This Odu predicts a blessing that comes as the result of being singled out. Beware that you are not blinded by the limelight, lest you curse your loss of insight. Bow neither too often nor too low to your audience. The best cure for what ails you is to learn from your reviews. *In choosing between alternatives—the right hand is chosen. Okanran Osa has spoken.*

1 + 10   Okanran Ofun

With Okanran falling first and Ofun falling next, we have found Okanran Ofun—the head troublemaker. This Odu says a blessing results from someone stepping out of line. But in bending the rules, beware that the rule makers do not curse you with oppression. Honor your personal taboo. Avoid acting as if you are immortal. The best cure for what ails you is a swift kick in the buttocks. *In choosing between alternatives—the left hand is chosen. Okanran Ofun has spoken.*

1 + 11   Okanran Owonrin

With Okanran falling first and Owonrin falling next, we have found Okanran Owonrin—the head procrastinator. This Odu predicts a promise that in fact may not materialize in the end. Watch out for the curse that circles endlessly inside your head. Avoid making the same decision again and again. The best cure for what ails you is to—once and for all—choose. *In choosing between alternatives—the right hand is chosen. Okanran Owonrin has spoken.*

1 + 12   Okanran Iwori

With Okanran falling first and Iwori falling next, we have found Okanran Iwori—the head of the warrior. This Odu foretells a blessing that comes out of bravery, strength, commitment, and action. Do not curse the difficult test, lest you seal your fate too fast. Avoid dissension. The best cure for what ails you is to fight for what you believe . . . to prove what you must about yourself. *In choosing between alternatives—the right hand is chosen. Okanran Iwori has spoken.*

1 + 13   Okanran Ika

With Okanran falling first and Ika falling next, we have found Okanran Ika—the head of a witch. This Odu says that a blessing from craft, skill, and mastery of some secret art is ordained. Watch out for those who are skeptical of you, lest they succeed in undermining your power. Avoid disparagement and ridicule. The best cure for what ails you is to keep your secrets to yourself. *In choosing between alternatives—the right hand is chosen. Okanran Ika has spoken.*

1 + 14   Okanran Oturupon

With Okanran falling first and Oturupon falling next, we have found Okanran Oturupon—the head guardian. This Odu foretells a blessing that results from a humble, generous, and protective spirit. Watch out for those who would blindside you just to prove they could. Avoid letting others mislead you. The best cure for what ails you is to listen when your spirit voices speak. *In choosing between alternatives—the right hand is chosen. Okanran Oturupon has spoken.*

1 + 15   Okanran Otura

With Okanran falling first and Otura falling next, we have found Okanran Otura—the head of the peacemaker. This Odu foretells a blessing that comes from spiritual enlightenment and passive strength. Beware the curse of self-doubt, lest it curse you with a weakening of your potential. Avoid the disbeliever in yourself. The best cure for what ails you is already rooted in your own self-confidence. *In choosing between alternatives—the right hand is chosen. Okanran Otura has spoken.*

1 + 16   Okanran Irete

With Okanran falling first and Irete falling next, we have found Okanran Irete—the head that has fallen. This Odu foretells a blessing that comes from getting rid of what is no longer needed. Beware the fear of success. Avoid the fear of failure. It is curses either way. The best cure for what ails you is to turn your shortcomings into strengths. *In choosing between alternatives—the right hand is chosen. Okanran Irete has spoken.*

1 + 0   Okanran Opira

With Okanran falling first and Opira falling next, we have found Okanran Opira. There is nothing wrong with your head. *In choosing between alternatives—neither hand is chosen. Okanran Opira has spoken through silence.*

TWO SHELLS

owo eeji

Oyeku is about difficulties that arise from doing things in a way that is wrong for you or at a time that is not right for you. It is about blessings that result from pursuing the unique track that your soul wants to follow. It is about living up to your personal destiny.

Combinations of Oyeku
(*Eyioko*)

2 + 1   Oyeku Okanran

With Oyeku falling first and Okanran falling next, we have found Oyeku Okanran—the personal secret. This Odu foretells of a blessing that comes out of seeming chaos. Do not curse the destiny that you yourself requested. Avoid clinging to a worn-out shell. The best cure for what ails you is to take a leap of faith—believe in yourself. *In choosing between alternatives—the right hand is chosen. Oyeku Okanran has spoken.*

2 + 2   Oyeku Meji

With Oyeku falling first and Oyeku falling again, we have found Oyeku Meji (two Oyekus)—the deep, dark secret. This Odu says a blessing will result from honoring your taboo—that thing which you feel instinctively you should not do at this time. Beware those who would beguile you into cheating on yourself. Avoid revealing your fantasies to others. The best cure for what ails you is to protect your own secrets. *In choosing between alternatives—the left hand is chosen. Oyeku Meji has spoken.*

2 + 3   Oyeku Ogunda

With Oyeku falling first and Ogunda falling next, we have found Oyeku Ogunda—the male secret. This Odu predicts a blessing that comes out of an overt act. Be wary of your partners, lest you become cursed with their afflictions. Avoid sex with strangers. The best cure for what ails you is a permanent relationship. *In choosing between alternatives—the left hand is chosen. Oyeku Ogunda has spoken.*

2 + 4   Oyeku Irosun

With Oyeku falling first and Irosun falling next, we have found Oyeku Irosun—the secret to success. This Odu foretells a blessing that comes as a result of dressing for the part. Beware the curse that may result from wearing red on a solemn occasion. Avoid things that clash with who you are. The best cure for what ails you is to use your better judgment. *In choosing between alternatives—the left hand is chosen. Oyeku Irosun has spoken.*

2 + 5   Oyeku Oshe

With Oyeku falling first and Oshe falling next, we have found Oyeku Oshe—the secret touch. This Odu foretells a blessing that comes as a result of direct experience. Beware the curse that comes as a result of distancing yourself from others. Avoid insensitivity. The best cure for what ails you is to touch and be touched. *In choosing between alternatives—the right hand is chosen. Oyeku Oshe has spoken.*

2 + 6   Oyeku Obara

With Oyeku falling first and Obara falling next, we have found Oyeku Obara—the secret dream. This Odu foretells a blessing that comes from out of a vision of the future. Beware that you do not scoff at your dreams. A curse is sure to result from ignoring a timely warning. A curse is sure to result from scoffing at a favorable forecast. Avoid impatience and discontent. The best cure for what ails you is to trust in your premonitions. *In choosing between alternatives—the right hand is chosen. Oyeku Obara has spoken.*

2 + 7   Oyeku Odi

With Oyeku falling first and Odi falling next, we have found Oyeku Odi—the secret, sacred place. This Odu predicts a blessing that results from a birth or rebirth experience. Beware the curse that comes from stagnation. Avoid predictability. The best cure for what ails you is to pursue your personal evolution. Go to your personal space. *In choosing between alternatives—the right hand is chosen. Oyeku Odi has spoken.*

2 + 8   Oyeku Ogbe

With Oyeku falling first and Ogbe falling next, we have found Oyeku Ogbe—the great secret. This Odu foretells a blessing that comes from a life's work. Beware the curse that comes from lack of commitment. Avoid distractions. The best cure for what ails you is to follow the dream that you dream and dream again. *In choosing between alternatives—the left hand is chosen. Oyeku Ogbe has spoken.*

2 + 9   Oyeku Osa

With Oyeku falling first and Osa falling next, we have found Oyeku Osa—the female secret. This Odu foretells a blessing that comes as a result of following your "female intuition." Beware the curse that comes from entirely rational thinking. Avoid the facts in this case. The best cure for what ails you is to trust in your hunches. *In choosing between alternatives—the right hand is chosen. Oyeku Osa has spoken.*

2 + 10   Oyeku Ofun

With Oyeku falling first and Ofun falling next, we have found Oyeku Ofun—the terrible secret. This Odu foretells a blessing that comes from admitting your shortcomings. Beware the curse that comes out of false denial. Avoid pretenses. The best cure for what ails you is to take your punishment and resolve to do better next time. *In choosing between alternatives—the left hand is chosen. Oyeku Ofun has spoken.*

2 + 11   Oyeku Owonrin

With Oyeku falling first and Owonrin falling next, we have found Oyeku Owonrin—the secret admirer. This Odu foretells a blessing that comes from a change of heart. Beware the curse of clinging to a false idea. Avoid traps laid by others. The best cure for what ails you is to start thinking for yourself. *In choosing between alternatives—the right hand is chosen. Oyeku Owonrin has spoken.*

2 + 12   Oyeku Iwori

With Oyeku falling first and Iwori falling next, we have found Oyeku Iwori—the secret flame. This Odu says a blessing will result from an emotional outpouring. Beware the curse that comes from stifling a burning passion. Avoid those who would ridicule you for pursuing your dream. The best cure for what ails you is to go where your spirit leads. *In choosing between alternatives—the right hand is chosen. Oyeku Iwori has spoken.*

2 + 13   Oyeku Ika

With Oyeku falling first and Ika falling next, we have found Oyeku Ika—the secret ingredient. This Odu foretells a blessing that comes as a result of adding a magical touch. Beware the recommendations of others, lest they curse your winning formula with dilution. Avoid all snarls and snares. The best cure for what ails you is to work—and trust in—your own magic. *In choosing between alternatives—the right hand is chosen. Oyeku Ika has spoken.*

2 + 14   Oyeku Oturupon

With Oyeku falling first and Oturupon falling next, we have found Oyeku Oturupon—the secret pact. This Odu speaks of a blessing that comes from giving the secret handshake. Beware the curse that comes from telling others more than they need to know. Avoid betraying the trust others have placed in you. The best cure for what ails you is to make your reputation for yourself. *In choosing between alternatives—the right hand is chosen. Oyeku Oturupon has spoken.*

2 + 15   Oyeku Otura

With Oyeku falling first and Otura falling next, we have found Oyeku Otura—the secret word. This Odu foretells a blessing that comes as a result of achieving inner peace. Beware the curses that you lay upon your own head. Avoid feeling guilty about who and what you are. The best cure for what ails you is to pump up your self-image. Say the magic word. *In choosing between alternatives—the right hand is chosen. Oyeku Otura has spoken.*

2 + 16   Oyeku Irete

With Oyeku falling first and Irete falling next, we have found Oyeku Irete—the secret wish. This Odu foretells a blessing that yet will come from longing, planning, hoping, and dreaming. Beware the curse that is assured by your having given up. Avoid all thoughts that sabotage. The best cure for what ails you is to center yourself. *In choosing between alternatives—the right hand is chosen. Oyeku Irete has spoken.*

2 + 0 Oyeku Opira

With Oyeku falling first and Opira falling next, we have found Oyeku Opira. What is secret must be left at that. *In choosing between alternatives—neither hand is chosen. Oyeku Opira has spoken silently.*

THREE SHELLS

owo eeta

Ogunda is about difficulties that arise out of doing things in a male way. It is about blessings that result from working to achieve your ambitions. It is about controlling your passions and directing sexual energy into constructive works.

Combinations of Ogunda
(*Oggunda*)

3 + 1 Ogunda Okanran

With Ogunda falling first and Okanran falling next, we have found Ogunda Okanran—the top man. This Odu foretells a blessing that comes as a result of displaying courage. Beware of taking the curses of others to heart. Avoid the things that incite you to violence. The best cure for what ails you is to keep a level head. *In choosing between alternatives—the right hand is chosen. Ogunda Okanran has spoken.*

3 + 2   *Ogunda Oyeku*

With Ogunda falling first and Oyeku falling next, we have found Ogunda Oyeku—the bottom man. This Odu decrees a blessing that comes by doing what comes naturally. Do not curse your genitals even though they rule you sometimes. Avoid intimate contact with total strangers. The best cure for what ails you is sex with precaution. *In choosing between alternatives—the right hand is chosen. Ogunda Oyeku has spoken.*

3 + 3   *Ogunda Meji*

With Ogunda falling first and Ogunda falling again, we have found Ogunda Meji (two Ogundas)—the man's man. This Odu says that a blessing is in store for two buddies. Watch out for the curse of friends who bring out the worst in each other. Avoid excessive use of expletives (deleted). The best cure for what ails you is to combine resources with someone you can not only confide in, but trust. *In choosing between alternatives—the left hand is chosen. Ogunda Meji has spoken.*

3 + 4   *Ogunda Irosun*

With Ogunda falling first and Irosun falling next, we have found Ogunda Irosun—the red-eyed man This Odu says a blessing will come from burning the midnight oil. Beware the color of your eyes does not give you away in the morning. Avoid overexertion. The best cure for what ails you is to set a reasonable goal. *In choosing between alternatives—the left hand is chosen. Ogunda Irosun has spoken.*

3 + 5   *Ogunda Oshe*

With Ogunda falling first and Oshe falling next, we have found Ogunda Oshe—the man's penis. This Odu foretells a blessing that comes out of something that turns you on. Beware that the purveyors of erotica do not curse you with an aching frustration. Avoid going too long without a healthy release. The best cure for what ails you is a handshake—if not also a kiss. *In choosing between alternatives—the right hand is chosen. Ogunda Oshe has spoken.*

3 + 6   *Ogunda Obara*

With Ogunda falling first and Obara falling next, we have found Ogunda Obara—the man's dream. This Odu foretells a blessing that comes out of a well-conceived action plan and the motivation to complete it. Beware the figments of your illusion, lest they curse you with the perpetual chasing of windmills. Avoid deluding yourself. The best cure for what ails you is to pick a goal and mark your territory. *In choosing between alternatives—the right hand is chosen. Ogunda Obara has spoken.*

3 + 7   *Ogunda Odi*

With Ogunda falling first and Odi falling next, we have found Ogunda Odi—the self-contained man. This Odu says that a blessing is ordained as a result of covering your bases. Beware the curse that comes from trying to be entirely self-sufficient. If you remain independent from others, they may leave you completely alone. Avoid making others' mistakes for them. The best cure for what ails you is to give others a fair chance. *In choosing between alternatives—the right hand is chosen. Ogunda Odi has spoken.*

3 + 8   *Ogunda Ogbe*

With Ogunda falling first and Ogbe falling next, we have found Ogunda Ogbe—the perfect man. This Odu foretells a blessing that comes from the hand of one who can do everything and yet do no wrong. Beware that your overtures are welcome—and your intentions sincere—lest you wind up being cursed in court. Avoid seeing challenges as obstacles. The best cure for what ails you is to keep everything respectable and to be respectful. *In choosing between alternatives—the left hand is chosen. Ogunda Ogbe has spoken.*

3 + 9   *Ogunda Osa*

With Ogunda falling first and Osa falling next, we have found Ogunda Osa—the lady's man. This Odu foretells a blessing that results from charisma, finesse, and romance. Beware the curse that comes from playing a stereotypical role. You may be typecast. Avoid being indirect. The best cure for what ails you is to respect the power of your charms. *In choosing between alternatives—the right hand is chosen. Ogunda Osa has spoken.*

3 + 10   *Ogunda Ofun*

With Ogunda falling first and Ofun falling next, we have found Ogunda Ofun—the dirty old man. This Odu foretells a blessing that comes as a result of the position of respect you have attained. Beware the curse that results from assuming that others want the same things as you. Avoid taking your position of authority for granted. The best cure for what ails you is to remain humble in the face of the wisdom you should have gained by now. *In choosing between alternatives—the left hand is chosen. Ogunda Ofun has spoken.*

3 + 11   *Ogunda Owonrin*

With Ogunda falling first and Owonrin falling next, we have found Ogunda Owonrin—the penetrating man. This Odu says that a blessing comes out of sensitivity and tenderness. Beware the curse that comes as a result of bullying others. Avoid bragging. The best cure for what ails you is to take a walk in someone else's shoes. *In choosing between alternatives—the right hand is chosen. Ogunda Owonrin has spoken.*

3 + 12   *Ogunda Iwori*

With Ogunda falling first and Iwori falling next, we have found Ogunda Iwori—the fiery man. This Odu says that you are on the verge of a blessing that comes from controlling your rage. Beware that you do not destroy the things you love, lest regret be your curse to bear. Avoid a quiet life of silent desperation. The best cure for what ails you is to direct your rage into your passion. *In choosing between alternatives—the right hand is chosen. Ogunda Iwori has spoken.*

3 + 13   *Ogunda Ika*

With Ogunda falling first and Ika falling next, we have found Ogunda Ika—the witch doctor. This Odu predicts a blessing that comes as a result of a magic moment. Do not curse the moonlight. Avoid reality for this one night. The best cure for what ails you is to get under the spell . . . go into the mood . . . let yourself be hypnotized. (Look into my eyes.) *In choosing between alternatives—the right hand is chosen. Ogunda Ika has spoken.*

3 + 14   Ogunda Oturupon

With Ogunda falling first and Oturupon falling next, we have found Ogunda Oturupon—the determined man. This Odu foretells a blessing that results from taking a defensive stand. Beware getting caught with your pants down, lest you be cursed with the need for humility. Avoid bragging about what you haven't got. The best cure for what ails you is to make the most of your strengths and minimize your weaknesses. *In choosing between alternatives—the right hand is chosen. Ogunda Oturupon has spoken.*

3 + 15   Ogunda Otura

With Ogunda falling first and Otura falling next, we have found Ogunda Otura—the initiated man. This Odu foretells of a blessing that comes as a result of passing through a spiritual gauntlet. Avoid cursing those whose job it is to make you stronger. Avoid copping out. The best cure for what ails you is to grit your teeth—or grin—and bear it. *In choosing between alternatives—the right hand is chosen. Ogunda Otura has spoken.*

3 + 16   Ogunda Irete

With Ogunda falling first and Irete falling next, we have found Ogunda Irete—the defeated man. This Odu says that a blessing comes out of reassertion. Beware that you do not curse yourself for being the nice guy who finishes last—or you just might. Avoid a defeatist attitude. The best cure for what ails you is to come out and ask for what you want. *In choosing between alternatives—the right hand is chosen. Ogunda Irete has spoken.*

3 + 0   Ogunda Opira

With Ogunda falling first and Opira falling next, we have found Ogunda Opira. The man in your life has nothing to say. *In choosing between alternatives—no hand is chosen. Ogunda Opira has spoken without speaking.*

FOUR SHELLS

owo eerin

Irosun is about things that go wrong on account of forgetting the past. It is about things that get corrected through the proper alignment. From the dusty history of your people comes a vision of truth.

Combinations of Irosun
(Eyorosun)

4 + 1   *Irosun Okanran*

With Irosun falling first and Okanran falling next, we have found Irosun Okanran—the red head. This Odu foretells of a blessing that comes as a result of keeping your temper. Beware the curse of words said in anger, lest their echo doubly curses you back. Avoid getting so mad you see red. Avoid jealousy. The best cure for what ails you is to take a few deep breaths. *In choosing between alternatives—the right hand is chosen. Irosun Okanran has spoken.*

4 + 2   *Irosun Oyeku*

With Irosun falling first and Oyeku falling next, we have found Irosun Oyeku—the container of blood. This Odu says a blessing emerges from out of your lifeblood . . . your bloodline . . . your life force. Do not curse the one who feeds you. Do not curse the one who clothes you. Do not curse the one who puts a roof over your head. Avoid conflict with kin. The best cure for what ails you is to show some respect for your roots. *In choosing between alternatives—the right hand is chosen. Irosun Oyeku has spoken.*

4 + 3   Irosun Ogunda

With Irosun falling first and Ogunda falling next, we have found Irosun Ogunda—the engorged penis. This Odu says a blessing will flow from your lips . . . a blessing will flow from your loins . . . a blessing will pump from inside. Beware the curse of unrequited love. Avoid heartache . . . as well as break. The best cure for what ails you is to make your desire seen as well as felt. *In choosing between alternatives—the right hand is chosen. Irosun Ogunda has spoken.*

4 + 4   Irosun Meji

With Irosun falling first and Irosun falling again, we have found Irosun Meji (two Irosuns)—the doubly red. This Odu predicts a blessing that comes as a result of an inherited tendency, inclination, or trait. Beware the family curse! . . . both in yourself and your offspring. Avoid repeating the sins of your fathers and mothers, brothers and sisters, aunts and uncles and even second cousins. The best cure for what ails you is to live up to your legacy, not down. *In choosing between alternatives—the left hand is chosen. Irosun Meji has spoken.*

4 + 5   Irosun Oshe

With Irosun falling first and Oshe falling next, we have found Irosun Oshe—the red sea. This Odu says a blessing is about to come to you from some secret source. Do not try to second-guess the direction of the underground currents here, lest you curse the fact that you have been misguided. Avoid deep subjects. The best cure for what ails you is to buoy yourself up and float where the waters take you. *In choosing between alternatives—the right hand is chosen. Irosun Oshe has spoken.*

4 + 6   Irosun Obara

With Irosun falling first and Obara falling next, we have found Irosun Obara—the red streak. This Odu predicts a blessing that comes at you like a shooting star. Quick—look up and make a wish! . . . before the spark disintegrates. And better yet, duck! . . . or else have reason to curse. Avoid the path of the fallout. The best cure for what ails you is to spot a sign for what it is. Read one when you see it. *In choosing between alternatives—the right hand is chosen. Irosun Obara has spoken.*

4 + 7   *Irosun Odi*

With Irosun falling first and Odi falling next, we have found Irosun Odi—the container of red dust. This Odu ordains a blessing that comes as the result of something done—or not done—in the past. Beware the skeleton in your closet. It may yet come into the light and curse you with a haunted life. Avoid dwelling upon what cannot be undone now. The best cure for what ails you is to act in the present so that you will have no cause later for regret. *In choosing between alternatives—the right hand is chosen. Irosun Odi has spoken.*

4 + 8   *Irosun Ogbe*

With Irosun falling first and Ogbe falling next, we have found Irosun Ogbe—the red mark. This Odu foretells a great blessing coming at the hand of your family, relatives, and friends. Heed the warning of someone older and more experienced in these matters, or risk the curse of repeating past mistakes. Avoid getting stuck in a cultural rut. The best cure for what ails you is to live, watch, and learn. *In choosing between alternatives—the left hand is chosen. Irosun Ogbe has spoken.*

4 + 9   *Irosun Osa*

With Irosun falling first and Osa falling next, we have found Irosun Osa—the reddened vagina. This Odu predicts a blessing arising out of a confrontation with a woman in your household. Beware the curse of PMS, and try not to take harsh words or glances either too personally or—on the other hand—for granted. Avoid arguing for argument's sake. The best cure for what ails you is to wait a week or so and start fresh. *In choosing between alternatives—the right hand is chosen. Irosun Osa has spoken.*

4 + 10   *Irosun Ofun*

With Irosun falling first and Ofun falling next, we have found Irosun Ofun—the red passion. This Odu says that a blessing will come as a result of inherited proclivities and inclinations that no one ever told you about and no one ever talks of. Beware the curse of abusive, sexist, racist, or other self-destructive behavior patterns passed down to you. Avoid acting on incestuous urges. The best cure for what ails you is quite possibly a cold shower. *In choosing between alternatives— the left hand is chosen. Irosun Ofun has spoken.*

4 + 11   Irosun Owonrin

With Irosun falling first and Owonrin falling next, we have found Irosun Owonrin—the red obsession. This Odu predicts a blessing arising out of discipline and diligence. Beware that you neither give up too quickly on your dream nor hold on too fast, too long. Either way is a curse. Avoid overconfidence in the way things were done in the past. The best cure for what ails you is to let your spirit guide you. *In choosing between alternatives—the right hand is chosen. Irosun Owonrin has spoken.*

4 + 12   Irosun Iwori

With Irosun falling first and Iwori falling next, we have found Irosun Iwori—the red flame. This Odu foretells a blessing that comes as the result of seeing through to completion something of importance to you. Beware that your efforts to achieve your goals do not become all-consuming, lest those you love wind up cursing you for your self-gratifying passion. Avoid procrastination, perfectionism, and paranoia. The best cure for what ails you is to get your priorities in order. *In choosing between alternatives—the right hand is chosen. Irosun Iwori has spoken.*

4 + 13   Irosun Ika

With Irosun falling first and Ika falling next, we have found Irosun Ika—the red menace. This Odu predicts a blessing that results from believing hard enough, long enough, true enough. Beware words, actions, and attitudes that undermine your ambitions and thus curse you with poor performance. Avoid superstitious notions. The best cure for what ails you is to see your fears clearly and confront them bravely. *In choosing between alternatives—the right hand is chosen. Irosun Ika has spoken.*

4 + 14   *Irosun Oturupon*

With Irosun falling first and Oturupon falling next, we have found Irosun Oturupon—the red fang. This Odu indicates that a blessing will yet result from the ill wishes of others. Beware those who put you down or make light of your ambitions. They will curse you with a jaundiced eye and their jealous mouth. Avoid taking naysayers to heart. The best cure for what ails you is to develop a thick skin and a tough hide. *In choosing between alternatives—the right hand is chosen. Irosun Oturupon has spoken.*

4 + 15   *Irosun Otura*

With Irosun falling first and Otura falling next, we have found Irosun Otura—the red flag. This Odu indicates a blessing that yet results from a weakness in physical, emotional, or spiritual character. Beware actions that curse you with penalties, prices, persecution, or prosecution. Avoid means that the ends do not justify. The best cure for what ails you is to focus on your personal strength and achieve peace with yourself. *In choosing between alternatives—the right hand is chosen. Irosun Otura has spoken.*

4 + 16   *Irosun Irete*

With Irosun falling first and Irete falling next, we have found Irosun Irete—the bleeding heart. This Odu foretells of a blessing that comes as the result of personal sacrifice. Beware your doubts and insecurities—they will curse you with paralysis in a pinch. Avoid a tendency to worry too much in advance. The best cure for what ails you is to make the necessary sacrifice for those you love. *In choosing between alternatives—the right hand is chosen. Irosun Irete has spoken.*

4 + 0   *Irosun Opira*

With Irosun falling first and Opira falling next, we have found Irosun Opira. You have avoided seeing red. *In choosing between alternatives—no hand is chosen. Irosun Opira has spoken without moving its lips.*

131

FIVE SHELLS

owo aarun

Oshe is about things that go wrong on account of lack of sensitivity. It is about the things that go right because of the burning sensuality inside you. Though the love of two may not always prove to be everlasting, there is eternity in the moment that it endures.

Combinations of Oshe
(Oche)

5 + 1   Oshe Okanran

With Oshe falling first and Okanran falling next, we have found Oshe Okanran—the solitary love. This Odu predicts a blessing resulting from self-admiration, self-adulation, and self-love. Beware the curse of hairy palms and waning vision (only kidding!). Beware the curse of despising yourself. Avoid feeling guilty. The best cure for what ails you is to take matters into your own two loving hands. *In choosing between alternatives—the left hand is chosen. Oshe Okanran has spoken.*

5 + 2   Oshe Oyeku

With Oshe falling first and Oyeku falling next, we have found Oshe Oyeku—the virgin love. This Odu predicts a blessing resulting from a period of deliberate inaction. Beware the curse of naïveté. May no one wish to take advantage of you. Avoid unwelcome overtures. The best cure for what ails you is to keep your fingers crossed . . . as well as your legs. *In choosing between alternatives—the left hand is chosen. Oshe Oyeku has spoken.*

5 + 3   Oshe Ogunda

With Oshe falling first and Ogunda falling next, we have found Oshe Ogunda—the sensuous man. This Odu predicts a blessing re-

132

sulting from the sharing of emotions as well as body parts. Beware the tendency to bottle things up inside, lest you be cursed with anguish, heartache, and loneliness. Avoid pining from a distance. The best cure for what ails you is to let your feelings out. *In choosing between alternatives—the left hand is chosen. Oshe Ogunda has spoken.*

5 + 4   Oshe Irosun

With Oshe falling first and Irosun falling next, we have found Oshe Irosun—the red-eyed lover. This Odu foretells a blessing that results from singing the blues. Beware a tense feeling—it will curse you to the point of distraction. Avoid dwelling on the past. The best cure for what ails you is to cry into your beer and get it over with. *In choosing between alternatives—the left hand is chosen. Oshe Irosun has spoken.*

5 + 5   Oshe Meji

With Oshe falling first and Oshe falling again, we have found Oshe Meji (two Oshes)—the sensuous waters. This Odu says a blessing will result from going with the flow. Beware the curse of stagnation. Avoid remaining in the same place for too long. The best cure for what ails you is to get out and join the mainstream. *In choosing between alternatives—the right hand is chosen. Oshe Meji has spoken.*

5 + 6   Oshe Obara

With Oshe falling first and Obara falling next, we have found Oshe Obara—the passionate cause. This Odu says a blessing will come from righteous devotion to a cause. Beware placing your trust in ephemeral or transient things that will betray your confidence in the wake of their passing. Avoid fads. The best cure for what ails you is to take social responsibility. Come to the aid and assistance of others. *In choosing between alternatives—the left hand is chosen. Oshe Obara has spoken.*

5 + 7   Oshe Odi

With Oshe falling first and Odi falling next, we have found Oshe Odi—the sensuous drum. This Odu predicts a blessing that arises from keeping a finger to the earth's pulse. Beware the undulations of enticing buttocks or swaying breasts, lest your panting breath betray you. Is it love—or lust? Avoid scandalous affairs. The best cure for what ails you is to reconfirm your faith. *In choosing between alternatives—the left hand is chosen. Oshe Odi has spoken.*

5 + 8   Oshe Ogbe

With Oshe falling first and Ogbe falling next, we have found Oshe Ogbe—the physical path. This Odu says a blessing flows naturally from the pursuit of your individual destiny. But do not disrupt the harmony of your people on the way, lest they curse you for your evil ways. Avoid breaking the peace. The best cure for what ails you is to work your will within the confines of the group you wish to be with. *In choosing between alternatives—the left hand is chosen. Oshe Ogbe has spoken.*

5 + 9   Oshe Osa

With Oshe falling first and Osa falling next, we have found Oshe Osa—the sensuous woman. This Odu speaks of a blessing coming out of warmth, tenderness, and fluid motion. Beware the beguilement of others, lest they latch on to you like a curse. Avoid using your wiles for destructive purposes. The best cure for what ails you is better left unsaid, but—I suspect—you know what I mean. *In choosing between alternatives—the left hand is chosen. Oshe Osa has spoken.*

5 + 10   Oshe Ofun

With Oshe falling first and Ofun falling next, we have found Oshe Ofun—the sensuous brother. This Odu tells of a blessing emerging from the privacy of your own home. Beware that your secrets are not actually indiscretions in disguise, lest you wind up being cursed by the ones you love. Avoid letting the family ghosts out of the closet. The best cure for what ails you is to quit fooling yourself. *In choosing between alternatives—the left hand is chosen. Oshe Ofun has spoken.*

5 + 11   Oshe Owonrin

With Oshe falling first and Owonrin falling next, we have found Oshe Owonrin—the romantic fool. This Odu predicts a blessing arising from a casual affair. But beware the advances of someone already committed to someone else, lest you be cursed as the home wrecker or the family breaker. Avoid those who would borrow your body from you for the sake of their fantasy. The best cure for what ails you is to think better of it once, twice, and even thrice. *In choosing between alternatives—the left hand is chosen. Oshe Owonrin has spoken.*

5 + 12   *Oshe Iwori*

With Oshe falling first and Iwori falling next, we have found Oshe Iwori—the burning love. This Odu speaks of a blessing revealed by an acid test. You may have to walk on water yet! Beware those who want more from you than you want to give, lest they push you too far, too fast, too much. Avoid self-punishment. The best cure for what ails you is to look within yourself. Seek there the courage and the strength to pass the test worth passing . . . to prove a thing worth proving. *In choosing between alternatives—the left hand is chosen. Oshe Iwori has spoken.*

5 + 13   *Oshe Ika*

With Oshe falling first and Ika falling next, we have found Oshe Ika—the love spell. This Odu foretells of a blessing coming as a result of a concerted effort by someone toward an object of his or her desire—namely, you. Beware the intentions of those who want to sail away with you, lest they lure you into a situation you might later curse. Avoid compromising positions. The best cure for what ails you is to keep a safe distance . . . keep your guard up. *In choosing between alternatives—the right hand is chosen. Oshe Ika has spoken.*

5 + 14   *Oshe Oturupon*

With Oshe falling first and Oturupon falling next, we have found Oshe Oturupon—the erotic dancer. This Odu speaks of a blessing that comes as a consequence of something enticing and graphic. Beware the person who promises to give you everything you want—no questions asked—lest you wind up cursing your lost innocence. Avoid heavy breathers. The best cure for what ails you is to get got a couple of times. *In choosing between alternatives—the right hand is chosen. Oshe Oturupon has spoken.*

135

5 + 15   Oshe Otura

With Oshe falling first and Otura falling next, we have found Oshe Otura—the burning sensuality. This Odu says a blessing will come as if from between the legs. Beware that the fires that you let smolder for too long aren't doused one night by an erotic dream. Avoid fitful sleeps. The best cure for what ails you is to find a way to express yourself. *In choosing between alternatives—the right hand is chosen. Oshe Otura has spoken.*

5 + 16   Oshe Irete

With Oshe falling first and Irete falling next, we have found Oshe Irete—the sex slave. This Odu speaks of a blessing resulting from voluntary submission to a higher authority. Beware that your limits are respected, lest you curse the day you might have escaped a debasing captivity. The best cure for what ails you is a healthy dose of self-respect. *In choosing between alternatives—the right hand is chosen. Oshe Irete has spoken.*

5 + 0   Oshe Opira

With Oshe falling first and Opira falling next, we have found Oshe Opira. Sex is not your problem. *In choosing between alternatives—no hand is chosen. Oshe Opira has spoken in a whisper.*

SIX SHELLS

owo eefa

Obara is about things that go wrong on account of lack of honesty—with others and with self. It is about things that go right on account of keeping focus on the light. Though your vision of the future may not always be clear as a sky the rain has just left, you will from time to time get a glimpse of a rainbow.

Combinations of Obara
(Obbara)

6 + 1   *Obara Okanran*

With Obara falling first and Okanran falling next, we have found Obara Okanran—the personal truth. This Odu speaks of a blessing coming from silence, solitude, and the quiet within you. Beware the unwanted distraction and the sudden interruption, lest you curse the loss of your train of thought. Avoid sulking. The best cure for what ails you is a little time alone with your thoughts. *In choosing between alternatives—the left hand is chosen. Obara Okanran has spoken.*

6 + 2   *Obara Oyeku*

With Obara falling first and Oyeku falling next, we have found Obara Oyeku—the absolute truth. This Odu speaks of a blessing that arrives out of the great mysteries of the Universe. Beware that you do not lose faith in powers greater than science, lest you be cursed to live by the facts alone. Avoid being hypnotized by the voices of reason. The best cure for what ails you is to listen to your tribal voice. *In choosing between alternatives—the left hand is chosen. Obara Oyeku has spoken.*

6 + 3   *Obara Ogunda*

With Obara falling first and Ogunda falling next, we have found Obara Ogunda—the male truth. This Odu is about a blessing that comes from behaving "like a man" at a time when one ought to behave as such. Beware a tendency to vacillate at the last moment, lest you curse yourself later for your failure to act like a hero. In general, avoid deals wherein no one wins. The best cure for what ails you is to take a firm stance and stick to your ground. *In choosing between alternatives—the left hand is chosen. Obara Ogunda has spoken.*

6 + 4   *Obara Irosun*

With Obara falling first and Irosun falling next, we have found Obara Irosun—the bright red truth. This Odu speaks of a blessing coming from facing up to both the facts and feelings. Try not to feel blue. Try not to turn red. Beware the curse that makes you feel better only for a moment. Avoid acting on an illusion. The best cure for what ails you is accepting what is . . . and what is not. *In choosing between alternatives—the left hand is chosen. Obara Irosun has spoken.*

6 + 5   Obara Oshe

With Obara falling first and Oshe falling next, we have found Obara Oshe—the watered-down truth. This Odu says a blessing comes as a result of sparing the feelings of others. Beware that the little white lie does not turn around and bite you in the buttocks. Avoid confusing the issues. The best cure for what ails you is to do what you have to do . . . and hope that the good prevails. *In choosing between alternatives—the right hand is chosen. Obara Oshe has spoken.*

6 + 6   Obara Meji

With Obara falling first and Obara falling again, we have found Obara Meji (two Obaras)—the elusive truth. This Odu predicts a blessing arising out of an attempt to do what is best for everyone concerned. Beware that in attempting to please everyone, you do not wind up pleasing no one . . . not even yourself. Avoid overintellectualizing everything. The best cure for what ails you is to do what you can and leave the rest to God. *In choosing between alternatives—the right hand is chosen. Obara Meji has spoken.*

6 + 7   Obara Odi

With Obara falling first and Odi falling next, we have found Obara Odi—the container of truth. This Odu refers to a blessing that comes out of a combination of legend and lore . . . tradition and precedence. Beware that you do not place too much confidence in the rising star of the moment, lest you curse the face of fleeting fame. Avoid speculation. The best cure for what ails you is to place your bets carefully, and when in doubt, hedge. *In choosing between alternatives—the left hand is chosen. Obara Odi has spoken.*

6 + 8   Obara Ogbe

With Obara falling first and Ogbe falling next, we have found Obara Ogbe—the perfect truth. This Odu tells of a blessing that comes from following the feelings of the heart and gut—the balls and bowels—and listening to the voice in the head. Beware the temptation to place your own needs first, lest the others in your life curse you for it. Avoid old excuses. The best cure for what ails you is to make—and keep—your resolutions. *In choosing between alternatives—the left hand is chosen. Obara Ogbe has spoken.*

6 + 9   *Obara Osa*

With Obara falling first and Osa falling next, we have found Obara Osa—the female truth. This Odu speaks of a blessing resulting from maternal instincts. Beware that the basic urge to nest does not curse you with the role of primary caretaker. Avoid always placing yourself second. The best cure for what ails you is to nurture yourself as well as nurturing the others in your life. *In choosing between alternatives— the left hand is chosen. Obara Osa has spoken.*

6 + 10   *Obara Ofun*

With Obara falling first and Ofun falling next, we have found Obara Ofun—the infernal truth. This Odu says that a blessing will emerge as the result of a great temptation. Beware your serpent when it speaks to you, lest the "truth" it tells is truly a curse. Avoid divulging another's secrets. The best cure for what ails you is to let this fantasy remain just that. *In choosing between alternatives—the left hand is chosen. Obara Ofun has spoken.*

6 + 11   *Obara Owonrin*

With Obara falling first and Owonrin falling next, we have found Obara Owonrin—the eternal truth. This Odu portends a blessing of lasting emotional involvement. Beware the coming and going of the moon and the rise and fall of tides, lest the patterns in your life elude you . . . and bring you curses instead of blessings. Avoid doing things at the wrong time. The best cure for what ails you is to take things in sequence. *In choosing between alternatives—the left hand is chosen. Obara Owonrin has spoken.*

6 + 12 *Obara Iwori*

With Obara falling first and Iwori falling next, we have found Obara Iwori—the fiery truth. This Odu says a blessing comes even from words spoken in anger. Beware the face value of a message. Don't let yourself be cursed by the sting of a word's literal meaning. Avoid cursing back. The best cure for what ails you is to try to understand what's behind it. *In choosing between alternatives—the left hand is chosen. Obara Iwori has spoken.*

6 + 13 *Obara Ika*

With Obara falling first and Ika falling next, we have found Obara Ika—the indiscernible truth. This Odu speaks of a blessing that has a bittersweetness to it. Beware that you neither mourn nor celebrate too much, lest the poignant mood be broken and the magic be undone. That would be a curse indeed. Avoid things at the extremes if you can. The best cure for what ails you is: think of your situation in terms of heavenly signs and symbols. *In choosing between alternatives—the right hand is chosen. Obara Ika has spoken.*

6 + 14 *Obara Oturupon*

With Obara falling first and Oturupon falling next, we have found Obara Oturupon—the honest truth. This Odu says that a blessing comes from letting your thoughts be known—and do not spare the words. Beware the risk of rejection, but at least you will not have to curse an opportunity lost. Avoid rehearsing too much in advance. The best cure for what ails you is to say it in your own words. They will surely come to you at the right moment. *In choosing between alternatives—the right hand is chosen. Obara Oturupon has spoken.*

6 + 15 *Obara Otura*

With Obara falling first and Otura falling next, we have found Obara Otura—the half-truth. This Odu says a blessing of peace is sure to come to the underdog. Beware the tendency to see only innuendo. Don't curse yourself with the burden of carrying a chip on your shoulder. Avoid self-defamation of character. The best cure for what ails you is to get hostility out of your system. *In choosing between alternatives—the right hand is chosen. Obara Otura has spoken.*

6 + 16   *Obara Irete*

With Obara falling first and Irete falling next, we have found Obara Irete—the untruth. This Odu foretells of a blessing that comes out of chaos. Beware the making of idle threats, lest someone calls your bluff. Avoid making obscene gestures that you do not mean to back up. The best cure for what ails you is to avoid an altercation in the first place. *In choosing between alternatives—the right hand is chosen. Obara Irete has spoken.*

6 + 0   *Obara Opira*

With Obara falling first and Opira falling next, we have found Obara Opira. There is no peace for you tonight. Wash your shells. *In choosing between alternatives—no hand is chosen. Obara Opira has spoken nothing but said much.*

SEVEN SHELLS

owo eeje

Odi is about things that go wrong on account of underachievement. It is about things that go well, because they are fresh, new, and eager to put themselves forward. Though a birth may yet prove to be difficult, you will not regret having conceived this "child" of your own creativity.

Combinations of Odi
(*Oddi*)

7 + 1   *Odi Okanran*

With Odi falling first and Okanran falling next, we have found Odi Okanran—the soul's container. This Odu speaks of a blessing that comes from the back of your own head. Beware that you do not forget the promises you have made to yourself in the past. Remember, it is a terrible thing to deceive yourself. And a wasted mind is its own curse. Avoid small concepts. The best cure for what ails you is to feed your head. *In choosing between alternatives—the left hand is chosen. Odi Okanran has spoken.*

7 + 2   Odi Oyeku

With Odi falling first and Oyeku falling next, we have found Odi Oyeku—the container of life. This Odu says that blessings are coming as if from the womb—something new is about to be born to you. Beware a tendency to consider these creative mysteries as a guarantee. Neither try to hurry up nor slow down this process. The best cure for what ails you is to incubate . . . await . . . and see. *In choosing between alternatives—the left hand is chosen. Odi Oyeku has spoken.*

7 + 3   Odi Ogunda

With Odi falling first and Ogunda falling next, we have found Odi Ogunda—the container of male energy. This Odu says that a blessing comes to you as if from the testicles of a man. Beware that you do not abuse the power that emanates from you, lest others tell you to take a flying . . . curse. Neither over- nor underindulge your parts. The best cure for what ails you is to exercise a little control . . . expend your energy wisely. *In choosing between alternatives—the left hand is chosen. Odi Ogunda has spoken.*

7 + 4   Odi Irosun

With Odi falling first and Irosun falling next, we have found Odi Irosun—the container of blood. This Odu speaks of a blessing from—and for—the heart. Beware that you do not wear yours on your sleeve, lest others take advantage of your sensitivity. Neither shed nor draw blood yourself. The best cure for what ails you is to be open and honest . . . both outwardly and inwardly. Trust your feelings. *In choosing between alternatives—the left hand is chosen. Odi Iro-sun has spoken.*

7 + 5   Odi Oshe

With Odi falling first and Oshe falling next, we have found Odi Oshe—the container of water. This Odu speaks of a blessing that results from remaining fluid . . . malleable . . . and flexible. But beware the tendency to follow the path of least resistance, lest your destiny be shaped by the rigidity of others. Avoid conformity at any price. The best cure for what ails you is to let yourself go. *In choosing between alternatives—the right hand is chosen. Odi Oshe has spoken.*

7 + 6   Odi Obara

With Odi falling first and Obara falling next, we have found Odi Obara—the container of stars. This Odu says that a blessing comes upon you as if it in answer to a prayer. A blessing comes to you as if from heaven. Beware that you do not take the Forces of Nature for granted, lest you be caught off guard by an Act of God. Swear not by the inconstant moon, which is always changing its mind. The best cure for what ails you is to show some respect for the Powers that Be . . . and remain constant and consistent in your own prayers. *In choosing between alternatives—the right hand is chosen. Odi Obara has spoken.*

7 + 7   *Odi Meji*

With Odi falling first and Odi falling again, we have found Odi Meji (two Odis)—the container of existence. This Odu says a blessing is coming—even as we speak. The wheels are in motion within you. Cause is having its effect. Effect is having its cause. Beware that the body, mind, and spirit—all three—are tended to, lest curses grow within your shadow. The best cure for what ails you is to seek the proper balance of your spiritual, intellectual, and physical powers. *In choosing between alternatives—the right hand is chosen. Odi Meji has spoken.*

7 + 8   *Odi Ogbe*

With Odi falling first and Ogbe falling next, we have found Odi Ogbe—the container of blessings. This Odu ordains a blessing that is beyond your imagining—so perfect and beautiful is its nature . . . even though it may disappoint you at first. But beware that you do not act disappointed, lest you curse the full joy that might have come from this moment. Avoid looking on the dark side of everything. The best cure for what ails you is to sit back and let this blessing flow over you. Enjoy! *In choosing between alternatives—the left hand is chosen. Odi Ogbe has spoken.*

7 + 9   *Odi Osa*

With Odi falling first and Osa falling next, we have found Odi Osa—the container of female energy. This Odu says a blessing is coming as if from the ovaries. A blessing is about to hatch as if from an egg. Be careful not to place all of yours in one basket. Be careful not to count your chickens in advance of hatching. Avoid jinxing yourself. The best cure for what ails you is to wait until things complete themselves. *In choosing between alternatives—the left hand is chosen. Odi Osa has spoken.*

7 + 10   *Odi Ofun*

With Odi falling first and Ofun falling next, we have found Odi Ofun—the container of wrongs. This Odu says that a blessing will result from closing in on the difficulties that trouble your life. Take care that the little things do not mount up to major issues, lest you be cursed with worries of your own making. Avoid doing things to yourself. The best cure for what ails you is to learn from your own past. *In choosing between alternatives—the left hand is chosen. Odi Ofun has spoken.*

7 + 11   *Odi Owonrin*

With Odi falling first and Owonrin falling next, we have found Odi Owonrin—the container of rhythms. This Odu talks about a blessing that comes out of keeping in step with the times. Beware the curse of classifying yourself into old-fashioned categories, lest the passage of time leave you disenfranchised. Avoid clinging. The best cure for what ails you is to adapt to contemporary standards, while pursuing your own personal expression. *In choosing between alternatives—the left hand is chosen. Odi Owonrin has spoken.*

7 + 12   Odi Iwori

With Odi falling first and Iwori falling next, we have found Odi Iwori—the container of impulses. This Odu says that a blessing comes to you as the result of good reflexes. Beware approaching a flame without caution, lest you curse the fact that you ever played with fire. Avoid the unexpected backlash. The best cure for what ails you is to stay on your toes. *In choosing between alternatives—the left hand is chosen. Odi Iwori has spoken.*

7 + 13   Odi Ika

With Odi falling first and Ika falling next, we have found Odi Ika—the container of medicine. This Odu says that a blessing will come as the result of a prescribed remedy. Beware disobeying the doctor's instructions, lest you be cursed with a relapse. Avoid paying too much just to feel a little better. The best cure for what ails you is to keep your spirits up. *In choosing between alternatives—the right hand is chosen. Odi Ika has spoken.*

7 + 14   Odi Oturupon

With Odi falling first and Oturupon falling next, we have found Odi Oturupon—the container of words. This Odu says that a blessing is written for you . . . in fact, the writing is already on the wall. Beware that you do not judge a book by its cover, lest you find the inner pages blank. Avoid using too many big words. The best cure for what ails you is to listen carefully to both what is said and what is implied. *In choosing between alternatives—the right hand is chosen. Odi Oturupon has spoken.*

7 + 15   *Odi Otura*

With Odi falling first and Otura falling next, we have found Odi Otura—the container of adversity. This Odu promises a blessing that comes as a result of sealing off troubles so that they can no longer get to you. Beware the petty anger that brews like a fire in your belly, lest it bring curses to your digestive tract. Avoid the wrath of others. The best cure for what ails you is to dispense with all conflicts of interest. *In choosing between alternatives—the right hand is chosen. Odi Otura has spoken.*

7 + 16   *Odi Irete*

With Odi falling first and Irete falling next, we have found Odi Irete—the container of ire. This Odu foretells a blessing fraught at first with grief—and all wrapped up with stress—yet turning into a blessing nonetheless at last. Beware the temptation to wish that excitement be avoided, lest someday you wind up cursing an uneventful existence. Avoid neither laughter nor tears. The best cure for what ails you is to see the good amidst the bad . . . and cherish both extremes. *In choosing between alternatives—the right hand is chosen. Odi Irete has spoken.*

7 + 0   *Odi Opira*

With Odi falling first and Opira falling next, we have found Odi Opira. Put your shells into a bowl for a while. They would like to be contained. *In choosing between alternatives—no hand is chosen. Odi Opira has spoken very quietly.*

EIGHT SHELLS

owo eejo

Ogbe is about things that go bad on account of two parties being at odds. It is about things that go good due to achieving a perfect balance. Though your spiritual double may not always seem to be on your side, it is the two of you who will get through heaven and hell together . . . and crossing all points in between.

Combinations of Ogbe
(Eyeunle)

8 + 1   *Ogbe Okanran*

With Ogbe falling first and Okanran falling next, we have found Ogbe Okanran—the perfect loner. This Odu speaks of the greatest blessing an individual can achieve . . . the perfect accomplishment of divine will. Beware that you do not look your destiny in the face and curse it still. No good comes from a failure to sacrifice. Avoid taking things that are not yours. The best cure for what ails you is to say an earnest prayer that you might achieve the purpose given you when you were down on your knees in heaven asking God to reveal your destiny. *In choosing between alternatives—the right hand is chosen. Ogbe Okanran has spoken.*

8 + 2   *Ogbe Oyeku*

With Ogbe falling first and Oyeku falling next, we have found Ogbe Oyeku—the perfect womb. This Odu says that at least two blessings can be expected in rapid succession if you remain open and receptive to the possibility of twin events. Beware a tendency to hide your tenderness behind a veil of secrecy, lest you deny your being its glorious existence. Avoid being too glib. Avoid being too loose. The best cure for what ails you is to allow yourself to be fulfilled. *In choosing between alternatives—the right hand is chosen. Ogbe Oyeku has spoken.*

8 + 3   *Ogbe Ogunda*

With Ogbe falling first and Ogunda falling next, we have found Ogbe Ogunda—the perfect penis. This Odu speaks of a blessing that comes as the result of a physical transformation. Beware the tendency to believe that length, girth, and tensile strength are more important than staying power. Do not curse your lovers with recurring disappointment. Avoid a cocksure attitude. The best cure for what ails you is to learn to withstand a little friction. *In choosing between alternatives—the right hand is chosen. Ogbe Ogunda has spoken.*

8 + 4   Ogbe Irosun

With Ogbe falling first and Irosun falling next, we have found Ogbe Irosun—the blue blood. This Odu tells of a blessing that comes directly from your ancestors and their forebears. Beware a genetic strength that may yet become a tragic flaw. Beware the family curse, lest it yet become your claim to infamy. Give away neither the family secrets nor the family jewels. The best cure for what ails you is to use your legacy as if it were a tool. *In choosing between alternatives— the right hand is chosen. Ogbe Irosun has spoken.*

8 + 5   Ogbe Oshe

With Ogbe falling first and Oshe falling next, we have found Ogbe Oshe—the perfect waters. This Odu says a blessing is coming like the breaking of the water at a birth and the gushing of a newborn from the womb. Beware the impending arrival of a stranger. Beware you do not curse the father of this unknown one too much. Avoid being overbearing. The best cure for what ails you is to take a few deep breaths and push only when Mother Yemaya says. *In choosing between alternatives—the right hand is chosen. Ogbe Oshe has spoken.*

8 + 6   Ogbe Obara

With Ogbe falling first and Obara falling next, we have found Ogbe Obara—the great illusion. This Odu says a blessing comes out of the vast depths of the imagination. Beware the dark pockets that also exist behind closed doors, lest your own whims curse you. Avoid a dangerous idea. The best cure for what ails you is to pursue only the recurring passion. *In choosing between alternatives—the right hand is chosen. Ogbe Obara has spoken.*

8 + 7   Ogbe Odi

With Ogbe falling first and Odi falling next, we have found Ogbe Odi—the great crucible. This Odu predicts a blessing that comes from mixing things up and combining the old pieces into something new. Be careful not to create an explosion in the process, lest your landlord curse you with an eviction notice. Avoid traditional ways of looking at things. The best cure for what ails you is to develop a new angle. *In choosing between alternatives—the right hand is chosen. Ogbe Odi has spoken.*

8 + 8   Ogbe Meji

With Ogbe falling first and Ogbe falling again, we have found Ogbe Meji (two Ogbes)—the great goodness. This Odu predicts blessing upon blessing . . . and soon, my friend, you are sure to know them all—for this is the most perfect combination of them all. Be sure to take the time to enjoy the good luck that has found you today. Do not later find yourself cursing the loss of the good old days. Avoid wishing time away. The best cure for what ails you is nothing, since nothing is the matter—noway, nohow, not now. *In choosing between alternatives—the left hand is chosen. Ogbe Meji has spoken.*

8 + 9   Ogbe Osa

With Ogbe falling first and Osa falling next, we have found Ogbe Osa—the perfect woman. This Odu says that there is someone in your life who makes everything all right. Beware that she does not get away, lest you curse yourself for letting her escape. Avoid anything that might destroy this relationship. The best cure for what ails you is to adore her . . . praise her . . . serve her. *In choosing between alternatives—the right hand is chosen. Ogbe Osa has spoken.*

8 + 10   Ogbe Ofun

With Ogbe falling first and Ofun falling next, we have found Ogbe Ofun—the great taboo. This Odu talks about a blessing that is only such if something is avoided completely. This is your weak spot, your downfall, your Achilles' heal. Do not do the thing that is forbidden of you . . . your great secret desire—and you know exactly what I mean. Avoid that which could destroy you. The best cure for what ails you is to abstain. *In choosing between alternatives—the right hand is chosen. Ogbe Ofun has spoken.*

8 + 11   *Ogbe Owonrin*

With Ogbe falling first and Owonrin falling next, we have found Ogbe Owonrin—the greatest love of all. This Odu predicts a blessing that comes out of your most poignant, passionate depths. This is deep desire, my friend. And you are standing deep within it. Beware that you are not engulfed, overwhelmed, swept away with yourself—or else you might wind up being cursed. But just the same, avoid toning down your art to meet contemporary mood swings. The best cure for what ails you is to do what God tells you to do . . . to go where your Great Spirit leads you—even though it be politically incorrect. *In choosing between alternatives—the right hand is chosen. Ogbe Owonrin has spoken.*

8 + 12   *Ogbe Iwori*

With Ogbe falling first and Iwori falling next, we have found Ogbe Iwori—the perfect flame. This Odu reveals a blessing that mere mortals cannot usually know. It comes from purity of essence and of soul. Beware that the reward that is coming does not frighten you into voicing a startled expletive, lest you break the magic spell. Avoid disenchantment. The best cure for what ails you is to believe what all your senses reveal to you. View the world with wonder. *In choosing between alternatives—the right hand is chosen. Ogbe Iwori has spoken.*

8 + 13   *Ogbe Ika*

With Ogbe falling first and Ika falling next, we have found Ogbe Ika—the perfect spell. This Odu foretells a blessing that comes as the direct result of weaving a web around an unsuspecting victim. Beware that the intentions of others are not as good as they might at first appear. Be sure to cover your buttocks, lest you become overexposed and exploited in the process. The best cure for what ails you is to wear around your neck an amulet. *In choosing between alternatives—the right hand is chosen. Ogbe Ika has spoken.*

8 + 14   *Ogbe Oturupon*

With Ogbe falling first and Oturupon falling next, we have found Ogbe Oturupon—the great doubt. This Odu portends a blessing of uncertainty. But this only proves to be fortuitous for you at this time. Be careful not to talk yourself out of a certain reservation. Do not curse an intuitive—but timely—foreshadowing. Avoid poo-pooing an ill wind. The best cure for what ails you is to take all necessary measures to assure that you are protected. *In choosing between alternatives—the right hand is chosen. Ogbe Oturupon has spoken.*

8 + 15   *Ogbe Otura*

With Ogbe falling first and Otura falling next, we have found Ogbe Otura—the great peace. This Odu speaks loudly and emphatically of a blessing that will follow a certain hostility. Beware a cunning adversary, lest you take false curses to heart. Avoid standoff and stalemate positions. The best cure for what ails you is to call the other one's bluff. *In choosing between alternatives—the right hand is chosen. Ogbe Otura has spoken.*

8 + 16   *Ogbe Irete*

With Ogbe falling first and Irete falling next, we have found Ogbe Irete—the great disaster. This Odu speaks of a blessing that results from great vengeance, great wrath, great vindictiveness, great animosity, or great ambivalence. Be sure that your name is written on the right list, lest you wind up cursing and gnashing your teeth along with the missionaries. Avoid prophecies of doom's coming—for of this, neither oracle nor prophet knows. The best cure for what ails you is to keep your own nose blown and your own anus fanned dry. *In choosing between alternatives—the right hand is chosen. Ogbe Irete has spoken.*

8 + 0   *Ogbe Opira*

With Ogbe falling first and Opira falling next, we have found Ogbe Opira. The omens are at least half good. *In choosing between alternatives—no hand is chosen. Ogbe Opira has spoken but said nothing.*

NINE SHELLS

owo eesan

Osa is about things that go wrong as a result of attempting to figure them out. It is about things that go right as a result of trusting in your women's premonitions. Though the winds may change without notice, listen for the silence that precedes the storm and you will always be forewarned.

Combinations of Osa
(Ossa)

9 + 1   Osa Okanran

With Osa falling first and Okanran falling next, we have found Osa Okanran—the single woman. This Odu talks about a blessing that follows on the heels of a woman who goes her own way. Beware that you do not fall victim to others' ideas of what is right for you. Avoid those who would limit you. Avoid being cursed by them and their ideas. The best cure for what ails you is to go away for a while. But you might find what you need in your own backyard. *In choosing between alternatives—the left hand is chosen. Osa Okanran has spoken.*

9 + 2   Osa Oyeku

With Osa falling first and Oyeku falling next, we have found Osa Oyeku—the pregnant woman. This Odu foretells a blessing of fertility. Before your creative juices dry up, be sure to put them to good use. Do not later curse the fact that you have nothing to show for your youth. Just the same, avoid becoming a slave to your biological clock. The best cure for what ails you is to give birth to whatever stirs within you. *In choosing between alternatives—the left hand is chosen. Osa Oyeku has spoken.*

9 + 3   Osa Ogunda

With Osa falling first and Ogunda falling next, we have found Osa Ogunda—the half man, half woman. This Odu says that a blessing will come from the union of male and female. Beware that a partnership is equal or that a bargain is fair, or else you will live to curse your partner later. Avoid consummating a marriage prematurely. The best cure for what ails you is to strive for equity . . . truth, good, and light. Peace. *In choosing between alternatives—the left hand is chosen. Osa Ogunda has spoken.*

9 + 4   Osa Irosun

With Osa falling first and Irosun falling next, we have found Osa Irosun—the menstruating woman. This Odu speaks of a blessing that comes as a result of shedding something that is no longer needed. Be careful not to panic over the sight of a little blood. It is not a curse after all, but a sign that there will soon be a healing. Avoid intercourse right now. But in the long run, it is the best cure for what ails you. *In choosing between alternatives—the left hand is chosen. Osa Irosun has spoken.*

9 + 5   Osa Oshe

With Osa falling first and Oshe falling next, we have found Osa Oshe—the undulating woman. This Odu says a blessing is coming from the rolling of hips, the jostling of breasts, and the trembling of lips. Beware the signals you send are the signals you mean. Beware the signals you pick up are the ones you were intended to receive. Do not wind up later cursing each other in court. Avoid innuendo. Yet be discreet. The best cure for what ails you is to come out and say what you mean. *In choosing between alternatives—the right hand is chosen. Osa Oshe has spoken.*

9 + 6   Osa Obara

With Osa falling first and Obara falling next, we have found Osa Obara—the queen of heaven. This Odu predicts a blessing that comes directly from "our mother, who art in heaven." Be a little care-

153

ful with such creative energy lest you wind up destroying more than you have the ability to create. Avoid erratic behavior. Do not curse Mother Yemaya later for your own mistakes. The best cure for what ails you is to focus on the things that last. *In choosing between alternatives—the right hand is chosen. Osa Obara has spoken.*

9 + 7   Osa Odi

With Osa falling first and Odi falling next, we have found Osa Odi—the belly of a woman. This Odu says that the force that stirs within you is the source of your blessing. Be careful in being prolific that you don't end up overdoing, lest your offspring curse their overcrowded conditions. Avoid too much—even of a good thing. The best cure for what ails you is simply to wait for the blessed event to take place. *In choosing between alternatives—the right hand is chosen. Osa Odi has spoken.*

9 + 8   Osa Ogbe

With Osa falling first and Ogbe falling next, we have found Osa Ogbe—the wise woman. This Odu says that a blessing will come if you listen carefully to the words of the diviner. Beware that you reveal nothing to her in advance, lest she tell you what you want to hear and not what you need to know. Do not curse her later for the truth she tells. Say nothing now, but avoid those you do not trust. The best cure for what ails you is to take a few words of advice from your own shells. *In choosing between alternatives—the left hand is chosen. Osa Ogbe has spoken.*

9 + 9   Osa Meji

With Osa falling first and Osa falling again, we have found Osa Meji (two Osas)—the twin girls. This Odu foretells of a blessing that involves two women of equal stature. Be careful that you do not confuse two opposite things that look very much alike. Do not find yourself in a position later to curse the trick that's been played on you. The best cure for what ails you is to look below the surface of the waters. Eat some fish. *In choosing between alternatives—the right hand is chosen. Osa Meji has spoken.*

9 + 10   Osa Ofun

With Osa falling first and Ofun falling next, we have found Osa Ofun—the fallen woman. This Odu says that a blessing may yet result from an error in judgment. Beware that an acquaintance or trusted friend does not prove to be your enemy. Avoid being alone with those who make you feel uneasy. The best cure for what ails you is preventive measures. . . . Do not lightly invite symptoms you do not want to fight. *In choosing between alternatives—the left hand is chosen. Osa Ofun has spoken.*

9 + 11   Osa Owonrin

With Osa falling first and Owonrin falling next, we have found Osa Owonrin—the fickle woman. This Odu ordains a blessing that results from a changing of heart, a reversal of thought, or a change of mind. Beware that this may not be the final word. Avoid indecision. Act fast before you have cause to curse your moment of hesitation. The best cure for what ails you is to do what your shells tell you to. *In choosing between alternatives—the left hand is chosen. Osa Owonrin has spoken.*

9 + 12   Osa Iwori

With Osa falling first and Iwori falling next, we have found Osa Iwori—the fiery woman. This Odu says that a blessing comes from showing your true colors. Wear plenty of scarves or put your heart on your sleeve. Beware that some may curse you for selling out to "lesser" ideals than theirs. So what? They are just jealous that you might have an idea of your own. Avoid them. The best cure for what ails you is to go forward with pride and good intent no matter what the others think. *In choosing between alternatives—the left hand is chosen. Osa Iwori has spoken.*

9 + 13   Osa Ika

With Osa falling first and Ika falling next, we have found Osa Ika—the witchy woman. This Odu speaks of a blessing that results from a woman working her magic on things. Beware that a charm does not ricochet. Beware of cheap tricks. Do not curse yourself later for having miscalculated the situation. The best cure for what ails you is to think again before making your move or countermove. *In choosing between alternatives—the right hand is chosen. Osa Ika has spoken.*

9 + 14   *Osa Oturupon*

With Osa falling first and Oturupon falling next, we have found Osa Oturupon—the jealous woman. This Odu tells of a blessing that comes out of proper conduct. Beware that a minor vice does not become a habit. Do not curse your luck later for something you might have prevented by changing your ways. Avoid making pale excuses. The best cure for what ails you is to live your life as if it were a truth. *In choosing between alternatives—the right hand is chosen. Osa Oturupon has spoken.*

9 + 15   *Osa Otura*

With Osa falling first and Otura falling next, we have found Osa Otura—the wronged woman. This Odu says a blessing will yet come out of a rejection. But be careful you are not outwitted or unnerved in a house where curses prevail. Avoid stooping too low. Avoid stretching too high. The best cure for what ails you is to hold your own, like a secret to your brow. *In choosing between alternatives—the right hand is chosen. Osa Otura has spoken.*

9 + 16   *Osa Irete*

With Osa falling first and Irete falling next, we have found Osa Irete—the lost woman. This Odu says that a blessing is coming from the family matriarch. A mother, grandmother, or elder sister plays a part. Beware that you do not dismiss wise words spoken through ancient lips. Do not curse an old idea only because it is old. Avoid being too modern. The best cure for what ails you is to listen twice as much as you speak. *In choosing between alternatives—the right hand is chosen. Osa Irete has spoken.*

9 + 0   *Osa Opira*

With Osa falling first and Opira falling next, we have found Osa Opira. No woman wants to answer this question. Blow on your shells and ask again. *In choosing between alternatives—no hand is chosen. Osa Opira has spoken without saying a word.*

TEN SHELLS

owo eewaa

Ofun is about things that go wrong on account of an ethical error. It is about things that come out right as a result of good character. Though the ends may not always justify your means, act in good faith and all will work out.

Combinations of Ofun
(*Ofun Mafun*)

10 + 1   *Ofun Okanran*

With Ofun falling first and Okanran falling next, we have found Ofun Okanran—the lone one. This Odu speaks of a blessing that comes as if from masturbation. An act of self-gratification is involved. Beware that self-indulgence does not blind you to the fact that others would like your company. Do not curse commitment. Avoid indecent exposure. The best cure for what ails you is a little palm oil. *In choosing between alternatives—the right hand is chosen. Ofun Okanran has spoken.*

10 + 2   *Ofun Oyeku*

With Ofun falling first and Oyeku falling next, we have found Ofun Oyeku—the orphan child. This Odu tells of a blessing that yet results from a physical, emotional, or spiritual abandonment. Beware the mother who has given up on her child. Beware the child who has given up on its mother. Curses go both ways. Avoid participating in malice—either on the giving or receiving side. The best cure for what ails you is to forgive yourself first, and then you will be able to forgive the other. *In choosing between alternatives—the right hand is chosen. Ofun Oyeku has spoken.*

10 + 3   *Ofun Ogunda*

With Ofun falling first and Ogunda falling next, we have found Ofun Ogunda—the roving penis. This Odu ordains that a blessing will yet come as a result of a man's indulgence of his manhood. Beware that the conquest is worth the price—or else you will surely curse the fact that a bargain was not a bargain. Avoid the risk of contracting sores. The best cure for what ails you involves looking without touching. *In choosing between alternatives—the right hand is chosen. Ofun Ogunda has spoken.*

10 + 4   *Ofun Irosun*

With Ofun falling first and Irosun falling next, we have found Ofun Irosun—the red rage. This Odu foretells a blessing that yet results from a temper that explodes. Beware that it is not your own excesses that get revealed in the process. Though you may be surrounded by the sounds of curses, avoid joining in them. The best cure for what ails you is to keep your tongue. *In choosing between alternatives—the right hand is chosen. Ofun Irosun has spoken.*

10 + 5   *Ofun Oshe*

With Ofun falling first and Oshe falling next, we have found Ofun Oshe—the prostitute. This Odu speaks of a blessing that comes from selling a favor of some kind. Beware that you not use sex as a tool for personal advantage. Do not later curse yourself for everything you get as a result of this. Avoid false pretenses. The best cure for what ails you is honesty. *In choosing between alternatives—the right hand is chosen. Ofun Oshe has spoken.*

10 + 6   Ofun Obara

With Ofun falling first and Obara falling next, we have found Ofun Obara—the fallen angel. This Odu predicts a blessing that comes from someone totally unexpected. Be careful not to assume that because you were deceived once, there is no way to be innocent again. Avoid holding a grudge against yourself. Do not later curse yourself for having been afraid to take a risk. The best cure for what ails you is to keep getting back up. *In choosing between alternatives— the right hand is chosen. Ofun Obara has spoken.*

10 + 7   Ofun Odi

With Ofun falling first and Odi falling next, we have found Ofun Odi—the broken container. This Odu says that a blessing will come following the picking up of scattered pieces. Beware the mistaken belief that everything can be the same again. Curses to the home wrecker. Avoid breaking an oath and you will not have this problem. The best cure for what ails you is to salvage what you can and get on to more important things. *In choosing between alternatives—the right hand is chosen. Ofun Odi has spoken.*

10 + 8   Ofun Ogbe

With Ofun falling first and Ogbe falling next, we have found Ofun Ogbe—the contenders. This Odu tells of a blessing that comes from fighting for the honor. Beware that you do not become cocksure of your position, or else you might have to curse your successor. Avoid childish political battles. The best cure for what ails you is to perform with honor the duties you have agreed to carry out. *In choosing between alternatives—the left hand is chosen. Ofun Ogbe has spoken.*

10 + 9   Ofun Osa

With Ofun falling first and Osa falling next, we have found Ofun Osa—the other woman. This Odu ordains a blessing that yet will emerge from an extracurricular affair. Beware that you do not enter this tryst lightly, lest you curse yourself later for the pain you have caused to the one you truly love. Avoid relationships that must be kept secret. The best cure for what ails you is to work on the love you've already got. *In choosing between alternatives—the right hand is chosen. Ofun Osa has spoken.*

10 + 10   *Ofun Meji*

With Ofun falling first and Ofun falling again, we have found Ofun Meji (two Ofuns)—double trouble! This Odu tells of a blessing that looks, at first, like a tremendous curse. Beware that you do not curse it too hard, lest the blessing that is due you as a result never materializes. Avoid seeing only the bad side. The best cure for what ails you is to consider the benefits of a temporary sacrifice. *In choosing between alternatives—the left hand is chosen. Ofun Meji has spoken.*

10 + 11   *Ofun Owonrin*

With Ofun falling first and Owonrin falling next, we have found Ofun Owonrin—the trickster. This Odu says that a blessing will appear before it disappears. Beware that you do not mistake a mirage for the real thing, lest your dry mouth curse your eyes for telling lies. Avoid buying in on something that appears better than it should. The best cure for what ails you is to think twice before you bite into something unfamiliar. *In choosing between alternatives—the right hand is chosen. Ofun Owonrin has spoken.*

10 + 12   *Ofun Iwori*

With Ofun falling first and Iwori falling next, we have found Ofun Iwori—the transgressor. This Odu says that a blessing comes from obeying the rules of the road. Beware that in going a familiar route, you do not become overconfident in what lies beyond the next bend. Do not curse later your belief that some things never change. The best cure for what ails you is to stay awake and alert. *In choosing between alternatives—the right hand is chosen. Ofun Iwori has spoken.*

10 + 13   *Ofun Ika*

With Ofun falling first and Ika falling next, we have found Ofun Ika—the conspirator. This Odu predicts a blessing that comes out of some kind of secret activity or even a plot. Beware that your well-laid plans do not get out. Do not curse later the fact that you confided in someone, especially the diviner. Avoid saying too little or too much. The best cure for what ails you is to tell no one what you're up to, lest everyone finds out. *In choosing between alternatives—the right hand is chosen. Ofun Ika has spoken.*

10 + 14   *Ofun Oturupon*

With Ofun falling first and Oturupon falling next, we have found Ofun Oturupon—the wicked one. This Odu speaks of the kind of blessing that comes from an obscene gesture. Beware those who grab their crotches, lest you find them grabbing yours. Avoid those who talk dirty, lest they mean what they whisper in your ear. Do not later curse the fact that the danger thrilled you. The best cure for what ails you is not to humor the one who follows you home. *In choosing between alternatives—the right hand is chosen. Ofun Oturupon has spoken.*

10 + 15   *Ofun Otura*

With Ofun falling first and Otura falling next, we have found Ofun Otura—the willing martyr. This Odu says that a blessing comes to those who sacrifice. But beware the self-declared messiah, lest you wind up cursing the fact that you have given all your money away to a charlatan. Avoid causes that sound too good for mortal words. The best cure for what ails you is to place your confidence in others with care. Leave a little bread out for the birds. *In choosing between alternatives—the right hand is chosen. Ofun Otura has spoken.*

10 + 16   *Ofun Irete*

With Ofun falling first and Irete falling next, we have found Ofun Irete—the willing slave. This Odu tells of the kind of blessings that come to someone who has willingly submitted to another's authority. Beware that you trust completely the one who holds your hands down. Do not find yourself cursing later the fact that the keys to your shackles have been misplaced. Avoid a cruel master. Avoid a harsh mistress. The best cure for what ails you is to draw the line when the line needs to be drawn. *In choosing between alternatives—the right hand is chosen. Ofun Irete has spoken.*

10 + 0   *Ofun Opira*

With Ofun falling first and Opira falling next, we have found Ofun Opira. There is nothing to be said, except do not curse the oracle. *In choosing between alternatives—no hand is chosen. Ofun Opira has spoken, but only a silent prayer.*

ELEVEN SHELLS

owo ookan laa

Owonrin is about things that go wrong on account of a change in conditions. It is about things that go right on account of patience and the willingness to adapt. Though a moment of uncertainly may yet cross your mind, the decisions you are about to make are life-altering.

Combinations of Owonrin
(*Ojuani Chober*)

11 + 1   *Owonrin Okanran*

With Owonrin falling first and Okanran falling next, we have found Owonrin Okanran—the selfish conclusion. This Odu tells of a blessing that comes as a result of pursuing a selfish course of action. Beware that the good of the many does not outweigh your grand ambition, lest you rue the day you tried to gain power over them. Avoid using others as if they were stones in a river. The best cure for what ails you is to get what you want by giving others what they need. *In choosing between alternatives—the left hand is chosen. Owonrin Okanran has spoken.*

11 + 2   *Owonrin Oyeku*

With Owonrin falling first and Oyeku falling next, we have found Owonrin Oyeku—the calm diligence. This Odu tells of a blessing that comes from quietly waiting for things to come to term. Be careful about rushing into things. Do not later curse the fact that you have hurried to meet failure. Avoid shoving. Avoid pulling. Avoid pushing. The best cure for what ails you is to show some patience and restraint. *In choosing between alternatives—the left hand is chosen. Owonrin Oyeku has spoken.*

11 + 3   **Owonrin Ogunda**

With Owonrin falling first and Ogunda falling next, we have found Owonrin Ogunda—the miraculous penis. This Odu says that a blessing is coming due to a sudden change in shape, form, and substance. Be neither too rigid nor too soft. Neither enter too fast, nor withdraw too quick. Do not later curse the fact that you came too soon or lingered beyond your welcome. Avoid having to excuse yourself. The best cure for what ails you is to take your cues from the others in the room. *In choosing between alternatives—the left hand is chosen. Owonrin Ogunda has spoken.*

11 + 4   *Owonrin Irosun*

With Owonrin falling first and Irosun falling next, we have found Owonrin Irosun—the reddening eyes. This Odu tells of a blessing that comes as a result of tears being shed. Do not hold back a good cry. Do not hold in a good sneeze. Beware that you do not curse the hand that would wipe both your tears and phlegm away. Avoid bottling things up inside. The best cure for what ails you is to find a strong arm to lean on . . . or a soft bosom to embrace. *In choosing between alternatives—the left hand is chosen. Owonrin Irosun has spoken.*

11 + 5   **Owonrin Oshe**

With Owonrin falling first and Oshe falling next, we have found Owonrin Oshe—the shifting tides. This Odu speaks of a blessing that emerges out of the never-ending cycles of rain and drought. All things—like the sea—are inclined to ebb and flow. Beware that you do not miss the signs in the sky or at your feet. Do not later curse the fact that you were caught unprepared. The best cure for what ails you is to watch, wait . . . and you will see. *In choosing between alternatives—the right hand is chosen. Owonrin Oshe has spoken.*

11 + 6   *Owonrin Obara*

With Owonrin falling first and Obara falling next, we have found Owonrin Obara—the unexpected rainbow. This Odu tells of a blessing that emerges out of thin air—and for no apparent reason. But beware—something so false can only be inclined to fade. If you are not careful, you may find yourself cursing yourself for not being sure of what you really saw. Avoid the doubting of your inner senses. The best cure for what ails you is to trust the feeling more than the figment. *In choosing between alternatives—the right hand is chosen. Owonrin Obara has spoken.*

11 + 7   *Owonrin Odi*

With Owonrin falling first and Odi falling next, we have found Owonrin Odi—the melting pot. This Odu says that a blessing is coming as the result of things heating up and at the same time softening. Beware that there are not too many artists involved in making the same bronze sculpture. Do not later curse the uneven results of a joint project. Avoid unnecessary tampering with a work of art. The best cure for what ails you is to remain yourself like clay on the potter's wheel. Trusting in divine hands, you will be spun into something worth keeping. *In choosing between alternatives—the right hand is chosen. Owonrin Odi has spoken.*

11 + 8   *Owonrin Ogbe*

With Owonrin falling first and Ogbe falling next, we have found Owonrin Ogbe—the persistent one. This Odu speaks of a blessing that results from a relentless search. Beware that you do not grow tired in the process of seeking, lest you curse the fact that you were too tired to return once you had found. Avoid giving up. Avoid giving out. Avoid giving in. The best cure for what ails you is to turn to your gods for whatever assistance they might bring. *In choosing between alternatives—the left hand is chosen. Owonrin Ogbe has spoken.*

11 + 9   Owonrin Osa

With Owonrin falling first and Osa falling next, we have found Owonrin Osa—the stalwart woman. This Odu says that a blessing comes out of constancy, loyalty, devotion, and dedication to a noble cause. Beware that you do not tire of your position, lest you start to curse the blessing of stability you have achieved. Avoid all manner of resentment and disdaining. The best cure for what ails you is to draw enjoyment from the daily task of surviving. *In choosing between alternatives—the right hand is chosen. Owonrin Osa has spoken.*

11 + 10   Owonrin Ofun

With Owonrin falling first and Ofun falling next, we have found Owonrin Ofun—the wayward son. This Odu says that a blessing comes yet from that which is lost . . . from one who has abandoned you, or one you have given up upon. Take care that you do not hope too much to restore things exactly as they were, lest you curse the day you received a vain and idle wish. Avoid passing judgment. The best cure for what ails you is to fill the days while you wait for someone who is lost to return to you. *In choosing between alternatives—the left hand is chosen. Owonrin Ofun has spoken.*

11 + 11   Owonrin Meji

With Owonrin falling first and Owonrin falling again, we have found Owonrin Meji (two Owonrins)—the chameleon. This Odu tells of a blessing that is constantly changing . . . growing, evolving, developing. That which was, no longer is. That which is, will not remain the same. That which is to come, will not stay long once it gets here. Beware that you do not curse things passing, lest the blessing that is coming not find you where you need to be. Avoid clinging like vines to the ankles of passersby. The best cure for what ails you is do what you must to get ahead. *In choosing between alternatives—the left hand is chosen. Owonrin Meji has spoken.*

11 + 12   Owonrin Iwori

With Owonrin falling first and Iwori falling next, we have found Owonrin Iwori—the passing dream. This Odu says that a blessing will be revealed to you by your spiritual double in a dream. Be careful that you do not dismiss a message that comes in the night, lest you curse the fact that a premonition went unacted upon. Just the same, avoid interpreting the signs too literally. The best cure for what ails you is to figure out what someone is trying to tell you. *In choosing between alternatives—the left hand is chosen. Owonrin Iwori has spoken.*

11 + 13   *Owonrin Ika*

With Owonrin falling first and Ika falling next, we have found Owonrin Ika—the inflicted change. This Odu talks about a blessing that is dictated by someone in a position of power and authority. Beware that you neither coerce nor entice the people you control, lest they curse you when your back is turned. Beware that you do not curse the person who has control over you, lest you be overheard by him or her. Avoid both harassment and insubordination. The best cure for what ails you is to behave in a way that merits mutual respect. *In choosing between alternatives—the right hand is chosen. Owonrin Ika has spoken.*

11 + 14   **Owonrin Oturupon**

With Owonrin falling first and Oturupon falling next, we have found Owonrin Oturupon—the covetous old one. This Odu says that a blessing does not come to you that someone else is not envious of. Beware that in winning, you do not alienate the loser. Avoid cursing the good things that have come to pass. The best cure for what ails you is to be more gracious and less proud. *In choosing between alternatives—the right hand is chosen. Owonrin Oturupon has spoken.*

11 + 15   *Owonrin Otura*

With Owonrin falling first and Otura falling next, we have found Owonrin Otura—the giant weakling. This Odu says that a blessing comes as a result of something becoming the opposite of what it appears to be. Be careful that you do not overlook the power of a weakness played to the hilt. Avoid trusting in ideas that no longer carry weight in the marketplace. Do not later curse the fact that you did not see a rival coming. The best cure for what ails you is to use the eyes in the back of your head. *In choosing between alternatives—the right hand is chosen. Owonrin Otura has spoken.*

11 + 16   Owonrin Irete

With Owonrin falling first and Irete falling next, we have found Owonrin Irete—the disintegrating factor. This Odu says that a blessing will come as a result of cataclysmic change. What you thought was stable is crumbling around you. Beware that you do not try to hold on as the walls come tumbling down, lest you fall with them. Avoid attempts to prop things up. The best cure for what ails you is to seek cover until the winds of change have blown the dust away. *In choosing between alternatives—the right hand is chosen. Owonrin Irete has spoken.*

11 + 0   Owonrin Opira

With Owonrin falling first and Opira falling next, we have found Owonrin Opira. Nothing is revealed. *In choosing between alternatives— no hand is chosen. Owonrin Opira has spoken, but nothing was said.*

TWELVE SHELLS

owo eeji laa

Iwori is about things that go wrong on account of a lack of commitment. It is about things that go right on account of pursuing a dream—wherever it leads. Though a doubt or two may cross your mind along the way, in the final analysis, you will know what to do when the road opens up to you.

Combinations of Iwori
(Eyila Chebora)

12 + 1   *Iwori Okanran*

With Iwori falling first and Okanran falling next, we have found Iwori Okanran—the fire within. This Odu speaks of a blessing that comes from a passion that burns within your soul. Beware that in your efforts to burn as bright as you can, you do not consume yourself in a short while. Avoid burning your candle at both ends. The best cure for what ails you is to learn how to handle pressure and control time. *In choosing between alternatives—the left hand is chosen. Iwori Okanran has spoken.*

12 + 2   *Iwori Oyeku*

With Iwori falling first and Oyeku falling next, we have found Iwori Oyeku—the spark of a flame. This Odu refers to a blessing that comes from lighting a fire under someone or something. Beware that in breathing life into a smoldering ash, you do not blow it out completely. Do not curse a dying ember. Avoid playing with matches. The best cure for what ails you is to first light a fire under yourself—then you will have the power to ignite others. *In choosing between alternatives—the left hand is chosen. Iwori Oyeku has spoken.*

12 + 3   *Iwori Ogunda*

With Iwori falling first and Ogunda falling next, we have found Iwori Ogunda—the burning penis. This Odu says that a blessing is sure to come yet from allowing a sleeping passion to build. . . up to the point of bursting. Be careful to keep the home fires burning neither too fast nor too low. Do not live to curse the fact that a flame burned out too soon. Avoid standing too close to a boiling kettle . . . especially while naked. Avoiding girding your loins too tight. The best cure for what ails you is to wait until it is your turn. *In choosing between alternatives—the left hand is chosen. Iwori Ogunda has spoken.*

12 + 4   *Iwori Irosun*

With Iwori falling first and Irosun falling next, we have found Iwori Irosun—the red ember. This Odu predicts a blessing that comes in the last hours of work . . . in the ending seconds of play . . . or in the final days of an endeavor. Beware that you do not give up hope before all hope is needed, lest you surrender too soon and live to curse your resulting bad luck. Avoid spending all of your energy up front. The best cure for what ails you is to save a little in reserve for the moment when it's needed most. *In choosing between alternatives— the left hand is chosen. Iwori Irosun has spoken.*

12 + 5   *Iwori Oshe*

With Iwori falling first and Oshe falling next, we have found Iwori Oshe—the churning sea. This Odu talks of a blessing that swells over you. Beware that it does not sweep you up and carry you away at the same time. Do not later curse yourself for having taken Mother Nature for granted. Avoid believing that a calm sea cannot grow suddenly dangerous. The best cure for what ails you is to give Mother Yemaya the respect that she deserves. *In choosing between alternatives—the right hand is chosen. Iwori Oshe has spoken.*

12 + 6   *Iwori Obara*

With Iwori falling first and Obara falling next, we have found Iwori Obara—the fire in the sky. This Odu tells of a blessing that comes as the result of a sudden revelation. Look for the signals and you will not be disappointed this time. Beware that the voices you listen to are not just the ones that say what you want to hear, lest you curse an unexpected truth when it is spoken to you. Avoid circular thought. The best cure for what ails you is to rethink an old conclusion. *In choosing between alternatives—the right hand is chosen. Iwori Obara has spoken.*

12 + 7   *Iwori Odi*

With Iwori falling first and Odi falling next, we have found Iwori Odi—the cooking pot. This Odu predicts a blessing that results from mixing things together in a stew and seeing what you get. Beware that you do not get carried away with adding spice to your life. It is impossible to undo the curse of too much garlic. Avoid overindulgence in any one thing. The best cure for what ails you is to temper, temper, my friend, until you get the secret recipe right. *In choosing between alternatives—the right hand is chosen. Iwori Odi has spoken.*

12 + 8   Iwori Ogbe

With Iwori falling first and Ogbe falling next, we have found Iwori Ogbe—the constant flame. This Odu predicts that a great blessing is coming that will be sealed with a kiss. Handle a burning passion with care. And beware that in a moment of unthinking you do not cheapen with curses the great love you share. Avoid lashing out against those whom you can lash out against at will. The best cure for what ails you is to take comfort in the fire that you share. *In choosing between alternatives—the left hand is chosen. Iwori Ogbe has spoken.*

12 + 9   Iwori Osa

With Iwori falling first and Osa falling next, we have found Iwori Osa—the burning womb. This Odu says that a blessing is coming out of an itch you cannot control. Beware that in attempting to scratch it, you do not scratch yourself open. (Or else you might have to curse the fact that you are too sore.) Avoid contact with those who have no sympathy for your anatomy. The best cure for what ails you is to do for yourself what cannot be done by others. *In choosing between alternatives—the right hand is chosen. Iwori Osa has spoken.*

12 + 10   Iwori Ofun

With Iwori falling first and Ofun falling next, we have found Iwori Ofun—the infernal fire. This Odu predicts a blessing arising from out of the quiet voices that keep calling your name. Beware! And be careful that your voices are not rationalizing a wrong into a right, lest you wind up being cursed by those whose own voices have not yet grown loud enough to hear in public. Avoid incestuous relationships at all costs. The best cure for what ails you is to keep your unseemly desires in the closet. *In choosing between alternatives—the left hand is chosen. Iwori Ofun has spoken.*

12 + 11   Iwori Owonrin

With Iwori falling first and Owonrin falling next, we have found Iwori Owonrin—the firestorm. This Odu foretells of a blessing that rises from the ashes of a burnt-out past. Beware that, as you go sifting through the rubble for some remnant to take away, you do not burden yourself with curses better left buried. Avoid dragging old things along into your new life. The best cure for what ails you is to let the field be entirely leveled so that you may set down fresh roots. *In choosing between alternatives—the right hand is chosen. Iwori Owonrin has spoken.*

12 + 12   Iwori Meji

With Iwori falling first and Iwori falling again, we have found Iwori Meji (two Iworis)—the double-tongued fire. This Odu speaks of a blessing that involves two interconnected, interwoven, or intersected things. Beware that in pursuing joint interests, neither party's dream becomes too great, lest one has cause to curse what the other has taken away. Avoid legal arguments later. The best cure for what ails you is to draw up a letter of intent. *In choosing between alternatives—the left hand is chosen. Iwori Meji has spoken.*

12 + 13   Iwori Ika

With Iwori falling first and Ika falling next, we have found Iwori Ika—the fiery venom. This Odu tells of a blessing that comes as the result of something that stings a little at first. Beware that the bite that follows is not worse! Wipe the curse from your lips. And above all else, avoid revenge. The best cure for what ails you is to learn your lesson so that you can avoid disaster next time. *In choosing between alternatives—the right hand is chosen. Iwori Ika has spoken.*

12 + 14   Iwori Oturupon

With Iwori falling first and Oturupon falling next, we have found Iwori Oturupon—the cold sweat. This Odu foretells a blessing that results from a physical challenge. Be aware that a fever is only a symptom. Beware that a greater malady is the real curse. Avoid things that make you feel sick to your stomach. The best cure for what ails you is to take care of yourself a little better. *In choosing between alternatives—the right hand is chosen. Iwori Oturupon has spoken.*

12 + 15   Iwori Otura

With Iwori falling first and Otura falling next, we have found Iwori Otura—the relentless fire. This Odu tells of a blessing that comes from sticking to your guns, holding fast to your ground. Beware that in standing up for your own rights, you do not violate the rights of others, lest they have just cause to curse you to your face. Avoid despising others. The best cure for what ails you is to give them their fair space, so that you can insist on having some room of your own. *In choosing between alternatives—the right hand is chosen. Iwori Otura has spoken.*

12 + 16   Iwori Irete

With Iwori falling first and Irete falling next, we have found Iwori Irete—the funeral pyre. This Odu speaks of a blessing that comes after all else is said and done. Be careful in assuming that just because something has petered out, it has lost all its influence. Do not curse the popular figure, lest he later turn into an icon. Avoid speaking ill of the dead. The best cure for what ails you is to keep your heroes alive in you. *In choosing between alternatives—the right hand is chosen. Iwori Irete has spoken.*

12 + 0   Iwori Opira

With Iwori falling first and Opira falling next, we have found Iwori Opira. Nothing is decided. Perhaps it's better that way. *In choosing between alternatives—no hand is chosen. Iwori Opira has spoken, but nothing was said.*

THIRTEEN SHELLS

owo eeta laa

Ika is about things that go wrong on account of pits, snares, and traps. It is about things that turn out right, only after having been turned back upon themselves. Though others may seem at times to have you under their spell, it is your feelings of self-doubt that keep you there.

Combinations of Ika
(*Metanla*)

13 + 1   *Ika Okanran*

With Ika falling first and Okanran falling next, we have found Ika Okanran—the wicked one. This Odu speaks of a blessing that comes to you on account of your own wickedness. Take care the spell you cast does not come back to curse you! Avoid wishing others ill. The best cure for what ails you is a dose of your own medicine. *In choosing between alternatives—the left hand is chosen. Ika Okanran has spoken.*

13 + 2   *Ika Oyeku*

With Ika falling first and Oyeku falling next, we have found Ika Oyeku—the wicked woman. This Odu speaks of a blessing that comes out of seductive gestures and suggestive ideas. Take care that you are not all talk and no play! But beware that your words do not turn curses back upon your own head. Avoid entrapment. The best cure for what ails you is to know your own mind and control your own body. *In choosing between alternatives—the left hand is chosen. Ika Oyeku has spoken.*

13 + 3   *Ika Ogunda*

With Ika falling first and Ogunda falling next, we have found Ika Ogunda—the wicked penis. This Odu speaks of a blessing that comes from throwing your weight around. Be careful that you do not spread yourself too far and wide or you might later curse the fact that you have worn yourself thinner than a needle. Avoid physical contact sports (unless you are wearing the proper equipment). The best cure for what ails you is to take responsibility for the tool in your fist. *In choosing between alternatives—the left hand is chosen. Ika Ogunda has spoken.*

13 + 4   *Ika Irosun*

With Ika falling first and Irosun falling next, we have found Ika Irosun—the wicked color. This Odu speaks of a blessing that comes from wearing red to a funeral and black to a wedding. Beware that you not make too bold a statement, lest someone curse you loud enough that all might hear. Avoid raising your voice, unless you mean to yell. The best cure for what ails you is to utter a moan instead of a scream. *In choosing between alternatives—the left hand is chosen. Ika Irosun has spoken.*

13 + 5   *Ika Oshe*

With Ika falling first and Oshe falling next, we have found Ika Oshe—the wicked waves. This Odu says that a blessing is coming as if on an angry sea. Some things will be washed in on the tides. Some things will be carried away. Beware! Avoid shouting into the wind. The sea absorbs curses and washes them back to your feet. The best cure for what ails you is to weather the storm, my friend. Ride it out until it ends. *In choosing between alternatives—the left hand is chosen. Ika Oshe has spoken.*

13 + 6   *Ika Obara*

With Ika falling first and Obara falling next, we have found Ika Obara—the wicked sky. This Odu speaks of a blessing that you can watch gathering and taking shape. Beware that what appears to be a harmless piece of fluff does not yet turn and bark. Avoid discordance. The best cure for what ails you is to keep a constant watch. *In choosing between alternatives—the left hand is chosen. Ika Obara has spoken.*

13 + 7   *Ika Odi*

With Ika falling first and Odi falling next, we have found Ika Odi—the wicked receptacle. This Odu predicts a blessing that comes as a result of depositing something vile in a hidden place. Beware that in secreting jewels within body cavities, no one of authority asks to inspect. Curses! Avoid the taking of contraband out into public places. The best cure for what ails you is to keep a lid on your secrets. *In choosing between alternatives—the left hand is chosen. Ika Odi has spoken.*

13 + 8   *Ika Ogbe*

With Ika falling first and Ogbe falling next, we have found Ika Ogbe—the wickedest. This Odu tells that a blessing is not a blessing if it has to be kept hidden from others. Be careful that you do not develop a passion for something that cannot be discussed in polite company. Do not later curse the fact that your great success at what you do cannot be shared with those you would like to tell the most. Avoid admitting that you learned this lesson from the diviner, but . . . the best cure for what ails you is to practice your beliefs openly. *In choosing between alternatives—the left hand is chosen. Ika Ogbe has spoken.*

13 + 9   *Ika Osa*

With Ika falling first and Osa falling next, we have found Ika Osa—the wicked breasts. This Odu predicts a blessing that attracts the eye of a secret admirer (who will not remain secret much longer). Beware that you do not encourage a superficial attachment, lest you find yourself cursing the shallow relationship that results. Avoid overpackaging. The best cure for what ails you is to look beneath the surface of a body's curves and protuberances. *In choosing between alternatives—the left hand is chosen. Ika Osa has spoken.*

13 + 10   *Ika Ofun*

With Ika falling first and Ofun falling next, we have found Ika Ofun—the wicked and despicable. This Odu talks of a blessing that comes at first with neither fear nor shame—yet bears in time a certain price. Beware that you do not start to think of everything you do as normal, or else you may yet curse the things that you are able to get away with temporarily. Avoid spoiling your reputation. The best cure for what ails you is to suppress the evil thought. *In choosing between alternatives—the left hand is chosen. Ika Ofun has spoken.*

13 + 11   *Ika Owonrin*

With Ika falling first and Owonrin falling next, we have found Ika Owonrin—the wicked way. This Odu foretells of a blessing that comes at the end of a winding road. Beware that the vines and creepers on this path do not become your snares, lest you fall in the mud and wind up cursing that you have come this way at all. Avoid dependency. The best cure for what ails you is to get your kicks some other way. *In choosing between alternatives—the left hand is chosen. Ika Owonrin has spoken.*

13 + 12   *Ika Iwori*

With Ika falling first and Iwori falling next, we have found Ika Iwori—the wicked flame. This Odu foretells a blessing that emerges from a burning, but destructive, passion. Beware that your artistic pursuits do not become all-consuming, lest you find yourself cursing from within the belly of your own beast. Avoid that which could consume you for no good purpose. The best cure for what ails you is to choose your poison selectively. *In choosing between alternatives— the left hand is chosen. Ika Iwori has spoken.*

13 + 13   *Ika Meji*

With Ika falling first and Ika falling again, we have found Ika Meji (two Ikas)—the doubly wicked. This Odu tells of a blessing that comes as the result of a showdown between two negative forces. Be aware that two pluses do not make a minus. (But two minutes do have a way of adding up.) Curses and countercurses! Avoid them both and do not step into the cross fire. The best cure for what ails you is to wait for things to settle down and even out—then it will be safe again to go out at night. *In choosing between alternatives—the right hand is chosen. Ika Meji has spoken.*

13 + 14   Ika Oturupon

With Ika falling first and Oturupon falling next, we have found Ika Oturupon—the wicked lie. This Odu talks about a blessing that comes as the result of a propaganda campaign backfiring on itself. Curses! You have duped others or been duped yourself. Beware that when the truth is revealed, it does not blind you with anger. Avoid backlash—but remove impostors from the king's chair. The best cure for what ails you is to choose less savvy criminals to hold high office. *In choosing between alternatives—the right hand is chosen. Ika Oturupon has spoken.*

13 + 15   Ika Otura

With Ika falling first and Otura falling next, we have found Ika Otura—the wicked words. This Odu says that a blessing will yet come—someday—as the result of this damnation. Beware that the curses clinging to your lips on that day will not have to be eaten, for they are bitter, foul, and rank. Avoid speaking too boldly of what you cannot know. The best cure for what ails you is to keep silence in the presence of the gods. Ashe. *In choosing between alternatives—the right hand is chosen. Ika Otura has spoken.*

13 + 16   Ika Irete

With Ika falling first and Irete falling next, we have found Ika Irete—the end of wickedness. This Odu foretells of a blessing that comes from a conscious decision to give up diabolical ways. Beware that the halo round your head does not shatter—and you wind up cursing the weakness you might have overcome. Avoid putting off the chance to change things now. The best cure for what ails you is to turn over a new leaf while you still can. *In choosing between alternatives—the right hand is chosen. Ika Irete has spoken.*

13 + 0   Ika Opira

With Ika falling first and Opira falling next, we have found Ika Opira. No answer has been revealed. Perhaps you wouldn't want to know anyway. *In choosing between alternatives—no hand is chosen. Ika Opira has spoken, but not a word was said.*

FOURTEEN SHELLS

owo eerin laa

Oturupon is about things that go wrong because of miscommunication. It is about things that go right as a result of keeping channels open. Though all conflicts do not result in noble ends, it is the victor who writes the history in the end.

Combinations of Oturupon
(Merinla)

14 + 1   Oturupon Okanran

With Oturupon falling first and Okanran falling next, we have found Oturupon Okanran—the conflict with self. This Odu says that a blessing will come as the result of one half winning out over the other. Beware that it is the better half of you that rises to the challenge, lest you be cursed forever with your own bad company. Avoid self-infatuation. The best cure for what ails you is to settle the grudge you hold against yourself. *In choosing between alternatives—the left hand is chosen. Oturupon Okanran has spoken.*

14 + 2   Oturupon Oyeku

With Oturupon falling first and Oyeku falling next, we have found Oturupon Oyeku—the inner doubt. This Odu speaks of a blessing

178

that comes from overcoming a niggling, nagging thought. Beware that what's eating you does not succeed. Curse only what you cannot bear. Avoid what you cannot abide. The best cure for what ails you is to trust in the voices inside. *In choosing between alternatives—the left hand is chosen. Oturupon Oyeku has spoken.*

14 + 3 *Oturupon Ogunda*

With Oturupon falling first and Ogunda falling next, we have found Oturupon Ogunda—the doubtful penis. This Odu says that a blessing comes from trying less hard. Beware that you do not worry a little thing to death. Avoid thinking that something will not work. The best cure for what ails you is to be less fearful and more brave. *In choosing between alternatives—the left hand is chosen. Oturupon Ogunda has spoken.*

14 + 4 *Oturupon Irosun*

With Oturupon falling first and Irosun falling next, we have found Oturupon Irosun—the ruddy doubt. This Odu talks about a blessing that will result from a moment of possible embarrassment. Beware being caught without a contingency plan in place, lest you curse the fact that you could have recovered better. Avoid thinking this one thing is the most important thing in the world. The best cure for what ails you is to lie back and let the music flow through you. *In choosing between alternatives—the left hand is chosen. Oturupon Irosun has spoken.*

14 + 5 *Oturupon Oshe*

With Oturupon falling first and Oshe falling next, we have found Oturupon Oshe—the reluctant rain. This Odu foretells of a blessing that comes after a period of watching and waiting. Take care that you conserve your basic resources, lest you curse the fact that you have run out of water (and therefore steam). Avoid assuming that a situation is only temporary. The best cure for what ails you is to settle in for the duration. *In choosing between alternatives—the left hand is chosen. Oturupon Oshe has spoken.*

14 + 6   *Oturupon Obara*

With Oturupon falling first and Obara falling next, we have found Oturupon Obara—the doubtful cause. This Odu says that a blessing will come to someone who takes the steps to assure it. Be careful that you do not hope for too much too fast. Be careful that you do not get too little too late. Both outlooks will curse you. Avoid both defeatist and supremacist attitudes. The best cure for what ails you is to plot things out one step at a time. *In choosing between alternatives—the left hand is chosen. Oturupon Obara has spoken.*

14 + 7   *Oturupon Odi*

With Oturupon falling first and Odi falling next, we have found Oturupon Odi—the dubious container. This Odu foretells of a blessing that comes out of a dark pit in your stomach. Beware that you do not curse a sinking feeling when it gives you the forewarning that you sought. Avoid going against the inklings of your gut. The best cure for what ails you is to read the signs in yourself. *In choosing between alternatives—the left hand is chosen. Oturupon Odi has spoken.*

14 + 8   *Oturupon Ogbe*

With Oturupon falling first and Ogbe falling next, we have found Oturupon Ogbe—the doubt that turns to faith. This Odu says that a blessing is coming. All you must do is believe. Beware that not even a shadow of a doubt creeps into your positive thinking, lest you curse your prayers with negative energy. Avoid jinxing things. The best cure for what ails you is to give it time. *In choosing between alternatives—the left hand is chosen. Oturupon Ogbe has spoken.*

14 + 9   *Oturupon Osa*

With Oturupon falling first and Osa falling next, we have found Oturupon Osa—the pouting breasts. This Odu speaks of a blessing that comes from the young of body, mind, spirit, and heart. Beware that you do not take these things for granted, lest you curse the day when you might have looked longer in the mirror. Avoid thinking yourself old even now—for this, too, is youth, my friend, looking back from a latter year. The best cure for what ails you is to consider the good things that pass before you now. *In choosing between alternatives—the left hand is chosen. Oturupon Osa has spoken.*

14 + 10   *Oturupon Ofun*

With Oturupon falling first and Ofun falling next, we have found Oturupon Ofun—the overconfident one. This Odu predicts a blessing that comes from a bold, yet charming source. Beware that you do not become a party to a nefarious plot, lest you find later that you are cursing the fact that "he made me do it." Avoid blaming others for sucking you in. The best cure for what ails you is to show a little more discretion. *In choosing between alternatives—the left hand is chosen. Oturupon Ofun has spoken.*

14 + 11   *Oturupon Owonrin*

With Oturupon falling first and Owonrin falling next, we have found Oturupon Owonrin—the incessant worry. This Odu says that a blessing cannot be stopped despite your efforts to head it off at the pass. Beware that you not try to coach a thing along that wants to unfold at its own rate, lest you curse yourself later for pushing too hard too soon. Avoid impatience like the plague. The best cure for what ails you is to bide and abide. *In choosing between alternatives—the left hand is chosen. Oturupon Owonrin has spoken.*

14 + 12   *Oturupon Iwori*

With Oturupon falling first and Iwori falling next, we have found Oturupon Iwori—the flaming doubt. This Odu says that a blessing comes from a passion that waxes and wanes and waxes again. Beware that in the interims, you do not give up all hope, lest you curse the fact that the manic mood never rises and shines again. Avoid tempting fate. The best cure for what ails you is to put yourself within a trance. *In choosing between alternatives—the left hand is chosen. Oturupon Iwori has spoken.*

14 + 13   Oturupon Ika

With Oturupon falling first and Ika falling next, we have found Oturupon Ika—the external conflict. This Odu predicts a blessing that comes from fending off something that would interfere in your life. Be careful of those who see you as a threat, lest they turn you into an enemy who curses them back. Avoid rising to the bait. The best cure for what ails you is to let evil slip off your skin. *In choosing between alternatives—the left hand is chosen. Oturupon Ika has spoken.*

14 + 14   Oturupon Meji

With Oturupon falling first and Oturupon falling again, we have found Oturupon Meji (two Oturupons)—the double-dog-dare. This Odu ordains a blessing for true friends who might yet be enemies in the bitter end. Beware that a healthy rivalry does not disintegrate into outright war, lest you curse each other to the same ironic fate. Avoid doing something that might damage your friendship. The best cure for what ails you is to remain still, neither rising nor sinking to the other's place. *In choosing between alternatives—the right hand is chosen. Oturupon Meji has spoken.*

14 + 15   Oturupon Otura

With Oturupon falling first and Otura falling next, we have found Oturupon Otura—the shock effect. This Odu speaks of a blessing that comes from taking an extreme position. Beware that if you intimidate others too much, you may curse the loss of your popular support. Avoid hurling barbs at easy victims. The best cure for what ails you is to live and let live. *In choosing between alternatives—the right hand is chosen. Oturupon Otura has spoken.*

14 + 16   Oturupon Irete

With Oturupon falling first and Irete falling next, we have found Oturupon Irete—the crumbling doubt. This Odu says that a blessing will reach you when the limitations you have placed on yourself suddenly disintegrate into dusty ruins. Beware that you not laugh too hard at your past folly, lest its lesson escape you and you have to go through it all again. Avoid making the same errors over and over. The best cure for what ails you is to not forget what you should already know. *In choosing between alternatives—the right hand is chosen. Oturupon Irete has spoken.*

14 + 0   Oturupon Opira

With Oturupon falling first and Opira falling next, we have found Oturupon Opira. Tough luck. *In choosing between alternatives—no hand is chosen. Oturupon Opira has spoken without uttering a word.*

FIFTEEN SHELLS

owo eedogun

Otura is about things that go wrong on account of spiritual weakness. It is about things that work out for the best, because they have come to a point of peace. Though everyone may not always feel exactly the same way about everything all the time, a truce assures that something constructive will get done.

Combinations of Otura
(*Manunla*)

15 + 1   *Otura Okanran*

With Otura falling first and Okanran falling next, we have found Otura Okanran—the peace of mind. This Odu says that a blessing will come to the head that comes to terms with its own reality. Be careful that in making your peace with yourself, you strike a fair compromise between what you need and what you are willing to give up, lest you wind up warring with yourself again. Avoid all-or-nothing propositions. The best cure for what ails you is to accept what you are and go from there. *In choosing between alternatives—the left hand is chosen. Otura Okanran has spoken.*

15 + 2   *Otura Oyeku*

With Otura falling first and Oyeku falling next, we have found Otura Oyeku—the peace of knowing. This Odu says that a blessing comes as a result of finding out something. Beware that in your search for knowledge you also search for truth, lest the facts curse you with their blind insensitivity. Avoid one-sided arguments. The best cure for what ails you is to keep what you learn in perspective. *In choosing between alternatives—the left hand is chosen. Otura Oyeku has spoken.*

15 + 3   *Otura Ogunda*

With Otura falling first and Ogunda falling next, we have found Otura Ogunda—the contented penis. This Odu foretells of a blessing that comes in the aftermath of sex. Beware that in your sublime mood you do not fall prey to yet another cigarette, lest you one day curse the consequence of your excesses. Avoid complacency, but also take time to languish. The best cure for what ails you is a little lethargy. *In choosing between alternatives—the left hand is chosen. Otura Ogunda has spoken.*

15 + 4   *Otura Irosun*

With Otura falling first and Irosun falling next, we have found Otura Irosun—the blood pact. This Odu tells of a blessing that comes as the result of passing safely through an ordeal of some sort. Beware that if blood is shed, none gets on you, lest unspeakable injustice curse you with the fate of becoming a medical fact. Avoid going all the way. The best cure for what ails you is to seal your vow with something other than blood, spit, or semen. *In choosing between alternatives—the left hand is chosen. Otura Irosun has spoken.*

15 + 5   *Otura Oshe*

With Otura falling first and Oshe falling next, we have found Otura Oshe—the peaceful waters. This Odu tells of a blessing that comes as a result of remaining relatively still, at least on the surface. But beware the placid exterior, lest you someday curse the fact that you did not suspect what evil lay hidden underneath. Avoid rising or falling too fast. The best cure for what ails you is to float on your back. *In choosing between alternatives—the left hand is chosen. Otura Oshe has spoken.*

15 + 6   *Otura Obara*

With Otura falling first and Obara falling next, we have found Otura Obara—the peaceful blue skies. This Odu foretells of a blessing that comes from calm resolve and clarity of thinking. Beware that in this moment of clear and unadulterated sanity, no curse enter your mind, lest the mood be broken. Avoid thinking of tomorrow or what needs to be done later. The best cure for what ails you is to cherish this moment right now. *In choosing between alternatives—the left hand is chosen. Otura Obara has spoken.*

15 + 7   *Otura Odi*

With Otura falling first and Odi falling next, we have found Otura Odi—the container of peace. This Odu speaks of a blessing that comes out of a truce of some kind, and unfolds in an orderly way. Be careful that you do not break your part of the bargain, lest you be cursed with a grievance yourself. Avoid trespassing where there are signs posted. The best cure for what ails you is to draw a line in the sand. *In choosing between alternatives—the left hand is chosen. Otura Odi has spoken.*

15 + 8   *Otura Ogbe*

With Otura falling first and Ogbe falling next, we have found Otura Ogbe—the prince of peace. This Odu ordains a blessing that results from the unity and harmony of all peoples. Beware that in your efforts to be fair and equal, you do not tip the scales too far left or right. Curses. Avoid believing that the ends justify the means. The best cure for what ails you is to open up your heart to others, so that others may open theirs to you. *In choosing between alternatives—the left hand is chosen. Otura Ogbe has spoken.*

15 + 9   *Otura Osa*

With Otura falling first and Osa falling next, we have found Otura Osa—the pendulous breasts. This Odu says that a blessing is coming as a result of hanging loose. Beware that when the tempo of the music picks up, you do not curse yourself with self-inflicted bruises. But otherwise, be free. Avoid the things that would constrict you. The best cure for what ails you is to fling off your restrictions. *In choosing between alternatives—the left hand is chosen. Otura Osa has spoken.*

15 + 10   *Otura Ofun*

With Otura falling first and Ofun falling next, we have found Otura Ofun—no rest for the wicked. This Odu predicts a blessing that comes at the end of a marathon session. Be aware that agony and ecstasy are intimately related. And beware, lest you curse the fact that when your runner's high wears off, your muscles are killing you. Avoid physical excesses, be they vice or virtue in the eyes of others. The best cure for what ails you is to soak in a hot tub and think things over. *In choosing between alternatives—the left hand is chosen. Otura Ofun has spoken.*

15 + 11   *Otura Owonrin*

With Otura falling first and Owonrin falling next, we have found Otura Owonrin—the peaceful acceptance. This Odu foretells a blessing that comes out of a quiet acknowledgment of the truth about something . . . perhaps even about yourself. Beware that in your efforts to come to grips with who and what you are, you do not curse yourself for being the way God made you. Avoid placing blame as much as feeling guilt. The best cure for what ails you is to come out into the light. *In choosing between alternatives—the left hand is chosen. Otura Owonrin has spoken.*

15 + 12   *Otura Iwori*

With Otura falling first and Iwori falling next, we have found Otura Iwori—the burnt offering. This Odu says that a blessing of this magnitude must come at some certain price. Be careful to give neither too little nor too much—for both gestures will meet only with curses in the end. Avoid misinterpretation. The best cure for what ails you is to play it on the safe side by going down the middle. *In choosing between alternatives—the left hand is chosen. Otura Iwori has spoken.*

15 + 13   Otura Ika

With Otura falling first and Ika falling next, we have found Otura Ika—the dreaded peace. This Odu predicts that a blessing is more likely to come from victory right now than from surrender. Be aware that if you wave the white flag, you are cursing yourself with the need to save face. Avoid an unfair settlement. The best cure for what ails you is to negotiate better than you fought. *In choosing between alternatives—the left hand is chosen. Otura Ika has spoken.*

15 + 14   Otura Oturupon

With Otura falling first and Oturupon falling next, we have found Otura Oturupon—the tenuous peace. This Odu says that a blessing will come from maintaining the balance of power. Beware that neither pro nor con gets weighted too heavily here, or else you will be cursed with the conflict that results. Avoid displays of might. The best cure for what ails you is to try to see both sides. *In choosing between alternatives—the left hand is chosen. Otura Oturupon has spoken.*

15 + 15   Otura Meji

With Otura falling first and Otura falling again, we have found Otura Meji (two Oturas)—the great peace. This Odu speaks of a blessing that comes at the hand of divine powers working in your life. Be careful that in your impatience you do not curse the gods for only doing their jobs. Avoid a direct confrontation. The best cure for what ails you is to let the will of God be known. *In choosing between alternatives—the right hand is chosen. Otura Meji has spoken.*

15 + 16   Otura Irete

With Otura falling first and Irete falling next, we have found Otura Irete—the broken peace. This Odu says that a blessing is coming from the falling apart of something that was good while it lasted. Be careful that in asserting yourself you represent the interests of your people. Do not later curse the fact that you have brought calamity upon yourself instead of justice. Avoid arrogance. The best cure for what ails you is to think carefully before you make the first move. *In choosing between alternatives—the right hand is chosen. Otura Irete has spoken.*

15 + 0   *Otura Opira*

With Otura falling first and Opira falling next, we have found Otura Opira. There is no answer, but I can't say why. *In choosing between alternatives—neither hand is chosen. Otura Opira has spoken not a word.*

SIXTEEN SHELLS

owo eerin din logun

Irete is about things that go wrong because they just fall apart. It is about things that go right as a result of picking up the pieces. Though freedom may, in fact, just be another word, it is also a state of mind. Take care, lest you prove to work against yourself sometimes.

Combinations of Irete
(Mediloggun)

16 + 1   *Irete Okanran*

With Irete falling first and Okanran falling next, we have found Irete Okanran—the downcast spirit. This Odu speaks of a blessing that comes from the depths of despair. Be careful that once you have ranted, raved, and cursed, you do not remain despondent. Avoid taking it all so personally. The best cure for what ails you is to get out and move among the people. *In choosing between alternatives—the left hand is chosen. Irete Okanran has spoken.*

16 + 2   *Irete Oyeku*

With Irete falling first and Oyeku falling next, we have found Irete Oyeku—the aborted effort. This Odu predicts a blessing that yet will come from a half-baked idea. Be careful about mourning the loss of something you never had, lest you curse yourself with idle thoughts of what might have been. Avoid crying over spilt milk. The best cure for what ails you is to get on with your next project. *In choosing between alternatives—the left hand is chosen. Irete Oyeku has spoken.*

16 + 3   *Irete Ogunda*

With Irete falling first and Ogunda falling next, we have found Irete Ogunda—the shriveled-up penis. This Odu says that a man is more than his manhood—a blessing comes from somewhere other than his loins. But beware that in attempting to rise above your carnal knowledge, you do not sacrifice the thing that made you tick. Avoid too much celibacy. The best cure for what ails you is to use it or lose it. *In choosing between alternatives—the left hand is chosen. Irete Ogunda has spoken.*

16 + 4   *Irete Irosun*

With Irete falling first and Irosun falling next, we have found Irete Irosun—the red scourge. This Odu portends a blessing that comes from a source of pandemic proportions. Beware that in trying to forestall the inevitable changes that are coming, you do not curse yourself to live through them all. Avoid resisting the winds of change. The best cure for what ails you is to jump on the bandwagon. *In choosing between alternatives—the left hand is chosen. Irete Irosun has spoken.*

16 + 5   *Irete Oshe*

With Irete falling first and Oshe falling next, we have found Irete Oshe—the receding waters. This Odu says that a blessing comes at the end of the season, when things are turning back upon themselves. Beware that in saying farewell to another summer, you do not lament too much that it might have lasted longer, lest you curse the sweetness of the good time you had. Avoid regrets and bitter tears. The best cure for what ails you is to clutch these things to your breast and hold them there. *In choosing between alternatives—the left hand is chosen. Irete Oshe has spoken.*

16 + 6   Irete Obara

With Irete falling first and Obara falling next, we have found Irete Obara—the passing rainbow. This Odu says that the blessing of a climax is coming. There is no time for taking notes here. And don't even try to speak, lest the thing you utter is a curse you did not mean. Avoid letting your thoughts wander. The best cure for what ails you is to simply take it all in, but quick—before it passes. *In choosing between alternatives—the left hand is chosen. Irete Obara has spoken.*

16 + 7   Irete Odi

With Irete falling first and Odi falling next, we have found Irete Odi—the container of sorrows. This Odu predicts a blessing that comes—in the end—out of grief. Beware that you do not reach too deep into the pot of anguish, lest your own heart be cursed to wallow there. Beware that you do not put a lid on the feelings you have inside, lest one day your feelings explode. Avoid denial. The best cure for what ails you is a good, hard cry. *In choosing between alternatives— the left hand is chosen. Irete Odi has spoken.*

16 + 8   Irete Ogbe

With Irete falling first and Ogbe falling next, we have found Irete Ogbe—the purification. This Odu portends a blessing that comes as the result of a personal ritual. Be careful that by force of habit, you do not curse yourself by simply going through the motions. No good can come of it. Avoid trying to impress others with devotion. The best cure for what ails you is to anoint yourself with oil. *In choosing between alternatives—the left hand is chosen. Irete Ogbe has spoken.*

16 + 9   *Irete Osa*

With Irete falling first and Osa falling next, we have found Irete Osa—the sagging breasts. This Odu says that a blessing comes from seeing many ages and witnessing many changes. Beware that you do not curse the fact that you have lived long enough to see these natural events. Avoid wearing black to a birthday party. The best cure for what ails you is to see it all in context. Everything is relative. *In choosing between alternatives—the left hand is chosen. Irete Osa has spoken.*

16 + 10   *Irete Ofun*

With Irete falling first and Ofun falling next, we have found Irete Ofun—the moral collapse. This Odu speaks of a blessing that comes out of the revelation that foul and disgusting things have been going on. Beware that in your efforts to get out from under, you do not extend this curse with further lies. Though you might avoid punishment by getting a good lawyer, the best cure for what ails you is to get things off your chest. *In choosing between alternatives—the left hand is chosen. Irete Ofun has spoken.*

16 + 11   *Irete Owonrin*

With Irete falling first and Owonrin falling next, we have found Irete Owonrin—the falling out of love. This Odu says that a new blessing is coming to take the place of the old. Beware that you do not go too eagerly on the rebound, lest you curse yourself with the first warm puppy that comes along. Avoid acts of quiet desperation. The best cure for what ails you is to let time heal these wounds. *In choosing between alternatives—the left hand is chosen. Irete Owonrin has spoken.*

16 + 12   *Irete Iwori*

With Irete falling first and Iwori falling next, we have found Irete Iwori—the burnt-out flame. This Odu predicts a blessing that comes from putting out a fire. Beware that in your efforts to stamp out the flames, you do not curse yourself with singes. In fact, avoid playing with fire in the first place. The best cure for what ails you is to learn something from your hurts and pains. *In choosing between alternatives—the left hand is chosen. Irete Iwori has spoken.*

16 + 13   Irete Ika

With Irete falling first and Ika falling next, we have found Irete Ika—the lost magic. This Odu predicts a blessing that is accompanied by smoke and mirrors. These things are not what they seem, but soon will be revealed for what they are. Beware that you do not see the clever line for the curse it is. Avoid scams. The best cure for what ails you is to just say no this time. *In choosing between alternatives—the left hand is chosen. Irete Ika has spoken.*

16 + 14   Irete Oturupon

With Irete falling first and Oturupon falling next, we have found Irete Oturupon—the estranged friends. This Odu predicts a blessing that comes out of a temporary separation. Take care that you do not gradually grow apart, lest you later curse the error of your separate ways. Avoid a petty hostility that only makes things as bad as they could be. The best cure for what ails you is to come to your decision of your own free will. *In choosing between alternatives—the left hand is chosen. Irete Oturupon has spoken.*

16 + 15   Irete Otura

With Irete falling first and Otura falling next, we have found Irete Otura—the peaceful passing. This Odu speaks of a blessing that comes to you in your sleep. Take care that you dwell upon your dreams until you figure them out, lest you be cursed with a recurring idle thought. Avoid taking nightmares as bad signs. The best cure for what ails you may prove yet to be the opposite of what you believe. *In choosing between alternatives—the left hand is chosen. Irete Otura has spoken.*

16 + 16   Irete Meji

With Irete falling first and Irete falling again, we have found Irete Meji (two Iretes)—the utter destruction. This Odu ordains a blessing that only comes when all is said and done, over and gone. Beware that the past you are creating does not add up to something that you would look back and curse upon. Avoid. Avoid. The best cure for what ails you is to start your life anew right now. *In choosing between alternatives—the right hand is chosen. Irete Meji has spoken.*

16 + 0   *Irete Opira*

With Irete falling first and Opira falling next, we have found Irete Opira. It might be best to say a little prayer. *In choosing between alternatives—no hand is chosen. Irete Opira has spoken silently.*

NO SHELLS

Opira is about things that go wrong for no apparent reason. It is about things that go right again for no discernible cause. It would be best to wash your shells now and move on to the next question, for there is no answer known for the one you just asked.

Combinations of Opira

0 + 1   *Opira Okanran*

With Opira falling first and Okanran falling next, we have found Opira Okanran. *In choosing between alternatives—neither hand is chosen.*

0 + 2   *Opira Oyeku*

With Opira falling first and Oyeku falling next, we have found Opira Oyeku. *In choosing between alternatives—neither hand is chosen.*

0 + 3   Opira Ogunda

With Opira falling first and Ogunda falling next, we have found Opira Ogunda. *In choosing between alternatives—neither hand is chosen.*

0 + 4   Opira Irosun

With Opira falling first and Irosun falling next, we have found Opira Irosun. *In choosing between alternatives—neither hand is chosen.*

0 + 5   Opira Oshe

With Opira falling first and Oshe falling next, we have found Opira Oshe. *In choosing between alternatives—neither hand is chosen.*

0 + 6   Opira Obara

With Opira falling first and Obara falling next, we have found Opira Obara. *In choosing between alternatives—neither hand is chosen.*

0 + 7   Opira Odi

With Opira falling first and Odi falling next, we have found Opira Odi. *In choosing between alternatives—neither hand is chosen.*

0 + 8   Opira Ogbe

With Opira falling first and Ogbe falling next, we have found Opira Ogbe. *In choosing between alternatives—neither hand is chosen.*

0 + 9   Opira Osa

With Opira falling first and Osa falling next, we have found Opira Osa. *In choosing between alternatives—neither hand is chosen.*

0 + 10   Opira Ofun

With Opira falling first and Ofun falling next, we have found Opira Ofun. *In choosing between alternatives—neither hand is chosen.*

0 + 11   *Opira Owonrin*

With Opira falling first and Owonrin falling next, we have found Opira Owonrin. *In choosing between alternatives—neither hand is chosen.*

0 + 12   *Opira Iwori*

With Opira falling first and Iwori falling next, we have found Opira Iwori. *In choosing between alternatives—neither hand is chosen.*

0 + 13   *Opira Ika*

With Opira falling first and Ika falling next, we have found Opira Ika. *In choosing between alternatives—neither hand is chosen.*

0 + 14   *Opira Oturupon*

With Opira falling first and Oturupon falling next, we have found Opira Oturupon. *In choosing between alternatives—neither hand is chosen.*

0 + 15   *Opira Otura*

With Opira falling first and Otura falling next, we have found Opira Otura. *In choosing between alternatives—neither hand is chosen.*

0 + 16   *Opira Irete*

With Opira falling first and Irete falling next, we have found Opira Irete. *In choosing between alternatives—neither hand is chosen.*

0 + 0   *Opira Meji*

With Opira falling first and Opira falling again, we have found Opira Meji (two Opiras). *In choosing between alternatives—neither hand is chosen.*

Appendix A

WHICH HAND WAS SELECTED?

African Oracles in 10 Minutes presents three different methods for asking any yes/no question you want to bring to the seashell oracle (*erindinlogun*). These techniques can also be applied to helping you make any choice between two possible options, choices, or outcomes. This Appendix reviews the methods, provides a place to check your answers, and (for those who are dying to know) discusses the mathematical workings of this oracle.

All of the methods presented here are based on casting your 16 shells (beads or coins) once <u>or</u> twice. Each time the shells are cast, a number of them will land mouth side up. By counting the number of mouths, you derive a figure. In some of the methods, this number alone will determine the sign the oracle has given. Or it may mean that you have to cast your shells again to produce a second figure, which then will reveal whether your left or right "hand" has been chosen. (I'll tell you how to interpret which hand has been chosen in a minute. But first let's consider what a choice between the left or right hand proves. . . .)

Prior to casting the shells—of course—an object of your choice has been placed to your left or right side (or if reading the shells for another, the client has placed an object in his or her left and right hands). The objects that the book recommends using are a white shell and a black stone. For a yes/no question, let's say you designate the white shell as meaning YES and the black stone as meaning NO.

After you have used your 16 shells to cast one <u>or</u> two figures, the oracle will either have not made a choice (meaning there is no answer to this question) or it will have selected the left or right hand—let's say it's the left. The object that you have placed to the left, then,

196

is your answer. Or at this point the person you are reading the shells for reveals the object in his or her left hand. If it's the white shell, then YES. If it's the black stone, then NO.

It's quite a marvelous trick, really—and unlike anything else I have encountered in studying other divination systems. Try it. I think you'll like the feel of it.

Once you have mastered yes/no questions, you can also use any of these three methods to choose among specific alternatives. Just designate your white shell as one of the choices open to you right now; and designate your black shell as an opposing or alternate choice. Then cast your shells once or twice as before.

To figure out whether your shells have pointed to the left or to the right, you can use the tables provided here to compute the results for yourself, or you can just look up your figures in the tables that immediately follow. Enjoy.

METHOD I

According to observers, this is the method that is most frequently used in Africa to answer yes/no questions and choose among specific alternatives. To find your answer, just look up your first figure in the left-hand chart. Then, if based on that look-up, you need to cast again, do so. Look up your second figure in the chart on the right. (See Reading #4 if you want to know more.)

First Cast:			Second Cast:		
Major (+)	Major (-)	Minor	Major (+)	Major (-)	Minor
1	13	5	1	13	5
2	14	6	2	14	6
3	15	7	3	15	7
4	16	9	4	16	9
8	0	11	8	0	11
10			10		
12			12		
Right Hand	No Comment	Throw Again	Left Hand	No Comment	Right Hand

BUT CAUTION!! Though highly authentic, this method tends to either choose the right hand or no hand at all. If you ask the oracle 100 questions, the odds are that the oracle will select the right hand 50 times—the same odds as flipping a coin. In 38 cases the oracle will simply not choose a hand at all. And only in the remaining 12 will the left hand be chosen.

This system's built-in bias against the left hand may be due to an Arab influence, for in the Arab world, the left hand is regarded as being unclean. This method seems to be implying, "It is better to choose no hand at all than to choose the left one." And so, the oracle will either choose the right hand, or it will choose neither hand.

This bias might seem (at first blush) to give the diviner plenty of room to influence the results. By placing the object that represents the less-desired outcome to the left, the diviner could almost assure that it will <u>not</u> be chosen. In practice, however, her power to influence the outcome in this way is negated by the fact that the person she is reading the shells for—and not she herself—is the one who places the objects to the left or right. As long as this person does not know that the system is biased against the left hand, no premeditated manipulation of the results should occur.

When reading for yourself, however, **I recommend you use Method II or III instead.** This will keep you from being tempted to avoid placing disfavored choices to the left—where they are unlikely to be chosen.

METHOD II

This is a method you might want to use after taking Method I for a test drive. Though the second method has the same "look and feel" as the first, it will produce more even-handed results. Here's all you have to do to check it out: After you have placed your objects to the left or right . . . after you have asked your question . . . and after you have cast your 16 shells once, look up the number of shells that has fallen mouth side up in the left-hand table below. . . .

First Cast:			Second Cast:		
Major (+)	Major (-)	Minor	Major (+)	Major (-)	Minor
1	13	5	1	13	5
2	14	6	2	14	6
3	15	7	3	15	7
4	16	9	4	16	9
8	0	11	8	0	11
10			10		
12			12		
Right Hand	Left[1] Hand	Throw Again	Left Hand	No Comment	Right Hand

If the table tells you to throw again, do so now. Count up the number of shells that have fallen mouth up and look up your number in the table to the right. This table will reveal your answer.

Or you can just ask your question, cast your shells twice, and look up your two figures in the table at the end of this appendix.

This new method reduces the left-hand bias of the original system, while retaining a lot of the original charm. If you ask 100 questions using Method II, the odds are that the oracle will select the right hand 50 times. It will select the left hand 41 times. And it will choose neither hand just 9 times.

METHOD III

Finally, Method III eliminates the bias against the left hand entirely. After you have placed your objects to the left and right and after you have asked your question, just automatically cast your shells twice, and look up each resulting figure (the number of shells mouth up) in the following chart. In general, if your second number appears to the

---

[1] By changing this answer to "LEFT HAND," the oracle will more evenly choose between both the left hand and the right hand—as can be observed by scanning the lists in this Appendix.

left of the first, choose the left hand. If it is to the right, choose the right hand.[2]

$$\longleftarrow \text{ Left } / \text{ Right } \longrightarrow$$

8, 10, 4, 3, 2, 1, 12, 11, 9, 7, 6, 5, 13, 14, 15, 16	
8+8, 10+10, 4+4, 3+3	9+9, 7+7, 6+6, 5+5
2+2, 1+1, 12+12	13+13, 14+14
11+11	15+15, 16+16

If a 0 occurs on either the first or second casting of the shells—neither hand is chosen.

Some additional rules: If you cast two of the same figure, the left hand is automatically chosen when the numbers involved are: 1+1, 2+2, 3+3, 4+4, 8+8, 10+10, 12+12, or 11+11. The right hand is automatically chosen if the combination is: 5+5, 6+6, 7+7, 9+9, 13+13, 14+14, 15+15, or 16+16.

If you ask 100 questions using Method III, the odds are that the right hand will be chosen 43 times, and the left hand will be chosen 43 times. In other words, no preference is being shown toward either the right or the left hand. But just as in the original method, you will sometimes receive no answer at all.

For any of the 3 methods . . .

The results you will receive using any of these three methods can be checked against the tables that follow.

Additional Hint: Whenever you cast two figures, you also have the option of looking them up in the Master Answer section (just preceding this Appendix). The Master Answer section will tell you what else the oracle wants to say to you tonight. (But please note: The left-hand and right-hand choices the text in the Master Answer section talks about were computed using Method III. If you are using Method I or II, your answer may actually be different from what the Master Answer section says it is—go by the tables here instead. The Master Answer section will still speak to you correctly in other ways.)

---

[2] This method makes use of the "secret" ranking system used in Africa for these figures.

Appendix A

Combo	Method I[3]	Method II[4]	Method III
1 + 1	Right	Right	Left
1 + 2	Right	Right	Left
1 + 3	Right	Right	Left
1 + 4	Right	Right	Left
1 + 5	Right	Right	Right
1 + 6	Right	Right	Right
1 + 7	Right	Right	Right
1 + 8	Right	Right	Left
1 + 9	Right	Right	Right
1 + 10	Right	Right	Left
1 + 11	Right	Right	Right
1 + 12	Right	Right	Right
1 + 13	Right	Right	Right
1 + 14	Right	Right	Right
1 + 15	Right	Right	Right
1 + 16	Right	Right	Right
1 + 0	Right	Right	Neither
2 + 1	Right	Right	Right
2 + 2	Right	Right	Left

[3] **Why have I listed all these answers?** If on the first cast of your shells you get a 1, 2, 3, 4, 8, 10, 12, 13, 14, 15, 16, or 0, you can ignore the number after the "+" sign. I've listed all the combinations ("1+1," "1+2," "1+3," etc.) so that you can see how the statistics are computed for each method. If you're not interested in the mathematical reasoning behind this, you can quit reading the footnote now and get back to work. If you want to know more, here's why I have listed each combination: Since the method allows for two casts of the shells (whenever you cast a 5, 6, 7, 9 or 11 on the first throw), theoretically speaking, two casts are always involved, even though in some cases you stop after making the first one. The practical reason that you don't go on to make the second cast (in the case of throwing a 1, 2, 3, 4, 8, 10, 12, 13, 14, 15, 16, or 0) is that—as you can see from the chart—it will not change the answer you have already received. In other words, even when you stop after the first throw, what you are really doing is casting twice. All you save by not making the second cast is your time. Statistically speaking, every one of the 289 combinations listed here is a possible answer whenever you use this method to ask a question. (There, I hope that clears everything up!)

[4] Ditto (see footnote 3).

Combo	Method I	Method II	Method III
2 + 3	Right	Right	Left
2 + 4	Right	Right	Left
2 + 5	Right	Right	Right
2 + 6	Right	Right	Right
2 + 7	Right	Right	Right
2 + 8	Right	Right	Left
2 + 9	Right	Right	Right
2 + 10	Right	Right	Left
2 + 11	Right	Right	Right
2 + 12	Right	Right	Right
2 + 13	Right	Right	Right
2 + 14	Right	Right	Right
2 + 15	Right	Right	Right
2 + 16	Right	Right	Right
2 + 0	Right	Right	Neither
3 + 1	Right	Right	Right
3 + 2	Right	Right	Right
3 + 3	Right	Right	Left
3 + 4	Right	Right	Left
3 + 5	Right	Right	Right
3 + 6	Right	Right	Right
3 + 7	Right	Right	Right
3 + 8	Right	Right	Left
3 + 9	Right	Right	Right
3 + 10	Right	Right	Left
3 + 11	Right	Right	Right
3 + 12	Right	Right	Right
3 + 13	Right	Right	Right
3 + 14	Right	Right	Right
3 + 15	Right	Right	Right
3 + 16	Right	Right	Right
3 + 0	Right	Right	Neither
4 + 1	Right	Right	Right
4 + 2	Right	Right	Right
4 + 3	Right	Right	Right

Combo	Method I	Method II	Method III
4 + 4	Right	Right	Left
4 + 5	Right	Right	Right
4 + 6	Right	Right	Right
4 + 7	Right	Right	Right
4 + 8	Right	Right	Left
4 + 9	Right	Right	Right
4 + 10	Right	Right	Left
4 + 11	Right	Right	Right
4 + 12	Right	Right	Right
4 + 13	Right	Right	Right
4 + 14	Right	Right	Right
4 + 15	Right	Right	Right
4 + 16	Right	Right	Right
4 + 0	Right	Right	Neither
5 + 1	Left	Left	Left
5 + 2	Left	Left	Left
5 + 3	Left	Left	Left
5 + 4	Left	Left	Left
5 + 5	Right	Right	Right
5 + 6	Right	Right	Left
5 + 7	Right	Right	Left
5 + 8	Left	Left	Left
5 + 9	Right	Right	Left
5 + 10	Left	Left	Left
5 + 11	Right	Right	Left
5 + 12	Left	Left	Left
5 + 13	No Comment	No Comment	Right
5 + 14	No Comment	No Comment	Right
5 + 15	No Comment	No Comment	Right
5 + 16	No Comment	No Comment	Right
5 + 0	No Comment	No Comment	Neither
6 + 1	Left	Left	Left
6 + 2	Left	Left	Left
6 + 3	Left	Left	Left
6 + 4	Left	Left	Left

Combo	Method I	Method II	Method III
6 + 5	Right	Right	Right
6 + 6	Right	Right	Right
6 + 7	Right	Right	Left
6 + 8	Left	Left	Left
6 + 9	Right	Right	Left
6 + 10	Left	Left	Left
6 + 11	Right	Right	Left
6 + 12	Left	Left	Left
6 + 13	No Comment	No Comment	Right
6 + 14	No Comment	No Comment	Right
6 + 15	No Comment	No Comment	Right
6 + 16	No Comment	No Comment	Right
6 + 0	No Comment	No Comment	Neither
7 + 1	Left	Left	Left
7 + 2	Left	Left	Left
7 + 3	Left	Left	Left
7 + 4	Left	Left	Left
7 + 5	Right	Right	Right
7 + 6	Right	Right	Right
7 + 7	Right	Right	Right
7 + 8	Left	Left	Left
7 + 9	Right	Right	Left
7 + 10	Left	Left	Left
7 + 11	Right	Right	Left
7 + 12	Left	Left	Left
7 + 13	No Comment	No Comment	Right
7 + 14	No Comment	No Comment	Right
7 + 15	No Comment	No Comment	Right
7 + 16	No Comment	No Comment	Right
7 + 0	No Comment	No Comment	Neither
8 + 1	Right	Right	Right
8 + 2	Right	Right	Right
8 + 3	Right	Right	Right
8 + 4	Right	Right	Right
8 + 5	Right	Right	Right

Combo	Method I	Method II	Method III
8 + 6	Right	Right	Right
8 + 7	Right	Right	Right
8 + 8	Right	Right	Left
8 + 9	Right	Right	Right
8 + 10	Right	Right	Right
8 + 11	Right	Right	Right
8 + 12	Right	Right	Right
8 + 13	Right	Right	Right
8 + 14	Right	Right	Right
8 + 15	Right	Right	Right
8 + 16	Right	Right	Right
8 + 0	Right	Right	Neither
9 + 1	Left	Left	Left
9 + 2	Left	Left	Left
9 + 3	Left	Left	Left
9 + 4	Left	Left	Left
9 + 5	Right	Right	Right
9 + 6	Right	Right	Right
9 + 7	Right	Right	Right
9 + 8	Left	Left	Left
9 + 9	Right	Right	Right
9 + 10	Left	Left	Left
9 + 11	Right	Right	Left
9 + 12	Left	Left	Left
9 + 13	No Comment	No Comment	Right
9 + 14	No Comment	No Comment	Right
9 + 15	No Comment	No Comment	Right
9 + 16	No Comment	No Comment	Right
9 + 0	No Comment	No Comment	Neither
10 + 1	Right	Right	Right
10 + 2	Right	Right	Right
10 + 3	Right	Right	Right
10 + 4	Right	Right	Right
10 + 5	Right	Right	Right
10 + 6	Right	Right	Right

Combo	Method I	Method II	Method III
10 + 7	Right	Right	Right
10 + 8	Right	Right	Left
10 + 9	Right	Right	Right
10 + 10	Right	Right	Left
10 + 11	Right	Right	Right
10 + 12	Right	Right	Right
10 + 13	Right	Right	Right
10 + 14	Right	Right	Right
10 + 15	Right	Right	Right
10 + 16	Right	Right	Right
10 + 0	Right	Right	Neither
11 + 1	Left	Left	Left
11 + 2	Left	Left	Left
11 + 3	Left	Left	Left
11 + 4	Left	Left	Left
11 + 5	Right	Right	Right
11 + 6	Right	Right	Right
11 + 7	Right	Right	Right
11 + 8	Left	Left	Left
11 + 9	Right	Right	Right
11 + 10	Left	Left	Left
11 + 11	Right	Right	Left
11 + 12	Left	Left	Left
11 + 13	No Comment	No Comment	Right
11 + 14	No Comment	No Comment	Right
11 + 15	No Comment	No Comment	Right
11 + 16	No Comment	No Comment	Right
11 + 0	No Comment	No Comment	Neither
12 + 1	Right	Right	Left
12 + 2	Right	Right	Left
12 + 3	Right	Right	Left
12 + 4	Right	Right	Left
12 + 5	Right	Right	Right
12 + 6	Right	Right	Right
12 + 7	Right	Right	Right

Combo	Method I	Method II	Method III
12 + 8	Right	Right	Left
12 + 9	Right	Right	Right
12 + 10	Right	Right	Left
12 + 11	Right	Right	Right
12 + 12	Right	Right	Left
12 + 13	Right	Right	Right
12 + 14	Right	Right	Right
12 + 15	Right	Right	Right
12 + 16	Right	Right	Right
12 + 0	Right	Right	Neither
13 + 1	No Comment	Left	Left
13 + 2	No Comment	Left	Left
13 + 3	No Comment	Left	Left
13 + 4	No Comment	Left	Left
13 + 5	No Comment	Left	Left
13 + 6	No Comment	Left	Left
13 + 7	No Comment	Left	Left
13 + 8	No Comment	Left	Left
13 + 9	No Comment	Left	Left
13 + 10	No Comment	Left	Left
13 + 11	No Comment	Left	Left
13 + 12	No Comment	Left	Left
13 + 13	No Comment	Left	Right
13 + 14	No Comment	Left	Right
13 + 15	No Comment	Left	Right
13 + 16	No Comment	Left	Right
13 + 0	No Comment	Left	Neither
14 + 1	No Comment	Left	Left
14 + 2	No Comment	Left	Left
14 + 3	No Comment	Left	Left
14 + 4	No Comment	Left	Left
14 + 5	No Comment	Left	Left
14 + 6	No Comment	Left	Left
14 + 7	No Comment	Left	Left
14 + 8	No Comment	Left	Left

Combo	Method I	Method II	Method III
14 + 9	No Comment	Left	Left
14 + 10	No Comment	Left	Left
14 + 11	No Comment	Left	Left
14 + 12	No Comment	Left	Left
14 + 13	No Comment	Left	Left
14 + 14	No Comment	Left	Right
14 + 15	No Comment	Left	Right
14 + 16	No Comment	Left	Right
14 + 0	No Comment	Left	Neither
15 + 1	No Comment	Left	Left
15 + 2	No Comment	Left	Left
15 + 3	No Comment	Left	Left
15 + 4	No Comment	Left	Left
15 + 5	No Comment	Left	Left
15 + 6	No Comment	Left	Left
15 + 7	No Comment	Left	Left
15 + 8	No Comment	Left	Left
15 + 9	No Comment	Left	Left
15 + 10	No Comment	Left	Left
15 + 11	No Comment	Left	Left
15 + 12	No Comment	Left	Left
15 + 13	No Comment	Left	Left
15 + 14	No Comment	Left	Left
15 + 15	No Comment	Left	Right
15 + 16	No Comment	Left	Right
15 + 0	No Comment	Left	Neither
16 + 1	No Comment	Left	Left
16 + 2	No Comment	Left	Left
16 + 3	No Comment	Left	Left
16 + 4	No Comment	Left	Left
16 + 5	No Comment	Left	Left
16 + 6	No Comment	Left	Left
16 + 7	No Comment	Left	Left
16 + 8	No Comment	Left	Left
16 + 9	No Comment	Left	Left

Combo	Method I	Method II	Method III
16 + 10	No Comment	Left	Left
16 + 11	No Comment	Left	Left
16 + 12	No Comment	Left	Left
16 + 13	No Comment	Left	Left
16 + 14	No Comment	Left	Left
16 + 15	No Comment	Left	Left
16 + 16	No Comment	Left	Right
16 + 0	No Comment	Left	Neither
0 + 1	No Comment	Left	Neither
0 + 2	No Comment	Left	Neither
0 + 3	No Comment	Left	Neither
0 + 4	No Comment	Left	Neither
0 + 5	No Comment	Left	Neither
0 + 6	No Comment	Left	Neither
0 + 7	No Comment	Left	Neither
0 + 8	No Comment	Left	Neither
0 + 9	No Comment	Left	Neither
0 + 10	No Comment	Left	Neither
0 + 11	No Comment	Left	Neither
0 + 12	No Comment	Left	Neither
0 + 13	No Comment	Left	Neither
0 + 14	No Comment	Left	Neither
0 + 15	No Comment	Left	Neither
0 + 16	No Comment	Left	Neither
0 + 0	No Comment	Left	Neither

STATISTICAL SUMMARY

Allowing for Opira, there are 289 possible combinations in the seashell divination method. So, using any of these three methods, there are 289 possible "answers" that could result. (Even in cases where you stop after the first casting of the shells, there are 289 possible answers lurking in the background.) The preceding charts list each of the possible answers you might receive using any of the three methods. If you wanted to count up each answer in each column, you would quickly know how many chances each method gives you to select the right hand, the left hand, or neither hand. Thankfully, my computer has done the work for you. . . .

	Method I		Method II		Method III	
Left	35	12%	120	41%	128	44.3%
Right	144	50%	144	50%	128	44.3%
No Comment	110	38%	25	9%	33	11.4%

What the table means is that using Method I, every time you ask a question, the odds are: You have a 12% chance of having the oracle choose the left hand. You have a 50% chance of having the oracle choose the right hand. And you have a 38% chance of having the oracle choose neither hand.

Looking at the table above, you can see that Method III is the most "fair." Using this method, you have an equal chance of having the oracle select the left or the right hand. But the oracle still has the chance to answer "NO COMMENT" if it is so inclined.

I should point out, of course, that these are only the odds. The odds themselves are computed based on an assumption that all of the 16 shells you are casting are perfectly (and I mean perfectly) matched. Since every set of shells—being a creation of nature—is unique, your own set is going to perform in its own idiosyncratic way. In other words, your own set of shells will probably have some kind of "statistical bias." Some of your shells (due to their shape and weight) may be more inclined to fall mouth side up than others. Some may prefer to land mouth down. But these individual anomalies are just part of the charm of this method. Your shells are your shells. Choose a set that serves you well by answering you right—no matter what its own odds are.

In practice, there is also a chance that your results will vary considerably from the "norms" listed above. This is particularly true if you do not consult the oracle often or if you do not ask very many questions in a single session. (You could, for example, use Method I, ask 10 questions, and have the shells consistently point to the left hand, even though it is unlikely.) It is only after looking at the results you receive from many castings that the statistics will tend to reveal themselves. I say, you be the judge. Choose the method that feels right to you and that works consistently for you over time.

The odds also assume that nothing else is involved in the oracle's work. Though the Yoruba inventors of these systems are very skilled in math, they might well scoff at this rather scientific analysis. Could it be that—in addition to being good with numbers—those who invented this system knew something about forces greater than statistics? Well . . . I'll let you be the judge of that.

PART II

The Melon Seed Road (The Male Path)

Deathly-Regains-His-Strength
on his way to consult the father of secrets . . .
Passing through the great forest
he heard the gong-gonger,
strolling back, strolling forth—
no mistaking that voice . . .
So he turned off onto Melon-seed road,
and there he found the divining board.

—NIGERIAN DIVINER AWOTUNDE AWORINDE
RECITATION ON THE FIGURE OBARA MEJI
JUDITH GLEASON TRANSLATION, 1973

THE READINGS

Reading #11

WHERE DO I STAND?
(What's My Lucky Name?)

Welcome to the Melon Seed Road, the way of the male diviner. . . .
Here we do things little by little, bit by bit, and each hoeing his
own row. In this Reading, you will start at the very beginning of
your initiation into the male secrets by getting your African name
and learning the purpose of your mission here.

TOOLS

In West Africa, it is the men who—by tradition—go to the farm . . .
or to the hunt . . . or off to war. It is the men who put their hands to
work in everything they do . . . including divination. Therefore, if
you want to fortune-tell like a man, you must first learn how to use
your hands like one.

Interestingly enough, some of the rudimentary skills you will need
can only be learned from your African "mother." This Reading
makes use of the skills you might have picked up from your mother as
you watched her count out money in the market or cast her shells to
divine the future. Her deft hands would have taught you how to cast
objects and "count" them quickly.

These same skills are also used in many of the leisure games that
are played by African men. For the Extra Credit section of this Reading, we'll be borrowing a popular dice game from the Igbo people who
live just to the northwest of the Yoruba in Nigeria. It uses either
cowry shells or coins. If cowries are used, the game is called *Igbo-ita*.
If coins are used, it's called *Igbo-ego*.

BACKGROUND

The method of African fortune-telling you will be learning in this part of the book is called Ifa. At its most basic level, it requires good hand-eye coordination. So that's what we're going to be working on in the first few Readings. For starters, we're just going to loosen up our wrist by first consulting the female version of this oracle and then—if you have your wallet with you—playing a friendly round of "African dice."

The dice game itself was adopted and adapted by the men from the method of fortune-telling practiced by women—and demonstrated in Part I of this book. Ironically enough, though women consult the Powers that Be with their cowry shells, men are just as inclined to gamble with them!

According to firsthand accounts, the game involves placing a wager. Then shells or coins are cast, and the number of heads are counted up. Based on the fall of the coins, winnings are either collected or opponents' wagers are paid off. In practice, the game is said to take place so rapidly that a cloud of dust is likely to encircle the gamblers.

I'll show you how to actually play the dice game in the Extra Credit section of this Reading. (And if you want to go on for the Extra Extra Credit, I'll even show you how to pick lottery numbers.) But first let's cast the coins in the traditional fortune-telling way of the women to see if we can get a quick Reading of how you can expect your luck (at dice, love, or whatnot) to go today . . . or, better still, what you can expect to get out of working your way through this book.

HOW TO

If you have already completed Part I of this book, just use the 16 shells you made in Reading #2. Otherwise just use 16 pennies, nickels, dimes, or quarters from your pockets.

 Gather up your 16 shells or coins and cup them in your hands, just like you'd cup a pair of dice.

 Say a silent prayer.

216

Blow on them for good luck, and . . .

 Ask your question. For starters, let's see if we can get an indication of what kind of luck you'll have today. And while we're at it, and as the first step in your initiation, we'll also get you a "lucky" name to go by here. . . .

As you cup your shells or coins, just ask: **Where do I stand today?** with regard to _____? (work, love, money, dice—you fill in the blank.) How do I sit? What's my relative position? to others? my brothers? my family? my group? Or simply, **What's my African name?** What name should I go by here? What name will bring me luck?

 Toss your shells or coins on the floor, and count up how many have landed mouth side up, if actually using shells 🐚 , or heads up if using coins Ⓐ . (Your answer will be a number between one and 16, with zero also a possibility.)

Scratch Pad

Jot down your numbers here.

 Consult the following Answer section.

THE ANSWERS

Using the combination you have just thrown, find your figure in this list—but first a small explanation.

If you completed Reading #0 (The Starting Point) before turning down this road, don't be confused by the answers here. The system you learned in Reading #0 for counting heads as one dot (tails as two dots) is the male way that you will be using in this part of the book. But in this Reading, we're using the female way, which simply counts up the number of heads that have fallen. Based on this number alone, an Odu figure is created. For those who are coming along from Part I of the book, this table will illustrate how the two systems mesh. You can continue to use your 16 shells for every Reading in the book. Just use this table to translate your shells into the Odu figures used by men.

Your combination . . .		*Your figure . . .*
1 Shell	1 Head	Okanran
2 Shells	2 Heads	Oyeku
3 Shells	3 Heads	Ogunda
4 Shells	4 Heads	Irosun
5 Shells	5 Heads	Oshe
6 Shells	6 Heads	Obara
7 Shells	7 Heads	Odi

218

8 Shells   8 Heads   Ogbe

9 Shells   9 Heads   Osa

10 Shells   10 Heads   Ofun

11 Shells   11 Heads   Owonrin

12 Shells   12 Heads   Iwori

13 Shells   13 Heads   Ika

14 Shells   14 Heads   Oturupon

15 Shells   15 Heads   Otura

Your combination . . .   Your figure . . .

16 Shells   16 Heads   Irete

No Shells   0 Heads   Opira

Now look up your figure (by name) in Part II's Master Answer section (starting on page 275). Once you find your figure, read the section of text called "For DESTINY Readings."

This portion of the text will give you an indication of what kind of luck accompanies you today. And—as a bonus—it will also assign you an African name to go by as you journey through this book.

EXTRA CREDIT

To play African dice. To play dice, you'll only need four of your coins or shells. You'll also need a gambling partner—two or more can play. Here are the rules. Players, ante up—a penny gets you in. First player, it's your turn. Shake up your four shells or coins and cast them. The rules are easy: All heads, you win. All tails, you win again. Congratulations, take the other guy's money and cast again. Half and half, shoot again (all money rides). Three heads or three tails, you lose. Pay each of the other players even money on their bet. You also forfeit your turn. Hand the "dice" over to your opponent. Here's a little cheat sheet to help you remember the rules . . .

2 heads—shoot again   2 tails—shoot again
3 heads—shooter loses   3 tails—shooter loses
4 heads—**shooter wins**   4 tails—**shooter wins**

EXTRA, EXTRA CREDIT!

To pick four. Need some numbers for tonight's big drawing? You can use nine shells or coins to pick each winning digit in the lottery. Just concentrate on winning. Saying a prayer might help! Then toss your nine shells or coins on the floor. Count up the number of heads that have landed. It will be a number between 0 and 9. This is your first winning digit. Now pick three more and you're all set to go down and buy your ticket. Good luck, my friend. *Ashe*. And so be it.

Go on to the next Reading whenever you are ready to continue.

Reading #12

TABOO OR NOT TABOO?
(True or False?)

In this Reading, you'll learn an African technique for quickly answering absolutely any question on your mind . . . as long as it can be answered "true" or "false" . . . yes or no. In the process you'll learn some additional preparatory techniques that will sharpen your overall divination skills.

TOOLS

For this Reading, we will be using a method of African fortune-telling known simply as "four-nut divination." The original method uses four sections of a kola nut that has been split apart. But since kola nuts are hard to find in the States, we'll have to settle for an un-kola solution here. Any four coins from your pocket will do. In keeping with the idea of splitting the nut into fourths, how about four quarters?

BACKGROUND

Throughout Africa, divination by four kola nuts (or alternatively four pieces of ivory or four coins) is widely practiced as a quick-and-dirty method of getting answers to urgent, everyday questions. You don't even have to be a full-fledged diviner to practice this ubiquitous art. But as part of your training in these mysteries, it will help you develop dexterity and learn the Odu figures.

To practice this art, the Yoruba of Nigeria simply split a kola nut into its four natural parts. Once split, the pieces of the nut appear to have male and female—heads and tails—sides. To find the answer to a yes/no or true/false question, the would-be diviner simply asks the question and casts the four pieces of nut on the ground. Each piece will land heads or tails.

The fortune-teller counts up the number of heads. Using this method, there are just five possible outcomes: four heads, three heads, two heads, one head, and no heads.

Each of these combinations is regarded as affirmative or negative. It's that easy. Let's give it a spin.

HOW TO

 First, you'll need four quarters. Dig into your pants pocket, sock drawer, or piggy bank now.

 Say a prayer for guidance and understanding.

 Hold your quarters in your hand while you ask your question. You can ask any yes/no question on your mind, but—to make it a little more interesting—let's express the question in a way that the oracle can answer true or false. And let's use a love question to sweeten the stakes. Some examples . . .

Pat loves me more than anyone else? D. J. is only interested in my body? X and I could really hit it off? You catch my drift. Whatever relationship "thing" is going on in your life, ask about it now. (You can ask as many of these questions as you like, but ask them one at a time and remember exactly how you phrased each, since you know how true/false tests are! One word can make all the difference.)

With your question in mind, shake up your coins and toss them on the floor or ground. Count up the number of heads that have landed and jot it down on the Scratch Pad.

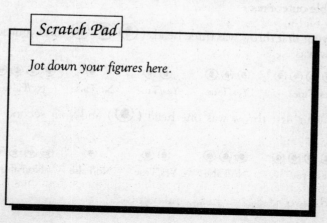

Scratch Pad

Jot down your figures here.

Consult the Answers. . . .

THE ANSWERS

By tossing your four coins, you will get one of five answers, depending on how many coins have landed heads. . . .

4 Heads   ● ● ● ●   2 Heads   ● ●
YES/TRUE   YES/TRUE

3 Heads   ● ● ●   1 Head   ●
MAYBE   MAYBE

4 Tails   ✦ ✦ ✦ ✦
NO/FALSE

If your answer was a definite yes or no—true or false—go on and ask another question. You can ask as many as you like. If you got a "maybe" for your answer, go on to do the Extra Credit section.

EXTRA CREDIT

To clarify certain answers. If either three heads or one head has turned up, the meaning of your answer is uncertain. To learn more, cast your coins again to produce a second Odu diagram. There are ten possible outcomes:

If your first throw was three heads (● ● ●) and your second throw was . . .

● ● ● ●   ● ● ●   ● ●   ●   ✦ ✦ ✦ ✦
Yes/True   Yes/True   Yes/True   No/False   No/False

If your first throw was one head (●) and your second throw was . . .

● ● ● ●   ● ● ●   ● ●   ●   ✦ ✦ ✦ ✦
Yes/True   No/False   Yes/True   No/False   No/False

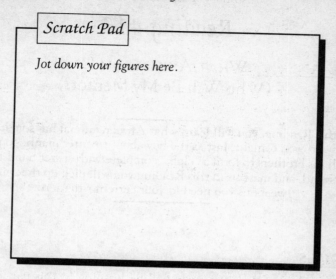

Scratch Pad

Jot down your figures here.

EXTRA, EXTRA CREDIT!

How must I refrain? There are certain things that are off limits to any athlete in training, any pledge in hazing, and any initiate at divination. To learn what your "taboo" is for the duration of this journey, cast the 16 objects (shells or coins) you used in Reading #11. Note how many of your objects have landed heads. Then, using the table in Reading #11, look up your resulting figure in Part II's Master Answer section. Interestingly enough, you'll find your answer in the section titled "For LOVE questions."

Go on to the next Reading whenever you are ready to continue.

Reading #13

WHAT ANIMAL AM I?
(Who Will Be My Mentor?)

In this Reading, you will learn what African animal has something to say to you tonight. Just as the boy about to enter manhood joins with his brothers to form a "club," complete with secret handshake, password, and mascot, in this Reading you will pick up the spiritual weapons you need in your current situation.

TOOLS

The method of divination you will be learning in this part of the book is called Ifa—which means "secret." It was adopted as many as a thousand years ago by the king's diviners in the City of Ife, located in present-day Nigeria.

To go any further, you will need some tools of this trade. For those who practice Ifa, a set of 16 palm nuts provides the basic equipment. But any 16 *things* will work just as well, provided these *things* are relatively small, rounded objects, that—taken all together—will fit comfortably into the palm of one of your hands.

Though palm nuts (which are black ovals, about an inch in diameter and marked with "eyes") are the most authentic way to consult this oracle, they are not readily available here in the United States. Good substitutes are (from smallest to largest) dried chick peas, whole coffee beans, chestnuts, or hazelnuts. Craft shops sometimes sell nut-shaped wooden beads that might suit you just as well—select 14-millimeter beads for medium-sized hands, 10-millimeter for smaller hands.

BACKGROUND

To consult the oracle, the diviner takes his palm nuts into the one hand. In a rapid motion with the opposite hand, he then snatches away all but one or two of these nuts. If one nut remains, he notes down two marks, like this: **●●** . If two nuts remain, he notes down one mark, like this: **●** . If more than two nuts remain, the attempt doesn't count. He tries again.

To get the answer he is looking for, he must repeat this process four times, each time noting with one dot or two the result. Starting from the top with his notations and writing each new dot or two under the preceding one, these patterns ultimately form the 16 Odu figures you saw previously in Readings #0 and #11: **⋮ ⦂ ⦂ ⁞** . . . .

With your new divination nuts in hand, let's see if we can get the hang of the technique for snatching up or "beating" nuts, as this process is known.

If it looks familiar to you, it's the same method you used in Reading #0 to get your initial sense of direction through this book.

HOW TO

 Round up your 16 *nuts* or substitutes, as described in this Reading's Tools section. (For an authentic touch, add a 17th nut. Before you begin, just set it aside. This is the "money of Ifa" and stands for the things you cannot know.)

 Squat down on the floor, and say a prayer.

 Gather your nuts into the palm of your hand. Right-handers, put them in the palm of your left hand. Lefties, palm them in your right. Ambidextrous? Do whatever feels right.

 Ask your question. **What animal am I?** Or, What is my mascot? You can also turn the question around: **Who is my mentor?** my hero? my role model? **Who will lead me through this part of the book?** Who is my spirit guide?

For good effect—and in keeping with tradition—you should whisper your question to your set of divination nuts, breathing on them in the process. By doing this, it is said, you give them breath to speak.

 Now—with your other hand—snatch! Snatch away all of the nuts but one or two. If two nuts remain, make a single mark

on the scratch pad: •• . If one nut remains, make a double
mark: •• .

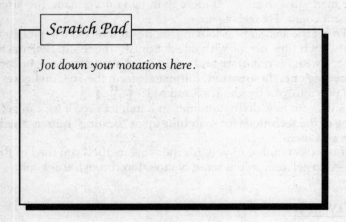

Scratch Pad

Jot down your notations here.

Repeat the process three more times, each time noting down
your double or single mark, <u>under</u> the one your wrote previously.

THE ANSWERS

Your completed figure will look like one of these 16 Odu figures (in
the order that they are recited in the City of Ife and the order that
they appear in the Master Answer section for Part II of this
book). . . .

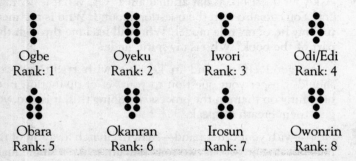

| Ogbe | Oyeku | Iwori | Odi/Edi |
| Rank: 1 | Rank: 2 | Rank: 3 | Rank: 4 |

| Obara | Okanran | Irosun | Owonrin |
| Rank: 5 | Rank: 6 | Rank: 7 | Rank: 8 |

| Ogunda | Osa | Irete | Otura |
| Rank: 9 | Rank: 10 | Rank: 11 | Rank: 12 |

| Oturupon | Ika | Oshe | Ofun |
| Rank: 13 | Rank: 14 | Rank: 15 | Rank: 16 |

Look up your figure in Part II's Master Answer section. Read the sections of the text called "For SPIRITUAL questions."

EXTRA CREDIT

To conduct this Reading using your age. If you don't have your divination nuts yet—or if you haven't quite gotten the hang of beating them yet—here's a way to conduct this Reading using your age in years, instead. Just jot down your current age in years on the Scratch Pad. If you have a birthday coming up within the next six months, round up. Then divide by 16.

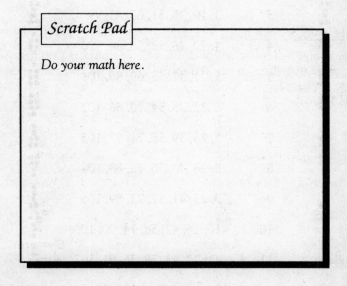

Scratch Pad

Do your math here.

Let's say you're 42 this year—42 divided by 16 is . . .

$$
\begin{array}{r}
2 \\
16 \overline{)\ 42} \\
\underline{32} \\
10 \quad \leftarrow \textbf{Your Figure}
\end{array}
$$

Your answer is the "remainder" at the end of the division process. This number will clue you to your animal mascot. Just consult the chart in this Reading's Answer section. Find the Odu figure whose rank is the same as your number. If you should wind up with a zero at the end of the division process—which means that your age has been evenly divisible by 16—then 16 is your figure, not zero.

Or what the heck, just look up your age in this chart, and let the book do the math for you. . . .

Your Answer		Your Age in Years	
⦂	1	1, 17, 33, 49, 65, 81, 97	⦂
⁛	2	2, 18, 34, 50, 66, 82, 98	⁛
⦂	3	3, 19, 35, 51, 67, 83, 99	⦂
⁛	4	4, 20, 36, 52, 58, 84, 100	⁛
⁛	5	5, 21, 37, 53, 69, 85, 101	⁛
⁛	6	6, 22, 38, 54, 70, 86, 102	⁛
⁖	7	7, 23, 39, 55, 71, 87, 103	⁖
⁛	8	8, 24, 40, 56, 72, 88, 104	⁛
⁖	9	9, 25, 41, 57, 73, 89, 105	⁖
⦂	10	10, 26, 42, 58, 74, 90, 106	⦂
⦂	11	11, 27, 43, 59, 75, 91, 107	⦂

12	12, 28, 44, 60, 76, 92, 108	
13	13, 29, 45, 61, 77, 93, 109	
14	14, 30, 46, 62, 78, 94, 110	
15	15, 31, 47, 63, 79, 95, 111	
16	16, 32, 48, 64, 80, 96, 112	

Look up your figure in Part II's Master Answer section and read the text titled "For *SPIRITUAL* questions."[1]

EXTRA, EXTRA CREDIT!

To do this Reading with shells. You can also conduct this Reading using the "shells" you made in either Reading #2 or #11. Instead of beating your divination nuts four times, just cast your shells once and count up the number that have fallen mouth up (or heads if you are using coins). Use this chart to find your Odu figure in Part II's Master Answer section:

Ogbe
8 shells

Oyeku
2 shells

Iwori
12 shells

Odi/Edi
7 shells

Obara
6 shells

Okanran
1 shell

Irosun
4 shells

Owonrin
11 shells

Ogunda
3 shells

Osa
9 shells

Irete
16 shells

Otura
15 shells

[1] Though this method of numerology is not actually practiced in Africa, the method uses the number 16 in a way that is not inappropriate for this oracle.

Oturupon
14 shells

Ika
13 shells

Oshe
5 shells

Ofun
10 shells

Go on to the next Reading whenever you are ready to continue.

Reading #14

WHAT MUST I PROVE?
(How Can I Improve?)

In this Reading, you will continue to use your divination nuts to get a "reading" on how you—yourself, the individual—can make your mark on the world . . . how you can win the respect of the others in your group . . . how you can play your part in the society of men and women.

TOOLS

For boys undergoing their initiation into manhood, the initiation test is one of strength and endurance. But instead of proving how much you can take all at once, let's focus on how you can build yourself up.

To find out then not "how much of a man you are," but how much of a person you could be, let's consult the palm nuts, using the same technique you learned in Reading #13.

All you need is your 16 nuts plus, of course, your dexterous hands and your increasing finesse at beating the nuts. But if you'd like to go on to do the Extra Credit section, I'll show you some additional divination equipment that would add to your experience with the palm nuts.

BACKGROUND

Boys in traditional Yoruba culture—having been "chosen," as it were, to become diviners—leave their homes at adolescence and move into the household of a master diviner, a man called a *Babalawo*—a keeper of the secrets of Ifa.

The initiation into these mysteries is long and arduous, with many initiatory steps—spanning many years and costing a great deal of

233

money. But suffice it to say, an apprentice in the house of Ifa learns his craft by practicing the art, and that is the tradition we will follow here. We will be learning by doing.

Once he has mastered certain introductory tests (like those you passed in Readings #11 and #12), and once he has learned his basic Ifa figures by name and rank (Reading #13), the young man would next be given a set of palm nuts of his own. On this auspicious occasion, all diviners who could come to the ceremony would cast their own palm nuts on his behalf, to see what advice they might give him on this great spiritual journey he has now taken on. In the process they might also predict things that would happen to him later on in life.

I think you've come far enough by now. What do you say we give it a shot? You'll have to do the casting, but I'll be happy to read for you. . . .

HOW TO

 Round up your sixteen *nuts* (coins or other substitutes) that you made in Reading #13.

 Light a candle if you will. Wear some token of your animal guide from Reading #13. Squat down on the floor. And be sure to say a prayer. Call to your God for the courage to achieve the best that you can be.

 Gather your nuts into the palm of your weaker hand. Southpaws, cup them in your right palm. All others, place them in your left.

 Ask your question. **What must I prove?** What challenge must I face? What hurdles must I leap? What bridges must I cross? **How can I improve myself?** What weakness should I focus on? What goal should I set? **How can I be a better man?** How can I become the person I was born to be?

 Now—with your other hand—swipe at the nuts in your palm and snatch away all but one or two. The rule is simple: If two remain, one. If one remains, two. If two nuts remain, make a single mark on the scratch pad: **•** . If one nut remains, make a double mark: **••** . (If 0, 3 or more, beat again.)

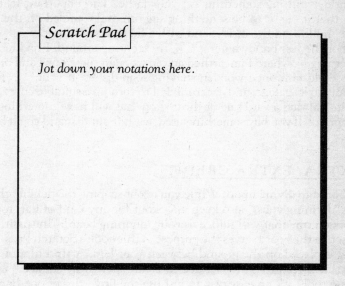

Scratch Pad

Jot down your notations here.

Repeat the process three more times, each time noting down your double or single mark, <u>under</u> the one your wrote just before.

THE ANSWERS

Look up your figure in Part II's Master Answer section. Consult the section of the text called "For STRATEGY questions."

EXTRA CREDIT

A place for your nuts. In addition to a set of divination nuts, the new apprentice receives a carved wooden divination cup to keep them in. To show your divination set the respect it deserves—and also to prevent yourself from losing any of the pieces—keep your eyes peeled for an appropriate container. A wooden lidded cup would be authentic. But your container can be made of pottery, wood, or virtually anything. If you're at all handy in the shop, you might even consider turning something on your lathe. The important features are that it ought to be something smooth and rounded on the outside, hollow on the inside, and with a lid that seals tight.

For the less handy among you, try scouting around. I had luck in my garage—where I unearthed an old wooden sugar bowl and one of those old-fashioned wooden shaving soap dishes. If your own basement, attic, garage, and car trunk fail to turn up a suitable container, there's always a yard sale or thrift shop that will have something appropriate. If you buy something used, wash it out first and you'll be all set.

EXTRA, EXTRA CREDIT!

A board to divine upon. While you're out scoping the neighborhood for "divining cups," also keep a lookout for any kind of flat, round, wooden tray that will suffice as your "divining board." In traditional practice the board serves the purpose of this book's Scratch Pads. The tray is placed on the ground between your legs. A thin film of sawdust[1] is spread over the surface to create a "writing surface." Using these tools, it's an easy task to just use the fingertips of one hand to note whether one dot or two has been made. To make one dot, press your middle finger into the dust on the tray. To make two dots, press your middle finger <u>and</u> index finger into the dust. Once your consultation is completed, it's a simple matter to note your figure, then wipe it out with the palm of your hand to get a clean slate again.

Go on to the next Reading whenever you are ready to continue.

---

[1] The African diviner uses a special dust that is the byproduct of termite activity. Let's hope you don't have any of this lying around your house! Substitute sawdust from your shop or you can also use sand, which is the medium that the Arabs use for a similar form of divination called *sand cutting*.

Reading #15

WHAT'S IN IT FOR ME?
(What Do I Have Coming to Me?)

Now that you have passed the first hurdles in your initiation to these male mysteries, it is time to <u>really</u> start consulting the oracle. In this Reading you will start to read the Ifa figures—the way they were meant to be read—in pairs.

TOOLS

Get your set of divination nuts (coins or whatever you've chosen to make in Reading #13) down from the place where you keep them. Bring them *down* to the mat, as they say. So that they can have the opportunity to speak . . . and say what they have to say.

If you made a divination board in Reading #14, get it out too, along with your sawdust. (Or you can continue to use the Scratch Pads in this book to note your Odu figures.) Sprinkle dust on your board, smooth it out. Set the money of Ifa (Reading #13) aside. And you're all set.

The only thing new you'll be learning in this Reading is to cast two Odu figures instead of just the one you have been using. And a last secret: You will always place the second figure to the <u>left</u> of the first. This is directly opposite to the way the women conducted their Readings in Part I, wherein the second figure was always placed to the right of the first.

BACKGROUND

Once the apprentice in the House of Secrets has learned the 16 basic Odu figures . . . once he is presented with his own set of palm nuts and his divining cup and board . . . once he has made his commitment, then he is ready to get down to the real work of Ifa divination.

Though learning the basic Odu figures is important, in practice a single figure is never read by itself. Two figures are cast, and the two are read in combination.

A quick bit of math will tell you how many possible combinations there are . . . 16 × 16 . . . 256 combinations . . . 256 possible outcomes . . . and each is unique.

Things will not be as hard for you as they are for the apprentice diviner in Africa, who must now begin the lifelong task of learning by heart the Ifa verses that go with each combination of figures. Everything you'll need to interpret the figures is in the Master Answer section! All you have to do is look up your pair of figures and read the "verses" there.

HOW TO

 Bring your sixteen *nuts* (coins or other substitutes) down to the mat (or floor). (And if you made a 17th nut, set is aside now as the money of Ifa.)

 Prepare yourself mentally by saying a prayer you know by heart. The Lord's Prayer is always a good one. But you can use anything that you learned as a part of your upbringing in any faith.

 Whenever you are ready, gather your 16 nuts into the palm of one hand.

 Ask your question. For this Reading, let's explore your job prospects and work life. Think of the place you work or the kind of job you do, and say: **What's in it for me?** What will I get out of working at this place? this job? this career? **What will I get if I take this new job?** The big promotion? The step down? What if I quit tomorrow? Or you can also ask something like: **What do I have coming to me?** as a result of the long hours I have put in? for my loyalty? **Will there be anything extra in my paycheck?** anytime soon?

 Now—beat your nuts: Swipe at them with your other hand and snatch away all but one or two. By now you know the rule.

If two remain, make a single mark on the scratch pad or with the middle finger of your right hand in the dust of your divining tray: • . If one nut remains, make a double mark by pressing two fingers into the dust or writing two dots on the Scratch Pad: •• .

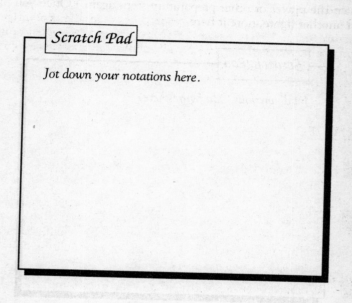

Repeat the process three more times, each time noting your double or single mark, <u>under</u> the one you made before.

THE ANSWERS

Look up your figure in Part II's Master Answer section. Consult the section of the text called "For WORK Questions." Depending on exactly what you asked, you might also want to read the section on "Money Questions."

But before you move on to the next Reading, come back and work the Extra Credit section here . . . because you're really only half done at this point.

EXTRA CREDIT

Two Odu are better than one. Now let's see what happens if you beat your nuts again to produce a second Odu figure. Follow the instructions in this Reading's How To section to produce another diagram for the same question you just asked. (You do not have to repeat the prayer or other preparatory steps again.) Once you have cast another figure, note it here.

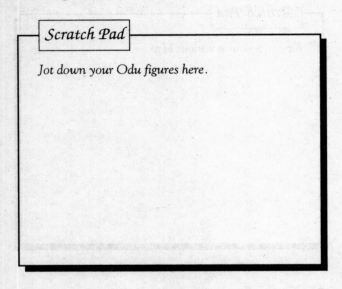

Scratch Pad

Jot down your Odu figures here.

Now, look up your second figure in Part II's Master Answer section. Read the appropriate section on Work or Money—which will give you a second angle on the issues you have raised in your question. The text may reaffirm what has already been said. It may contradict it. Or it may be just another dimension to the whole story. Once you have read your answer, be sure to come back here and work the Extra Extra Credit section for the kicker.

EXTRA, EXTRA CREDIT!

What does your combination mean? As the crowning step in this Reading, look up the specific combination of figures that you have cast for this question. You will find the answers for combinations right in the same Master Answer section you have been using at the back of the book—right behind the answers for the main Odu figures. Very important: Look up your first figure first. Then find your second figure (shown to the *left* of the first). The first few sentences of text will confirm that you have found the correct figure. Read your answer.

Go on to the next Reading whenever you are ready to continue.

Reading #16

WHO IS THE ENEMY?
(What Is the Game Plan?)

Now that you are well on your way to mastering the basic techniques involved in Ifa divination, in this Reading, you will learn how to make the oracle speak faster.

TOOLS

As you have no doubt experienced by now, the process of beating palm nuts is rather labor-intensive and time-consuming, considering that you have to beat the nuts eight times for every single question you want to ask.

The originators of this system saw this as a problem too, so they invented a special instrument to cast two single Odu figures in a single motion. It's called an Opele. And you're welcome to make yourself one in the Extra Credit section. But in the main part of the Reading, I'll be showing you an even simpler way to speed up the process of casting your Ifa figures.

BACKGROUND

In Reading #12 you cast four quarters on the ground in order to ask yes/no, true/false questions. Expanding on this basic idea— and borrowing an interesting innovation practiced by various peoples, including the Bushmen and Tonga, in Southern Africa—we will learn how to throw an Ifa figure all at once.

The key to this method is ingenious: Instead of using four quarters, use a penny, a nickel, a dime, and a quarter; just designate one coin as standing for the answer to the top line, another for the second line down, and so on. . . .

Top line	Quarter
2nd line	Dime
3rd line	Nickel
4th line	Penny

By tossing all coins at once, and translating the results into double and single dots, you will immediately arrive at your first Odu figure. Cast quickly again, and you will have the pair!

HOW TO

 Round up your coinage: a quarter, a dime, a nickel, and a penny.

 Say your prayers.

 You can ask any question on your mind, be it about work, love, money . . . anything. But to make things interesting, let's ask about it in terms of the challenges (and challengers!) you currently face in this area of your life. You might even be so bold as to ask: **Who are my enemies?** in the workplace? on the street? in this endeavor? **Who are my rivals?** my competitors? my challengers? Or to turn the tables a little more constructively: **How can I overcome my enemies?** What strategy should I use? **What's my winningest game plan?**

 Toss your four coins on the ground and note how they have landed, heads or tails. Every head counts as one dot (•), every tail as two (••). Jot them down on the Scratch Pad, based on the position in the diagram that each coin represents.

Top line	Quarter
2nd line	Dime
3rd line	Nickel
4th line	Penny

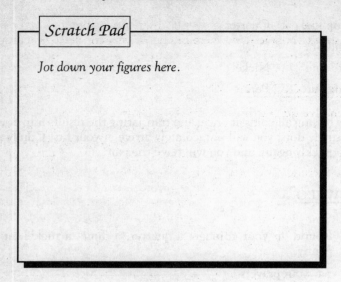

Let's say your quarter landed heads; your dime, heads as well; your nickel, tails; and your penny, heads. Your figure will be this one: .

Now ask your question a second time and cast the four coins again. Note how each coin has fallen.

THE ANSWERS

Look up each of your two figures in Part II's Master Answer section and read the section of text that most relates to your question (Work, Love, Money, Strategy, Destiny, or Spiritual).

Then look up the combination formed by your two figures. To find your combination, turn to the "Combinations" section of the Master Answer section. Look up the first figure, then find the second listed to the *left* of the first. Read this text in its entirety.

Your answer will be revealed by one or more of these text passages. However, you may have to do a little thinking about it, and you may have to pick and choose what you walk away with.

This is all part of the process of Ifa divination, wherein it is the person asking the question who must choose which "verse" is appropriate to the situation. As always, the choice, my friend, is yours.

EXTRA CREDIT

Alternative quick throw. For those among you who may worry that the use of four different coins somehow changes the odds that each might land heads or tails, I have an alternative for you. But it's a little trickier to do. Use four of the same coin (let's say U.S. quarters) and throw them all at once <u>away from you</u>. The one that lands farthest from you represents the top dot pattern in your Odu figure. The one next closest, the second line, and so on. Note whether each of these coins is heads or tails, and jot them down (from top to bottom) on the Scratch Pad. Now repeat the process to get your second figure.

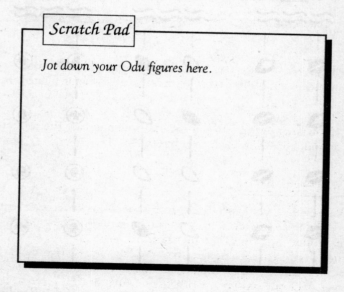

Scratch Pad

Jot down your Odu figures here.

What you are going to find is that sometimes it's hard to tell which coin is farthest away, which is next closest, and so on. You'll have to use your best judgment in making the call. And if judgment fails, well then, there's always intuition.

EXTRA, EXTRA CREDIT!

How to use an Opele. Another highly authentic way to make the oracle speak faster is to use an Opele, which is said to be more "talkative" than the palm nuts, because many questions can be asked of it in rapid succession without having to wait for the palm nuts to be beaten eight times in between.

An Opele is essentially two segments of rope that have been attached so that they form a U shape. Along each side of the U, four cowries are threaded and spaced so that they can rotate freely on the "chain." (Instead of shells, you could also use coins bored with a hole at the top or pieces of wood painted white on one side, black on the other).

An Opele looks like this:

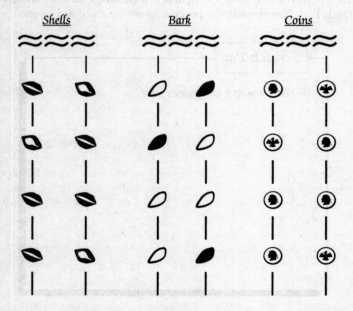

Just as we used different coins in the main part of this Reading to represent each of the four positions in an Odu figure, each of the shells on the Opele chain can be thought of as being in a particular position in the Odu figure, top to bottom. Depending on how each object landed (heads or tails) when the Opele was cast, the single or double Odu dot can be seen by the reader. . . .

Position		Cast		Translation	
≈≈≈	≈≈≈	≈≈≈	≈≈≈	≈≈≈	≈≈≈
1	1	●	●	•	••
2	2	●	●	••	•
3	3	●	●	•	•
4	4	●	●	•	••

In the example here, the double Odu figure that has been cast is ⋮ ⋮ —Iwori Otura—reading it from right to left, as is the Ifa way.

If you're good at tying knots, you might want to try making an Opele yourself. With a deft flick of the wrist, the chain is thrown to the ground. The coins, shells, or pieces of bark rotate freely, landing separately. Looking down each side of the strand, the keen-eyed diviner can quickly see two Odu figures lying side by side. And there is no need to cast anything again. Your Opele will also come in handy for the next Reading.

Go on to the next Reading whenever you are ready to continue.

Reading #17

How Can I Get Rich Quick?
(What If I Do This? What If I Do That?)

The last thing you need to learn how to do as a male diviner is to use your divination set to choose among specific alternatives. The Ifa system is so adept at this task that you can actually choose among as many as five different options at once!

TOOLS

This Reading makes use of the divination nuts you made in Reading #13, or the four coins (quarter, dime, nickel, and penny) you used in Reading #16. If you made an Opele as an Extra, Extra Credit exercise in the last Reading, it would also work ideally here.

You really don't need any other tools to do this Reading, but for an authentic touch—and an interesting experience—you'll want to round up some additional objects for your divination set. The items you will need are called Ibo bones (which are very similar to the Igbo bones used in Part I of this book).

Ibo bones are nothing more than a few small items that are used to represent each of the specific options or alternatives you want to consider. They can be anything "finger sized." Say . . .

A white pebble—to signify longevity, endurance, stamina, health

A wishbone or bean—to represent family, children, wishes in general

A pottery shard—to designate triumph, victory, conquest, defeat of an adversary

A snail shell or nut—to represent love, friendship, sex, and marriage

Extra cowries—to stand for money, business, trade, financial success

But you are free to use whatever objects you find lying around your home or neighborhood:

| Scallop Shell | Feather | Dog Biscuit | Bark | Root | Stick | Leaf |

And you are welcome to assign to each whatever meaning makes sense to you. (In fact, it doesn't even have to make sense, as long as you remember what the object is supposed to represent in this case.)

BACKGROUND

Once the apprentice diviner has learned to recognize at sight the 16 figures of Ifa by name and rank (Reading #13) . . . and once he has mastered the Opele (or the coin-tossing method we substituted in Reading #16) so that he can rapidly learn to recognize the 256 <u>pairs</u> of figures that are possible on any double throw . . . he has only yet to learn how these 256 combinations are ranked.

It is the rank order of the 256 pairs that gives the Ifa oracle its great versatility and dexterity in handling the choice among specific alternatives. To the diviners in the City of Ife—who pride themselves on the way things are done right there—knowing how to choose among specific alternatives is what separates the great diviner from the charlatan.

In a nutshell—as it were—here's how it works. The five Ibo bones are spread out on the table in front of the diviner. By tradition, each object stands for a specific blessing (and also a corresponding curse). By casting the Opele chain once for each of these Ibo bones and noting the double figure that the Opele has spoken each time it lands, the diviner then uses his knowledge of the ranking of the pairs to announce which object (and therefore which blessing or curse) the oracle has pointed to this time.

The rules for determining which figure will outrank another are not only quite intricate, but they vary from diviner to diviner. We're going to be using a totally authentic, but—comparatively speaking—simple version of this hidden knowledge.

If you'd like to use your palm nuts for this Reading—you will have your work cut out for you. Go to the Extra Extra Credit section to find out how it's done. For those who have made an Opele, you'll find your instructions in the Extra Credit section. All others—and for simplicity's sake—we'll just use the coins you used in Reading #16.

HOW TO

 You'll need your four coins (quarter, dime, nickel, and penny). If you like, you can also use Ibo bones, but if you don't have yours yet—no problem. Just use your imagination.

 As always, start off by saying a prayer for guidance.

 Ask your question. You can ask anything, but to illustrate the procedure, let's use this one: **What alternative will make me the most money?**

In this case, the Ibo bones could be said to stand for . . .

O	**Endurance**—a long-range strategy
ΥO	**Genius**—a sudden stroke of luck
▶	**Competition**—a challenge you meet
⊘❽	**Partnership**—a business dealing
❧❧	**Cash**—a good investment

But if you've got some specific moneymaking schemes in mind, just assign one to each of your bones.

 Now touch one of your coins to the white stone. (Or, if you don't have a stone, just whisper the name of your first alternative to your coins.) Cast them once . . . cast them again. Each time, note down the Odu figure that has been formed.

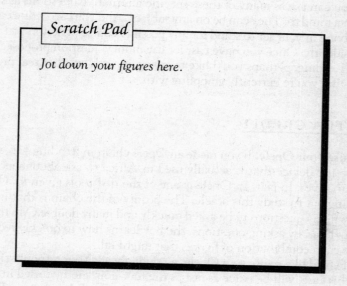

		If Heads . . .	*If Tails . . .*
Quarter	Top line	●	●●
Dime	2nd line	●	●●
Nickel	3rd line	●	●●
Penny	4th line	●	●●

Place your second figure to the *left* of the first. . . .

> ## Scratch Pad
>
> *Jot down your figures here.*

Repeat this operation for each of the options you want to explore. Perhaps two or three are plenty for a first time. But if you want to go for the money, you're welcome to cast for all five.

THE ANSWERS

Your answer will consist of two parts. First, look up each Odu combination your have thrown in Appendix B, immediately following Part II's Master Answer section. (The Appendix will also tell you the "rules" by which the Odu are ranked in case you're interested in learning it on your own time.)

Jot down each number beside your figures on the Scratch Pad. Now compare. In general, the highest-ranking number wins. Whichever of the five options scores highest is your answer. (But Note: <u>The higher the number, the lower the rank.</u>)

Now—as a bonus—look up each combination in Part II's Master Answer section, to see if the oracle has anything more to say to you on this subject.

You can ask as many of these specific alternative questions as you have a mind to. They can be on any subject. And you can define each Ibo bone in your set to stand for any possible course of action you are considering. Once you have cast for the money question proposed in this Reading, perhaps you'd like to try again with another real problem that you're currently grappling with.

EXTRA CREDIT

To use your Opele. If you made an Opele chain in Reading #16, you have the device that is actually used in Africa to ask about specific alternatives. In fact, an Opele is one of the first tools given to a boy setting out to study this oracle. The beauty of the chain is that it allows many questions to be asked quickly and many double Odu to be cast. Thus, by asking questions, the boy learns how to quickly recognize each combination of figures that might fall.

If you'd like to use your Opele, go right ahead. Your response time, in this case, will be twice as fast as the four-coin method used in the main part of this Reading, since a single throw of the chain will do what it takes two coin tosses to do. By tossing the Opele down once, the shells or nut casings will literally form a double Odu diagram before your very eyes. All you have to remember is, if a shell (coin or piece of bark) comes up heads, read one dot; if tails, two. . . .

Opele | Translation

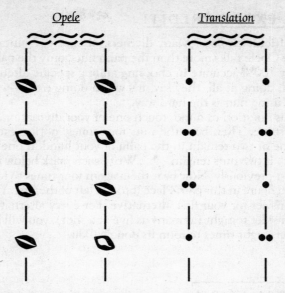

Just cast your Opele chain once for each of the alternatives you want to consider. Note your double Odu figure for each option. Then find the rank of each of these figures in the Appendix. The option that the oracle gave the highest-ranking figure to (which is to say, the lowest number) is your answer. Look it up in the "Combinations" section of Part II's Master Answer section.

Scratch Pad

Jot down your Odu figures here.

EXTRA, EXTRA CREDIT!

Making difficult choices. Many diviners, of course, maintain that though the Opele talks more than the palm nuts, only the palm nuts are actually 100% accurate in choosing among specific alternatives. If it's worth doing at all, they say, it's worth doing right—which in the case of using nuts is the hard way.

With this question in mind, touch one of your divination nuts to the white stone. Then beat the nuts four times, noting each time whether one or two remain in the palm of your hand. If one nut remains, •• . If two nuts remain, • . Write each mark below the one you cast just previously. Now beat them again four times to form the second Odu figure in this pair. Place it to the left of the first. You now have the answer for your first alternative. For every alternative you want to consider tonight (as many as five at a shot), you will have to beat the nuts eight times to form its double Odu.

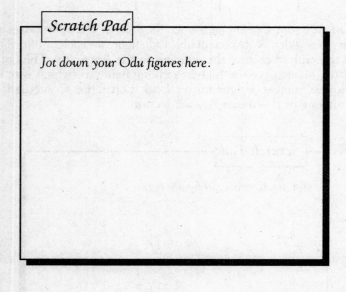

Scratch Pad

Jot down your Odu figures here.

Once you have all the double figures you need to consider all of your options, turn to the Appendix and find how each of your figures ranks. The choice that the oracle made is now obvious. The highest-ranking Odu pair you have thrown has pointed at the winning choice. Look it up among the combinations listed in Part II's Master Answer section.

Go on to the next Reading whenever you are ready to continue.

Reading #18

How Far Can I Go?
(How Far Will I Get?)

In this Reading you will put your skills in choosing among
alternatives to work . . . to determine the nature of the good things
that are coming in your life . . . the bad things to be avoided . . .
and the things you ought to do to assure your success.

TOOLS

You need nothing you don't already have . . . and nothing you don't
already know, to do this Reading. Just apply your skills as an African
diviner, and let Ifa do the rest.

BACKGROUND

In a full-fledged standard consultation with this Oracle, many steps
are involved in a single "reading." First two Odu figures are cast with
the palm nuts (or the Opele). This is the primary answer . . . the main
point that Ifa wants to make today.

But just as the women fortune-tellers do, the men at this point put
their skills at choosing among specific alternatives to work for the
questioner. They might ask first whether the double Odu that has
been cast should be read as a favorable or an unfavorable sign. The
choice here will be among just the two alternatives, in which case, if
Ibo bones are being used, one bone would represent an affirmative response and the other object, a negative response.

The diviner would then go on to find out what blessings were in
store for the questioner (for Ifa always brings blessings to the table).
Using the male way, the diviner would ask about five blessings at
once.

But no one's world is perfect, and the diviner would then go on to
find out what curses were in store for the questioner. Again a choice
would be made among five alternatives.

And finally, the diviner would determine what sacrifice the consultant should make to assure the blessings, while at the same time counteracting any curses that might be going on. Or he might use his knowledge of choosing among specific alternatives to zero in on an appropriate cure or remedy—for the skilled Ifa diviner is also a practitioner of herbal medicine.

In this Reading, I'll show you how you can take your Ibo bones, your divination nuts, and your coins (or Opele) and go step by step—little by little—through this entire process.

HOW TO

 Instead of using shells—which is the female way—you'll be using your nuts (or coins), of course. So bring them down now to the mat and say your prayers.

 Ask you question. As always, it can be about anything. But for demonstration purposes, let's ask: **How far can I go?** in my chosen line of work? in my present job? in love? at life in general? **How far can I get?** in my relationship with X? in my dealings with Z? in learning this oracle? in discovering myself? my heritage?

 Now, after whispering your question, beat your nuts eight times, toss your four coins twice, or cast your Opele to get two Odu figures. Write the second to the left of the first.

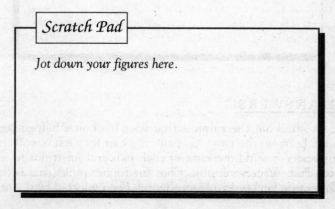

Scratch Pad

Jot down your figures here.

This is your main answer. Just set it aside for now.

Now, to determine whether it's a good sign or not, take two of your Ibo bones. Let's say the white pebble is one ⭘, and the pottery shard is the other ➤.

Touch your divination object (Opele, nut, or coin) to the white pebble and say: **Is this indication good?** Beat your nuts, cast your coins, or drop your Opele to construct another Odu pair. Then touch your divination object to the pottery shard and ask: **Is this indication not so good?** Cast again and get a second Odu pair.

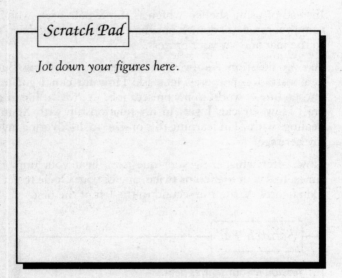

Scratch Pad

Jot down your figures here.

THE ANSWERS

First, let's find out the auspices that your Ibo bones helped you determine. Look up the two Odu pairs you cast for each of your bones in Appendix B. Find the rank of each pair and jot it down on the Scratch Pad. Whichever object has the higher rank (that is to say, the lower number) is the object that has been selected by the oracle.

The answer depends on which object it is, and what question you asked when you touched that object with your divination tools.

With this determination in mind, now turn to the "Combinations" in Part II's Master Answer section. Look up the Odu pair that you cast as the first step of doing this Reading. Read the text, and use the knowledge that your Ibo bones gave you to interpret what you read.

To go on with this line of questioning, continue in the Extra Credit section. . . .

EXTRA CREDIT

To determine your blessings. The next step would be to determine what blessings you can anticipate at this time—provided, of course, that your divination set has indicated that the auspices for your Odu pair are favorable. (On the other hand, you can also learn the nature of whatever difficulties might be lurking for you in the wings, based on an indication that your Odu pair is unfavorable.)

To do this step, you'll need all five of your Ibo bones from Reading #17. You can define each bone according to your own values about what constitutes either a blessing or curse, but the traditional designations are these. . . .

	Blessings	**Difficulties**
O	Long life	Argument
Y O	Birth	Life-altering change
▶	Triumph	Loss
ᴄᴏ ᴮ	Union	Separation
● ●	Riches	Poverty

To find which of these is your blessing (or curse), use your divination gear (nuts, Opele, or coins) and cast two double Odu figures for each alternative. Look up the resulting pairs in Appendix B, and note which is of the highest rank (i.e., the lowest number). The Ibo bone that the oracle points to in this way is your answer.

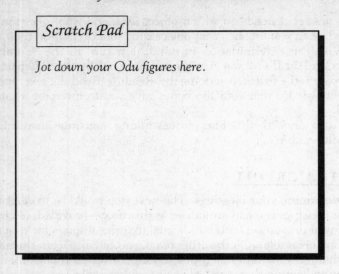

Look up the winning combination in Part II's Master Answer section to learn more about the blessing or difficulty in store.

EXTRA, EXTRA CREDIT!

To determine the required sacrifice or remedy. At this point, there is one last thing to do—but a very important one: The entire objective of this system of divination is to determine the right thing to do at the right time. Usually this involves both making a sacrifice and taking a remedy. Once again, the Ibo bones will point the diviner and his client in the right direction.

You will need to redefine your Ibo bones at this point to stand for possible sacrifices you might be willing to make or possible cures you might be willing to consider. Here is the list that the women used in Part I of this book to make a similar determination:

Spare . . .	Skip . . .
A dime	A cigarette
A little time	A beer
A bite to eat	A cup of coffee
A light	Sex

Lend . . .	Give . . .
A helping hand	Bread to the birds
A couple of bucks	Food to the homeless
Your time	Clothes to the needy

Offer . . .	Say . . .
An apology	A prayer
Praise	
Thanks	

I believe that these choices are best left up to the individual. But for the African diviner, various amounts of money, foodstuff, clothing, or other articles would be considered, in turn, as honest-to-goodness—and very serious—sacrifices to make. According to one adage from the sacred oral "texts" of Ifa itself, no good can come from not making a sacrifice.

Once you have assigned one of the sacrifices you are willing to make to each of your Ibo bones, all you need to do is cast a double Odu figure for each bone. Then, turn to the Appendix, jot down the rank of this combination. And note which sacrifice has "won." Then—finally!—to find your remedy as well, consult your winning combination in Part II's Master Answer section.

Congratulations. You have just done a complete consultation, using the full-blown Ifa system.

Go on to the next Reading whenever you are ready to continue.

Reading #19

EVERY MAN FOR HIMSELF
(Summary, Review, and Full Instructions for Consulting the Palm Nuts)

In this Reading you will combine everything you know about the palm-nut oracle. And with this Reading, your initiation into the secrets of male divination is complete. *Ashe*, my friend, so be it. And peace.

TOOLS

To review everything we've used in the past eight Readings . . . The basic tools that you need to work with this oracle are 16 palm nuts—which are quite plentiful in Nigeria. But since that's a pretty tall order for those living elsewhere, 16 chickpeas, 16 coffee beans, 16 hazelnuts, 16 chestnuts, or even 16 coins or beads will suffice. The only requirement is that all 16 need to fit into the palm of your outstretched hand.

In addition to your 16 nuts, coins, or beads, you will need five additional objects, called Ibo "bones":

O	A white pebble
YO	A wishbone or bean
▶	A pottery shard
↩🅑	A snail shell or nut
◖◗	Extra cowries

These Ibo "bones" not only play a very important role in the workings of this oracle, but they are fun and fascinating to use, adding an extra dimension and extended dynamic quality to the oracle.

262

For additional touches, you may add an extra nut, coin, or bead to serve as "the money of Ifa." The "money" is simply set aside at the start of a consultation and serves no other purpose than to honor the African spirits and symbolize your small offering to them.

To complete your collection of divination paraphernalia, you can also add a divining cup for housing your divination nuts when not in use. Use any kind of wooden or pottery vessel as long as it has a lid. You can also add a shallow round wooden tray as your divining board. By scattering a layer of sawdust (or sand) on this tray, you will be able to use it to mark your figures, instead of having to rely on this book's Scratch Pads.

And lastly, you might like to get yourself a comfortable straw mat to sit on, since these oracles are best consulted on the floor, if not the ground.

BACKGROUND

Ifa—or palm-nut divination—is practiced by the Yoruba of Nigeria and—in various altered forms—by other people in the region. The method, which the Yoruba borrowed from the Arabs' "science of sand," or sand cutting, is a form of geomancy, similar to the I Ching, an ancient Chinese divination art that uses the casting of coins to create a "diagram" or "figure."

The I Ching diagram, constructed from the bottom line up, has six lines. To cast it involves throwing three coins six times and noting each time how they have landed. The results can be a solid line, ▬▬▬▬▬▬▬▬, or a broken line, ▬▬▬ ▬▬▬. These lines are "stacked" on top of each other to form one of the I Ching's 64 figures, which look, for example, like this one. . . .

In the African version of geomancy, the palm nuts are manipulated in the hands of the diviner to produce a combination of nuts that, in turn, indicates whether a single or a double "fingerprint" should be sketched in the dirt, sand, or sawdust, thus: • or •• . The process is repeated just four times (in comparison to I Ching's six casts) to produce any of 16 figures (compared to I Ching's 64), built from the top line down (compared to I Ching's bottom-up construction):

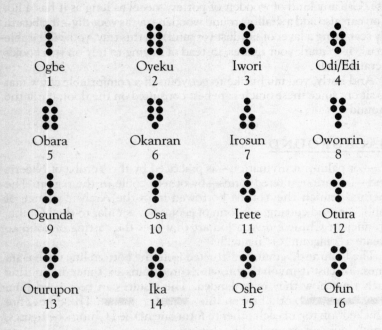

Ogbe	Oyeku	Iwori	Odi/Edi
1	2	3	4
Obara	Okanran	Irosun	Owonrin
5	6	7	8
Ogunda	Osa	Irete	Otura
9	10	11	12
Oturupon	Ika	Oshe	Ofun
13	14	15	16

Once learned, these single "Odu figures" are never interpreted by themselves during the process of a divination. A second figure is always cast, and the two are "read" together. There are 256 different combinations of these basic 16 forms. So any question you ask could produce any of 256 results!

The object of Ifa divination is not only to presage events of importance, but to determine "right action" on the part of the questioner . . . to assure that blessings materialize as they should, that evils are avoided, that personal character is built up, and that each person achieves individual destiny.

In an Ifa consultation, the diviner (an initiated priest called a *Babalawo*) executes a series of manipulations with his palm nuts and Ibo bones. In its full-blown form, a single consultation is long and quite complex, involving a whole series of considerations (see Reading #18). In the process of answering the consultant's original question or concern, blessings are foretold. Dangers are forewarned. Sacrifices are called for. And remedies are prescribed.

To its religious (and serious) practitioners, it is believed that this oracle is a direct communication channel to the gods, which in traditional Yorubaland include a great many spirits, any of whom may "speak" through the divination nuts. But the spirit who "owns" this particular method of divination is the Spirit of the Diviner, Orunmila.

The oracle speaks directly and indirectly. Directly, it speaks in a very literal (but poetic way), because the diviner has learned thousands of "verses" for the many and various signs that the process of beating the palm nuts generates. When a particular sign (two Odu figures side by side) is drawn in the dust on the divining board, the diviner's job is to recite all the verses that he knows for that particular diagram—it can be dozens, each the length of a chapter in the Bible and many in the style of a Psalm.

Though these verses are not written down anywhere—except lately in bits and pieces that have been collected by anthropologists—they are very much like the Scriptures of the Jews, Christians, and the Moslems who live far to the north of Yorubaland.

Nobody knows how many of these verses there actually are, but based on the few that have been collected and translated by scholars—and the voluminous size of the books they take up—we are talking in the thousands and thousands here. It is the questioner's job to listen to everything the diviner recites—a litany that tends to take on a hypnotic singsong quality—and pick out the passage that strikes home. This is the direct way that the oracle speaks. It also speaks indirectly, through the use of the Ibo bones and a sophisticated system of ranking the various figures that can be generated in this method. In these cases, the oracle "speaks" by pointing at a particular Ibo bone, which has had a certain meaning preassigned to it.

The five bones—each assigned to represent a specific blessing, curse, sacrifice, remedy, or any other specific alternative—are simply laid out in front of the diviner. Using his palm nuts, he generates a pair of Odu figures for each bone. Then he uses the ranking system to see which bone has scored the highest (which is to say, which has the lowest-ranking order number). The bone with the highest-ranking Odu pair thus assigned to it wins! This is the answer the oracle has pointed to and thus has "spoken" without "speaking."

It is this interaction between the palm nuts and the Ibo bones that gives the oracle its complete voice and endows it with an ability to speak in a consistent yet dynamic way.

Readings #10 through 18 walk you through the entire process, but if you'd just like to try out the oracle before you commit (or if, having completed the Readings, you'd like to go on to improvise), here's how to proceed. . . .

HOW TO

 A Reading starts with a prayer. Say one you know by heart.

 If you choose to use it, set the money of Ifa (your extra nut, coin, or bead) aside. This is your token offering to the Powers that Be.

If you choose to use a divining board, scatter some sawdust on it now, so it's ready to mark your Odu figures in.

 Take your remaining 16 nuts from their container. Place them in the palm of your left hand, unless you are left-handed, in which case, place them in your right.

Whisper your question to them.

Your question can be about anything, but this oracle is particularly good at "how" and "what" questions.

What can I do about _____ ?
How can I get _____ ?
What will result from _____ ?
How will _____ turn out?
What is the point of doing _____ ?
How can I overcome _____ ?

You can fill in the blank with just about anything. But you will have the best results if you bring real issues and problems to the oracle. Ask about something that's really on your mind.

Whisper your question to the nuts. Then take your free hand and swipe it across the nuts in the palm of your other hand. In a sweep similar to the technique you would use to play jacks, snatch up all of the nuts but one or two.

The rule of thumb is: If one nut remains in your palm, make two marks (••) on the Scratch Pad or in the dust of your divining board. If two nuts remain, make one mark (•).

Scratch Pad

Jot down your Odu figures here.

To complete the "first leg" of your figure, repeat this process three more times, each time noting your single or double dot <u>below</u> the one you just drew.

Now beat your divination nuts four more times to construct the "second leg" of your double Odu figure. Place this diagram to the <u>left</u> of the one you cast first.

THE ANSWERS

Though an African diviner would not interpret each of the two figures separately that make up your pair, you will get more out of this book if you think about each of these figures before you attempt to understand the combination that the two create.

To do this, just look up the first Odu figure you cast (the right leg) in the Master Answer section that immediately follows Reading #20. Read the whole answer if you like. Like the original methods used in Nigeria, this approach will simulate the experience of hearing the diviner recite his verses. You will hear various stories, any one of which may click with you today. Choose the one that does! Or you can choose to read just that portion of the text that relates to the question you have asked today, be it a Work, Love, Money, Strategy, Spiritual, or Destiny question.

Then look up the second figure you cast; read the whole text or the appropriate section.

Finally, look up your specific combination of Odu figures at the back of Part II's Master Answer section. This portion of the text will amplify or extend your overall interpretation of the diagram.

Since the Ifa divination system emphasizes free will and choice, don't feel at all reticent to read between the lines of this text, to draw your own conclusions, or to read into the ideas. This is exactly how the oracle is supposed to work. The final decision about what the message is, is always up to you . . . and so be it.

NEXT STEPS

To continue your Reading . . . Once you have consulted the "verses" in the Master Answer Section, you may continue your consultation by using your Ibo bones—your white stone $\bigcirc$; your wishbone (or bean) $\curlyvee(\oslash)$; your piece of broken pottery $\blacktriangleright$; your snail shell or acorn $\varpi(\bigodot)$; and your pair of cowries $\blacktriangleright\blacktriangleright$ (which you can string together if you like).

Your Ibo bones can be put to work at this point to clarify the meaning of your verses and to determine what exactly you need to do to assure a favorable outcome and—as important—to prevent things from going wrong.

At this point in the Reading it is traditional for questioners to ask whatever yes/no questions they want to put forward. You can ask them in the way described in Reading #12, as true/false questions and using coins. Or you can ask them by using two of your Ibo bones. You can choose any two, but let's say your cowry shells will indicate the yes (or true) portion of the question and your piece of broken pottery or china will represent the no portion.

Just place these two objects in front of you. Ask any yes/no or true/false question. Beat your divination nuts eight times for each of the Ibo bones. This process (as described above) will produce one pair of Odu figures for each of the Ibo bones on the floor. By consulting Appendix B and noting which of these pairs ranks higher than the other, you will have your answer. If the shells have the higher ranking, the answer is yes/true. If the piece of pottery has the higher-ranking pair, the answer is no/false.

To speed up this process, you can use four coins (as described in Reading #16) or an Opele, an authentic device that permits you to cast a pair of Odu figures with a single flick of the wrist (see Reading #16's Extra, Extra Credit section).

Using any of these three techniques, by asking a series of yes/no questions at this point, it's possible to zero in on anything you want to know about. You can ask as many yes/no questions as you want.

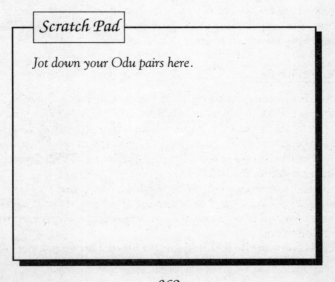

Scratch Pad

Jot down your Odu pairs here.

EXTRA CREDIT

To extend your consultation with the oracle . . . You can now continue your consultation by making use of all of your five Ibo bones and using this oracle's ability to choose among five alternatives at once. Reading #18's Extra Credit and Extra, Extra Credit sections explain this in full detail.

Go on to the next Reading whenever you are ready to continue.

Reading #20

To Each His Own
(Afterword)

In this final Reading—which is really something more to "read" than "do"—you will learn how the male system of divination you have just learned compares to the female system described in Part I of this book.

TOOLS

Whether you have come to this end by first taking the "female" path down the White Cotton Road or by actually starting on the "male" path up the Melon Seed Road—it makes no difference when all is said and done. Both paths—as it turns out—lead to the same place, which is right about here. So here you stand. Now, the only question remaining is, Which road do you prefer?

This is not a question of gender preference, sexual orientation, masculinity, femininity, or even sexual ambiguity, since both systems have male and female aspects. Rather, it is a spiritual question. Why limit yourself to either system when it is your own destiny at stake?

Just as in anything you want to look at in this world, you can't really understand something until you know what it is. But to really know what something is, you also have to appreciate what it is not.

These marvelous African oracles present a perfect case in point, since each can be thought of as a slightly different tool for accomplishing the same thing. By trying out each of the systems presented here, you will learn something about the other . . . and in learning about the other, you will learn about the first.

The choice, of course, is yours. For the sake of review, here are the similarities and differences between the two systems I observe. . . .

BACKGROUND

There are two aspects to both of these oracles, one technical and one artistic. The first aspect is totally procedural. Both the "male" system you have perhaps just learned and the "female" system you may now go on to explore involve deliberate and sometimes complex methodology, procedure, and ritual.

The male diviners would probably say that if it's worth doing a thing, it's worth doing it well. And if it's worth doing it well, it's worth doing it right. If you were a diviner in the City of Ife, where both methods are practiced, you would probably say that the painstaking "male" method of Ifa divination is therefore superior.

Even in the present-day practice of Santeria in the States (which uses the female method of shell casting), certain questions are referred to an Ifa priest. There is no question that the male way you have just seen in Part II is certainly more physically difficult to master, and generating the figures is more tedious. But both systems are otherwise technically similar.

HOW TO

The procedure of beating the palm nuts is (as you know) a skill that takes a little practice to master. Depending upon the size of your hands and your general level of manual dexterity, the technique of snatching the nuts so that only one—or at the most two—remains, can be downright vexing.

In contrast, the "female" way is much more forthright and more easily accessible to one and all. It just involves casting 16 shells on the ground and counting up how many have landed heads (which in the case of shells is mouth side up). This count translates directly into an Odu figure. So, in a single casting of the shells, the women manage to do what it takes men four snatches of the nuts to accomplish.

Can something so simple as the female shell-casting method possibly work for a matter so serious as divining the will of the gods? Having worked closely with both systems, I think you will not be disappointed with either system's performance. But it is only by trying out both systems that you can make this judgment for yourself.

There are, of course, many other procedural differences between the two systems. Though they both make use of "bones," for example, the number of bones that are used is different, and the method of selecting a bone to read varies considerably. In general, the male system tends to be more grandiose—but is bigger always better? Short of trying out both methods, I don't know how you'll ever know.

THE ANSWERS

As I noted earlier, there are two aspects to these oracles, and the first aspect is procedural, wherein you will see the most difference between the oracles in practice.

But procedural aspects are only half the story of these two marvelous oracular systems. The other aspect to the oracles is a "literary" one, for both of these devices combine "science" and "art" into a complete and fully balanced system.

It is not enough as a diviner to be able to beat the divination nuts and write the Odu figures on your divining board. It is not even enough to also be able to cast the shells and say what figure has been derived. All of this is child's play, really. It's what an apprentice or a novice does as an assignment. The hard part is knowing the <u>right</u> words to say when the figure has been cast.

African Oracles in 10 Minutes—being practical by nature—does not make you do this. But as these systems exist and have been practiced, memorizing the verses is a painstaking process that may take four, five, or even ten years to master even at a basic level. It is, in fact, said that a diviner of Ifa never quits learning new verses, which he picks up from other diviners over the course of his lifetime. (He or she may even add new verses as the result of dreaming them.)

For the real diviners who practice this art, there is no Master Answer section to consult. The verses must be memorized line for line and bit by bit—verse after verse after verse. Once again, the males have taken their system to epic proportions, by insisting that there are 256 different answers, each of which may have 10, 12, or more verses associated with it. The female system, on the other hand, stresses the 16 basic answers, though (as in this book) some female diviners also read for the 256 combinations.

In the "artistic" area of the divination verses, you will also note a difference between the two systems, though here the distinction is less easy to describe. Depending on whether you consult the answers for Part I or Part II, your message is going to be a little different. And you may find that one section works consistently better for you than the other . . . or one section may tend to be easier for you to relate to than the other. The only way to know, of course, is to try both.

EXTRA CREDIT

There is, in fact, nothing to prevent you from <u>always</u> looking up your answers in the Master Answer sections for Part I <u>and</u> Part II. Doing so will actually be more like a real-life consultation of either oracle, since in practice the diviner in either system would give you at least two different verses to choose from for any given answer you receive.

When you attempt to do this, the first thing you will note is that the Odu figures are ordered (and therefore numbered) differently in the two Master Answer sections of this book. This is because the men and women who invented these systems organized them differently in the first place. But with a little patience, I'm sure you will be able to find your answer in both sections.

EXTRA, EXTRA CREDIT!

I would hope that by now—despite whatever level of male pride you feel—you will swallow a bit of it now and go on in this book to learn the female way of doing things. Since the female method makes use of the math skills that American males are notoriously good at (at least on SAT tests), I think you'll like it—as much or maybe even more than the "male" system you have just learned.

So at this point, and without further ado, I invite you to follow me down the White Cotton Road, pal, to learn how our sisters do these things.

Master Answer Section for Part II

THE MELON SEED ROAD
(Palm-Nut Divination)

How to Find Your Answers

The 16 primary Odu figures of Ifa are presented in a sequence used in the Nigerian City of Ife:

Ogbe
1

Oyeku
2

Iwori
3

Odi/Edi
4

Obara
5

Okanran
6

Irosun
7

Owonrin
8

Ogunda
9

Osa
10

Irete
11

Otura
12

Oturupon
13

Ika
14

Oshe
15

Ofun
16

So that you can easily correlate them with the shell oracles from Part I, each figure is also keyed to its equivalent Odu in the *erindinlogun* (16-shell) system.

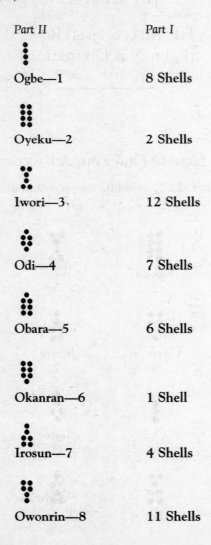

Part II	Part I
Ogbe—1	8 Shells
Oyeku—2	2 Shells
Iwori—3	12 Shells
Odi—4	7 Shells
Obara—5	6 Shells
Okanran—6	1 Shell
Irosun—7	4 Shells
Owonrin—8	11 Shells

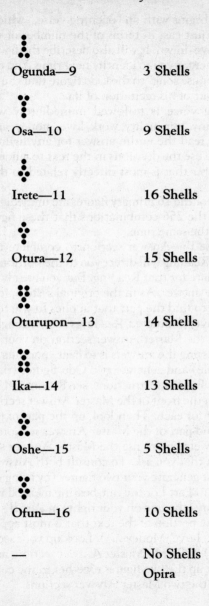

Ogunda—9   3 Shells

Osa—10   9 Shells

Irete—11   16 Shells

Otura—12   15 Shells

Oturupon—13   14 Shells

Ika—14   13 Shells

Oshe—15   5 Shells

Ofun—16   10 Shells

—   No Shells
                   Opira

Each answer begins with an "opening verse," which describes the figure you have just cast in terms of the number of single or double dots that you have drawn. It will also describe the figure in a way that may make it easier for you to identify next time. You can think of this section as the "praise song" to the Odu figure that the African diviner might offer as part of his recitation of Ifa.

The opening verse is followed immediately with additional "verses" on destiny, spirituality, work, love, money, and strategy. You are welcome to read the entire answer for any figure that you cast. But you can also use the divisions in the text to guide you to the portion of the answer that is most directly related to the question you asked.

The answers for the 16 primary figures are immediately followed by the answers for the 256 combinations that these figures form when you cast two at the same time.

When you use the Answer section to complete the Readings in this book, each Reading will direct you to the portion of the text that is most appropriate for that Reading. But you are always welcome to read more of the answer. As in the original system, it is up to you (as the consultant) to find the part that applies to you today.

After you have completed Readings #11 through #20, you can continue to use the Master Answer section on your own. The basic method for accessing the answers is to beat your nuts (toss your coins or use your Opele) and generate two Odu figures (the second to the left of the first). For full instructions, see Reading #19. Look up each of your figures in the front of the Master Answer section and read the appropriate text for each. Then look up the pair of figures you have cast in the second part of the Master Answer section.

You are also welcome to use the Master Answer section in Part I for any question that you ask. To consult both Answer sections on a regular basis, just generate your two figures (by using either the shell-casting method in Part I or the nut-beating method in Part II). Look up your first figure (the one on your right) in Part II's Master Answer section. Read the portion of the text that is most appropriate to your question (Work, Love, Money . . .). Look up your second figure (the one on your left) in Part I's Master Answer section, and read the text there. Now look up the two figures together in the combinations sections of each of the two Master Answer sections.

of attaining them. Your challenge is a moral, spiritual, physical, and mental one. All your skills must be combined if you will meet the challenge you have set for yourself. Whatever comes, you will be a "better man" for having gone for it. Don't forget to say your prayers . . . and make the appropriate sacrifice.

OYEKU

African Name (*Ifa*)	Oyeku
Ifa Rank	2
American Name (*Santeria*)	Eyioko
Part I Figure (*erindinlogun*)	2 Shells *owo eeji*
African Spirit	Obeji

KEYWORDS: Death. Night. West. The Reincarnate Soul. Death-dodging. Fertility. Progeny. Twins. The Voice of the Ancestors.

OPENING VERSE

Four double dots on the board—and the second elder is marked. Four double dots! Make way for Oyeku, the transforming one. She clears away a path. And Obeji, the Twins, are speaking. Your spir-

itual double in Heaven has something to say to you. Hear it out! It is your destiny that is being talked about . . . the destiny you chose for yourself . . . and now is yours to complete.

For DESTINY readings.

You, my friend, were born to be who you are . . . no more, no less, no other. It is, was, and always will be the way you dreamed. So choose then, carefully, and make your pick. Ifa says your female name is MARIAMA. Ifa says your male name is JAJA. They mean one and the same: You are "God's Gift." And where you stand is this: in the very shoes you, standing in heaven, once asked the Good Lord to give you.

For SPIRITUAL questions.

It is like a cicada with you. Your progress comes in fits and bursts—with long periods of rest in between. It is the only way for something so prolific to keep its own creativity in check. An Obeji twin is your mentor. Everything there is has its "evil" side. Everything there is has its "better" half. Look into your mirror, my friend. *If you are 2, 18, 34, 50, 66, 82, 98—having come of this age now, there is some fact of life you must accept.*

For WORK questions.

What's in it for you? What you put into it. What will you get? What you take out of it. A new job promises to be more of the same. But no two places are ever exactly alike. No two situations are ever quite the same. And no two endings are ever identical. What do you have coming to you? You will get what you see at the end of the day. What will be in your pay? Fair wages.

For LOVE questions.

You are like the locusts. You believe in keeping everything bottled up, until all at once . . . you explode in a fever, frenzy, and fervor. In a man you look for the one who satisfies you completely . . . again and again. In a woman you look for the one who reminds you of your mother—not that you love her in the same way. Your taboo is this: Do not avoid touching . . . yourself.

For MONEY questions.

What's in it for you? Easy come, easy go. But there will be plenty to go around if you put some aside for a rainy day now. What will you get? A return on an investment of your time. A special effort is sure to pay off down the line, especially if it's a creative project. A blessing of money will come at the moment it is due—and no sooner. Hold out, my friend, till then.

For STRATEGY questions. You are in a situation wherein you have to prove that the things you want most are worth waiting for the longest. Your challenge involves forces that are outside your realm and beyond your ken. Remain open to the various possibilities. Even as we speak the wheels are turning. Time is passing. And favorable things are cycling up. You must sacrifice your time. Be ready to act when the right moment comes.

IWORI

African Name (*Ifa*)	Iwori
Ifa Rank	3
American Name (*Santeria*)	Eyila Chebora
Part I Figure (*erindinlogun*)	**12** Shells *owo eeji laa*
African Spirit	Eshu

KEYWORDS: Life force. South. Water. Blood. Semen. Impregnation. Miracle of Birth and Rebirth. Energy. *Ashe* (Spiritual Vitality). Impetuousness.

OPENING VERSE

There are two single dots on the board and two doubles—the two inside the other. And now you see! It is the third elder that lies on the

*tray. No other. It is Iwori, the Unified One. Half male, half female
. . . and perfectly balanced. Eshu, the Messenger of gods, is speaking through him. Hear him out! He is telling you to become a whole,
well-balanced person.*

For DESTINY readings. You were born to be yourself—whatever that is . . . to go your own way—no matter where it leads . . . and
to discover the truth about and for yourself—regardless what it is.
Your luck comes from without . . . but also from within. It takes both
ways, both kinds, both alternatives. And so it is—that male or female
parts aside—your name is simply this: OLA, "Precious Wealth and
Precious Worth"—which is what each person is. And you, my friend,
are standing on your own two feet.

For SPIRITUAL questions. It is like a snail. Progress is inch by
inch. And it is only by sticking your neck out that you cover any
ground at all. Come out from the safety of your shell, or else stay forever in the dark. Eshu is your mentor. Go far and wide. Do as much
a you can. Be a messenger of the gods. *If you are 3, 19, 35, 51, 67, 83,
99—having come of this age now, you have reached a turning point.*

For WORK questions. What's in it for you? Something beyond
human measure . . . a life full of personal rewards. What else will you
get? Your own identity. Should you go somewhere else? Your destiny
will only follow after you. And you will have to learn its lesson one
place or the other. What do you have coming to you? The experience—from which you will gain much. What will be in your pay?
Enough to keep you in the style to which you are accustomed.

For LOVE questions. You are like the snails. It matters not what
sex the other snail is . . . since each is half and half! (And yes, they
do unto each other as you would have the other do unto you.) I guess
I'd say you'd best be prepared for anything and everything in this relationship. For in the best man, you will find the woman. And in a
best woman, you will find a man. Whatever . . . be each other's best
friend. Your taboo is this: Do not excite yourself . . . alone.

For MONEY questions. What's in it for you? The things that
money cannot buy or measure. What will you get? Enough to satisfy
your needs, whims, caprices, and even support your hobbies and
habits. Though your blessings in general have no cash value, the

things you have gathered around you are priceless in their sentimental way. Cherish the things in your life that could never be replaced. But when you need them no longer, give them up.

For STRATEGY questions. You are in a situation wherein you need to gather your personal strength and energy and apply yourself to the task at hand. Your challenge is to know yourself well enough to push when you need to . . . and otherwise pace. All your skills must be combined if you will meet the challenge you have set for yourself. You will have to sacrifice some of your hard-earned energies here.

ODI/EDI

African Names (Ifa)	Odi Edi
Ifa Rank	4
American Name (Santeria)	Oddi
Part I Figure (erindinlogun)	7 Shells owo eeje
African Spirit	Egungun

KEYWORDS: Containment. North (the direction faced to ask a question). The 16 Odu Figures. Ifa Itself. The Diviner's Cup. Prophecy. Divination. The Closer of Roads to Bad Things. The Container of Existence. The Womb.

<u>OPENING VERSE</u>

Four signs on the board—two doubles and two singles, the female marks inside. And it is Odi—the Fourth Elder . . . the Womb . . . the Container of Life's Secrets . . . the Crucible, where new life is formed. And it is the Voices of the Ancestors—the Egungun—that speak through her rounded belly. Hear them out! For she is whispering the secrets of the new life that is in store for you.

For DESTINY readings. You were born to be. It is that simple. And you are destined to have The Experience. You are lucky to be here. You are lucky to have come so far so fast. And—provided you make the right choices—you will be lucky to your last breath. Ifa says your female name is BELUCHI—"Provided God Approves." Ifa says your male name is CHINAKE—"Only God Decides." And where you stand is smack-dab in the middle of your own existence.

For SPIRITUAL questions. It is like a spider with you. You are a weaver of the tapestry of your own existence. You are a spinner of many fates around you . . . and also your own. The Egungun are your mentors. They go down to the river to wave their long cloths in the wind. They go down to the river to trap the wayward souls within. But only you can save your own destiny. All you have to do is choose to. *If you are 4, 20, 36, 52, 58, 84, 100—having come of this age now, you have a difficult choice to make . . . and a major transition.*

For WORK questions. What's in it for you? A chance to refit yourself and adjust to new employment conditions. What will you get? The chance to try something new for a change. Would it be better to go someplace else? Perhaps. But if you can cling to the past ways for a little while more, the inevitable will catch up to you for sure. What do you have coming to you? As much as you can adjust to. What will be in your pay? The same for a while, but there's potential for more here.

For LOVE questions. You are like the spiders . . . you hopeless romantic! A gift is almost expected, first. And before there's any foolishness, you'd best get in the mood. In a man you look for someone handsome enough to devour with your eyes. In a woman, you look for someone whom you can beguile into submission. You two! It was a match made in heaven . . . even if you hardly ever do see each other

. . . and even if the meetings are brief. Your taboo is this: Do not finger yourself . . . in public.

For MONEY questions. What's in it for you? A steady income. What will you get? A regular check. A blessing of big money may also come as if on cue, but only after things have had the time to incubate, and only if your performance measures up to expectations. It would not hurt to put some money into a little nest egg—you never know when there might be an additional mouth to feed.

For STRATEGY questions. You are in a situation that requires you to do some waiting, hoping, dreaming, and planning. Your challenge is to prepare for a future that you cannot entirely appreciate or understand before all the facts and circumstances are known. As you wait expectantly for the big event, try to find something to keep your hands occupied. Sacrifice something you want today for something you may need tomorrow.

OBARA

African Name (*Ifa*)	Obara
Ifa Rank	5
American Name (*Santeria*)	Obbara
Part I Figure (*erindinlogun*)	6 Shells *owo eefa*
African Spirit	Abiku

KEYWORDS: After the Rains. Rainbows. Summer. Cool Breezes. A Fan in the Heat. Prosperity. The Opener of Roads. New Avenues. Many Possibilities. But also, Illusions. Mirages. Figments of the Imagination. Everything is Ephemeral.

OPENING VERSE

Three double dots on the board, arching up and crowned by a lone single cap. It is Obara!—the Rainbow. It is the fifth elder you have cast. Take pause—but quick!—before the sign fades away. For it is the spirit of an Abiku—the child that dies young— who speaks here. Hear it out! Don't miss the elusive, ephemeral opportunity to grasp the glorious moment that is coming your way.

For DESTINY readings. You were born to die. But like a star in the heavens, there is no reason not to shine in the process of living out your days. You are lucky to have your own identity. You are lucky to have the opportunity to express yourself. So do it . . . now! Ifa says your male name is OLORUN—"Owner of the Sky." Your female name is IFEOMA—"It Is a Good and Beautiful Thing." And where you stand is this: Right here. Right now. This is your chance of a lifetime. This is your opportunity.

For SPIRITUAL questions. It is like a fruit fly with you. It all happens so fast. And there is hardly time left to take it all in, let alone to enjoy it. An Abiku is your mentor. Take your lesson from the "child who was born to die." It doesn't matter how long you spend in one place. It doesn't matter how long a good thing lasts . . . as long as you make the most of it while you still can. *If you are 5, 21, 37, 53, 69, 85, 101—having come of this age, you have arrived to a new respectability.*

288

For WORK questions. What's in it for you? As much as you are willing to stake on an idea. What will you get? As much as you can sell your ideas for. A new job? Why not . . . if the prospects seem bright. But just remember everyone who runs a business does not have a clear vision of the future. What do you have coming to you? Plenty if you are willing to risk believing in a grand dream. What will be in your pay? It all depends on whether the dream you are chasing is real, or just a pipe dream.

For LOVE questions. You are like a fly on the ceiling. You know how to dive after the things that you want . . . even if it's risky business . . . and even if it could result in a close encounter with a cowtail switch or (at the outside) cost you your very life! In a woman, you want one who's hard to resist—but doesn't. In a man—well—you always liked a good chase, even if it is a short race. The two of you are as compatible as two bugs in a rug (at least for tonight). Your taboo is this: Do not manipulate yourself . . . in a habitual way.

For MONEY questions. What's in it for you? A pot of gold at the end of the rainbow. What will you get? If nothing else, a good story to tell . . . an adventure to relate . . . and some experience to put under your money belt. A blessing of money may seem elusive at times. But eventually everyone wins . . . something. May yours be the best (and not the booby) prize.

For STRATEGY questions. You are in a situation wherein things are not exactly what they seem (but most things aren't!). Your challenge is to look beyond the hype. You must make your decision not on hope, but on the confidence you feel in your gut. When in doubt, pray. And tender your heartfelt sacrifice.

OKANRAN

African Name *(Ifa)*	Okanran
Ifa Rank	6
American Names *(Santeria)*	Okana Okana Sodde
Part II Figure *(erindinlogun)*	1 Shell *owo ookan*
African Spirit	Shango

KEYWORDS: Lightning. The Second Rainy Season. Fall. Thunderstorms. The Power of Rain to Wash Things Away. A Clean Slate. The Feast of Shango. [Pay the diviner extra whenever this figure falls on the tray.]

OPENING VERSE

Three double dots on the board—arching down to the single dot below. It is a bolt of lightning grounding itself! Thus you will know the sixth elder has struck its mark. And it is Shango—the God of Lightning—who speaks now in his rumbling, echoing, reverberating voice. Hear him out! And listen till he's done! There are sudden changes in store tonight . . . and fresh starts in the morning.

For DESTINY readings. You were born to make your mark. But it is up to you to enliven your own days and light up your own nights.

You are lucky at having your own say. You are lucky at working your own way. You are lucky at the things that come to you just in the nick of time— and in a flash. Ifa says your male name is KAMALU— "A Streak of White Light." Ifa says your female name is ORISHA— "The Great Spirits in Flight." And where you stand is this: The world is at your command.

For SPIRITUAL questions. It is like a firefly with you. Rising from out of the darkness around you, you make your own light. No wonder Shango is your mentor. Look up to the one who backlights the clouds at night. Look up to the one who strobes the dark with piercing light. Be one who jars us to our senses and rattles us to our bones. *If you are 6, 22, 38, 54, 70, 86, 102—having come of this age, you have crossed over into a new period of living, learning, and knowing.*

For WORK questions. What's in it for you? Something that falls unexpectedly from out of the blue. What will you get? A piece of the fallout. Just be prepared for anything—and you will not be caught off guard. Things at work are stirring up again. And what about a new job? Look for things to open up suddenly. Be ready to apply—and show no hesitation if it's something you've always wanted to do. What do you have coming to you? Manna from heaven. What will be in your pay? Something extra if you seize an opportunity to get ahead.

For LOVE questions. You are like the fireflies. In attracting your mates it never hurts to advertise, I guess. But aren't you going kind of heavy on the cologne? You like a man whom you can spot from 40 paces. You like a woman who turns your head . . . then follows through. The two of you are like a couple of prowlers on a hot tin roof. What a dance you do! (Have I got some music for you. See Acknowledgments.) Your taboo is this: Do not dance naked with yourself . . . unless the shades are closed.

For MONEY questions. What's in it for you? A moneymaking opportunity. But you'll have to strike faster than lightning. What will you get? Cashed in . . . or cashed out. An investment may be undertaken or alternatively abandoned as you suddenly see the light. Action is required. The operative idea here is speed. Financial change comes rapidly when this Odu appears.

For STRATEGY questions. You are in a situation wherein a change that was inevitable suddenly takes place. Your challenge is to size up the situation immediately and waste no time in responding the right way. There is no time to sleep on an idea. The best thing to do is consult your divination set and make whatever sacrifice the oracle chooses . . . then act.

IROSUN

African Name (*Ifa*)	Irosun
Ifa Rank	7
American Names (*Santeria*)	Eyorosun
Part I Figure (*erindinlogun*)	4 Shells *owo eerin*
African Spirit	Agayu

KEYWORDS: Fire. The Dry Season. Winter. Temporary Difficulties. Sleepless Nights. Reddened Eyes. Heat. Making it Through Hard Times. (Rub the eyelids thrice with chalk in order to overcome these difficulties.) Also, a Bird called Irosun, a Tree called Irosun (Camwood).

OPENING VERSE

Two double dots on the bottom . . . two singles on top. And the seventh elder has appeared on the tray to make its mark. It is Irosun,

the Red-Eye, that has landed this time. And it is Irosun . . . cam-
wood—the Dust of the Divining Tray itself—that speaks. Hear it
out! And hear all it has to say. There is a promise coming your way.
But it is also a warning: First you will have to pay.

For DESTINY readings. You were born, my friend—and that in
itself is nothing easy. All things have their price. Life demands its little sacrifice. You are lucky to have the option of making one. You are
lucky to have the power of choosing what you will give. You are lucky
to have the endurance to pay off what you have already obtained. Ifa
says your male name is OJO; your female name, AINA—both of
which signify a "Difficult Birth." Where you stand right now is on the
threshold of the new life you are about to build. It's entirely up to you
now to take the big leap.

For SPIRITUAL questions. It is like a termite with you. You
have taken on a lot to chew. And there are only so many hours in the
day. Would you consume them, too? Follow the example of Agayu—
the spirit of fire. Try not to burn out too soon. Let Agayu be your
mentor. Leave your mark on the world, even if it's just a trail of ashes
and dust to note your rapid progress. . . . Leave the others to rub it on
their lips. *If you are 7, 23, 39, 55, 71, 87, 103—having come of this*
age, you'll get the urge to either settle down . . . or roam.

For WORK questions. What's in it for you? Continuing employment if you are lucky—for these times are hard on employer and em-
ployee alike. What will you get? That which comes from the sweat of
your brow. A new job perhaps? It's not the best time to look. But
where you see a red flare, take it as a sign. What do you have coming
to you? Not as much from your employer as you think. What will be
in your pay? As much as can be afforded, not necessarily as much as
you are worth. Hang in there.

For LOVE questions. You are like the termites in their mound.
Yours is a relationship of convenience—for there is work to be done,
and no time left for foreplay. You look for a man who knows how to
get the job done. You look for a woman who can carry her own
weight around (on her head?). The two of you are red-eyed and tired
at the end of the day. It's a wonder you don't have twin beds. Your
taboo is this: Do not rub yourself . . . raw.

For MONEY questions. What's in it for you? Not much . . . not now—I'm sorry to say. But it is only the dry season you must weather away. What will you get? A light at the end of the tunnel. A blessing that time's passage bestows upon our heads and down our faces. Things will turn around in time. Money will free up again. Happy days will return again.

For STRATEGY questions. You are in a situation wherein things have simply dried up for a while. The work gets harder now. And everything becomes an effort. Your challenge is to rise to your highest limits and achieve your best work. It may not be a question of life or death, but it is certainly an issue of survival here. Sacrifice?? I'd say you'd best give it all you've got. . . and then some.

OWONRIN

African Name (Ifa)	Owonrin
Ifa Rank	8
American Name (Santeria)	Ojuani Chober
Part I Figure (erindinlogun)	**11** Shells *owo ookan laa*
African Spirit	Oshun

KEYWORDS: Rain. Spring. The Major Rainy Season. Thunderstorms or (alternatively) Drought. Striving (either way). Disease. Scars. Transcendence. Avoidance of Death. Atonement. Appeasement.

OPENING VERSE

Two double dots on top—two singles on the bottom. And the eighth elder makes an appearance on the tray. It is Owonrin—the Fluid One—that has come this time. And it is Oshun, the Spirit of the River in Flood, who takes this opportunity to speak. Hear her out! She is telling you how to find the path of least resistance . . . and therefore how to come safely to your destination just as fast as you can.

For DESTINY readings. You were born, my friend, to endure. You were born to adapt. You were born to learn. You were born to evolve. You were born to survive. You have been lucky in making your way to this turning point. You will be lucky again in choosing your way out. But luck is only the half of it. Ifa says your male name is AKINWOLE—"Bravery Enters this House." Ifa says your female name is FAYOLA—"Luck Walks with Honor." And where you stand right now is in the midst of a crisis you must weather with dignity and strength.

For SPIRITUAL questions. It is like a cockroach with you. You must be smarter than the ones who are against you . . . you must be quicker than even a superior mind. . . you must be clever to avoid those who would just as soon obliterate you. Take a lesson from Oshun. She is your mentor. Her great stream flows on and on as if there is no end in sight, other than a new beginning. *If you are 8, 24, 40, 56, 72, 88, 104—having come of this age, you'll bid a section of your past a fond farewell.*

For WORK questions. What's in it for you? A career path. What will you get? A job that grows with you and forms to fit your shape. A new job? Perhaps. But not necessarily at a new place. One thing becomes another with you. One job blends into the next seamlessly. What do you have coming to you? Not so much of a promotion as a better fit. What will be in your pay? Not much more, but you will be happier making it.

For LOVE questions. You are like the cockroaches in the walls. By the time the two of you are through, we'll have to move. Do you never get enough? It seems you're always locking feelers and climbing all over each other. You look for a man who prefers to be on the bottom. You look for a woman who likes it better on top. That's why the two of you are sure to hit it off. Your taboo is this: Do not go after yourself . . . morning, noon, <u>and</u> night.

For MONEY questions. What's in it for you? You'll get paid for doing something you like to do. What else will you get? What else would you have, my friend? You can always figure out how to live on what you make. Wouldn't you rather be poor and happy than rich and distressed? Granted, it's also possible to be rich and happy. But before you chuck it all to go for the gold, review your finances and see if you can swing it.

For STRATEGY questions. You are in a situation wherein all the advance planning in the world will not help you. For you must expect the unexpected twist of fate. You are being swept along by external waves. Your challenge is to keep up with the current trends. Hint?? You are being pushed in the direction you're supposed to go. Sacrifice?? Yes, but of course.

OGUNDA

African Name (*Ifa*)	Ogunda
Ifa Rank	9
American Name (*Santeria*)	Oggunda
Part I Figure (*erindinlogun*)	3 Shells *owo eeta*
African Spirit	Ogun

KEYWORDS: Male Aggressiveness. The New Moon. Impulses. The Penis. Testicles. Male Ritual. The Knife. Circumcision. Scarification. Male Professions. Male Compulsions. Male Obsessions. Tools. Weapons. Male Skills. Things Done with the Hands.

OPENING VERSE

Three single dots on top of a double. A phallus has fallen on the tray! It is Ogunda—the Male Member. It is Ogunda, the ninth elder, that is written in the dust. (Even graffiti makes a point!) And it is Ogun—the God of Iron—who has a story to tell. Hear him out! He says you must remain firm if you want to succeed at your business. He says if you are persistent, you will meet with success.

For DESTINY readings. You were born to seek your fortune, make your living, and find your place. You are lucky at things that require muscle power, elbow grease, and a touch of finesse. You are lucky at getting the things you go after. You are lucky at having your way with others. You are lucky at working your will upon the world. Ifa says your male name is AKIN—"The Proud Warrior." Ifa says your female name is ADEOLA—"Crown has Honor." Where you stand right now is upright. Stay firm, my friend. Walk tall.

For SPIRITUAL questions. It is like a dog with you. It is not enough to run on your own. It is not enough to be part of the pack. It is better yet to let others cook your food for you and pat you on the head. Take your cues from Ogun. Let Ogun be your guide. Everything is better when you have the right attitude. Use the tools in your hand, as well as your head. Adopt a pet and gain a spiritual companion. *If you are 9, 25, 41, 57, 73, 89, 105—having come of this age, it is time for getting back down to business.*

For WORK questions. What's in it for you? As much as you want to aim for . . . as high as you want to achieve. What will you get? As much as you succeed at. A new job, perhaps? A raise? A better position? Yes, you'll be poised upon the ladder of success. Yes, you'll be climbing, climbing, climbing up the ladder. What do you have coming to you? One rung after the other . . . a greater and greater challenge each time. What will be in your pay? The price you have put on your best years.

For LOVE questions. You are like two dogs. Snarling. Nipping. Biting. Licking. And then, there are those nights of the full moon! You like a man who comes sniffing around. You like a woman who likes to get down. So what if it's a mixed marriage? or if the two of you make for an odd couple? It happens . . . at various times . . . and in the strangest settings. As long as it works for you. Your taboo is this: Do not probe yourself . . . with things that might get stuck.

For MONEY questions. What's in it for you? That all depends on what kind of a bargainer you are and how much of a risk taker you are willing to be. What will you get? In direct proportion to your wager. But please don't go for broke. A blessing of money comes more surely as the result of a safe investment than a lucky lottery ticket. But somebody has to win those too. All things in balance, my friend. Consider it your investment portfolio.

For STRATEGY questions. You are in a situation wherein the male in you is having a heyday. Your challenge is to direct all of your aggressive tendencies, sexual impulses, and risk-taking attitudes into something constructive. (How about a nice contact sport?) You may be tempted to go out on a limb to prove your point . . . to do something daring . . . impetuous . . . foolish. I'd say best make a sacrifice (and take a cold shower).

OSA

African Name *(Ifa)*	Osa
Ifa Rank	10
American Name *(Santeria)*	Ossa
Part I Figure *(erindinlogun)*	9 Shells *owo eesan*
African Spirit	Oya

KEYWORDS: Female Aggressiveness. The Crescent Moon. Our Mother. Vagina. The Rim of Existence. Childbirth. Creativity. And alternatively: Destruction. Female Magic. Female Actions. Female Dreams. Female Skills. Success at Business. Luck with Money.

OPENING VERSE

A double dot astride three singles. And it is the tenth elder that has come to the tray this time. She is Osa—the Receptive One, but with a mind of her own. And it is the spirit of Oya—Shango's wife—who speaks now loud as the howling winds of the storm. Hear her out! She says there is no use in resisting the changes that are blowing in. She says let loose, and you will be pushed in the direction the Powers that Be would have you go.

For DESTINY readings. You were born, my friend, to be on the receiving end of things. But this does not mean you need to take things lying down. You are, in fact, lucky at staying on top of things (even if others think you are on the bottom). You are lucky with the things that come your way. You are lucky with the things that fall into your lap. You are lucky with the people who come into your life. Ifa says your female name is UCHENNA and your male name is UCHECHI. In either case, it is "God's Will." Where you stand right now is astride your world. You are in control. And God willing, you will remain so.

For SPIRITUAL questions. It is like a lioness with you. Everything is a question of your pride and duty. Life can be one big responsibility. But you have within you the skills of a hunter. Take your cues from Oya—the wind. Kick up the dust from time to time. Take your cues from Ochosi, the hunter. Be patient as you lie in wait. *If you are 10, 26, 42, 58, 74, 90, 106—having come of this age, you must come into your own some more.*

For WORK questions. What's in it for you? More than your mother could have dreamed. What will you get? More than your father ever reckoned. A new job in the offing? Why not? Sure. Just look for something that makes use of your moneymaking skills. Track down a lead or two on the grapevine. What do you have coming? Whatever you choose to go after. What will be in your pay? More and more as time goes by and your contribution is better appreciated.

For LOVE questions. You are like two lions. This relationship is close . . . when it's not distant. It's an "understanding" you have, as

300

much as a commitment. A recurring passion holds the two of you together during absence. In general, you like a man who—when you need him—is around. In general, you like a woman who's desired by everyone in town. Among consenting adults, your lifestyle is your own. Your taboo is this: Do not maul yourself . . . without first clipping your nails.

For MONEY questions. What's in it for you? Salary and wages, based on job level and performance. What will you get? As much as you demand, but be prepared to walk if you make an ultimatum. A blessing of money will come to those who negotiate well enough. But don't be a pest. Nothing's automatic, even for top-ranking men, in this world of ours.

For STRATEGY questions. You are in a situation in which your female nature takes charge. Your challenge is to turn all of those intuitive and emotional feelings of yours into constructive action. It doesn't do much good to have a hunch that goes unacted on but later turns out right. It doesn't do much good to share your feelings if nobody takes them seriously. Still, you must try. Put your ideas forward at this time. And it wouldn't hurt to make a little sacrifice beforehand.

IRETE

African Names (Ifa)	Irete
Ifa Rank	**11**
American Name (Santeria)	Mediloggun
Part I Figure (erindinlogun)	**16** Shells *owo erin din logun*
African Spirit	Yemoja

KEYWORDS: Earth. Ashes. Dust. The Garden Place. The Grave. The Fire Pit. A Person's Place, Fate, Fortune, and Number of Days. A Reborn Spirit. The Quarter Moon. Continuity. Cycles. Endurance. Passing through Phases. Growth. Changes.

OPENING VERSE

Three single dots, split by a double—an upside-down cross. The eleventh elder has fallen in this dust. And how appropriate. For it is Irete—the Earth Mother—who has surfaced this time. It is Yemoja—Our Mother of the Deep Waters—who has the floor to speak. Hear her out! She says that you should always do what comes

*naturally to you . . . you should always do what is instinctively right.
She says listen to your inner voice, and heed the words of the diviner.*

For DESTINY readings. You were born, my friend, to do what comes naturally . . . at least to you. You are lucky at feeling your way around. You are lucky at being in the right place at the right time. You are lucky at the simple (but important) things of life. Ifa says your female name is YORUBA—"The Meeting Place." Ifa says your male name is OBIKE—"The Strong Household." Where you stand right now is in perfect alignment. You are in sync with the natural world around you. It is as if you have come home.

For SPIRITUAL questions. It is like a fish with you. A particular environment suits you fine and helps you grow. But any other, and, well . . . Take your cues from Yemoja. Let the spirit of the waters be your mentor. Look into your own depths if you would find the answer. Be like a fish in water . . . keep moving around. *If you are 11, 27, 43, 59, 75, 91, 107—having come of this age, it is time to leave the past behind . . . and take a different route for a time.*

For WORK questions. What's in it for you? A new opportunity. A new chance to succeed. The possibility of making a significant contribution. What will you get? Maybe a little ahead (but only if you maintain your previous lifestyle). New job? An offer is coming just as sure as we speak. But you will have to see whether it feels right for you. Don't just go for the money. What do you have coming to you? If it's meant to be, it will be fair and timely. What will be in your pay? The possibility of a bonus. Ask around to see what you'd have to do.

For LOVE questions. You are like two fish. You are always swimming circles around each other. Or else you are always swimming in parallel. The two of you are always keeping your safe distance. And when it comes to sex, I think you'd just as soon have it in different rooms. Why are you so afraid to touch? Why do you fear getting close? You are looking for the one who does not slip away this time. Your taboo is this: Do not relieve yourself in the water . . . others might drink.

For MONEY questions. What's in it for you? A sterling opportunity that comes along only once every so many years. What will you get? Success perhaps from overseas. Assets may be liquefied now with greater ease. A loan is easier to float than it used to be. But interest—as always—fluctuates. A blessing of money will drift into your hand, but you must be the first to recognize it and snatch it up. Beware the competition. Careful not to spend your money all in one place.

For STRATEGY questions. You are in a situation wherein timing is of the essence. Your challenge is do the right thing at the right moment. Things that happen in recurring patterns or cycles are the easiest to predict. But you must also be sensitive to the fact that unexpected things happen, too. In general, you'll want to watch the signs and signals carefully . . . and read between the lines. What sacrifice should you make? In this case, I'd be generous.

OTURA

African Names (Ifa)	Otura
Ifa Rank	12
American Name (Santeria)	Manunla
Part I Figure (erindinlogun)	15 Shells owo eedogun
African Spirit	Orisha l'Oko

KEYWORDS: Sky. Heaven. Sun. Full Moon. Stars. The Place Where Olodumare, the Sky God, Dwells. The Place Where the Soul Goes. High Tide. Cowries. Sea Turtles. Things that Wash Up. Words. Speech. Sounds. Cries. The Shifting Balance. The Unity of All Faiths. Peace. [Hold a cowry shell while you read your answer.]

OPENING VERSE

Three single dots—and a double splitting the top. The twelfth elder has fallen in the dust. And it is Otura—the Crucifix. Now it is the God of the Christians who has the chance to speak. Now it is the God of the Muslims who talks. Hear them out! They will tell you how to sacrifice now, instead of later. And it is a certain peace of heart that you will come to know in the end.

For DESTINY readings. You were born, my friend, a spiritual being. And you feel the hand of God in your life. You are lucky at getting the things you pray for. But you are also lucky at seeing the good in prayers that go unanswered. Ifa says your female name is CHINARA—"May God Receive." Ifa says your male name is TOBECHUKWU—"Praise God." Where you stand right now is where you are "supposed to be." There is a reason (and a time) for everything.

For SPIRITUAL questions. It is like an elephant with you. It is all a matter of keeping things in perspective. For no matter how great you are, there is always something greater. Orisha l'Oko—god of hunt and god of farm—looks over you. Take your cues from the prophets and the saviors. Jesus Christ is your mentor. Mohammed. Abraham. Even Buddha . . . *If you are 12, 28, 44, 60, 76, 92, 108— having come of this age, it is time to make a new commitment.*

For WORK questions. What's in it for you? The sky's the limit. But there's a distinct possibility for martyrdom. What will you get?

As high up the building as you can stand to look down. A new job???
Only if it contributes to the mission you have chosen for yourself and
only if it serves the cause you have identified as your priority. What
do you have coming to you? Some people will look up to you. Some
will denounce you. But many more will accept you. It's the risk you
take in championing a point of view. What will be in your pay?
Nothing like what you bargained for, I'd say.

For LOVE questions. You are like the elephants. Your friends are
as important to you as your mate. And if you have children, well—
there is no question of who comes first. In a man, you are looking for
one who pretty much lets you alone. In a woman, you want someone
who has her own interests. This relationship has the long term going
for it. The two of you pass in the night sometimes—and it is mean-
ingful. Your taboo is this: Do not lower yourself . . . on anything too
sharp.

For MONEY questions. What's in it for you? Hazardous duty
pay. What will you get? Nothing for all the extra hours you put in.
But there are other rewards in life than cash disbursements. A blessing of money will come happiest to one who had no expectations
that money was due. If you sacrifice at first and do your work for the
love of it, money will follow and you will be taken care of.

For STRATEGY questions. You are in a situation wherein your
faith will see you through. Your challenge is to keep believing no
matter what happens to discourage you. Take a position and stick
with it. Do what is most important to do now. Stand up and be
counted. Give of yourself this time, and that will be sufficient sacrifice.

OTURUPON

African Name (*Ifa*)	Oturupon
Ifa Rank	**13**
American Name (*Santeria*)	Merinla
Part I Figure (*erindinlogun*)	**14** Shells *owo eerin laa*
African Spirit	Eshu

KEYWORDS: Difficulties. The Decreasing Moon. A Pit in the Earth. A Trap. The Grave You Dig for Yourself. Skull's Backyard [Your Personal Taboo]. A Scapegoat. [Turn your back on this figure. Turn your back on evil things.]

OPENING VERSE

Three double dots and a single near the bottom. The thirteenth elder has bitten the dust. And don't look now, but it is Oturupon, the Difficult One to Read . . . the Very Clever. Surely it is Eshu—the Trickster—who speaks through him. Better hear him out! But weigh every word this time! He says there's an opportunity you should not pass up. But he likes to kid around—and you will have to make up your own mind.

For DESTINY readings. You were born to strive for (and after) the things you want. You were born to want to improve your lot. But you are not always as lucky as you would like. Things do not always come easy, my friend. And luck matters to the things you are going after. Ifa says your female name is ONI—"The Desired." Ifa says your male name is MONGO—"The Famous." Where you stand right now is with your back turned to this sign. Don't take these things at face value. You will have to read between these lines.

For SPIRITUAL questions. It is like dogs coupling. Turn your back on such things, look the other way, and try not to laugh too hard behind your hand. Take your cues from Eshu. Let Eshu—the practical joker—be your guide. You are the hyena. See the humor in even the most serious things. But strive for common decency. *If you are 13, 29, 45, 61, 77, 93, 109—having come of this age, you will discover a new level of sensuality.*

For WORK questions. What's in it for you? Not much in this pit of a place. What will you get? A helping hand out. A new job??? I'd say you could use one. Keep your ears open for an opportunity that otherwise might pass you by. It is your ticket out. What do you have coming to you? Something better than this. What will be in your pay? It really doesn't matter . . . there are larger, overriding factors here.

For LOVE questions. You are like the hyenas. You run with a pack of "friends." But by the way you are constantly cutting on each other, it's hard to tell if you are friends or rivals. In a man, they all look the same to you—and they could hardly matter less. In a woman, you will defer to the one with the higher rank. You lead an active social life together. And you are always laughing. Your taboo is this: Do not tickle yourself . . . in only the one spot.

For MONEY questions. What's in it for you? A cut in pay, I'm afraid—if you don't protect yourself. What will you get? As little as they can get away with. A blessing of money comes first to those who insist upon it and won't work for less. Can you be so bold as to demand a higher wage? Can you be so meek as to take whatever they are willing to give? What kind of pit is that to dig for yourself?

For STRATEGY questions. You are in a situation wherein everything you do only seems to make things worse. Your challenge is to turn this trend around. You are in over your head. You are up to your knees. And you will probably need some help to get out. I suggest you sacrifice your pride and take the hand that is offered you . . . no matter what relative it is. Go no further into the trap you have dug.

IKA

African Names *(Ifa)*	Ika
Ifa Rank	**14**
American Name *(Santeria)*	Metanla
Part I Figure *(erindinlogun)*	**13** Shells *owo eeta laa*
African Spirit	Yemoja

KEYWORDS: The Snare. Fingers. Tendrils. The Dark of the Moon. Thickets. The Forest Floor. Creeping Vines. Snakes. Magic and Countermagic. Resistance. Perseverance. Caution.

OPENING VERSE

Three double dots and a single near the top. It is the fourteenth elder that has fallen to this dust. It is Ika—the Sinister—that has come this time to pass. And it is the Wicked Witches of the Forest Floor who want to speak—all at once. And in cacophony. Close your ears! And hum! There are people out there who want to trap you into doing things against your will. Vote them out of office at the next opportunity.

For DESTINY readings. You were born to use your wits and wisdom. You were born, my friend, to use your head to survive. You are lucky at spotting danger from a mile away. You are lucky at escaping those who would make you their prey. Ifa says your female name is NDULU—"The Dove." Ifa says your male name is AREN—"The Eagle." And thus, with these wings, you have the power to escape. Where you stand right now is knee-deep in a place you do not wish to remain for long. Stay calm. But now is the time to file calmly toward the nearest exit sign (and don't forget it may be behind you).

For SPIRITUAL questions. It is like chimpanzees chattering in the trees. Everyone must look out for everyone else. And if danger threatens, you must not forget to warn the rest. Take your cues from Yemoja, the Mother of Us All. Take care of your brothers and sisters. Let Yemoja be your guide. Take your cues from the chimps. Avoid the snakes. *If you are 14, 30, 46, 62, 72, 94, 110—having come of this age, you are ready to take on new responsibilities.*

For WORK questions. What's in it for you? The power to make a name for yourself. What will you get? The reputation you deserve. A new job, perhaps? If it gives you more power, yes. Otherwise pass it up. What do you have coming to you? All that you have the power to get. What will be in your pay? More than you probably deserve, but if you can get away with it, hey. All power to you.

For LOVE questions. You are like snakes. And when you get together you like to dance. It only adds to the sensuous mood . . . and the moonlight. In a woman you like the one who undulates. In a man you like the ones who are oh so smooth. The two of you go arm in arm into the bushes to entwine. And the rest is secret. Your taboo is this: Do not caress your own skin . . . so much it sheds.

For MONEY questions. What's in it for you? Ill-gotten gains that do not taste so good. What will you get? Exactly what you wanted, but at a fairly big price. A blessing of money will come to those who know how to perform magic. But the money that comes that way will not do anybody any good and it will not last. It is better to do things in an honest way.

For STRATEGY questions. You are in a situation wherein things are not exactly as they seem. Someone has deluded you some way, perhaps. You are not seeing things straight. Your challenge is to escape the hooks that someone has in you. Something is holding you back. Something is holding you down. Hint?? It's probably you. Sacrifice?? Yes, give up a foolish belief.

OSHE

African Name (*Ifa*)	Oshe
Ifa Rank	**15**
American Name (*Santeria*)	Oche
Part I Figure (*erindinlogun*)	**5** Shells *owo aarun*
African Spirit	Oshun

KEYWORDS: Violation. Abuse. Victimization. A Deep, Dark Secret. Remorse. Feelings of Guilt. Alternatively, Setting Things Right Again. Beating Ifa. Defeating Ifa. Overcoming the Things Others Have Done to You. High Tide.

<u>OPENING VERSE</u>

A single dot and a double. A single dot and a double. Two single dots alternating with two doubles—working from the top down. A stick doll is drawn. And the fifteenth elder falls on the board. It is Oshe, the Victim of Incest. And it is Oshun—the Spirit of the River in the Dry Season—that speaks now through her parched lips. Better hear her out! She is saying there is a price to pay for everything you do that you shouldn't do . . . even if it wasn't your idea . . . even if it really wasn't your fault. So take care.

For DESTINY readings. You were born to be resilient. You were born to be able to bounce back. You are lucky at keeping your feelings under control. You are lucky at holding on to your dignity, even in disgrace. You are lucky at making a comeback. Ifa says your female name is FOLA—"Honor." Ifa says your male name is ZBENJO—"Avoid Sin." Where you stand right now is at a decision point. Now is the time to correct what went wrong. Now is the time to set things straight . . . and move on. Here's to a speedy recovery.

For SPIRITUAL questions. It is like a frog with you. Every male in the area would have you—even if against your will, not that you feel you have any left. Take your cues from Oshun. Let the River Goddess be your guide. Run around the things that block your passage. Stay ahead of the things that come up from behind you. *If you are 15, 31, 47, 63, 79, 95, 111—having come of this age, you are vulnerable.*

For WORK questions. What's in it for you? A hostile workplace, I'm afraid . . . incestuous in a way . . . and nowhere you'd really like to be. What will you get? A better offer if you can hold out long enough. A new job? It's your only real hope of escaping where you are. What do you have coming to you? It's all on the other side of the fence. All you have to do is figure out how to get there. What will be in your pay? Security.

For LOVE questions. You are like the frogs. You are always croaking at one another. You are always hopping all over each other. And it all seems so repetitive sometimes. Still, the two of you hang on. In a man, you go for the guy with the deep voice. In a woman, you go for the one you can wrap your arms around. It's a kissy, huggy relationship, all right. But be careful not to squeeze too hard. Your taboo is this: Do not puff yourself up . . .unless you also plan to pump.

For MONEY questions. What's in it for you? Plenty if you defeat the odds against it. What will you get? Much more than you think possible right now. But you will have to play to win. A blessing of money will come to you. But more important this time, a blessing of honor will accompany it. In this case, money really does set you free . . . on all accounts. Perhaps you should consider selling your story?

For STRATEGY questions. You are in a situation wherein you are truly the underdog. Your challenge is to get back on your own two feet. Regain your dignity. And start a new life. In an oppressive situation, the only way out is to get out—even though that, too, may be a scary proposition. Weigh your alternatives. Choose among your choices with the bones. Sacrifice. And receive your remedy. But mostly pray.

OFUN

African Name (*Ifa*)	Ofun
Ifa Rank	16
American Name (*Santeria*)	Ofun Mafun
Part I Figure (*erindinlogun*)	10 Shells *owo eewaa*
African Spirit	Babalu Aye

KEYWORDS: Taboo. The Thing You are Not Supposed to Do. Chalk. Red Powder. Charcoal. Mud. The Thing You Must Do To Make Things Right. Also, The Fallen Hero. The Leader Who Has Lost His Place. Low Tide.

OPENING VERSE

A double dot and a single. A double dot and a single. Two double dots alternating with two singles—working from the top down. A person standing on his head is drawn in the dust, and the sixteenth and final elder falls on the tray. It is Ofun, the Perpetrator of Incest and the Breaker of Taboo. It is Babalu Aye—the Spirit of the Gong-Gonger of Death—that takes this chance to speak. But do not fear. Hear him out! He says honor your taboo. Stay away from what is forbidden you. And that is how you will not only survive in the days and years ahead, but you will be able to hold up your head.

For DESTINY readings. You were born to be set apart. You were born to stand out—and let it not be like a sore thumb! You are lucky at keeping your secrets to yourself (at least for a little while). You are lucky at pressing your luck (at least until you get caught!) Ifa says your male name is OBASI—"In Honor of the Supreme God." Ifa says your female name is KAMBIRI—"Allow Me to Join this Family." Where you stand right now is on the outside, looking in. You will have to prove that you are worthy to resume your place in line. Strive for right action at all times.

For SPIRITUAL questions. It is like a crocodile with you. Everything around you is carnivorous. Everything is cold-blooded. Take your cues from Babalu Aye. Let Baba be your guide. In this world of prey and predators, it is the strong that survive. *If you are 16, 32, 48, 64, 80, 96, 112—having come of this age, there is no telling what you might feel compelled to do.*

For WORK questions. What's in it for you? You are risking it all, my friend. You are stepping over the line. What will you get? Maybe away with it . . . but not forever . . . if not for long. A new job?? Pressing license plates perhaps. Or posing for your picture in the tabloids. What do you have coming to you? Exactly the sentence you deserve. What will be in your pay? Not much. But it is three square meals a day. And maybe even cable.

For LOVE questions. You are like the crocodiles. You are always snapping your jowls. You are always hurling low blows. You are always hitting it off. In a man you go for the one who could abuse you, yet doesn't. In a woman, you want the one who lets you feel like the man. Though it's kind of passé and a little old hat, whatever turns you on, my friend. Your taboo is this: Do not abuse yourself . . . by mistake.

For MONEY questions. What's in it for you? Everything. Nothing. You risk big this time. What will you get? Certainly not what you've bargained for. Alimony. Child support. Or other damages. A blessing of money may yet come to someone from a lawsuit, even if it's settled out of court. But are you the plaintiff or the defendant? You may have to spend money to save money in the end. (Careful it all doesn't go to the lawyers.)

For STRATEGY questions. You have gotten yourself into a bad situation this time. You've messed up . . . screwed up . . . maybe even fucked up. And the only way out would seem to be to fess up. But I'm not an attorney-at-law. And you'd be best off to consult one, right about now. The only final advice I have to give—and this is my counsel—is to sacrifice, my friend. Pay the price. And get on with your life.

The Combinations

OGBE'S FAMILY

Everything always goes right with Ogbe's Twins. Everything always turns out for the best. Because Ogbe's family knows the secrets . . . the secrets of the palm nuts . . . and the secrets of sacrifice.

Combinations of Ogbe

Eji Ogbe   Rank   1

Greetings. It is little by little that we learn to divine. It is bit by bit that the figures of Ifa are picked up. And it is only practice that makes the palm nuts beat smoothly through our hands. Ifa says that there is no escaping the inevitable. Therefore, you should do your own thing. You should hoe, seed, and tend the row you were given . . . the row you asked for. Ifa says your mission is important. You will be able to finish what you start. Sacrifice. And get with it.

Ogbe Oyeku   Rank   18

Greetings. It is not with the cowries that the truth is found. It is not by casting cowries on the ground that the right answer is found. Though you remove your clothes and practice stark naked . . . it does not open you up. Though like a lion you urinate in a circle around yourself, it does not keep danger out. Ifa says you can avoid any evil that might await you by making the right sacrifice.

Ogbe Iwori   Rank   19

Greetings. How would you rather come to earth then? As a bird that boys throw stones at? As a palm nut that is beaten for its oil? Or as a spirit that can safely dwell forevermore? Take care of the soul that is living behind your forehead right now . . . and let your Guardian Angel do the rest. Make a sacrifice to yourself. Sacrifice to your own head. Pamper your spirit. May it go on and on forever and ever.

Ogbe Odi   Rank   20

Greetings. A menstruating woman cannot conceive. A man who wants to make love to a menstruating woman will not be successful in fathering a child. Ifa says you must do the right things at the right times. You must avoid doing the wrong things at any time. Something is getting in the way of your success. Something is preventing you from achieving the destiny you would like. You must sacrifice so that you may have the "child" you wish. You must sacrifice so that you may give birth to your dream.

Ogbe Obara   Rank   21

Greetings. Rain touches heaven. Rain touches earth. And the rainbow makes a bridge between the two. Ifa says your spiritual double in heaven is looking out for you. Ifa says that your spiritual double will save you from losing what otherwise might be temporary gains. Ifa says you will not lose your position. Sacrifice to the part of your soul that has remained behind in heaven, so that it might send you advice in a dream.

Ogbe Okanran   Rank   22

Greetings. Rain touches earth. Rain touches heaven. And the lightning bolt unites the two. Ifa says you were born to be a diviner. Ifa says the God of the sky himself arranged for you to come here. Your destiny is to beat the palm nuts. Everything else you need to decide will be revealed through them. Ifa says the one and only God decrees it. You are being led by him (or her). Sacrifice in the way the palm nuts point, and all will be right with your world.

Ogbe Irosun   Rank   23

Greetings. The dust of the divining tray speaks. The dust of the diving tray whispers the message. The figures come quickly and are as swiftly wiped away. And you must listen carefully, for they speak fast when they are talking. And for you they are talking tonight. Voices are quavering. Breasts are quivering. Take care that the one you make love to is also the one you love. Sacrifice for them. They, too, belong to Ifa. Read for them.

Ogbe Owonrin   Rank   24

Greetings. The forces are at work. The forces are constricting you. The forces are restraining you. The forces are holding you back. Ifa says no evil eye can stop you. Ifa says no magic can bind you, trap you, make you do what you do not wish to do. Sacrifice and the forces attempting to work against you will be dispelled. The road will be opened. The way will be cleared.

317

Ogbe Ogunda   Rank   25

Greetings. Ifa says that a man's penis is doing his thinking for him. Ifa says that a man is letting his penis make his decisions for him. Ifa says a man's penis is setting his limits for him. Sacrifice, lest this penis fail from too much use. Sacrifice, lest injury is done to the one you love. Ifa says there is a way around everything. Ifa says you must regain control of your head.

Ogbe Osa   Rank   26

Greetings. What we hear is what we want to hear. What we see is what we choose to see. We hear things that are loud. We do not hear things that are soft. We see things that are near to us. We do not see things that are removed. Ifa says that the things you want must be done quietly and secretly. It is like two people making love. You do not need an audience. Sacrifice so that what you do in private will serve you well in public.

Ogbe Irete   Rank   27

Greetings. You never know until all is said and done. Though things may look difficult right now, the gods are on your side. And you have their ear tonight. Ifa says there is no such thing as an irreversible decision. Ifa says an apparent misfortune can be turned around yet. Sacrifice. And soon you will see the sheer coincidence. Sacrifice. And soon you will see all the pieces falling into their proper place. And you will know that for it all to work out, you had to stop here first.

Ogbe Otura   Rank   28

Greetings. You who carry the weight of others . . . you who take on the burden of others for yourself . . . Ifa says you will not always be an apprentice in this house of mysteries. You will not always be a servant to another. Ifa says your days of slaving for another diviner are almost through. Sacrifice. And you will not play the part of the servant . . . anymore.

318

Ogbe Oturupon   Rank   29

Greetings. Let us bow our heads. Let us turn inward. Let us look the other way. Where dogs are fucking, let's not watch. Ifa says that something is going on in your life that no one knows about but you. Ifa says that it's nobody's business, not even his. But Ifa offers this friendly word of advice. Avoid evil. Do not cheat on yourself. Sacrifice.

Ogbe Ika   Rank   30

Greetings. Night comes and we crawl into our sleeping bags. Day breaks and we roll them back up. There is someone here who wants to go home, wherever that is. Ifa says this is the Ogbe that wants to go home . . . for the night has been long, and enough absence has been felt in the dark and silence. Who needs a reminder of such fear? Sacrifice. And you will reach your destination faster than you think. Sacrifice. And you will avoid the bad things that might cross your path yet.

Ogbe Oshe   Rank   31

Greetings. The palm nuts are beaten in the hand. The palm nuts are beaten. And in beating them, all vile intentions are beaten. All bad things are defeated. All evil is overcome. Ifa says you must beat the palm nuts hard tonight, for there is something in your own life that must be defeated. There is something that must be overcome . . . and now. Sacrifice, my friend. And you will gain the strength to stand up against your enemies . . . even if they claim to be your relatives and friends.

Ogbe Ofun   Rank   32

Greetings. It is good you came. For the figure we call Pale Ogbe is on the mat. Take care at that. And mind your head . . . which is confused . . . troubled . . . even disturbed about something. Mind your head, which is in its muddled state; the voice of reason cannot get a word in edgewise. Ifa says there is no trouble that cannot be untangled. There is no web so tight it cannot be straightened out into a thread. Ifa says you must sacrifice completely. And then your head will clear and you will know.

OYEKU'S FAMILY

Oyeku's children are always getting into trouble. Oyeku's children are always having things happen to them. Oyeku's children are always having sad stories to tell. But each and every time, Ifa bails them out. All they have to do is make their sacrifice.

Combinations of Oyeku

Oyeku Ogbe   Rank   33

Greetings. Oyeku next to Ogbe has a story to tell about someone who was very ill once but recovered. Oyeku next to Ogbe has a story to tell about a woman who almost died, but fooled her would-be mourners. Ifa says that the problem you face may be dire. You may be in despair. But it will pass. For the gods have something to say in this. Say a prayer to your Guardian Angel that your soul not be taken from you in this long night. Sacrifice. And everything will be all right.

Oyeku Meji   Rank   2

Greetings. Would you defecate by the side of the road? Would you defecate in the field? Or would you rather defecate at home? Ifa says you should relieve yourself of some great burden you bear. Ifa says that a stranger is coming. We must let this stranger defecate in our house. For we never know what blessing he might give us in the morning. Ifa says, dung happens. Sacrifice. And take it in your stride.

320

Oyeku Iwori — Rank 34

Greetings. Vibrating Oyeku is what we call the figure you have cast. Vibrating Oyeku feels her baby kicking inside. Vibrating Oyeku feels her baby trying to get out. But it is not time yet. Ifa says there is a soul that wants to live in you. Ifa says a soul is vibrating inside you. Sacrifice. And take care of yourself. There is a soul that wants to live . . . it is yours . . . and only you can give it birth.

Oyeku Odi — Rank 35

Greetings. Oyeku Who Is Dead from the Waist Down is what we call this figure, for here is a man who's penis has failed him; and he cannot perform. Ifa says someone of power has grown impotent and ineffective. Ifa says someone who had power once has lost it. Ifa says someone who has taken a hard position in the past has softened on it. Sacrifice that your vitality might be restored. Sacrifice so that you might achieve your full potential. Sacrifice so that you might see your child.

Oyeku Obara — Rank 36

Greetings. Oyeku Who Is Transparent is what we call this figure, for no sooner is it born than the rainbow fades. No sooner is the baby born than the child it was has grown up. No sooner is the young girl a woman than her old breasts hang to her waist; and the boy no sooner a man than he stands hunched over his shriveled manhood. Ifa says these days are numbered. Ifa says all things are meant to pass. Ifa says it is a blessing to walk bent over with old age. Sacrifice. And so be it.

Oyeku Okanran — Rank 37

Greetings. The Flashing Oyeku is what we call this figure, for it is fast as a lion on the savannah. It is fast as the antelope that tries to get away. It is faster than lightning when Shango decides to strike. Ifa says that in the end everything passes too quickly. Ifa says that everything is happening too fast. What is it you are hurrying to? Sacrifice, my friend. But without delay. I know that you can find the time.

Oyeku Irosun　　　　Rank　38

Greetings. The Red Oyeku is what we call this figure, for whatever it is that's irritating you, your eyes have turned red . . . whatever it is that's bothering you has caused your skin to break out. Ifa says to dry your tears on the sleeve of your robe. Ifa says to wipe your eyes so that what is bothering you is wiped clear. Sacrifice. Then rub your skin with oil. And take a nice, warm bath.

Oyeku Owonrin　　　　Rank　39

Greetings. But watch out for the snakes! For there are those who look casually into the eye of their enemies. Watch out for the snakes! For there are those who stick their necks out . . . for yours. Constricting Oyeku we call it. Ifa says that something has coiled around you. Ifa says that something has wrapped itself around your happiness and is squeezing the life out of you. Sacrifice. And get this python off your back, before it unlocks its jaws and moves in on the meal.

Oyeku Ogunda　　　　Rank　40

Greetings. We call this figure Oyeku of the Loincloth, for it talks about something that is being kept hidden under clothes. It talks about something going on in your life that is not entirely aboveboard. Ifa says that a penis—though it be hidden—is still a distraction. Ifa says you are being distracted by the thing that is hidden beneath your clothes. Sacrifice. And get naked.

Oyeku Osa　　　　Rank　41

Greetings. The Virgin Oyeku is what we call this figure. It speaks about an opening that is kept closed. It speaks of a woman who wants to, but cannot have a child. It talks about any blessing that refuses to come. Ifa says that this person should sacrifice, so that the way may be opened. Ifa says that this person should sacrifice, so that a blessing that has refused to, comes.

⠞ ⠿   *Oyeku Irete*   Rank   42

Greetings. Oyeku of the Creepers is what we call this figure. Ifa says a worm has no teeth. Ifa sails a snail will not bite. No one should be afraid of worm. No one should be afraid of snail. Ifa says, had worm only sacrificed! Ifa says, had snail only paid the price! Then people would not despise them so. Ifa says someone is showing contempt for you. Sacrifice. Or else remain a worm. Sacrifice. Or else retreat into your shell.

⠅ ⠿   *Oyeku Otura*   Rank   43

Greetings. Oyeku of the Crossroads is what we call this figure. For this is not a subject of the marketplace. This is not a subject of the farm. Not even a household is involved. Ifa says that something is lurking in your own backyard. Ifa says something is still bothering you from behind. Ifa says there is a sacrifice—or two—to leave along your Road. Ifa says there is still a price to pay for something that is long done, past, and should be gone. Sacrifice. And let it alone.

⠭ ⠿   *Oyeku Oturupon*   Rank   44

Greetings. Oyeku of the Mask is what we call this figure. For it would be impolite to show your face at a time like this. Ifa says that there is a test you must pass. Ifa says there is a trial you must go through. There is a rite of passage you must undergo. Ifa says that death does not accept your bribe and then take you. Sacrifice, so that you might prove your level of endurance. Sacrifice, so that you might improve your stamina.

⠭ ⠿   *Oyeku Ika*   Rank   45

Greetings. Oyeku of the Forest is what we call this figure, for this is where Oyeku Ika lives . . . among the trees and creeping vines . . .

among the tangles of the forest floor. Ifa says it is not safe to walk around here, especially barefoot. Ifa says there is something here you do not want to step in. Ifa says there is something you do not want to stumble upon. Ifa says some secrets are best kept by their keepers. Sacrifice, lest you find out something you did not want to know.

⠃ ⠿ Oyeku Oshe   Rank   46

Greetings. Oyeku the Avenger is what we call this figure, for this Odu talks about Oyeku having her revenge. Ifa says it is good to beat palm nuts and laugh. Ifa says it is good to laugh and beat Ifa at Ifa's own game. Sacrifice, so that you might turn the tables on those who play you for the fool. Sacrifice so that you might overcome those who humiliate you. Sacrifice so that you might outshine those who ridicule you. Sacrifice, so that you might have the last laugh . . . on them.

⠅ ⠿ Oyeku Ofun   Rank   47

Greetings. The Toppled Oyeku is what we call this figure, for it talks about someone who has been stood on his head. Ifa says that someone in power falls on account of inner weakness. Ifa says that a person of great status is inclined to blow it. Ifa says Oyeku should have sacrificed in order to avoid this end. Ifa says you should sacrifice too, my friend.

IWORI'S FAMILY

Iwori's children are always running out of energy. Iwori's children are always having to restore their strength. Iwori's family is used to it. They have to fight constantly to stay in third place. Lucky they know how to sacrifice.

Combinations of Iwori

Iwori Ogbe   **Rank   48**

Greetings. Let us praise Iwori Ogbe: Iwori that Makes a Sacrifice in Advance. Ifa says that the truth shall be known through the palm nuts. Ifa says that through these palm nuts you will know in advance what you must do to assure blessings. Ifa says to sacrifice even when nothing is wrong with your life. Ifa says to sacrifice in order to keep the blessings coming into your life.

Iwori Oyeku   **Rank   49**

Greetings. Let us praise Iwori Oyeku: Iwori that Makes a Sacrifice After the Fact. Ifa says come here. Ifa says come here troubled. Ifa says come here distressed. Ifa says it is better to sacrifice sooner than later. It is better to come later than not at all. Ifa says it is not too late to make things better. Ifa says this is your second chance to sacrifice. Shall it be now? Or never?

Iwori Meji   **Rank   3**

Greetings. Let us praise Iwori Meji: Iwori that Fathers a Child. Ifa says things do not come out of nowhere. Ifa says good things do not come out of nothing. It is by having sex that a child is born . . . it is by making love. Ifa says there is an energy in your groin. There is a power in your loins. There is a force in your pelvis. Ifa says you must be a channeler of sexual energy. Ifa says you should energize each other. Ifa says the two of you should come together. But first sacrifice.

Iwori Odi   **Rank   50**

Greetings. Let us praise Iwori Odi: Iwori of Miracles. Why do you grieve for the money you do not have yet? Ifa says it will come by miracles. Why do you ask for the house you do not own yet? Ifa says it will come by miracles. Why do you grieve for the child you have not had yet? Ifa says it will all come to you . . . food, clothing, shelter, and a long life . . . by miracles. And therefore, sacrifice, so that miracles may play a part in your life.

Iwori Obara   Rank   51

Greetings. Let us praise Iwori Obara: Iwori of the Skies. As it is ordained on high, thus shall it be below. The hand that set the clouds in motion . . . the hand that changes the shape of the clouds . . . is the same hand that has set you on your road . . . the same hand that changes you along the way. Ifa says it is a question of the destiny you were given when you asked. Sacrifice so that your destiny might be fulfilled.

Iwori Okanran   Rank   52

Greetings. Let us praise Iwori Okanran: Iwori of the Storm. Ifa says smoke is fire's glory. Ifa says dust and bending grass belong to wind. Ifa says lightning is the glory of rain. Ifa says sacrifice to Shango . . . and that wife of his, Oya . . . so that two who quarrel with one another may yet work together. Sacrifice, so that the two of you may achieve your common glory.

Iwori Irosun   Rank   53

Greetings. Let us praise Iwori Irosun: Iwori of the Flame. Ifa says a woman has seen red. She has seen the red color of the embers. She has seen the red color of the sunset. She has seen the red color of the moon eclipsing. Ifa says a woman does not need to see the red beads on the wrist of a child that is not hers. Ifa says a woman does not need to be reminded that she is still menstruating. Sacrifice, so that a woman may not see red.

Iwori Owonrin   Rank   54

Greetings. Let us praise Iwori Owonrin: Iwori of the Mist. Drizzle settles on the sea and fogs your vision. Dew wets the surface of a lagoon, but will not cling to your eyelashes. Ifa says you should see straight. Ifa says you should splash cold water in your face. Ifa says you should sacrifice, lest you see some evil on the Road you are on.

Iwori Ogunda Rank 55

Greetings. Let us praise Iwori Ogunda: Iwori with His Trousers On. Ifa says there is a man who would like to have sex, but he is keeping his penis inside his pants. No good can come of it there. Ifa says there is something you want to do, but you are keeping yourself from doing it. There is some energy that needs to be released. Sacrifice. And why don't you just drop those pants. . . .

Iwori Osa Rank 56

Greetings. Let us praise Iwori Osa: Iwori with her Legs Crossed. Ifa says there is a woman who is keeping her breasts covered. There is a woman who has wrapped sashes around her waist. Ifa says there is someone who is ashamed of her vagina. No good can come of this. Ifa says someone has erected a false barrier around herself. Ifa says someone is holding things inside herself. Ifa says, sacrifice, so that you might open yourself to the possibilities. Sacrifice, so that you might know your potential.

Iwori Irete Rank 57

Greetings. Let us praise Iwori Irete: Iwori Who Needs a Helping Hand. Ifa says! Ifa says a sacrifice should be something to eat. Ifa says a sacrifice should be something to drink. Ifa says a sacrifice should be the clothes on your back. Ifa says a sacrifice should be six- pence. I say there is someone who will ask you for money on the street. I say give her your spare change. I say spare a buck if you've got one. Sacrifice. And generate some positive energy around yourself.

Iwori Otura Rank 58

Greetings. Let us praise Iwori Otura: Iwori of the Sacred Cross. Ifa says there are 165 kinds of trees. Ifa says there are 256 combinations

... 256 possible roads ... 256 rows to hoe ... 256 ways to go. Ifa says there are 400 deities. Ifa says you must be yourself. Ifa says you must follow your own Road. Sacrifice in doing so. And your energy will only grow.

⚇ ⚇ Iwori Oturupon Rank 59

Greetings. Let us praise Iwori Oturupon: Iwori of the Excrement. Ifa says a dog lifts its leg. Ifa says a dog urinates from its belly. Ifa says a dog turns in circles before it squats to defecate. Ifa says, turn your head. Ifa says, look the other way. Avoid the negative energy around here. Ifa says, sacrifice. And—even so—watch where you step.

⚇ ⚇ Iwori Ika Rank 60

Greetings. Let us praise Iwori Ika: Iwori of the Bones. Ifa says you should choose. You should choose among your choices. You should choose among your alternatives. Ifa says you should use your bones to decide. No diviner who does not is worth his salt. Do not pay for bad advice. Do what your bones tell you to do. Sacrifice. And gain the strength to make your choice.

⚇ ⚇ Iwori Oshe Rank 61

Greetings. Let us praise Iwori Oshe: Iwori of the House. Thin walls do not let you see what you are listening to. Thin walls obstruct the view, but not the noise of the neighbors. Ifa says there is something going on here that does not meet the eye. Ifa says there is something going on here that you are a party to anyway. Ifa says everyone involved should sacrifice. Only then will walls do their work. Only then will your energies not be distracted.

⚇ ⚇ Iwori Ofun Rank 62

Greetings. Let us praise Iwori Ofun: Iwori of the Farm. Ifa says it will come back. Ifa says it will return. Even the outcast has his opportunity to prove himself again. Ifa says someone has been slandered. Ifa says it is libelous . . . and deceitful. Ifa says this person will return to the city where he made his name. Ifa says you can make your comeback. Sacrifice. And honor will be restored. Sacrifice. And regain your power. Sacrifice, and your energy will return.

ODI'S FAMILY

Odi's children are always having to contain their problems, which, of course, they do through sacrifice. No wonder, since Odi itself is the "Container of Existence." Containment in this family is a way of life.

Combinations of Odi

Odi Ogbe   Rank   63

Greetings. Odi Ogbe was the one who made Ifa for Perplexed Stranger Who Disbelieved the Diviner. Ifa says if you are not satisfied with the message, ask again. Ifa says if you do not believe in the second message either, turn to the Answers for Part I. And if you are not satisfied with these, best find yourself another diviner! Ifa says that you are having doubts. You are questioning the advice of others. You are questioning others' intentions. Ifa says to sacrifice just in case . . . for that is the way to close the Road to bad things, while letting good things get through. That is the way to contain your doubts.

Odi Oyeku   Rank   64

Greetings. Odi Oyeku was the one who made Ifa for Uncertain Beater of the Palm Nuts, discouraged apprentice. Ifa says if two remain in your palm, mark one. If one remains, mark two. This is the way we do it in Ife, and it is the right way. Ifa says in the matter you have asked about, you are concerned about doing things right (which is good). Ifa says you are anxious to overcome your difficulties (which is good, too). Ifa says the answer is always sacrifice. That is the way to contain bad things.

⁞ ⁞   *Odi Iwori*   Rank   65

Greetings. Odi Iwori was the one who made Ifa for Exhausted Diviner, on the night when he was frustrated by the verses. Ifa says there is something that eludes you. And the harder you work at it, the less it comes. The harder you try to grasp it in the palm of your hand, the harder it is to contain. Ifa says it will happen. Ifa says it will come to you. But first you will need a second wind. Sacrifice, so that the energy you are lacking builds back up and flows through you.

⁞ ⁞   *Odi Meji*   Rank   4

Greetings. Odi Meji was the one who made Ifa for Sky God, when he wanted to dispatch a soul to earth. Ifa says that this child will be someone who uses his head. Ifa says this child's head will find its own destiny. Ifa says there is a specific place you want to go. And when you get there, everything will be good for you. Sacrifice, so that you arrive excellently to your destination. Sacrifice, so that evil is contained along the way. Sacrifice, so that everything you put your head to will turn out good.

⁞ ⁞   *Odi Obara*   Rank   66

Greetings. Odi Obara was the one who made Ifa for Man Who Felt Pangs in His Scrotum, frustrated lover. Ifa says there is someone who wants you as much as you want her (or him). Ifa says this person's soul is already sitting beside yours in heaven. Ifa says even if you have not met yet, your soul will recognize its mate. Sacrifice. So that the two of you may stay united on earth for as long as you possibly can.

⁙ ⁞ ***Odi Okanran***   *Rank*   **67**

Greetings. Odi Okanran was the one who made Ifa for Old Woman Who had Stopped Menstruating Completely, barren womb. Ifa says, I don't care. Ifa says she will conceive anyway. Ifa says something that you thought was impossible will yet come to pass . . . in an instant . . . in a flash. Sacrifice, so that the improbable can become possible for you. Sacrifice so that you may yet be surprised—even at your age.

⁞ ⁙ ***Odi Irosun***   *Rank*   **68**

Greetings. Odi Irosun was the one who made Ifa for Sleepless Eyes, on the night before an important meeting. Ifa says those who lie awake all night know when and where the moon sets. Ifa says those who lie awake all night know when and where the sun comes up. Ifa says your eyes have grown so red from sleeplessness that you had better use some eye drops. Ifa says your head has been so muddled from dreamlessness that you have lost the power to contain your fears. Sacrifice. And try at least to relax.

⁚⁙ ⁞ ***Odi Owonrin***   *Rank*   **69**

Greetings. Odi Owonrin was the one who made Ifa for Free Spirit Kept in Bondage, slave of oppressive master. Ifa says you are being held down by someone. Someone is exerting power over you. Someone is keeping you in your place. Someone is containing you. Sacrifice. And this person will lose his grip. Sacrifice, so that you become a free agent again.

⁞ ⁙ ***Odi Ogunda***   *Rank*   **70**

Greetings. Odi Ogunda was the one who made Ifa for Penis that Provides no Home to Crabs, scrotum that has no fuzz. Ifa says it is better to shave the hair that is your pride than to let it be a container for parasites. Ifa says there is something that is making you itch in places you can't scratch in public. Ifa says something has gotten under your clothes. Something has gotten to your skin. Sacrifice, so that you may contain the spread of this infection.

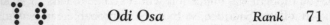 Odi Osa — Rank 71

Greetings. Odi Osa was the one who made Ifa for Buzzing Vagina, who had not been penetrated in over a year. Ifa says no good can come of this. Ifa says you have been keeping your mouth shut for too long. It is time to open up. Ifa says you have contained yourself long enough. It is time to reach out. Ifa says sacrifice, and your period of containment will end. Ifa says sacrifice, and then you will get laid.

Odi Irete — Rank 72

Greetings. Odi Irete was the one who made Ifa for Homeless Person in want of Spare Change. Ifa says the Road to bad things will be closed. The Road to poverty will be closed. The Road to unemployment will be closed. The Road to hunger will be closed. . . . Ifa says all Roads to bad things shall be closed. Ifa says you are in need of closing Roads. Sacrifice. And let the Road to bad things be closed. Let bad things be contained.

Odi Otura — Rank 73

Greetings. Odi Otura was the one who made Ifa for Martyr on the Road to Sainthood, good guy on the way to be hanged from a tree. Ifa says it is one of 16 ways. It is one of 16 fates . . . and 16 Roads. Ifa says you are about to achieve the destiny that is yours alone. Ifa says you are about to determine the destiny of many others at the same time. Sacrifice. Sacrifice. Sacrifice . . . lest others contain you before your life's work is complete.

⠧ ⠶   *Odi Oturupon*   Rank   **74**

Greetings. Odi Oturupon was the one who made Ifa for One Who Drinks Spirits, one who drinks white wine, one who drinks beer. Ifa says there is something that is keeping your head from seeing straight. Ifa says everything is getting blurred together in your head. Ifa says, close your eyes. Ifa says, you are getting sleepy. Ifa says, sacrifice. And in the morning things will be clear. In the morning your thoughts will be contained again.

⠧ ⠶   *Odi Ika*   Rank   **75**

Greetings. Odi Ika was the one who made Ifa for Drum, on the night that he went to the forest to beat loudly. Ifa says BATA-BAM. Ifa says, BATA-BUM. Ifa says the rhythm is calling you. Ifa says your feet are starting to move. BATA-BAM. BATA-BUM. And RAT-TAT-TAT-LE. Ifa says the music has put you in its trance. Ifa says there is a song you cannot get out of your head. Ifa says, listen to the words. Ifa says the lyrics contain your answer tonight. Get the message? Sacrifice. And—now—let's dance.

⠇ ⠶   *Odi Oshe*   Rank   **76**

Greetings. Odi Oshe was the one who made Ifa for Sister of Brotherly Love, on the night when he raped her. Ifa says those who appear to be your friends in public are not as important as those who remain friends behind closed doors. Ifa says those who curse you to your face do not count. Ifa says those who praise you when your back is turned, they count. Sacrifice, so that your friends remain true. Sacrifice so that lust is contained. Sacrifice so that your brother remains a brother to you.

⠧ ⠇   *Odi Ofun*   Rank   **77**

Greetings. Odi Ofun was the one who made Ifa for Downfallen Priest, man who liked young boys. Ifa says there are 16 ways . . . 16

Roads . . . 16 branches, from one of which is hung your "death." Ifa says, contain yourself. Ifa says, honor your taboo. Sacrifice. Reap the rewards of your sensitivity without paying its consequences.

OBARA'S FAMILY

Obara's children are always looking for immediate gratification. Things happen quickly in Obara's house, and all her children are constantly busy. Obara is herself the sign of Roads opening up to people. So it is no surprise that for Obara's children, there are always new avenues to explore.

Combinations of Obara

Obara Ogbe   Rank   78

Greetings. We have come to Obara Ogbe. We have come to the Melon Seed Road, fast track to immediate reward. Ifa says a blessing. Ifa says a blessing is in store. Something that you have been wanting lies just around the bend of the rainbow. Sacrifice, so that you do not miss an opportunity inclined to fade. We have looked at Obara Ogbe; may we get there soon.

Obara Oyeku   Rank   79

Greetings. We have come to Obara Oyeku. We have come to the White Cotton Road, safe exit ramp from imminent danger. Ifa says the storm has passed without killing you. Ifa says a rainbow has appeared in place of what you feared. You have been reprieved . . . again. Ifa says death always comes sudden in the end. But you can avoid it until then. Ifa says, sacrifice so that the inevitable may not

334

come early. We have looked at Obara Oyeku. May we not hear the distant drum . . . anytime soon.

⠃⠃ Obara Iwori   Rank   80

Greetings. We have come to Obara Iwori. We have come to the Road Where Two Paths Meet and then Diverge, place of random greetings. The Melon Seed and White Cotton Roads come together here, and then withdraw again. Ifa says there are two basic alternatives . . . two main ways to go . . . two routes to take to the same place . . . two ways through this. Ifa says you are at the point where you must choose. Ifa says you must pick between alternatives. Sacrifice so that you might choose correctly, left or right. We have seen Obara Iwori. May we not tire before we have collapsed into each other's arms.

⠃⠃ Obara Odi   Rank   81

Greetings. We have come to Obara Odi. We have come to the Calabash Road, path lined with swollen wombs, way of great expectancy. Ifa says things are developing, left and right. Ifa says things are coming along as they should, right and left. Ifa says in the end each birth occurs suddenly, but cannot be hurried until the time is ripe. Sacrifice so that your labor may be brief. We have seen Obara Odi; may our names not die out.

⠃⠃ Obara Meji   Rank   5

Greetings. We have come to Obara Meji. We have come to Parrot Road, the way strewn with bright-colored tail feathers. Red. Orange. Blue. Green. Indigo. And violet. Ifa says this is your moment to shine brightly. Ifa says, put a feather in your cap and shine. Praise comes swiftly when it is due this time. Sacrifice, so that the Powers that Be will eat the scraps you leave and remember you. We have seen Obara Meji; may new Roads open up to us.

⠃⠃ Obara Okanran   Rank   82

Greetings. We have come to Obara Okanran. We have come to the Road Leading to Storm's Approach, place where the sky darkens fast. Ifa says all hell is about to break loose—but only for a while. Ifa says, take cover at first sign of imminent danger. Ifa says, hold up and cover your head. Ifa says we need the rain. Sacrifice so that you are not caught off guard. We have seen Obara Okanran. May we not be struck by hail the size of palm nuts.

Obara Irosun   Rank   83

Greetings. We have come to Obara Irosun. We have come to the Red Dirt Road, way that bleeds instantly in rain, crusts over in sun. Ifa says it is worth the struggle to get where you are going. Ifa says it is worth blood, sweat, and tears. Ifa says it is worth making a sacrifice before you leave for somewhere. Sacrifice, so that the going will get you there in one piece. We have seen Obara Irosun. May the earth not soak up our blood.

Obara Owonrin   Rank   84

Greetings. We have come to Obara Owonrin. We have come to the Bush Cow Road, path littered with dung heaps and buzzing with flies. Ifa says you will need a cowtail switch to keep these bastards from biting your back. Ifa says you will need a fan to keep the stench out of your nostrils. Ifa says there are better ways to go. Sacrifice, so that a cleaner path may open up soon. We have glanced at Obara Owonrin. May it leave only scars of honor on our flesh.

Obara Ogunda   Rank   85

Greetings. We have come to Obara Ogunda. We have come to the Sweet Potato Road, berm scattered with phallic objects. Ifa says, nothing wrong with a big dick. (Who can complain?) Ifa says, nothing wrong with a little one. (Who will ever notice?) And nothing you can do about it now, except perform the best that you can. Sacrifice so that big fellow may not fail at the last moment. Sacrifice so that little fellow may yet stand proud. We have seen Obara Ogunda. May we not suffer too long from embarrassment.

Obara Osa   Rank 86

Greetings. We have come to Obara Osa. We have come to the Marketplace Road, way worn smooth by barefooted women with burdens on their heads. Ifa says a vagina counts children as they pass. One. Two . . . Ifa says a vagina counts the pushes of a penis as fast as the hands count shells. Ifa says there is something you need to get or give . . . buy or sell. Ifa says you must add quickly in your head. Sacrifice so that you may negotiate well. We have seen Obara Osa. May we not be swallowed up by the person taker.

Obara Irete   Rank 87

Greetings. We have come to Obara Irete. We have come to Road where Boys Go Out and Men Return, place of decapitated foreskin. Ifa says these are brief burdens you will have to bear. Ifa says these are short trials and tribulations. Ifa says proud scares will forever remain. It is the small price of admittance you must pay. Sacrifice so that you may prove yourself worthy at the moment of truth. We have seen Obara Irete. May we never forget what a brief lesson has taught us.

Obara Otura   Rank 88

Greetings. We have come to Obara Otura. We have come to Missionary Road, way of the white cannibals. Ifa says death dwells on the lonely savannah with its high grass. And those who do not sacrifice will not come back. If you do not remember your elders, they will not be able to help you now. Sacrifice, so that the ancestors of your people hear your urgent call. We have seen Obara Otura. May no crusader attempt to save us.

Obara Oturupon   Rank 89

Greetings. We have come to Obara Oturupon. We have come to the Road Down to Dump, place where all our wrongs are gathered up.

Ifa says, turn your back to the dung heap. Turn your eyes from the dung-load of trouble you are in. Turn you back and walk quickly away. And don't look back. Sacrifice, so that your troubles will decompose quickly. We have seen Obara Oturupon. May our eyes quit burning.

⸬ ⸬   Obara Ika   Rank   90

Greetings. We have come to Obara Ika. We have come to Road Slippery When Wet, place where sure footing is inclined to fail. Ifa says vines reach out to grab hold of your ankles. Ifa says, if you do not look where you are going, you may find yourself on your buttocks. Sacrifice, or it's your ass. We have looked at Obara Ika. May we foresee danger coming from a distance.

⸬ ⸬   Obara Oshe   Rank   91

Greetings. We have come to Obara Oshe. We have come to Water Bearer's Road, footpath worn thin to river. Many burdens have passed by here on women's heads. Many spirits have been gathered in the colorful cloths of the soul snatchers. Ifa says you are feeling weighted down. Ifa says your spirit is feeling flat. Ifa says, sacrifice, if you would remove the load from your back. We have seen Obara Oshe. May we not be raped on our way through the park.

⸬ ⸬   Obara Ofun   Rank   92

Greetings. We have come to Obara Ofun. We have come to Road that Goes Quickly Down, path that falls off suddenly. Ifa says he sees a madman dancing in silence. Ifa says he sees a crazy son of a bitch dancing without even a drumbeat. Ifa says you have come quickly to the end of your rope. Ifa says you have enough rope to hang yourself. Sacrifice, lest you be arrested further in your development. We have seen Obara Ofun. May we reel ourselves back to reality.

OKANRAN'S FAMILY

Okanran's children are all very musical. They are all very rhythmic, but each dances to a somewhat different beat. Okanran's family is always having to deal with things—like heavy drumming—that repeat and repeat and repeat. It is by sacrifice, they find the way to keep in sync.

Combinations of Okanran

Okanran Ogbe   Rank   93

Greetings. Here is Okanran Ogbe—heart ticking. It's a good sign. Ifa says, Heart, keep doing what you're doing on the inside, and everything will remain fine on the outside. Ifa says, Heart, keep playing your bata drum. *BATA-BUM. BATA-BUM.* Ifa says, take care of yourself, my friend. Ifa says, sacrifice, so that a recurrent blessing might continue unabated. Do you see how Ifa reached this decision? Do you see why Okanran Ogbe has come?

Okanran Oyeku   Rank   94

Greetings. Here is Okanran Oyeku—palpitating pulse. Ifa says there is a beat missing here and there. Ifa says, there is something you are skipping that you should not. Ifa says, sacrifice, so that an intermittent pause in your life might be filled up. Ifa says, sacrifice, so that a recurring alarm does not get ignored. Do you see how Ifa reached this decision? Do you see why Okanran Oyeku has come?

⠿ ⠿ Okanran Iwori   Rank 95

Greetings. Here is Okanran Iwori—bass thumping. Ifa says there is an underlying beat to everything. There is a tempo to life. There is a rhythm that touches your soul. Ifa says, marry the upbeat with the downbeat—harmonize with yourself—and you'll have a hit on your hands. Sacrifice, so that everything comes together for you in time. Do you see how Ifa reached this decision? Do you see why Okanran Iwori has come?

⠿ ⠿ Okanran Odi   Rank 96

Greetings. Here is Okanran Odi—gourd shaking. Ifa says, SHHHH! Ifa says, Shhhh-sha-sha-SHuuuu. Ifa says, sa-sa-sa-something has rattled your nerves. Ifa says, sa-sa-sa-someone has gotten under your skin. Ifa says, sa-sa-sa-something is poking you from the inside. Ifa says, sacrifice, so that a recurrent fear does not make you paranoid. Sacrifice so that existence might be a pleasure. Do you see how Ifa reached this decision? Do you see why Okanran Odi has come?

⠿ ⠿ Okanran Obara   Rank 97

Greetings. Here is Okanran Obara—hand thumping on drum. Hand down, BAM. Hand up, silence. Ifa says to play the drum, you have to know when to strike the head. To play the drum, you have to know when to let up and take your hand away. Ifa says two opposites are involved here. And neither can exist without the other. Ifa says, sacrifice, so that a recurring pattern may continue to recur. Sacrifice so that you—in the throes of drumming—can keep it. Do you see how Ifa reached this decision? Do you see why Okanran Obara has come?

⠿ ⠿ Okanran Meji   Rank 6

Greetings. Here is Okanran Meji—dueling drummers. Ifa says something here, but it's hard to hear above the din of thunderous rapping in the background. (Can someone turn down the volume?) Ifa says something, but it's hard to make out the message for the way it's said. (Can someone fucking help me here?) Ifa says, sacrifice, so that the message you are looking for gets through to you. Sacrifice so that a recurring noise does not confound you. Do you see how Ifa reached this decision? Do you see why Okanran Meji has come?

Okanran Irosun   Rank 98

Greetings. Here is Okanran Irosun—periodic moment of silence. Ifa says lightning does not strike in the dry season. Ifa says the drumming in your head has let up for a while. Ifa says there is a pregnant pause . . . a brief respite . . . a short intermission. Ifa says, sacrifice, so that you might use this time to catch your breath. Sacrifice so that you are ready to begin dancing when the recurrent drumming starts up again. Do you see how Ifa reached this decision? Do you see why Okanran Irosun has come?

Okanran Owonrin   Rank 99

Greetings. Here is Okanran Owonrin—bull-roarer making frightful noise. Ifa says, no need to be really scared. The weird sound you hear is just a test of the emergency broadcasting network. Ifa says cover your ears until this momentary distraction is done and gone. Ifa says, sacrifice, so that a periodic disturbance doesn't last for too long at any one time. Sacrifice, so that by the time it passes, you will only feel relief that it has gone. Do you see how Ifa reached this decision? Do you see why Okanran Owonrin has come?

Okanran Ogunda   Rank 100

Greetings. Here is Okanran Ogunda—cock crow at sunrise. Ifa says penis knows when it is time to get out of bed in the morning. Ifa says cock knows when it is time to crow the alarm for tired penis that sleeps in. Ifa says that you will know when it is time to go forward in the matter you have asked about. Ifa says, sacrifice, so that a recurring call to action does not go unheeded. Sacrifice, so that you might wake refreshed in the morning. Do you see how Ifa reached this decision? Do you see why Okanran Ogunda has come?

⁝ ⁝⁝ Okanran Osa Rank 101

Greetings. Here is Okanran Osa—beat of contractions coming seconds apart. Ifa says pelvis of a woman knows when it is time to issue forth—and no other diviner. Ifa says if all goes well, a child will be born in the tenth month following penis insertion. Ifa says, if you are lucky, it may even be twins! Ifa says, sacrifice, so that the labor you are about to undertake may be completed on time. Sacrifice so that a recurring urge may be fulfilled (for at least a little while). Do you see how Ifa reached this decision? Do you see why Okanran Osa has come?

⁝ ⁝⁝ Okanran Irete Rank 102

Greetings. Here is Okanran Irete—beat of American music. Ifa says nobody gets out of this world without singing the blues. And this is a sad song of woe and misery you sing tonight. Ifa says without the lows, there would be no highs. Sacrifice so that a recurring depression does not set in. Sacrifice so that you might count your blessings as well as your curses. Do you see how Ifa reached this decision? Do you see why Okanran Irete has come?

⁝ ⁝⁝ Okanran Otura Rank 103

Greetings. Here is Okanran Otura—extended beat of dragged-out missionary hymn. Ifa says, put down the book on this one. Put down the book and do your own thing. Ifa says, clap your hands. Ifa says, tap your toes. Ifa says, sway the way the spirit moves you. Ifa says, speak in your own tongue. Ifa says, sacrifice, so that a recurring refrain may not limit your range. Sacrifice so that you may feel the presence of the gods. Do you see how Ifa reached this decision? Do you see why Okanran Otura has come?

⁝⁝ ⁝⁝ Okanran Oturupon Rank 104

Greetings. Here is Okanran Oturupon—pounding beat of intercourse. Ifa says, turn your head (and cough). Ifa says, open wide (and say, Ahhh). Ifa says something has gotten through to you this time. Ifa says something has admitted you. Sacrifice, so that a recurring action does not wear you too thin. Sacrifice so that in the matter you have asked about, there is not much resistance. Do you see how Ifa reached this decision? Do you see why Okanran Oturupon has come? (Did you?)

Okanran Ika   Rank   105

Greetings. Here is Okanran Ika—secret drumbeat overheard from afar. Ifa says something's going on down there. Ifa says something's happening out there. Ifa says someone's up to something that's not perfectly clear. Ifa says you've picked up on the symptoms but not the cure. Sacrifice so that the intermittent signals from a distance are not misunderstood. Sacrifice so that you continue to sleep soundly in your own bed. Do you see how Ifa reached this decision? Do you see why Okanran Ika has come?

Okanran Oshe   Rank   106

Greetings. Here is Okanran Oshe—rhythmic drumming of the waves. Ifa says something you cannot escape is setting your dates for you. Ifa says, something outside your control is setting the rhythm and the pattern of your life. How can you get out from under this "oppression"? Ifa says, no need—for it is the course of Mother Nature that's gotten in your blood this time. But sacrifice anyway, lest something interrupt the recurring beat that's easy for you to dance to. Sacrifice anyway, lest someone try to take your music away. Do you see how Ifa reached this decision? Do you see why Okanran Oshe has come?

Okanran Ofun   Rank   107

Greetings. Here is Okanran Ofun—the bell tinkling. Ifa says there is a bell going off in your head. Ifa says one "rin-win," one "o-kan-ran," is the sound it makes. Ifa says in this case you need all the help you can get. Sacrifice, so that the intermittent clanging of an alarm does not drive you temporarily mad. Sacrifice, so that the pounding in your head might cease. Do you see how Ifa reached this decision? Do you see why Okanran Ofun has come?

IROSUN'S FAMILY

Irosun's children are all shades of red, which is the color of both the Irosun bird and the dust of the Irosun tree (used on the divining board). Irosun's children are always getting into hot water. But through a timely sacrifice, they usually get out before they get too badly burnt. (And if not, there's always camwood salve for them to apply.)

Combinations of Irosun

Irosun Ogbe   Rank   108

Greetings. Irosun Ogbe is written in its own dust. It is red. Very red. And it is getting very hot in here. Ifa says it is good for the crops. Things are growing bigger every night. Ifa says you are having a period of blessings yourself. And things for you are looking up and up. Sacrifice, so that your things keep improving—as they should—for you. You have cast Irosun Ogbe. It is red. Very red.

Irosun Oyeku   Rank   109

Greetings. Irosun Oyeku is written in its own dust. It is red. Very red. Red as blood. Ifa says it is good for the warrior. It is good for his son. Ifa says you are about to have your moment of glory. Ifa says you're next in line to prove your point. Here comes your big chance.

Sacrifice, so that you will not make a fool of yourself in the process. You have cast Irosun Oyeku. It is red. Very red.

⠢ ⠢   *Irosun Iwori*   Rank 110

Greetings. Irosun Iwori is written in its own dust. It is red. Very red. Red as sex feels. Hot as sex is. Ifa says you should never be ashamed to do as nature intended you to do. Ifa says you must pursue your passion, whatever it is. Ifa says diversity is what it's all about. There are 256 different combinations in all. Sacrifice, so that you may discover the 257th. You have cast Irosun Iwori. It is red. Very red.

⠢ ⠢   *Irosun Odi*   Rank 111

Greetings. Irosun Odi is written in its own dust. It is red. Very red. Red as Afterbirth. Ifa says you will experience a short period of recovery now. Mostly what you need is rest. Ifa says your condition will improve day by day now, and you will get more and more sleep. Ifa says we will mark Irosun Odi in the dust of the divining board and then pour the powder into a container as a cure for you. Sacrifice, so that a home remedy actually makes you better. You have cast Irosun Odi. It is red. Very red.

⠢ ⠢   *Irosun Obara*   Rank 112

Greetings. Irosun Obara is written in its own dust. It is red. Very red. Red as the rim of a rainbow. Red as dyed cloth. Ifa says if you've got it, flaunt it. And red is the hallmark of success. Ifa says you should wear red more often, especially if you want to get rich. Put red on your bottom. Put red on your top. Ifa says you should dress for success. Sacrifice so that your favorite clothes do not turn pink in the wash. You have cast Irosun Obara. It is red. Very red.

⠢ ⠢   *Irosun Okanran*   Rank 113

Greetings. Irosun Okanran is written in its own dust. It is red. Very red. Red as warning skies at evening. Ifa says, better lash down the

345

roofing . . . better bring in the wash. Ifa says you're in for some kind of weather, all right. And take this as your sign. Ifa says conditions are about to change suddenly. Sacrifice, so that you are ready to celebrate afterward. You have cast Irosun Okanran. It is red. Very red.

Irosun Meji Rank 7

Greetings. Irosun Meji is written in its own dust. It is red. Very red. Red as divining powder . . . red as camwood dust. Ifa says if you ask for trouble, you will find it here. If you ask for peace, you will find it too. Ifa says you get whatever you ask for . . . wish for . . . beg for . . . hope for . . . fight for. You get whatever you request around here—even Irosun Meji! Sacrifice first, and it will all come easier. You have cast Irosun Meji. It is red. Very red.

Irosun Owonrin Rank 114

Greetings. Irosun Owonrin is written in its own dust. It is red. Very red. Red as hateful eyes. But Ifa says—in this case—two wrongs make a right. In this case, there is sure to be a fight first. Ifa says, learn to stand up for yourself. See red when you must. Sacrifice, so that red does not cause permanent feelings of bitterness. Sacrifice, so that tomorrow you and your foe will be singing each other's praises again. You have cast Irosun Owonrin. It is red. Very red.

Irosun Ogunda Rank 115

Greetings. Irosun Ogunda is written in its own dust. It is red. Very red. Red as the head of a missionary's penis. (Ifa says belated congratulations on your initiation, Brother.) Ifa observes, funny how penis dangles precariously all day yet never falls off. Ifa says, hang in there, friend. Eat okra, oranges, cold water, and long yams. And be sure to sacrifice, so that you remain a healthy specimen for as long as you can. You have cast Irosun Ogunda. It is red. Very red.

Irosun Osa Rank 116

Greetings. Irosun Osa is written in its own dust. It is red. Very red. Red as menstrual blood. Ifa says you are going to start a new period soon . . . a new cycle . . . a new phase. Ifa says things are getting better every day for you. Sacrifice, so that you are not plagued with cramps. Sacrifice, so that one day this blood turns into someone else. You have cast Irosun Osa. It is red. Very red.

Irosun Irete   Rank   117

Greetings. Irosun Irete is written in its own dust. It is red. Very red. Red as eyes that have been crying. Ifa says, dry your tears now. Ifa says he knows. There is something you have not been able to achieve. There is something you have not been able to get. There is something you have not yet accepted. Sacrifice, so that you may avoid further depression and anguish. You have cast Irosun Irete. It is red. Very red.

Irosun Otura   Rank   118

Greetings. Irosun Otura is written in its own dust. It is red. Very red. Red as hellfire and brimstone. Ifa says you should believe what you believe. But in Yorubaland our souls do not have just one shot at it—all or nothing—but they keep coming back to know pleasure and pain. Ifa says you are worried that you are losing your religion. Ifa says, no. Ifa says you are only expanding your horizons. Sacrifice so that you may know your options before you select one. You have cast Irosun Otura. It is red. Very red.

Irosun Oturupon   Rank   119

Greetings. Irosun Oturupon is written in its own dust. It is red. Very red. Red as sore anus burning with hemorrhoids. Red as backside of monkey in heat. Ifa says, I know. It's hard to sit down . . . it's hard to walk . . . it's hard to bend over. Ifa says, I know. The matter that concerns you is a pain in the ass. Sacrifice. And get yourself some soothing ointment or take a hot bath. You have cast Irosun Oturupon. It is red. Very red.

Irosun Ika   Rank   120

Greetings. Irosun Ika is written in its own dust. It is red. Very red. Red as the plumage on a cardinal in mating season. Red as cedar and camwood. Red as fire. Red as disturbing dreams. Ifa says these are not the best signs. But we've got to work with what we've got. And Irosun Ika is what's shown up this time. Ifa says, take care. Take care that you do not get carried away with your beliefs. Take care that you do not get drawn in completely by someone else's version of truth. Ifa says sacrifice, so that you may awaken before a nightmare even begins. You have cast Irosun Ika. It is red. Very red.

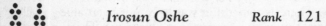

Irosun Oshe   Rank   121

Greetings. Irosun Oshe is written in its own dust. It is red. Very red. Red as the blood of a ruptured hymen. Ifa says in the matter that you asked about, you are a virgin—but not for long. Ifa says you are being too trusting . . . too innocent . . . too naive. Ifa says someone is setting you up . . . someone is making your date with destiny for you. Ifa says sacrifice anything and everything, but never your power of choice. You have cast Irosun Oshe. It is red. Very red.

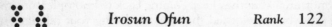

Irosun Ofun   Rank   122

Greetings. Irosun Ofun is written in its own dust. It is red. Very red. Red as potion made with divining dust. Ifa says there is someone who would do anything to get what he (or she) wants. Ifa says there is someone who might even slip you a Mickey before taking you for all you're worth. But even worse than this, Ifa says there are those who will tell you lies to your face. Sacrifice so that you might keep your wits about you at all times. You have cast Irosun Ofun. It is red. Very red.

OWONRIN'S FAMILY

Owonrin's children are always getting into trouble. Owonrin's children are inclined to seek the advice of the oracle, and then ignore it.

They do not always sacrifice as they should—and this only compounds their problems. Still, having learned from their own experience, they should know by now what the solution is.

Combinations of Owonrin

⸬ ⸭   *Owonrin Ogbe*   Rank   123

Greetings. It is the first Owonrin you see on the board. It is Owonrin Ogbe. And it goes like this: Proud Sun, Vain Moon, and Smug Stars did not sacrifice as told by *Babalawo,* Ifa's diviner. What happened? Rain came—obscuring all three. But Colorful Parrot, he sacrificed as told. What happened? His radiant feathers didn't even get wet! Ifa says, truth or consequences, my friend. Take your pick. Sacrifice, so that you might keep your position. Do not sacrifice, and risk being unseated by one who has.

⸬ ⸭   *Owonrin Oyeku*   Rank   124

Greetings. It is the second Owonrin you see on the board. It is Owonrin Oyeku. And it goes like this: Death coming out of the savannah, with his list in hand, arrived at last in town, and hurried to the home of Person Scheduled to Die, but it was too late. Person had already sacrificed. So it goes. Tough luck for Death. Ifa says the *New England Journal of Medicine* is correct. Don't smoke so much. Don't eat too much red meat. Watch your cholesterol intake, control your blood pressure, and who knows how old you might get? Ifa says, sacrifice, so that you might stymie all evil, even unto Death.

⸬ ⸭   *Owonrin Iwori*   Rank   125

Greetings. It is the third Owonrin you see on the board. It is Owonrin Iwori. And it goes like this: There was a woman who was crying when she came to see the diviner. Why? Because hard as she

349

and her husband tried, no child was conceived. Diviner, handing her a hanky, said, do not despair. Sacrifice, he said. Your name will continue. Ifa says you are trying to do something on your own that cannot be accomplished without help. Ifa says, don't bang your head against a brick wall. Sacrifice is called for, that's all. Dig into your pocket and go see a specialist.

Owonrin Odi   Rank   126

Greetings. It is the fourth Owonrin you see on the board. It is Owonrin Odi. And it goes like this: Obstinate Coconut, with a big hole in his head, was told by the diviners to sacrifice so that his milk might stay fresh longer. Obstinate Coconut did not comply. And pretty soon his milk had turned as hard as his head. Ifa says you are being a little too hardheaded yourself. Ifa says you are being cocky and arrogant. Ifa says, I am telling you to sacrifice for longevity . . . for endurance . . . for continuity in your life. But it is your choice, whether you do or don't take my advice.

Owonrin Obara   Rank   127

Greetings. It is the fifth Owonrin you see on the board. It is Owonrin Obara. And it goes like this: Foolish Rainbow went to the diviners, who said to sacrifice if he wanted to linger longer. He did not. Foolish Rainbow said his soul preferred to stay in heaven. Thus he goes on like a child born to die—remaining in one place only briefly. Ifa says you are moving around too much. You are shifting from job to job . . . lover to lover . . . house to house. Ifa says you are putting in appearances, that's all. Sacrifice so that you will be able to commit.

Owonrin Okanran   Rank   128

Greetings. It is the sixth Owonrin you see on the board. It is Owonrin Okanran. And it goes like this: Cocky Rooster, consulting Ifa, was told to sacrifice on account of his constant swearing. Fuck you, he said. And strutted off. When hail came suddenly the next day to pound his wives and children on the head, he thought better, and crowed out to the gods. But the only words he could utter were shhhh-it, gawd-damn, and Gezuus Christ. (Not even the missionary's God answered to this one.) Ifa says you better watch your mouth. Ifa says you better quit giving lip. Sacrifice so that your curses do not circle back to strike your own house.

⋮⋮ ⁝⁝   Owonrin Irosun   Rank   129

Greetings. It is the seventh Owonrin you see on the board. It is Owonrin Irosun. And it goes like this: New Knife, having consulted the diviners in Ife, was told to sacrifice so that he might remain sharp to cut. They told knife to sacrifice, lest he should rust and turn to red. New Knife did as he was told. And that is how he got to complete so much work down at the river and out in the woods. Ifa says there is some work you must do. And you will need to be sharp to pull it off. Sacrifice so that no one catches you slowing down on the job.

⁝⁝ ⁝⁝   Owonrin Meji   Rank   8

Greetings. It is the eighth Owonrin you see on the board. It is Owonrin Meji. And it goes like this: Seashell's Diviner, about to leave on a journey, thought better of trusting her shells and turned instead to Ifa for advice. Sacrifice, said Ifa, so that your journey is productive. Seashell's Diviner did, and that is why her trip paid off so well for her. Ifa says there is somewhere you want to go. There is something you want to do from afar. There is something that needs to be done at a distance. Ifa says, sacrifice, so that the trip is worth the effort.

⋮⋮ ⁝⁝   Owonrin Ogunda   Rank   130

Greetings. It is the ninth Owonrin you see on the board. It is Owonrin Ogunda. And it goes like this: Timid Gun, on his way to protect his family, stopped off at the diviner's to see if he could get the courage to discharge. The diviner told him to make a contribution to his favorite charity so that his voice would ring out loud and clear, if need be. Gun did as he was told, and he was able to get off. Ifa says you are afraid that you cannot live up to others' expectations of you. You are afraid that you cannot do the job. You are afraid you will fail. Ifa says, make a sacrifice and your courage will prevail.

⠒⠒ Owonrin Osa   Rank 131

Greetings. It is the tenth Owonrin you see on the board. It is Owonrin Osa. And it goes like this: Unmarried Woman Seeks Non-smoker went to the diviner to see what she should do. Diviner said, sacrifice lest you marry someone who has a worse habit. Unmarried Woman did not sacrifice and that was how she got a husband who only wanted to eat foods that made him fart. Ifa says you are being influenced too much by what you read in the papers and see on Headline News. Ifa says you are only getting half the story. Sacrifice so that you might know enough to make an informed decision.

⠦⠒ Owonrin Irete   Rank 132

Greetings. It is the eleventh Owonrin you see on the board. It is Owonrin Irete. And it goes like this: Hunter on the trail of a leopard ran into a diviner on the road who told him, sacrifice, so that you may not lose sight of rounded paw prints. Hunter sacrificed on the spot. And that is how he bagged a new area rug for his house. Ifa says you are hot on the trail of something. Ifa says you have the right idea. Ifa says your destiny is waiting around the next bend for you. Sacrifice, so that you might not give up before you reach it.

⠰⠒ Owonrin Otura   Rank 133

Greetings. It is the twelfth Owonrin you see on the board. It is Owonrin Otura. And it goes like this: Defendant on his way to court went to the diviner first to see how he could win his case. Diviner said, sacrifice, and you will be given the words to beat the plaintiff. Defendant sacrificed, and that was how he was able to get off with only a warning this time. Ifa says you are in some kind of trouble that is not too difficult to fix. But you must sacrifice anyway lest your own words come out wrong and cause you to convict yourself.

⠿ ⠇ Owonrin Oturupon   Rank   134

Greetings. It is the thirteenth Owonrin you see on the board. It is Owonrin Oturupon. And it goes like this: Accommodating Hornbill consulted the diviners at Ife before allowing snake to take up residence in his beak. Diviners said, Hornbill, this is a mistake. Hornbill thought better and invited snake into its mouth anyway. And that was how Hornbill was eaten from the inside. Ifa says something on the inside is eating you, too. Ifa says something is eating you up from the inside. Ifa says, learn a lesson from Hornbill, and start sacrificing so that you may quit accommodating your enemies.

⠿ ⠿ Owonrin Ika   Rank   135

Greetings. It is the fourteenth Owonrin you see on the board. It is Owonrin Ika. And it goes like this: Mealy Grub from Forest Floor went to the diviners on a whim, since nothing ailed him, he had plenty of food, and could get as much sex as he wanted. Diviners said, sacrifice anyway. Mealy Grub laughed and walked away. Next year developers came and slashed and burned the woods above his head. Rain suddenly fell where it didn't use to, and Mealy Grub was washed into oblivion. Ifa says one can never be too careful around these parts. Ifa says your life has been too easy and you do not appreciate what is at stake. Ifa says, sacrifice if you want your environment to remain conducive for your continued existence.

⠿ ⠿ Owonrin Oshe   Rank   136

Greetings. It is the fifteenth Owonrin you see on the board. It is Owonrin Oshe. And it goes like this: Sibling of Abusive Brother went for help to the diviners. Sacrifice, they said, and you will be able to overcome this humiliation. Sibling did. Ifa says someone who should love you is playing the part of an enemy. Ifa says you do not have to take it anymore. Ifa says, sacrifice everything but your self-esteem, and you will be able to come out on top.

Owonrin Ofun   Rank 137

Greetings. It is the sixteenth Owonrin you see on the board. It is Owonrin Ofun. And it goes like this: Bitter Child, on his way to exert revenge over others, came to a diviner in the fork of the road. Diviner said, Child, Child. It does not look good. This thing you are up to is not what you ought to do. Bitter Child spat at the diviner and went on. And that is how he wound up losing everything on account of his rage. Ifa says, think once. Think twice. Think three times before speaking. Think thrice before you go through with the thing you are planning. Ifa says, sacrifice, so that you might calm down in time to avert calamity.

OGUNDA'S FAMILY

Ogunda's is a family of many boys. And like many boys, they are inclined to act up from time to time, do what they know they're not supposed to do—exactly what their penises tell them to. But fortunately, when all is said and done, Ogunda's children also know how to pay the price that's due.

Combinations of Ogunda

Ogunda Ogbe   Rank 138

Greetings. Made Ifa for Ogunda Ogbe—he whose penis is long and straight with one eye in its head. Ifa says to penis, can you see anything out of Old One-Eye? Can any of life's blessings be seen from down there? Ifa says to you, you have not been using your own eyes. Or else you would know better. What is behind the question you have asked tonight? Ifa says you are not getting the point. Sacrifice, for good vision.

⠿ ⠇ Ogunda Oyeku   Rank 139

Greetings. Made Ifa for Ogunda Oyeku—penis about to lose foreskin. Ifa says to penis, all it ever did was slither about anyway—and make you itch. Be brave, friend. Ifa says to you, there is something you are clinging on to that you do not need anymore. Sever yourself from a relationship that never was very useful. Any pain there is at first will heal. Sacrifice something you no longer need.

⠿ ⠇ Ogunda Iwori   Rank 140

Greetings. Made Ifa for Ogunda Iwori—penis about to invade married woman's vagina. Ifa says to penis: Better slow down, friend. Are you sure this is your wife? Ifa says to you: Why are you considering having an affair? Ifa says, be careful. These things have a way of getting complicated. Sacrifice, so that you might not be tempted into places better left uninvaded.

⠿ ⠇ Ogunda Odi   Rank 141

Greetings. Made Ifa for Ogunda Iwori—penis who fathers a child. Ifa says to penis: Congratulations, friend. Good job. Nice work. Now, get back in your trousers and go to sleep. Ifa says to you: Your hard efforts are about to pay off in the matter you have asked about. Ifa says you are about to realize the fruits of your labor (if not also your loins). Sacrifice so that this offshoot will be something you will always take pride in.

⠿ ⠇ Ogunda Obara   Rank 142

Greetings. Made Ifa for Ogunda Obara—penis arched in its full glory. Ifa says to penis: It takes all kinds of destinies. It takes all kinds of chances. It takes all kinds of possibilities. Ifa says to you: You are so full of dreams and ideas. You are so full of hope and confidence. And with what you've got going for you, you can do just about anything . . . even spawn a miracle or two. Sacrifice, so that all your hopes and dreams will not go wasted.

Ogunda Okanran   Rank 143

Greetings. Made Ifa for Ogunda Okanran—penis in throes of orgasm. Ifa says to penis: Wow! How do you do that? But please don't stop now to answer. Ifa says to you: There are no words to describe how good you will feel about something that is soon going to happen to you. But let me try. . . . It is agony. It is ecstasy. Both at the same time. Ifa says you are about to be fulfilled. Sacrifice, lest the phone ring at just the right moment to spoil your climax.

Ogunda Irosun   Rank 144

Greetings. Made Ifa for Ogunda Irosun—penis worn thin by too much friction. Ifa says to penis: I'd say you've had enough for now. Here, let me toss you some cocoa butter. Ifa says to you: You, too, have been overstimulated lately . . . overworked . . . overused. And unless you get some rest, you're not going to be worth much to anybody pretty soon. Sacrifice, so that you might pace yourself a little better next time.

Ogunda Owonrin   Rank 145

Greetings. Made Ifa for Ogunda Owonrin—penis that withdraws at the last moment. Ifa says to penis: Well, that's one way to play it safe and avoid arguments later. But you better keep your wits about you and you better be quick. Ifa says to you: There is something you think you can back out of at the last minute. Or there is something you hope to pull off in the final seconds. But either way, you won't know until you get there how you will react and how you will respond. Sacrifice, so that you do not screw things up in the end.

⠃⠃ **Ogunda Meji**   Rank   9

Greetings. Made Ifa for Ogunda Meji—two penises lined up at a urinal. Ifa says to penises: Compare and contrast. It takes all kinds. Just be careful you don't get into a fight. Ifa says to you: There is a standard you feel you have to measure up to. There is a code you feel you must abide. But Ifa says, there are 16 kinds and 256 combinations. Sacrifice, so you do not wind up pigeonholing yourself.

⠊⠃ **Ogunda Osa**   Rank   146

Greetings. Made Ifa for Ogunda Osa—penis about to penetrate vagina. Ifa says to penis: Hold on to your hat. And if you've got protection on you, now's the time to try to get it out of its wrapper. Ifa says to you: There is someone you want to go to bed with. There is someone you want to see naked. There is someone you want to get to know better—on the inside, as well as out. Sacrifice, so that your relationship ends up being something more than this one night.

⠇⠊ **Ogunda Irete**   Rank   147

Greetings. Made Ifa for Ogunda Irete—penis gone limp. Ifa says to penis: Don't let it worry you. It happens to every man once in a while (Eshu's little joke). Ifa says to you: There is something you think you want to do, but you have been frustrated in an early attempt. Don't give up hope. Maybe next time—or the time after that—it will all turn out even better than you hoped. Sacrifice, so that you do not remain powerless and impotent.

⠇⠊ **Ogunda Otura**   Rank   148

Greetings. Made Ifa for Ogunda Otura—disused penis of missionary. Ifa says to penis: Hell-oooo! Is anybody home in there? Sorry to wake you, but it's been quite a while since you stirred. Just wanted to make sure you weren't dead. Ifa says to you: There is a matter of principle involved here. You have taken some kind of oath that you do not want to violate. It's understandable. But even though you have managed to keep your end of the bargain so far, you must continue to sacrifice if you want to hold out much longer.

⠮ ⠦ Ogunda Oturupon   Rank   149

Greetings. Made Ifa for Ogunda Oturupon—grip-locked penis of dog. Ifa says to penis: Just remain calm. Don't panic. In a little while, you'll get your independence back. Ifa says to you: This is a sticky situation you've gotten yourself into. And suffice it to say, you're in it up to your balls. You may even be suffering a moment of embarrassment. Grin and bear it. Sacrifice, lest you be caught with your pants down again.

⠮ ⠦ Ogunda Ika   Rank   150

Greetings. Made Ifa for Ogunda Ika—penis inspired by aphrodisiac. Ifa says to penis: Whatever works for you, friend . . . even if it is labeled "genuine placebo." (I recommend garlic myself, but you'll never get a date.) Ifa says to you: In the matter you have asked about, you are trying to reach new heights . . . set new limits . . . push yourself as far as you can go. And in your pursuit, you seem to be willing to try anything that might help you. Ifa says sacrifice, lest you become overly dependent on artificial sweeteners.

⠮ ⠦ Ogunda Oshe   Rank   151

Greetings. Made Ifa for Ogunda Oshe—penis scratched casually in front of family. Ifa says: Well, if it itches, what the hell. We all understand. Ifa says to you: It is a family matter you have asked about tonight. It is a family affair that brings you here. And in the end only the family can work it out. Sacrifice, so that you do not drive each other crazy in the process.

⠮ ⠦ Ogunda Ofun   Rank   152

Greetings. Made Ifa for Ogunda Ofun—penis being masturbated. Ifa says: Nothing you do could surprise me now. Well, at least it's safe sex. Ifa says to you: There is something you do on a periodic basis that you tell no one about. Yet it is something others also do, at least on occasion, but never admit or discuss. Ifa says there is something to be learned from everything that goes on in our lives—even what happens in the bathroom. Sacrifice, so that you might learn to understand what exactly makes you tick.

OSA'S FAMILY

Osa has a big family—and her children are also giving birth to more and more descendants. Osa's children are always trying to assure that they will bring children of good destiny into the world. And that is why Osa's children are always sacrificing so well.

Combinations of Osa

Osa Ogbe — Rank 153

Greetings. Here is Ogbe, child of Osa—Osa Ogbe by name. And he has this to say: If it is today, then it is not tomorrow. If it is today, it will not be like this tomorrow. If it is tomorrow, it will not be like today. Osa Ogbe was the one who made Ifa for Impaled Female, riding atop male counterpart. Ifa says, everything you do changes everything that results. No act goes unrecognized, and every move you make counts. Ifa says, sacrifice in order to retain your dominant position, whatever tomorrow brings.

Osa Oyeku — Rank 154

Greetings. Here is Oyeku, child of Osa—Osa Oyeku by name. And she has this to say: Each moment that passes is small death. Each day that goes by is small death. Each moon. Each season. Each year. Time going by is small death passing. Osa Oyeku was the one who made Ifa for Female in Menopause, on the day she was crying because she felt she had no future. Ifa says it is not your luck that's gone bad. Ifa says the future is not as bleak as it seems. Sacrifice, so that you may go on now—new with hope. It is just another small death this time; that, too, will pass.

:: : Osa Iwori   Rank 155

Greetings. Here is Iwori, child of Osa—Osa Iwori by name. And he has this to say: Today is not tomorrow. And what a difference a day can make. Osa Iwori was the one who made Ifa for Impregnated Female, on the very day she conceived. Ifa says there are so many children in the world already. But who can say how many souls there are awaiting birth . . . or how many individual destinies? Ifa says, even as your parents were coupling, you were kneeling in heaven requesting the Great Diviner to reveal your future. Get ready now. For it is coming. Get ready. It's coming. It's coming now. It's coming.

:: : Osa Odi   Rank 156

Greetings. Here is Odi, child of Osa—Osa Odi by name. And she has this to say: Nothing comes from nothing. Everything comes from something. Each thing comes into the world, squirming up over the rim of existence. Each thing goes back, feet dragging, at the end. It was Osa Odi who made Ifa for Vagina Stretched by Crowning Head, on the day she was complaining about everything—but especially the prick who did this to her. Ifa says everything is relative in your life right now. And all things are transitory. Nothing's permanent. Sacrifice, so that you might see the blessing in even life's uncertain moments.

:: : Osa Obara   Rank 157

Greetings. Here is Obara, child of Osa—Osa Obara by name. And she has this to say: Our parents do not choose us—we choose them. Our parents do no make us—we make them. Our parents do not

360

leave us—we leave them. It was Osa Obara who made Ifa for Three Children of the Same Mother, on the day they were born, each a little different from the other. Ifa says no two things are exactly alike, even though they may bear a resemblance. No two situations are precisely the same. No single remedy ever applies twice. Sacrifice, so that you might walk away from here knowing what it is that you alone can do to achieve your own rainbow destiny.

Osa Okanran   Rank   158

Greetings. Here is Okanran, child of Osa—Osa Okanran by name. And he has this to say: Everything destined to be makes it into existence. Everything destined to be is what it is. Everything that is, in being, achieves its own destiny. It was Osa Okanran who made Ifa for Woman with Intermittent Contractions—electric as lightning—on the day before her water broke. She wanted to know whether it would be a boy or a girl. Ifa says, in the matter you have asked about, it will be what it will be. It will have its own day. It will make its own way. And only when it has arrived shall you know what it is that you have helped to give birth to. Why spoil the surprise? Sacrifice, so that you might accept what is coming for what it is.

Osa Irosun   Rank   159

Greetings. Here is Irosun, child of Osa—Osa Irosun by name. And she has this to say: Nothing is wasted. Nothing goes to waste. That which we no longer need, earth takes back. And everything has its purpose. It was Osa Irosun who made Ifa for Woman Suffering from Menstrual Cramps, on the day before her bloodletting began. She wanted a remedy . . . and she wanted it fast. Ifa says the complaint that brings you here tonight is a fact of life you must face. Like all things that come upon you, it will pass. Until then, all we can do is treat the symptoms. Sacrifice, so that you might find an inexpensive drug that is a comfort to you.

Osa Owonrin   Rank   160

Greetings. Here is Owonrin, child of Osa—Osa Owonrin by name. And he has this to say: Twelve hundred needles. Twelve hundred pins. Fourteen hundred pieces of metal surrounding you for protection. That is the web we are weaving here. It was Osa Owonrin who made Ifa for Woman Suffering from Chronic Female Problems, on her way to put her feet in the stirrups. She wanted to know what the doctor would find out. Ifa says, you have come here on a matter of grave personal concern. Something has been troubling you so much, you would submit to even this depth. Something has been niggling you . . . nagging you. And it's time we found out what. Ifa says it's never too late to sacrifice. Temporary submission is a small price to pay for ultimate peace of mind.

Osa Ogunda   Rank 161

Greetings. Here is Ogunda, child of Osa—Osa Ogunda by name. And he has this to say: The moon folds and unfolds. The tides ebb and surge. Day becomes night. Rainy season gives way to dry spell. Everything goes up and down . . . back and forth . . . in and out. It was Osa Ogunda who made Ifa for Vagina About to Entertain Penis, on the night of their clandestine meeting. She wanted to know if he would be good in bed. Ifa says, in the matter you have asked about, there is a risk that things might not turn out to be as wild as your wet dreams. But it will be interesting to see what gives. Sacrifice so that your eyes might be opened wide.

Osa Meji   Rank   10

Greetings. Here is Osa, child of Osa—Osa Meji by name, the spittin' image of her mom. And she has this to say: A sister may be a friend. A friend may be a sister. A mother and a daughter may dress alike. Two twins may see the other in the mirror. It was Osa Meji who made Ifa for Two Women Formerly Married to the Same Louse, on the day when they were getting together for coffee. Ifa says, in the matter you have asked about, it would be best to lean on the shoulder of someone you share something in common with. Ifa says you should go see someone who has been through the same dung as you. Ifa says the answer to this one lies with your spiritual double. Sacrifice, so that you might yet see the common purpose in a past that has brought the two of you together.

⁖ ⁚   *Osa Irete*   **Rank 162**

Greetings. Here is Irete, child of Osa—Osa Irete by name. And she has this to say: Little by little, a bright cloth fades. Bit by bit, a pot rusts. Tree is devoured by a moth worm one nibble at a time. It was Osa Irete who made Ifa for Woman About to be Hysterical, who wanted to know why her period had stopped. Ifa says, I can see that something's been worrying you. Something's been changing your mood. Something's been making you ponder the possibilities. It is little by little that we develop. It is bit by bit that we bloom. It is one nibble at a time that we fade. Ifa says, I see a blessing of grandchildren for you. Sacrifice, so that your name will continue forever and ever.

⁖ ⁚   *Osa Otura*   **Rank 163**

Greetings. Here is Otura, child of Osa—Osa Otura by name. And he has this to say: Ibo. Ibo. Ibo. Ibo bones and Ibo stones. Which hand is chosen, left or right? Which route is to be taken to the bush that will bring you back out? It was Osa Otura who made Ifa for Mother of Church, on her way to give birth to Christianity. She wanted to know if her child would be a diviner. Ifa says, the answer to your question is preordained. The hand of God is in it . . . and things are turning out just as they should. You have been chosen. You have been blessed. Now all you have to do is sacrifice. Open your Bible and point to any chapter, point to any verse, and that is your answer for tonight.

⁖ ⁚   *Osa Oturupon*   **Rank 164**

Greetings. Here is Oturupon, child of Osa—Osa Oturupon by name. And he has this to say: Quarter. Nickel. Dime. And penny. Toss your coins and you'll see plenty. Heads is one dot. Tails is two. Fast as you can throw, your Ifa figures form upon the mat. It was Osa Oturupon who made Ifa for Woman Who Knew How to Act, on her way to freshen her mask. She wanted to know if anyone would ever discover her secret. Ifa says, in the matter you have asked about, there is someone looking over your shoulder. There is someone close to you whom you can confide in, and who can confide in you. Sacrifice, so that your best friends will honor the silent taboo you have set for one another.

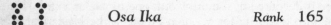

Osa Ika   Rank   165

Greetings. Here is Ika, child of Osa—Osa Ika by name. And she has this to say: White shell. Black stone. Broken dish. Wishbone of a chicken. Cowries tied on a line. The best way to find out something is to ask directly. Use you bones to decide. It was Osa Ika who made Ifa for Mother of Three Children, on the day when she was bringing them up over the rim of existence, each with a container of destiny in its hands. She wanted to know how it would turn out for each of them. Ifa says, in the matter you have asked about, there are numerous possibilities at this time. And each possibility has numerous options. It is not the fate you are handed, but the decisions you make, that determine your destiny. Sacrifice, so that you may make the right choices.

Osa Oshe   Rank   166

Greetings. Here is Oshe, child of Osa—Osa Oshe by name. And she has this to say: Thou shalt not mock my breasts. Thou shalt not pinch my buttocks. Thou shalt not even look at me in that way . . . again. It was Osa Oshe who made Ifa for Woman Standing Up for Her Rights, on the day she was going to the council to file a grievance. She wanted to know if the law would side with her. Ifa says, the matter that brings you here is a personal dispute. In some way you feel as if you have been taken by one you trusted. Ifa says, in this matter, it's not a matter of right and wrong—justice or injustice—but of precedent. Sacrifice, so that the law may come down on your side this time. Sacrifice, so that the guilty party will even have to pay your diviner's fees.

Osa Ofun   Rank   167

Greetings. Here is Ofun, child of Osa—Osa Ofun by name. And he has this to say: Gidi. Gidi. Gidigidi. Animal that wears the skin of a human to deceive you. Gidi. Gidi. Gidigidi. Animal that would just as soon eat you. It was Osa Ofun who made Ifa for Son of Abusive Father, on the day it was discovered he preferred little boys. He wanted to know what could be done. Ifa says, in the matter you have asked about tonight, there is a precedent that you are following. But it is not necessarily the one you should follow. Sacrifice so that you might have the courage to break with tradition this time.

IRETE'S FAMILY

Irete's children are always seeing additional blessings in their lives. But each typically has a specific blessing in mind. It seems Irete's children are always wishing for something they do not have yet. For Irete's children are always putting off sacrifice until the last moment.

Combinations of Irete

Irete Ogbe   *Rank*   168

Greetings. Irete Ogbe was the one who was seeking the blessings of life. The diviners told him that he could get money, he could get land, he could build a house, he could marry a wife, and he could have plenty of progeny. They told him that he could watch what he ate, he could count his beers, and he could reduce the amount that he smoked, but not even such extreme measures would assure him eternal life. Ifa says, sacrifice, lest you depart before collecting your grandchildren around you.

Irete Oyeku   *Rank*   169

Greetings. Irete Oyeku was the one who was seeking the blessings of better health, for she lay sick in bed. The diviners made herbal medicine for her, and for good measure threw in a pinch of dust from a divining tray upon which her figure had been marked. Ifa says, when you have your health it does not necessarily mean much to you. It is only when your health goes away that you even miss it. Little by little. Day by day. Bit by bit, we have deteriorated. Little by little. Day by day. Bit by bit, we shall repair. Ifa says sacrifice, so that you may return yourself to a healthy condition.

⠗ ⠮ Irete Iwori Rank 170

Greetings. Irete Iwori was the one who was seeking the blessing of having a mate for life. But though he looked near and wide, he could not find the one who was meant for him. And though he had many dates, none of them satisfied him completely. He did not know where else to turn, so he went to the diviners. They said, it is clear you are frustrated. But just as sure as you were born, so was your double . . . so was your equal . . . so was your match. Ifa says there is someone coming into your life, sure as we speak. Sacrifice, so that you might not miss the opportunity to know this person, even if but for a short while.

⠇ ⠮ Irete Odi Rank 171

Greetings. Irete Odi was the one who was seeking the blessing of having a home to call her own, though she did not have the money for a down payment and she didn't own any land to use as collateral at the bank. She went to the local diviners to see what advice they might give. They told her, the things that you think matter in this case do not. A house is not a home, they said, a home is not a house. Ifa says you might think about reexpressing the question you have asked. Ifa says, I take things literally. Sacrifice for the ones you love, I say. And that is how you will find where your home is.

⠗ ⠮ Irete Obara Rank 172

Greetings. Irete Obara was the one who was seeking the blessing of peaceful dreams. For though she slept at night, she drifted in and out of disturbing scenes . . . tossed and turned and counted cowries in her head until her mental fingers bled. Next day, she went to the diviners. They said they would give her hypnotic leaves, but these would only cause her to forget her dreams and not to quit having them. For that, it would require a sacrifice to her own head. Ifa says there is a list of worries that keeps your eyes busy even when they are closed. There is a problem that keeps your mind occupied. Sacrifice so that it might work itself out in your sleep.

Irete Okanran   Rank   173

Greetings. Irete Okanran was the one who was seeking the blessing of inspiration. For though he sat at his computer late into the night, no words filled the strobing screen. He went onto the Internet and networked his way to Nigeria to the compound of the Ifa priests who beat palm nuts on the spot. They said it is little by little. It is bit by bit. And there is no way to force it to come any faster than it wants to come. Ifa says there is something you are trying to do that is going nowhere right now. Sacrifice tonight, so that you might have better luck tomorrow.

Irete Irosun   Rank   174

Greetings. Irete Irosun was the one who was seeking the blessing of bearing a child from her own womb. But every month she was frustrated when her period came again, and the blood of her womb did not form itself into a child. She went to the diviners for fertility counseling. They said, You are a creative person. You are a fertile person. You are a prolific person. They said there are many things you could do with your time. Ifa says timing is everything. Sacrifice so that next time things will come together for you.

Irete Owonrin   Rank   175

Greetings. Irete Owonrin was the one who was seeking all manner of blessings. But it always seemed as if things were coming up short in the end. And he was always having to run to the diviners to see what had gone wrong with his well-laid plans. On this particular occasion, the diviners told him that he was not a hypochondriac (at least not this time). They told him he was not being paranoid (not now). They told him his troubles were real. Ifa says life is full of troubles. That is why you must sacrifice on a regular basis.

Irete Ogunda   Rank 176

Greetings. Irete Ogunda was the one who was seeking the blessing of orgasmic pleasure. But for some reason that he could hardly contemplate and could scarcely admit, his penis had fallen asleep at a most inappropriate moment and could not be woken up. He went so fast to the diviners that in his haste he forgot to dress. The diviners took one look at him and said, ah-ah, uh-hum, we can see at once why you have come. Why did you not come sooner? Ifa says, for some reason that you do not want to admit—and can scarcely contemplate—something that has always worked for you before suddenly has failed. Sacrifice now, so that your best performance will not be a thing of the past.

Irete Osa   Rank 177

Greetings. Irete Osa was the one who was seeking a blessing for her daughter. But it seemed no matter what she said or did, her daughter would not recognize her, let alone obey her wishes. She turned to the diviners to see how she could make her daughter straighten up. They said, aha. Sometimes we learn as much from the question as the answer. Next time you might want to whisper it so that you know we have not sold you a bundle of lies. Ifa says you are thinking that someone else is the problem, when in fact the problem is with your own outlook. Sacrifice, so that you might achieve your own destiny, by letting others achieve theirs.

Irete Meji   Rank 11

Greetings. Irete Meji was the one who was seeking the blessing of wealth for herself and her family. But no matter how many hours she put in down at the market, wealth did not amount for her, and she amassed no riches to speak of. Finally, after many years of toil and labor, she turned to the diviners to see if she might yet hold out hope for a financially secure retirement. They said, we will grind leaves for you. We will mix medicine in our mortar. We will add bright-colored extracts. And we will mix it all up with plenty of water and a touch of ash. Ifa says there is a remedy for every problem. And you know what it is. Sacrifice so that you need not toil and weep any longer for the good life that you wish.

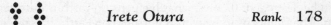

Irete Otura   Rank   178

Greetings. Irete Otura was the one who was seeking the blessing of eternal remembrance. For she had no children, and she feared that after she had gone back to heaven, no one on earth would speak to her anymore. She turned to the diviners. They told her that even though it was a fact she had no children of her own this time, all of the living and all of the dead are one. And as long as one is remembered, so are all. Ifa says, do not forget to tend the graves of your ancestors. Do not forget to speak well of the dead. Ifa says there is someone in your past who has something to say to you from a great distance. Sacrifice, so that the message might get through to you.

Irete Oturupon   Rank   179

Greetings. Irete Oturupon was the one who was seeking the blessing of avoidance of evil. But everywhere he turned, all he saw was filth. Everything he looked up, heard, witnessed, and observed was full of filth—even this book—at least in his jaded eyes. When he sat down opposite the diviners, he noticed the dust on the tray. He noticed the obscene marks the diviner's pointed finger made in the dust (and his filthy fingernails). They smiled when they read Irete Oturupon on the tray. And then they proceeded to tell the story of Dog Penis Stuck in Reluctant Bitch (a tale that really goes with the mirror image of this figure). Ifa says, in the matter you have asked about, you are seeing only what you want to see. Ifa says the redeeming social content in this matter ought to be clear. Sacrifice, so that you might overcome your fear of common things.

Irete Ika   Rank   180

Greetings. Irete Ika was the one who was seeking the blessing of long life—extended death avoidance. The diviners said a very long prayer before beating their nuts for her. When at last they saw the sign in the dust, they immediately erased it, but told her not to fear. An apprentice was sent out to dig a pit. What happens in heaven is mirrored on earth, they told her. What we do on earth, is also done in heaven. Thus it was they built for her a death house and made it collapse into the pit so that the death house built for her in heaven might also be destroyed. Ifa says, what happens on earth is mirrored in heaven, what happens in heaven is mirrored on earth. Ifa says, in order to get what you desire you must extend a symbolic gesture. Ifa says sacrifice so that you may avoid for as long as possible whatever it is you wish to avoid—even the inevitable.

 Irete Oshe   Rank   181

Greetings. Irete Oshe was the one who was seeking the blessing of inner peace. But everywhere she went, it seemed someone was prodding her from behind. It seemed like her space was always being invaded. She took it to the diviners and sat down opposite them. They took one look at her and then at the sign and said, in no uncertain terms, they understood what she meant. They said she was indeed being prodded from behind. Her space was indeed being invaded. And they understood that in such a situation one might long for peace. But they also said she was taking it too seriously. For it was not she who had been prodded and invaded, but only her body. Ifa says your body is your own and you can do whatever you want with you. Ifa says your body is your own and you do not have to allow anyone else to have any part of it. But it is so important that you would consider leaving it to science. Ifa says, sacrifice, so that your soul may find its inner peace.

 Irete Ofun   Rank   182

Greetings. Irete Ofun was the one who was seeking the blessing of a title. But every time he was coming up on the promotion, it seemed he managed to fuck up somehow. And so he was always going the wrong way up the ladder. He went to the diviners to find out how he could quit fucking things up all the time. They told him he could not have come at a better time, because they had just the job for him. Now, it's entry level, they told him, but if you work hard enough, you can get back to the top someday. And then—just for starters they taught him how to cast seashells. Ifa says there are 16 palm nuts, there are 16 figures of Ifa, there are 16 Roads to take, there are 256 different outcomes. Sacrifice, so that you might choose the right answer for you.

OTURA'S FAMILY

Otura's children are always being reborn. Otura's children are always getting christened with their names. They are always being told to sacrifice . . . some cash.

Combinations of Otura

      Otura Ogbe   *Rank* **183**

Greetings. On the day this figure went to the diviner to get his name—it was nine days after his birth—the diviner cast the sign and at once proclaimed, Otura Ogbe is his name. Ifa says this is a child who will have the opportunity to achieve all the good things in life, but only if he sacrifices. Ifa says, in the matter you have asked about, there is a price you must pay to get the things that you want. There is a price you must pay now, and you know what it costs. Put a dollar in someone else's pocket.

      Otura Oyeku   *Rank* **184**

Greetings. On the day this figure went to the diviner to get her name—it was seven days after her birth—the diviner cast the sign and said, Otura Oyeku, it is you. Ifa says this is a child who is born to struggle, for that is the name of the game. But sacrifice will see her through. Ifa says, in the matter you have asked about, there is going to be a struggle. It is a fight from the start. It is a fight all along. It is a fight to the finish. And only the strong survive. Put a dollar in an outstretched hand.

Otura Iwori   Rank 185

Greetings. On the day this figure went to the diviner to get his name—it was nine days after his birth—the diviner cast the sign and at once said, Otura Iwori is his name. Ifa says this is a child who is born to the breed—and that is what he will do. By way of sacrifice, his family will get through. Ifa says the matter you have asked about involves everyone around you—not just yourself. You must always look out for each other. You must always help each other. Put a dollar in the offering plate.

Otura Odi   Rank 186

Greetings. On the day this figure went to the diviner to get her name—it was seven days after her birth—the diviner cast the sign and said, Otura Odi is her name. Ifa says this is a child who was born to do great things. And if she only will sacrifice, she will accomplish much. Ifa says the matter you have asked about is critical, and not just to you. What you are involved in is something crucial to you and those you love. Drop a dollar in the mail to your favorite charity.

Otura Obara   Rank 187

Greetings. On the day this figure went to the diviner to get her name—it was seven days after her birth—the diviner cast the sign and said, Otura Obara is her name. Ifa says this is a child who was born to aspire. But she must sacrifice, lest the thing she aspires to vanishes just as she reaches it. Ifa says the matter you have asked about involves a lofty goal, a high ambition, and a glorious ending.

But do not be taken in by illusions of grandeur. Drop a dollar in the mail to an old friend who needs the dough.

⠇ ⠆   *Otura Okanran*   Rank 188

Greetings. On the day this figure went to the diviner to get his name—it was nine days after his birth—the diviner cast the sign and at once said, in a thunderous voice, Otura Okanran is his name. Ifa says this is a child who was born to fight fire with fire. But if he fails to sacrifice, he will surely meet his match. Ifa says the matter you have asked about involves an argument of some kind. But it is not exactly clear what you are fighting about . . . today. Give a dollar to your favorite cause.

⠰ ⠆   *Otura Irosun*   Rank 189

Greetings. On the day this figure went to the diviner to get her name—it was seven days after her birth—the diviner cast the sign and at once said, Otura Irosun is her name. Ifa says this is a child who will have her work cut out for her. All the more reason to sacrifice. If she resists, she will come directly to an impasse. Ifa says the matter you have asked about involves a roadblock of some kind. You have come to an obstacle that is difficult to surmount. Tip the waitress an extra buck.

⠅ ⠆   *Otura Owonrin*   Rank 190

Greetings. On the day this figure went to the diviner to get his name—it was nine days after his birth—the diviner cast the sign and at once said, Otura Owonrin is his name. Ifa says this is a child who, the more he gets, will always want for more. If he does not sacrifice, he will lead a frustrated life. Ifa says the matter you have asked about involves needs, hopes, desires, and wants. Yet you already have many blessings you could count. The more you get, the more you want. If you lose a dollar, let it drop.

Otura Ogunda   Rank   191

Greetings. On the day this figure went to the diviner to get his name—it was nine days after his birth—the diviner cast the sign and at once said, Otura Ogunda is his name. Ifa says this is a child who is well endowed—both from the waist up and the bottom on down. But unless he sacrifices, his penis will go to his head. Ifa says the matter you have asked about involves keeping things in proper perspective and right balance. The battle is always going on between the one extreme . . . and the other. Give a dollar to your favorite youth group.

Otura Osa   Rank   192

Greetings. On the day this figure went to the diviner to get her name—it was seven days after her birth—the diviner cast the sign and at once said, Otura Osa is her name. Ifa says this is a child who will carry her work out as she should. But unless she sacrifices, she will have trouble being terribly productive. Ifa says the matter you have asked about involves hard work and dedication. You have a responsibility here. You have a commitment to make . . . and keep. Give a dollar to a women's group.

Otura Irete   Rank   193

Greetings. On the day this figure went to the diviner to get her name—it was seven days after her birth—the diviner cast the sign and at once said, Otura Irete is her name. Ifa says this is a child who will see things from both angles. But if she does not sacrifice, such a broad perspective will only confuse her. Ifa says, in the matter you have asked about, there are two opposing views to be considered. Everything has its pros and cons, and only you can decide. Give a dollar to the needy.

Otura Meji   Rank   12

Greetings. On the day this figure went to the diviner to get its name—it was eight days after her birth—the diviner cast the sign and at once said, Otura Meji is the name. Ifa says this pair of twins will both be diviners. But unless they each set aside a shell from their divination set, they will have a hard time of it. Ifa says, the matter you have asked about involves a certain procedure you must adhere to. There is a certain ritual you must go through. There are motions you must make, but it will be better for you if you mean them. Give a dollar to your favorite diviner.

Otura Oturupon   Rank 194

Greetings. On the day this figure went to the diviner to get his name—it was nine days after his birth—the diviner cast the sign and at once said, Otura Oturupon is his name. Ifa says this is a child who will witness his share of violence and perversity—for the world is a violent and perverse place. If he only will sacrifice, he will come through it all unscathed. Ifa says the matter you have asked about involves something you have seen or realized lately that changes your perception of the world around you. Both good and bad are to be seen in everything, but sometimes you will have to look carefully. Give a buck to some civic-minded group.

Otura Ika   Rank 195

Greetings. On the day this figure went to the diviner to get her name—it was seven days after her birth—the diviner cast the sign and at once said, Otura Ika is her name. Ifa says this is a child who will be good with words. But if she fails to sacrifice, her words will turn to curses. Ifa says the matter you have asked about involves an exchange of words. What you actually say, of course, is as important as what you meant. But everything is subject to misinterpretation these days. Give a buck to an alternative newspaper.

Otura Oshe   Rank 196

Greetings. On the day this figure went to the diviner to get her name—it was seven days after her birth—the diviner cast the sign and at once said, Otura Oshe is her name. Ifa says this is a child who will rise above the things that others do intentionally to her. She must sacrifice, however, so that the things they say to her do not get stuck in her head. Ifa says the matter you have asked about involves people who take advantage of each other . . . in every which way they can imagine. It is difficult to do sometimes, but you must also hold your head up. Give a buck to your favorite support group.

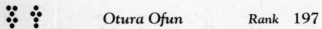 *Otura Ofun* Rank 197

Greetings. On the day this figure went to the diviner to get his name—it was nine days after his birth—the diviner cast the sign and at once said, Otura Ofun is his name. Ifa says this is a child who will be ambitious. But unless he sacrifices, he may start believing he has risen above the law. Ifa says the matter you have asked about involves a question of values, morals, and ideals. If you want to get ahead, you will have to toe the line and abide by the same rules as others. Give a dollar to the cause you identify the most with.

OTURUPON'S FAMILY

Parental Warning: Oturupon's children like to swear and curse. If you are easily offended, you have turned to the wrong place. Turn your back immediately to any figure containing Oturupon. Oturupon's family is not something you want to look upon for long.

Combinations of Oturupon

 Oturupon Ogbe Rank 198

Greetings. It was She with Drooping Breasts who made Ifa for Oturupon Ogbe, a banker, an appraiser, and a realtor—three children of the same mother—who had gathered to conspire against both the seller and the buyer. She with Drooping Breasts cast just eight cowries for them, instead of the normal 16, for she did not want to spend more time with them than she needed. She said if they land four faceup and four mouth down, you lose, otherwise screw both the seller and the buyer to your heart's content. Ifa says, turn you back and bend over so that three children born of the same mother can have their turn fucking you. Sacrifice so that you can get it over with sooner.

⠇⠇ ⠦⠦ *Oturupon Oyeku*   Rank 199

Greetings. It was Skull and Bones that made Ifa for Oturupon Oyeku, a corpse rotting in a place that no one remembered and everyone had forgotten. The diviner beat the palm nuts as fast as he could, for the stench was pretty bad, and he wanted to collect his fee and get out of there just as fast as he could. The nuts pounded, and the sign of Oturupon Oyeku appeared in the dust. The diviner took two steps back, and—if I am not mistaken—crossed himself. Ifa says you have forgotten someone you need to remember. Ifa says this person is someone who—for all intents and purposes—is far away and forgotten, and therefore dead to you. Sacrifice so that you do not lose contact forever.

⠦⠦ ⠦⠇ *Oturupon Iwori*   Rank 200

Greetings. It was I Will Show You Mine who made Ifa for Oturupon Iwori—person of voyeuristic tendencies. . . person who liked to watch others doing their thing. The diviners had gathered in a circle behind him to beat their palm nuts in unison while he watched in the mirror. When they all proclaimed that the marks had come into the trays simultaneously and identically the same, he turned back to face them. They said, we see who you are and we know what you do. Ifa says, in the matter you have asked about, you are standing back and watching someone else do things. You are standing on the sidelines and letting others call your plays for you. You are letting others make your moves. Sacrifice, so that the tables do not turn and others turn their gaze on you.

⁝⁝ ⁝⁝   *Oturupon Odi*   Rank 201

Greetings. It was Look Before You Flush who made Ifa for Oturupon Odi—person whose bowel movements are as explosive as enemas. The diviners turned their heads while she expelled what she was holding. (Has something died in here? they thought, but they said nothing as they lit a fragrant candle and brought the palm nuts down to the mat where they were casting.) Ifa says you are holding an anguish inside you that is making you feel distressed. Hold it just a few seconds longer—but no more. Then let it go, like caustic dung that burns your ass; but then you are rid of it for good. Sacrifice, so everything vile and disgusting passes in a single episode.

⁝⁝ ⁝⁝   *Oturupon Obara*   Rank 202

Greetings. It was Pinch Yourself to Wake Up who made Ifa for Oturupon Obara—person troubled by vile and disgusting dreams from which she could not pull herself awake. As she sat there across from the diviners, her frightened eyes looking down at the dust on the ground, they suspected ghosts. But they cast the figures anyway and found it was not a ghost at all but a dream that possessed her in this way. Ifa says there is an illusion that has taken up residence in your sleep. There is an idle analogy that has taken on a grim reality of its own. Ifa says something is fucking with your head. Sacrifice so that you are not deluded by a figment of your own invention.

⁝⁝ ⁝⁝   *Oturupon Okanran*   Rank 203

Greetings. It was Cowtail Whip's Diviner who made Ifa for Oturupon Okanran—person with a self-destructive impulse. Okanran prostrated himself before the diviners. And when next he asked to borrow Cowtail's whip, they all winked at each other as if they understood. There is no need to ask, they said. Let us consult Ifa. Their fingers marked the answer slowly in the dust (for they wanted to do things the hard way themselves). But when the figure came at last, they knew it all by sight. Ifa says, no pain, no gain. Ifa says, it is little by little. It is inch by inch. Ifa says you are doing things the hard way.

You are making things hard on yourself. Ifa says, what can I say that you do not already know? Sacrifice, and may it make you feel good in the aftermath.

⁝⁚ ⁝⁚   *Oturupon Irosun*   Rank   204

Greetings. It was Diviner of the White Cloth who made Ifa for Oturupon Irosun—person stirring a vat of red dye. As she came forward, sloshing red dye on the ground, the diviners lifted their white robes above their waists and moved a foot or so back. Fuck this, one said. And they got to arguing about whose turn it was to do the readings. It was Diviner of the White Cloth who drew the short lot while the others went out for a smoke. And after he marked the figure of Oturupon first, worse came to worst. As the figure for Irosun emerged next, the vat of red dye, becoming agitated, leaned forward to watch. Ifa says someone is going to get something on you. Sacrifice so that it all comes out in the wash.

⁚⁝ ⁝⁚   *Oturupon Owonrin*   Rank   205

Greetings. It was Supreme Sacrifice who made Ifa for Oturupon Owonrin—person in dire straits, on the day when he was going out to seek his destiny in some other place. As Owonrin hunkered down on the diviner's floor, sirens sounded out of doors and Owonrin looked back over his shoulder. It was no surprise to the diviner when the figure that was drawn came. Ifa says you are in some kind of serious dung. And all in all, it looks like you are doubly fucked. Damned if you do. Damned if you don't. Man, you'd better sacrifice before you leave town. Sacrifice, so that those you have left behind do not sacrifice in order to catch up with you.

⁝⁚ ⁝⁚   *Oturupon Ogunda*   Rank   206

Greetings. It was the Diviner of Soap who made Ifa for Oturupon Ogunda—penis that stinks to high heaven, on the day after fucking. As penis squatted down in the dust, the diviner on the other side of the board shook his head and wiped his nose. Is it hot weather we have been having? he said, as he gathered up his divination nuts and started to beat them. When he saw he had marked the figure of Oturupon Ogunda on the tray, he turned his head again and coughed. Ifa says you have been sticking your penis into places and then forgetting to wash it off. Sacrifice, so that dogs from all over do not want to sniff your crotch.

⦂⦂ ⦂⦂ Oturupon Osa   Rank 207

Greetings. It was the Diviner of Bitter Kola who made Ifa for Oturupon Osa—vagina frothing with yeast infection. When she arrived at the diviners, she refused to come inside. The diviners said it didn't matter if she came inside or not, they would still consult Ifa for her. They were not at all surprised when the figure that they cast appeared on the tray. Ifa says, have you been fucking around again? Ifa says, if not, then someone has been inserting dirty fingers into you. Someone who does not wash his hands after pissing has been shaking hands with you. Sacrifice, so that you do not pass along this vile favor to anyone else.

⦂⦂ ⦂⦂ *Oturupon Irete*   Rank 208

Greetings. It was the diviner named No Answer Is an Answer who made Ifa for Oturupon Irete—person upset about a raw deal she was getting. When the diviners saw her coming, they could tell from the way she carried herself that she was mad. They wiped out the sign that was currently on the divining board and started their rituals all over from the beginning by saying their opening prayers again. When at last the prayers had droned on long enough for everyone to relax, the nuts were beaten and then the diviners pointed out the figure on the divining tray. Ifa says you feel as if you have been shafted. You feel as if you have been pissed upon. You feel as if someone has placed dung on you. And that is why your body is walking angrily to the diviners this time. There can be no answer you will accept, until you calm down. Sacrifice, and take a cold shower—then we will see what Ifa has to say.

⦂⦂ ⦂⦂ Oturupon Otura   Rank 209

Greetings. It was I, The Author, who made Ifa for Oturupon Otura—a person who thought he would go to hell for Reading *African*

Oracles in 10 Minutes. (This is why, I suppose, he kept it hidden among his other books, where none of his religious friends would ever see it.) As he approached tonight, I saw that his curiosity had gotten the better of him. Was his preacher right? Is all this stuff really the work of the devil? Unfortunately, when he fumbled through the book—his heart racing with the thrill of coming so close to the forbidden—he landed right here. And thus saw what he expected to see. Ifa says someone is fucking you from behind. Someone has enchanted you with a charismatic spell. Someone has bewitched you with threats of hell. Someone is telling you what books to buy—and what books to burn . . . what channel to turn to and what charity to contribute to. Is that why the Good Lord gave you a brain? Sacrifice—because a mind is a terrible thing to waste, especially if it's yours.

⁝ ⁝   *Oturupon Meji*   Rank   13

Greetings. It was the diviner named Think It Over Twice who made Ifa for Oturupon Meji—two children of the same mother who had gotten together to reminisce about the difficulties of childhood. After a while they decided they really ought to go see the diviner if they ever hoped to get over their childhood traumas. So—encouraged by each other—they went. The diviners—who are inclined to favor all twins—smiled warmly when the two came in. And with a flourish the palm nuts were beaten, and the figure was cast. When they saw the figure that it was, they turned away from the board and said, go out of the room for two minutes—and don't come back until two minutes are up. Then you may read the answer, which is printed for you in the footnote.[1]

⁝ ⁝   *Oturupon Ika*   Rank   210

Greetings. It was the diviner named How Can I Explain This Better who made Ifa for Oturupon Ika—a person who wanted to become

---

[1] Now we may turn back to the figure again. Ifa says there is a grim secret harbored between two people. There is a certain something that you feel you can talk about only with a certain someone. Ifa says you are both fucked up. Sacrifice, so that you won't make any further trouble for yourself.

a certified psychic. While traveling in Southern California, she decided to stop by the Corner New Age Shop to see if she could find any good esoteric bull-dung to read on the plane home. But all she found was The Author signing copies of *African Oracles*. (He's shorter than you thought.) She decided what the hell and forked over a couple of bucks. (Most of it went to the store.) After she was done reading the music credits at the back, her thumbing fingers landed here. Ifa says you <u>must</u> be psychic. Ifa says something has happened that is just too uncanny to be a coincidence. Sacrifice, so that you might not doubt the truth when it bites you on the ass.

⠆ ⠒   ### Oturupon Oshe   Rank   211

Greetings. It was the diviner named Taboo who made Ifa for Oturupon Oshe—a person who had inadvertently done something she wasn't supposed to do. As she hurried to the diviners, the question on her mind was, what could she do to keep it a secret? But when she got there and the diviners started performing their rituals over the divining nuts, the question she ended up asking of herself was, why should I believe this fucking mumbo-jumbo? That was the thought on her mind as the nuts were beaten and the sign for her was cast. Ifa says the question you have asked is not the matter that brings you here. Your real problem is that you have unwittingly done something you were not supposed to do. And now you are afraid you will be found out. The diviners said, we can help you, but you will have to sacrifice, lest your disbelieving undoes all of our hard work.

⠒ ⠒   ### Oturupon Ofun   Rank   212

Greetings. It was the diviner named Public Affairs who made Ifa for Oturupon Ofun—a person who had intentionally done something he wasn't supposed to do, but he didn't care. As he sat opposite the diviners scratching his balls, they stared politely (into his eyes) and talked about sports. But once the pleasantries were behind them, and the divining nuts had done their casts, they looked back into his eyes to see if it was true. They said, you have intentionally violated the rules. But since this is a professional consultation—and the client/diviner relationship is sacred—we will gladly keep it just between us friends of the cloth, but is it true you have been fucking your brother's wife? Ifa says, Taboo. If you persist in doing the things you are doing to others, it will be bad for you. Ifa says, quit while you are still ahead. Sacrifice! Sacrifice! And keep sacrificing until I tell you to quit.

IKA'S FAMILY

Ika's family is a wicked brood. And her children are not the sort of people you would want to encounter by mistake. Fortunately, as long as you see them coming, you can avoid them. And avoiding difficulty is exactly what we're here to do.

Combinations of Ika

 Ika Ogbe   Rank 213

Greetings. Ika comes first, Ogbe comes next. Ika Ogbe is cast. Ika comes right. Ogbe comes left. Ika Ogbe comes to the mat. Do you confirm? Ika Ogbe coming in. Is this the sign you cast? Okay then. Let the drums begin. Ifa says even wickedness cannot get in our way. Ifa says even wickedness can spawn blessings for you yet. But you must turn it back upon itself. Sacrifice so that the wickedness that attempts to interfere with your blessings is turned back.

 Ika Oyeku   Rank 214

Greetings. Ika comes first, Oyeku comes second. Ika Oyeku is cast on the mat. Ika comes right. Oyeku comes left. Ika Oyeku—is the count correct? (If two remain, then one dot; if one, then two?) Count confirmed? Then true. Ika Oyeku comes to you. Let us counteract. Ifa says someone is intentionally trying to wear you thin. Someone is holding your nose to the ground, in hopes you will cave in. Sacrifice so that the trap that has been laid for you has no spikes in the bottom of it. Sacrifice so that if you fall for it, you can still get out.

Ika Iwori Rank 215

Greetings. Ika came first? Iwori came next? And not the other way—is this correct? Ika Iwori has been cast on the mat, and not its opposite? You pressed it top to bottom, right? Iwori came second? Ika came first? Confirm or deny it. And if in doubt, cast again. All right, then, Ika Iwori is your figure. What can you do? Ifa says there is wickedness in a relationship that goes nowhere, except deeper and deeper into itself, until it becomes an obsession. Ifa says, sacrifice, so that you do not surrender completely to one who enchants you with bedroom eyes. Sacrifice so that you do not crawl into bed with someone you are sorry to wake up with.

Ika Odi Rank 216

Greetings. Ika on the right. Odi on the left. Ika Odi climbing out of the dust. Ika Odi coming up to the top. Recognize it? Ika Odi, right? Exactly like the figures shown above? Confirmed. Then let's consider the cure. Ifa says, open wide. All the things the mouth takes in come out the other end . . . even medicine. Ifa says that there is something you have been eating. (There is something eating you.) There is something you have been taking. (There is something taking you.) Sacrifice, so that an illness abates. Sacrifice, so that a remedy takes hold.

Ika Obara Rank 217

Greetings. Ika cast first. Obara cast second. Ika Obara is cast. Ika on the right. Obara on the left. Mostly single nuts remaining? (If one, then two finger marks?) Ika Obara has come. (Are you sure you have the hang of beating nuts?) No time for a recount. Quick, before Ika Obara fades. We must read. . . . Ifa says there is a mirage in the road. Ifa says something appears to be more beautiful than it is. Wickedness that wears a sublime smile is the most beguiling wickedness of all. Sacrifice, so that you are able to see the truth behind an illusion.

Ika Okanran   Rank   218

Greetings. Ika counted first. Okanran counted second. Ika Okanran. Have you counted it correctly, then, right to left? All right, Ika Okanran has been counted, then. Let the counting be done. Ifa says someone is counting on you this time. Someone is counting you in on something you may not want to be a party to. Someone is counting you as if you were something belonging to someone else's warehouse of things. Sacrifice so that your head remains yours alone to count upon.

Ika Irosun   Rank   219

Greetings. Ika counted first. Irosun counted second. Ika Irosun. Icky Ika on the right hand. Red Irosun on the left. Are these the marks you made on your Scratch Pad? For sure? If so, it can only be true. Red Ika has come. Ika Irosun is pressed in the dust. Nothing left to do but determine what it means. Ifa says it is like a fire racing through dry grass. Wherever fire chooses to go, dry grass bends down before it. Wherever fire chooses to spread, dry grass cannot resist giving way. Ifa says sweeping change is coming on the winds. And you cannot stand in its way. Ifa says, sacrifice, so that it might yet blow in a direction other than yours.

Ika Owonrin   Rank   220

Greetings. Ika counted on the right hand. Owonrin counted on the left. Ika Owonrin has appeared on the divining tray. But are you sure you marked it correctly? Ika came first, and to the right? Owonrin came second? If so, Ika Owonrin is right. Here's what it means. Ifa says the diviner's cat has just used Ifa's board as a litter box. Ifa says a secret has been betrayed. The cat is out of the bag. Ifa says a truth has been covered up. A place has been ruined. A thing has been spoiled. Sacrifice, so that the filth heaped upon you comes out in the next wash.

Ika Ogunda   Rank   221

Greetings. Ika counted first. Ogunda counted second. Ika Ogunda has brushed itself in the dust. Half single dots, half double, in this combination. And arrayed thus: ⋮ ⋮ . Are these the marks you made? Okay. We have confirmed the count. And Ika Ogunda is on the mark. Ifa says a penis is the easiest thing in the world to enchant. A penis is the easiest thing to beguile. A penis tends to respond to any invitation it gets. Ifa says someone is making casual offers. Someone is making false promises. Ifa says, sacrifice, lest you not realize there are snarling strings attached to the offer you are about to take.

Ika Osa   Rank   222

Greetings. Ika coming first. Osa coming next. Ika Osa on the try. Ika on the right. Osa on the left. Ika Osa written in the dust. Sometimes it is right. But sometimes it is only Eshu playing tricks with your mind. So please confirm. You have jotted it down top to bottom? right to left? Only then may we go on. . . . Ifa says, north, south, east, west, and not a good witch to be found, even in Kansas. Ifa says there are these three weird sisters. And you should not trust any of them. Sacrifice, so that you are able to avoid the fingers of others meddling in your life.

Ika Irete   Rank   223

Greetings. Ika on the first cast. Irete on the second. Ika Irete has fallen in the dust of the divining board. It is a very difficult sign. So before you listen to the verse, make sure you have not looked it up wrong. Ifa says there is something that was almost in your grasp. Ifa says there was something close enough to taste, feel, touch, smell, and have intercourse with. But it did not ever really come to pass. Ifa says, sacrifice, so that something so close to be sure of does not yet slip through your fingers.

⠮ ⠳   Ìka Otura   Rank 224

Greetings. Ika has come first. Otura has come second. It is Ika Otura then that you have written. But if you cast shells for it, you are in the wrong part of the book. Look it up in the Answers for Part I. But if you beat your nuts to get here, it's certain then. This is Ika Otura. And here is your answer: Ifa says it is a complex web the spider weaves. And the spider never runs out of string. Ifa says you have gotten all wrapped up in something. Ifa says something has you all tied up in knots and sticky stuff. Ifa says, sacrifice, so that you are not permanently bound up by your present predicament.

⠳ ⠪   *Ika Oturupon*   Rank 225

Greetings. Ika is counted. Oturupon is counted. It is Ika Oturupon—in that order. We trust that you have marked the figure right this time. But turn your head now and compare this figure to your notes: 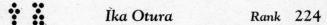 . . . . Greetings again now that you are back. It is confirmed then. We shall talk of Ika Oturupon. (I myself am turning away.) Ifa says that someone has turned their back to you. Ifa says someone has turned away. And it is not just the diviner. Someone does not want to see your face right now. Sacrifice, so that you might yet be redeemed in their sight. Sacrifice so that you might avoid each other's gaze until then.

⠳ ⠳   *Ika Meji*   Rank 14

Greetings. Ika is counted first. Ika is counted again. It is two Ikas on the tray. It is Ika Meji we have found. It is Ika Meji who has found us. Are you sure you did not jot down the same figure twice by mistake? If there's any doubt, cast again. If not, it's Ika Meji, then. Wipe it clean from the dust. Scratch it out on the pad. Get rid of it first, and then we'll talk about it. Ifa says something is wiped out. Something is erased. Something is gone for good now. And the slate has been made clean. Sacrifice, so that the next figure that appears will indicate a blessing instead of a curse.

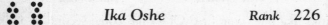

Ika Oshe   Rank 226

Greetings. Ika has come. Oshe has come. The combination of Ika Oshe has come . . . like two stick figures in the dust. Ika to the right. Oshe to the left. How is it then? Is this the way you wrote it down? Ifa says, on this one, don't count me in. Ifa says there is something going on here that cannot be condoned. Ifa says you must sacrifice, so that a wrong is not heaped upon a mound of wrongs.

Ika Ofun   Rank 227

Greetings. Ika has come. Ofun has come. The combination of Ika Ofun has come. Ika to his right. Ofun to her left. Ika Ofun in an obscene embrace. Are you sure you marked it down correctly on your paper? Are you sure your fingers made the marks right? Provided you are absolutely sure . . . Ifa says something incestuous is going on in your life. Ifa says there is a conflict of interest. Ifa says strange bedfellows are sleeping together. Sacrifice, so that you may not be permanently haunted by your mistakes.

OSHE'S FAMILY

Oshe's children are always bumping up against the things they are not supposed to do. Oshe's children are always having to cope with their taboos. But for the most part, Oshe's family makes it through. That's because they know how to defeat Ifa at his own game.

Combinations of Oshe

Oshe Ogbe   Rank 228

Greetings. It was Oshe Ogbe who appeared in the dust of the divining board this time. The diviner took one look at the sign and opened a cola. He sipped. Spat. And said, Taboo. Ifa says there are two people who are involved in a forbidden relationship. And it will not turn out well for either of them, unless they are both willing to sacrifice. Even so, it will not be easy. But this is one reason there is Ifa. Consult the oracle on a regular basis until you have achieved inner peace—regardless of what anyone else thinks.

Oshe Oyeku   Rank 229

Greetings. It was Oshe Oyeku who appeared on the board this time. The diviner took one look at it and ordered a bowl of chicken soup from the kitchen. Into this he dropped a smidgen of dust that the sign had been written in and handed it to the person asking the question. Ifa says you have been doing something to yourself that you should not do. Ifa says you have been running your own body into the ground. How long do you think you can keep on doing this to yourself? Sacrifice, lest the next time the cure will be worse than chicken soup.

Oshe Iwori   Rank 230

Greetings. It was Oshe Iwori who now appeared. The diviner looked at the figure for a split second, and popped a cowry shell into the cheek of his mouth before uttering the name. Ifa says there are two consenting adults here—and that is a fact. But they are engaging in something that is against the law in Georgia and other similar places. Ifa says, regardless of how stupid the law is (and how long it has remained unchallenged on the books), it is still taboo to do what you are doing. Ifa says sacrifice, or else move to California, where they don't care what you do as long as you have a green card while you're doing it and you don't smoke a cigarette afterward.

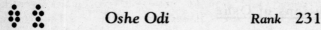

Oshe Odi   Rank 231

Greetings. It was Oshe Odi who appeared in the dust. The diviner looked at the sign and said, don't you see? Don't you see the way Ifa has come to be? Ifa says that we must do the right things at the right time. Ifa says that we must avoid doing the wrong things at any time. Ifa says in this case, a woman must not have her clitoris circumcised. What once was accepted is now taboo. Ifa says that there is something that everybody did once, but it has now become taboo. Ifa says sacrifice, lest you become a social outcast on account of being old-fashioned.

Oshe Obara   Rank 232

Greetings. It was Oshe Obara who showed up in the dust of the divining board. It was Oshe Obara that was formed when the diviner's hands had quit beating the palm nuts and when the diviner's fingers had quit pressing the dust. Ifa says, taboo today . . . not taboo tomorrow. Ifa says not taboo yesterday . . . taboo today. Ifa says the rules are changing, bending, breaking. (And how many Republicans does it take in Washington to reinvent the wheel?) What is wrong? What is right? It all depends on what day and year this is (and what press release the American Medical Association has issued for the media this week). Ifa says it is important that you obey the lighted placards at all times, even if there are so many rules to read, you can hardly make out the walls they're written on. Sacrifice, lest you inadvertently light up at the wrong place and time. Sacrifice, so that you don't lose your place in single file.

Oshe Okanran   Rank 233

Greetings. It was Oshe Okanran who turned up this time. And when he saw it in the dust of the divining board, the diviner exhaled air through his teeth. Shhhhhhh. And—in a low voice, almost a whisper, in fact—he began to tell the story of a mortal, who back when time began, had been raped by a god (for at that time they could get away with anything). But then his voice came back to normal tones as he explained that Ifa can be used to overcome even the most degrading circumstances. Ifa says someone feels as if she (or he) has been invaded. Ifa says someone has been forced to do something they did not want to do. Ifa says in the old days it would not have mattered who was to blame. Taboo was taboo. But Ifa says times have changed. Sacrifice, lest others fail to understand what you have been through.

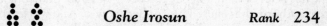

Oshe Irosun   Rank 234

Greetings. It was Oshe Irosun who turned up this time. And when it bit the red dust, a puff went up. The diviner poured some oil on the lip of the divining tray and started to recite all the verses he knew for Oshe Irosun. There were only a few. The one who had come for the divination listened to the verses patiently. But the thought that struck home today was this. . . . Ifa says there is a rock that lies on the bottom of the cool river, but it does not feel the cool water on its skin. There is a rock that lies on top of a sunlit hill, but if feels no warmth from the sun on its face. There is a rock entwined by the roots of an Irosun tree, but it feels no pleasure from the root's caress. Ifa says it is taboo for the rock to feel pleasure or pain. Ifa says, lucky you are not a rock. Ifa says, sacrifice, so that you do not have to give any sensitivity up.

Oshe Owonrin   Rank 235

Greetings. It was Oshe Owonrin who materialized in the dust of the divining tray this time. The diviner did not even lift his finger from making the last mark before he launched into his recitation of the appropriate verses. And as he droned on and on, he spoke of many blessings that had been lost to folks because, in the end, they had refused to make the sacrifice. Ifa says you are a candidate for many benefits. You are the heir apparent for many blessings. And all things are possible. But only if you honor your own taboos. Ifa says make some resolutions. Ifa says set some limitations for yourself. Ifa says sacrifice, lest you violate your own rules and think you can get away with it.

⠿ ⠿ Oshe Ogunda   Rank   236

Greetings. It was Oshe Ogunda who appeared now on the tray. And when the diviner saw it, he touched his tongue against the roof of his mouth. *CLICK*. He looked deeply into the eyes of the questioner. And then he started to recite a verse about a father who had lost visitation rights with his children, because there was something the courts said he had done that he shouldn't ever do. Ifa says an unwritten law has been broken. A code has been violated. Someone in a position of authority has abused his (or her) power. And worse, she (or he) is about to be discovered. Sacrifice, lest you fall victim to your own aggressiveness.

⠿ ⠿ Oshe Osa   Rank   237

Greetings. It was Oshe Osa who crawled up on Ifa's examining table. And when the diviner saw her lying there in the dust, his diviner's penis lurched inside its white cloth. He studied the eyes of his beautiful and naively innocent client, and nearly made divination in his pants. Ifa says there are two people who have a professional association, but they must be careful not to get involved with one another. There are two things going on in your life that may need to remain close but cannot get any closer. For now, at least, this is your taboo. Sacrifice, lest you be tempted into breaking it again.

⠿ ⠿ Oshe Irete   Rank   238

Greetings. It was Oshe Irete that appeared on the tray next. As the diviner's middle finger pressed the last dot of the upside-down cross on the left side, he saw it was Oshe Irete and not Oshe Irosun who had fallen in the dust of the divining board this time. He reached for another cigarette and said, it is red, very red. This is hot. Very hot. And, backing off, the diviner said, I do not want to come within six to nine inches of this one. Ifa says, there is a cross burning. Let us throw cold water on it. Diviner says, do not come within six to nine inches of anything that might burn you. Sacrifice, and take a cold shower.

Oshe Otura   *Rank*   17

Greetings. It was Oshe Otura that was scratched on the dust this time. Oshe Otura, the 17th Odu in the line. As the diviner's middle finger finished the sign and it turned out to be Oshe Otura and not Oshe Meji, he smacked his lips and said, aah. Ifa says this is the Great Mother of all Odu, the one who gave birth to all the other combinations. Let us consider it. Ifa says the stakes here are big, very big. Ifa says it's all in the odds that are evens, and the evens that are odds. (If two nuts are left in your palm, mark one dot; if one, two. It is diviner's taboo to do it any other way.) Ifa says, do not bet more than you can afford to lose. Sacrifice, lest the evens become evens and the odds become odds for you. (If two nuts are left, would you press twice? It is forbidden. It is diviner's taboo.) Sacrifice lest you wind up with an opposite destiny to the one you deserved.

 Oshe Oturupon   *Rank*   239

Greetings. It was Oshe Oturupon that appeared next on the divining tray. (It was Oshe Oturupon that you have penciled on your Scratch Pad.) The diviner looked at the sign and thought we should doodle it out now. And he started extending the dots into vertical dashes. (You can follow along on your Scratch Pad if you like.) The diviner's longest finger scratched casually at the dot's margins, turning them into lines running up and down. He took his good old time before he said, well, we're really not supposed to look too long on this one, so I had to doodle it out. Ifa says there are things to be learned even from the pornographic. Ifa says there is something written between the lyric of each rapper's words. You must read between the lines, for nothing is spoken of directly here. Ifa says, sacrifice, lest you try to impose your taboo on someone else's head.

 Oshe Ika   *Rank*   240

Greetings. It was Oshe Ika that was written next on the tray. The diviner stared at the figure for a moment while he reflected on whether he had just written two dots, when it should have been one.

Was it really Oshe Ika? Or should he have written Oshe Ofun (:: ::) instead? No, it was correct as is. The diviner glanced off into space as the opening verse started flowing through his mouth. Ifa says there are things that you do not want to come within six to nine feet of. And yet it's still too near—better make it miles. Ifa says there is something at a distance that you want to keep your distance from. It is taboo for you. Sacrifice so things happening at a distance do not happen any closer.

Oshe Meji   Rank   15

Greetings. It was Oshe Meji that was marked in the dust of the tray next time. The diviner rose from the floor, took chalk, and wrote the figure on the wall of his diviner's workshop. He explained, it's just a Pennsylvania Dutch hex sign. It's just a decoration that makes us feel lucky. (And besides, it will keep the witches away.) Ifa says there is someone for whom it is not taboo to do what you believe to be un-thinkable, unspeakable, undignified, and impolite. What else might this person stoop to? Who knows? Ifa says it's not a game you can attempt to play, for the rules are taboo to you. Sacrifice, so that you may at least erect a barrier of protection around yourself. Sketch Oshe Meji in chalk on the wall, but only if you truly believe it will help. Sacrifice, lest another person build a pocket of aggravation in your mind.

Oshe Ofun   Rank   241

Greetings. It was Oshe Ofun who fell on the divining board this time. The diviner took one look and started reciting. Ifa says it is a glutton who takes the biggest piece of meat when others are hungry too. It is a wild boar who attacks the others for no reason. It is the di-viners who beat Ifa at his own game. It is the diviners who know how to cast palm nuts who know how to defeat Ifa. It is the diviners who know about remedies and sacrifice. Sacrifice, so that you might de-feat your own obsessive-compulsive urges. This is your taboo. Sacri-fice so that you do not wind up getting yourself in trouble.

OFUN'S FAMILY

Ofun's family has a closet full of skeletons. And Ofun's children are always adding to the legacy. The problem is that Ofun's children are inclined to self-indulgence, which is inclined to result in scandal. But to Ofun's helpless, hopeless brood, sacrifice remains an ever-present escape route.

Combinations of Ofun

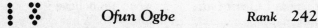

Ofun Ogbe   Rank 242

Greetings. It is Ofun Ogbe who has come out of the divining jar this time. It is Ofun Ogbe who is out of the closet and sitting on the divining board. Ifa says it is such a piddling violation you have come about today. And no, you will not go blind. Hairs will not grow on the palm of your hand. Ifa says there is something you are doing that is a form of masturbation. Ifa says there is something you are doing that is about nothing other than self-gratification. Sacrifice so that you don't get carried away with yourself. Sacrifice, so that you do not get caught doing it.

Ofun Oyeku   Rank 243

Greetings. It is Ofun Oyeku who has come out of the divining jar this time. It is Ofun Oyeku who is out of the closet and lying before us. Ifa says these are inanimate things you are getting involved with. Ifa says it's no big deal, of course. But never stick anything larger than a finger in your ear. Ifa says you are making love to someone who just lies there and says nothing. (Perhaps you forgot to change the batteries?) Sacrifice, so that your friend does not get discovered in the bottom of your drawer.

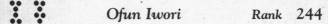

Ofun Iwori   Rank 244

Greetings. It is Ofun Iwori who has come out of the divining jar this time. It is Ofun Iwori who is out of the closet and standing naked before us. Ifa says someone who has seen you naked knows at least one of your secrets. Ifa says someone who has seen you naked has already seen you better than you see yourself. Ifa says, sacrifice; you have been showing what you've got to others. Ifa says they have been showing you something of theirs in return. Sacrifice, so that a confidence is kept. Don't worry. It's just between you and me. (Nice birthmark, by the way. Wanna see my tattoo?)

Ofun Odi   Rank 245

Greetings. It is Ofun Odi who has come out of the divining jar this time. It is Ofun Odi who is out of the closet and scratching her name faintly in the dust before us. Ifa says we aren't exactly sure who the father of this one was. (And even if we were, we'd have to let on that we didn't know.) Ifa says we will raise it like one of our own, and who will ever know the difference? There is a family resemblance, after all. Ifa says these things happen. But we are willing to overlook them for the sake of the innocent. Sacrifice so that keeping the family secret hidden does not become a greater burden than letting it escape.

Ofun Obara   Rank 246

Greetings. It is Ofun Obara who has come out of the divining jar next. It is Ofun Obara who is out of the closet this time. It is Ofun Obara written in the dust. Ifa says it's difficult to nail this one down. Ifa says it has shifty eyes, this one. Ifa says you are involved in something clandestine and furtive. Ifa says, you have a little something going on, on the side. Ifa says it means nothing to you. Sacrifice, so that it does not cost you more than you bargain for.

⁝ ⁝   **Ofun Okanran**   Rank   247

Greetings. It is Ofun Okanran who has come out of the divining jar next. It is Ofun Okanran who is out of the closet this time. It is Ofun Okanran flashing before us, like a streaker in the spring of '74. (Diviner says I would have picked a warmer place for nakedness myself, but we are nonetheless impressed with your balls.) Ifa says in some way you are exposing yourself. In some way, you have been exposed. Sacrifice so that others do not take advantage of the vulnerability you have invited upon your own head.

⁝ ⁝   **Ofun Irosun**   Rank   248

Greetings. It is Ofun Irosun who has come out of the divining jar next. It is Ofun Irosun who is out of the closet this time. It is Ofun Irosun written in its own dust. Our fingers have touched it. And it is hot, very hot to the touch. Ifa says you have been putting your fingers into places where they do not necessarily go, as a rule of thumb. Ifa says be sure to wash them off thoroughly when you are done. (And clean your fingernails before you shake hands with the diviner upon departing.) Sacrifice so that you may not rue the day you stuck your fingers into sticky places.

⁝ ⁝   **Ofun Owonrin**   Rank   249

Greetings. It is Ofun Owonrin who has come out of the divining jar next. It is Ofun Owonrin who is out of the closet now. It is Ofun Owonrin who has made his confession in the dust of the divining board. It is Ofun Owonrin giving testimony before us. Ifa says you have taken an oath. And now you must tell the truth, the whole truth, and nothing but the truth. Ifa says, take your nuts in your hand and swear to me that you will never do what you have been doing again. Ifa says, all right then. I will give you blessings and let you go in peace. But first you must sacrifice, lest I have gone too easy on you.

⸬ ⸬   ## Ofun Ogunda   Rank 250

Greetings. It is Ofun Ogunda who has come out of the divining jar next. It is Ofun Ogunda who is out of the closet now. It is Ofun Ogunda that has marked the dust with his splattering wad. Ifa says spit sits on the ground, but semen rolls. Ifa says now that you have brought something out in the open, we can all take it for the sign that it is. Ifa says you have been planting seeds in places they will not take hold. Ifa says it does no harm, of course. As long as no one comes along and slips on it. Sacrifice so that your energies may not be wasted in the effort you have undertaken.

⸬ ⸬   ## Ofun Osa   Rank 251

Greetings. It is Ofun Osa who has come out of the divining jar next. It is Ofun Osa who is out of the closet now. It is Ofun Osa who has left a trail of blood in our divining dust. Ifa says you feel as if you have been bled yourself, even if no blood actually flowed from any body cavity or any superficial flesh wound. Ifa says something you have done has caused you to bleed. The wound itself will surely heal. But sacrifice just in case, lest your soul continue bleeding from the wound to your ego.

⸬ ⸬   ## Ofun Irete   Rank 252

Greetings. It is Ofun Irete who has come out of the divining jar next. It is Ofun Irete who is out of the closet now. It is Ofun Irete written upside down and backwards in the dust. Ifa says that something that goes counter to popular thinking is involved. Ifa says, stand by. For you never know when fads might fade and general opinions change. Even the wacky has a way of becoming the norm. Ifa says, sacrifice, so that your kinky fetish may yet come back in style. (Do you think the diviner's too old to get an ear pierced? And would you tell me which ear means what again?)

⸬ ⸬   ## Ofun Otura   Rank 253

Greetings. It is Ofun Otura who has come out of the divining jar next. It is Ofun Otura who is out of the closet now. It is Ofun Otura crossing itself before us. (Diviner wonders if someone thinks he is a vampire now, too.) Ifa says it is like sweet potato shoots that grow leafy but neither flower nor fruit. It is an abomination. It is a mutation. What good can come of this? Ifa says you have only been using half a penis. Ifa says you have only been using half a vagina. Ifa says you have been using only half a brain. And for all your self-righteousness, you are no less obsessed with sex than those who make full use of the equipment that God gave them. No good can come from a penis shriveled up in its foreskin. No good can come from a vagina sealed in its shrink-wrap. No good can come from a mind that limits its beliefs. Sacrifice so that you may realize your full potential here.

⁙ ⁙   *Ofun Oturupon*   Rank   254

Greetings. It is Ofun Oturupon who has come out of the divining jar next. It is Ofun Oturupon who is out of the closet now. And whoa now. It is Ofun Oturupon before us. (Apprentice! Go get the cowtail switch in case we need to beat him back.) Ifa says it is dark, very dark. And we must not look on it too long. Ifa says you are flagellating yourself for something you have done. Ifa says you are beating yourself up. Ifa says you are trying to escape your own feelings of inadequacy and guilt. Ifa says it is dark, very dark. Sacrifice, lest you add injury to your own insults.

⁙ ⁙   *Ofun Ika*   Rank   255

Greetings. It is Ofun Ika who has come out of the divining jar next. It is Ofun Ika who is out of the closet now. It is Ofun Ika who has imposed herself upon this dust. Shall we recognize her? Shall we sing praises to her then? Are we sure it is she? Ifa says yes. Ofun Ika has come. And we should not go out of our way to insult her. Let's proceed. Ifa says there is a woman who wants to be our mistress. But we must not let her sink her claws into us. Ifa says there is a man who wants to be our master. But we must not let him sink his teeth into us. Ifa says, sacrifice, so that someone without morals does not wrestle you down to the ground.

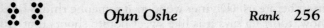

Ofun Oshe   Rank   256

Greetings. It is Ofun Oshe who has come out of the divining jar next. It is Ofun Oshe who is out of the closet now. It is Ofun Oshe who tumbles over and over in the dust before us. It is Ofun and Oshe who are copulating on the tray. Ifa says, okay, as long as you're not sisters and brothers by blood. Okay, as long as you're not parents and children. Okay, as long as you're not first cousins. Ifa says you must avoid incest like the plague. Ifa says it is the great taboo. Sacrifice, so that you do not get in bed with someone who is too closely related. Sacrifice so that an incestuous relationship does not become your downfall.

Ofun Meji   Rank   16

Greetings. It is Ofun Meji who has come out of the divining jar next. It is Ofun Meji who is out of the closet now. And at this point, the diviners stood and with a bit of camwood dust, wrote the figure of Ofun Meji on the wall, beside the one they had written earlier in chalk of Oshe Meji, his sister. This will serve to protect us further, they said. For despite his indiscretions, Ofun Meji has great power. Ifa says someone is not as bad as you think, after all is said and done. Ifa says one who appears to be in last place is actually more prominent than you think. Ifa says power is everything. But even the powerful need to sacrifice to keep their position. Ifa says sacrifice, then, and let us get on with our lives. Sacrifice, and let us achieve our personal destinies, no matter what they might be.

All Odu have spoken. *Ashe*. And praises.

Appendix B

The Ranking of the Odu Pairs

This listing of the 256 Odu figures of Ifa is consistent with the methods used in the City of Ife, historic center of Nigerian divination.

The Appendix comes in handy for choosing among specific alternatives (see Readings # 17, #18, and #19). All you have to do is look up your Odu pairs and note which rank each one is. The higher-ranking figure (which is to say the one with the lower number) is the winner. It points to your answer.

If you'd like to learn how to compute the ranks for yourself (thus avoiding having to turn to this Appendix all the time), here's how it works. . . .

Just remember that the single figures (or half legs) of Ifa are ranked from 1 to 16 like this. . . .

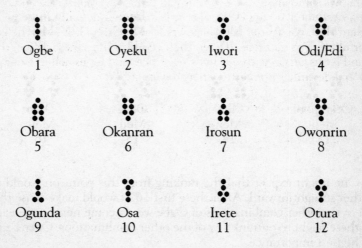

| Ogbe | Oyeku | Iwori | Odi/Edi |
| 1 | 2 | 3 | 4 |

| Obara | Okanran | Irosun | Owonrin |
| 5 | 6 | 7 | 8 |

| Ogunda | Osa | Irete | Otura |
| 9 | 10 | 11 | 12 |

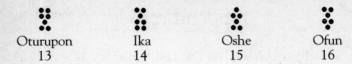

Oturupon	Ika	Oshe	Ofun
13	14	15	16

The highest-ranking Odu pairs (or twins) are also ranked in the same way. . . .

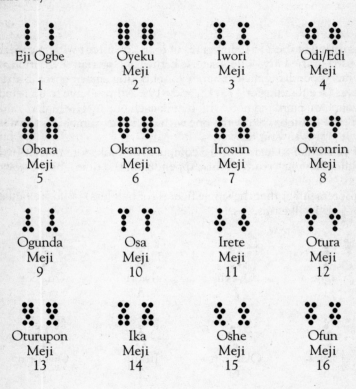

Eji Ogbe	Oyeku Meji	Iwori Meji	Odi/Edi Meji
1	2	3	4

Obara Meji	Okanran Meji	Irosun Meji	Owonrin Meji
5	6	7	8

Ogunda Meji	Osa Meji	Irete Meji	Otura Meji
9	10	11	12

Oturupon Meji	Ika Meji	Oshe Meji	Ofun Meji
13	14	15	16

One might expect that the ranking from this point on would be rather straightforward. After these first 16, it would make sense that all of the other combinations of Ogbe would come next, since each of these ought to outrank any of the other combinations, Ogbe being of highest importance.

That would be easy to remember. But a good diviner needs a mystery or two to keep his magic secret, so the sequence of the remaining Odu is encrypted with a further rule. . . .

The 17th figure is not—as one would expect—Ogbe Oyeku (▦ ▌), but rather Oshe Otura (⸪ ⸪). To appreciate why, you have to know the myth of how all these Odu figures got their ranks.

According to legends told by the diviners in Africa, the 16 Odu twins were born of the god of divination himself, Ifa (also known as Orunla or Orunmila). Their rank in the sequences represents the order in which they were born. Except . . . for Ofun Meji, (⸪ ⸪), who comes last. This was not always so. In fact, Ofun Meji was once not last in line, but first. How did he land up in last, instead of first place? Well, accounts range from incest to ineptness in public office, but at any rate he did something very, very wrong with the power that had been bestowed on him.

Oshe Otura comes 17th in line, because under Ofun Meji she was the servant of Ofun and all the other Meji (perfect pairs). When Eji Ogbe came to overthrow Ofun Meji, it was Oshe Otura who greeted him first. And therefore, she has the honor of coming directly after the perfect pairs.

After her come all of Ogbe's "children," the other pairs (15 in all) formed first by Ogbe and each of the other figures in turn:

Oshe Otura 17	Ogbe Oyeku 18	Ogbe Iwori 19	Ogbe Odi 20
Ogbe Obara 21	Ogbe Okanran 22	Ogbe Irosun 23	Ogbe Owonrin 24
Ogbe Ogunda 25	Ogbe Osa 26	Ogbe Irete 27	Ogbe Otura 28

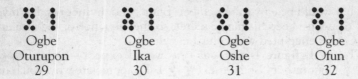

Ogbe	Ogbe	Ogbe	Ogbe
Oturupon	Ika	Oshe	Ofun
29	30	31	32

Then come Oyeku's children, Iwori's children, Odi's children, and so on . . . until at last the lowest-ranking figure of them all (number 256) is Ofun Oshun.

Some diviners had an additional twist, which you are welcome to try—but it gets awfully confusing.

First a bit more mythology as background: For, according to legend, it seems Ofun Meji, being a man who once had tasted power, was not satisfied to be in last place for very long. So he started up the ranks, fighting each Odu twin ahead of him. And he defeated all of them, all the way up to Owonrin Meji (in eighth place). Since his fight with Owonrin was a draw, that is the place where he had to be satisfied to remain, smack-dab in the middle.

To honor Ofun Meji for his spirited comeback, the ranking of the Odu figures can be modified to illustrate the point that Owonrin and Ofun are actually tied. In this interesting twist . . .

First of all, Owonrin Meji ( ) and Ofun Meji ( ) share eighth place among the primary Odu pairs. Any child of an Odu that contains either Owonrin and Ofun also shares the same rank; for example, among Ogbe's kids . . .

Oshe	Ogbe	Ogbe	Ogbe
Otura	Oyeku	Iwori	Odi
17	18	19	20

Ogbe	Ogbe	Ogbe	Ogbe
Obara	Okanran	Irosun	Owonrin
21	22	23	24

Ogbe Ogunda 26	Ogbe Osa 27	Ogbe Irete 28	Ogbe Otura 29
Ogbe Oturupon 30	Ogbe Ika 31	Ogbe Oshe 32	Ogbe Ofun 24

You are welcome to use either ranking system, both of which are indicated in the tables in this Appendix. Just look up each Odu pair you have cast, and jot down its rank number. The Odu pair with the higher rank (lower number) is the one that points to your answer. The rank order listed with each figure in the Master Answer section is the "simple" rank in the following chart.

		Simple RANK	*Complex* RANK
	Eji Ogbe	1	1
	Ogbe Oyeku	18	18
	Ogbe Iwori	19	19
	Ogbe Odi	20	20
	Ogbe Obara	21	21

		Simple RANK	Complex RANK
	Ogbe Okanran	22	22
	Ogbe Irosun	23	23
	Ogbe Owonrin	24	24
	Ogbe Ogunda	25	26
	Ogbe Osa	26	27
	Ogbe Irete	27	28
	Ogbe Otura	28	29
	Ogbe Oturupon	29	30
	Ogbe Ika	30	31
	Ogbe Oshe	31	32
	Ogbe Ofun	32	24

		Simple RANK	Complex RANK
	Oyeku Ogbe	33	33

			Simple RANK	Complex RANK
		Oyeku Meji	2	2
		Oyeku Iwori	34	34
		Oyeku Odi/Edi	35	35
		Oyeku Obara	36	36
		Oyeku Okanran	37	37
		Oyeku Irosun	38	38
		Oyeku Owonrin	39	39
		Oyeku Ogunda	40	41
		Oyeku Osa	41	42
		Oyeku Irete	42	43
		Oyeku Otura	43	44
		Oyeku Oturupon	44	45
		Oyeku Ika	45	46
		Oyeku Oshe	46	47
		Oyeku Ofun	47	39

		Simple RANK	Complex RANK
Iwori Ogbe		48	48
Iwori Oyeku		49	49
Iwori Meji		3	3
Iwori Odi		50	50
Iwori Obara		51	51
Iwori Okanran		52	52
Iwori Irosun		53	53
Iwori Owonrin		54	54
Iwori Ogunda		55	56
Iwori Osa		56	57
Iwori Irete		57	58
Iwori Otura		58	59
Iwori Oturupon		59	60
Iwori Ika		60	61
Iwori Oshe		61	62
Iwori Ofun		62	54

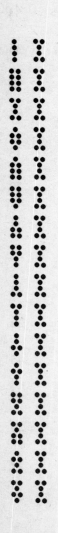

	Simple RANK	Complex RANK
Odi Ogbe	63	63
Odi Oyeku	64	64
Odi Iwori	65	65
Odi Meji	4	4
Odi Obara	66	66
Odi Okanran	67	67
Odi Irosun	68	68
Odi Owonrin	69	69
Odi Ogunda	70	71
Odi Osa	71	72
Odi Irete	72	73
Odi Otura	73	74
Odi Oturupon	74	75
Odi Ika	75	76
Odi Oshe	76	77
Odi Ofun	77	69

	Simple RANK	Complex RANK
Obara Ogbe	78	78
Obara Oyeku	79	79
Obara Iwori	80	80
Obara Odi	81	81
Obara Meji	5	5
Obara Okanran	82	82
Obara Irosun	83	83
Obara Owonrin	84	84
Obara Ogunda	85	86
Obara Osa	86	87
Obara Irete	87	88
Obara Otura	88	89
Obara Oturupon	89	90
Obara Ika	90	91
Obara Oshe	91	92
Obara Ofun	92	84

			Simple RANK	Complex RANK
		Okanran Ogbe	93	93
		Okanran Oyeku	94	94
		Okanran Iwori	95	95
		Okanran Odi	96	96
		Okanran Obara	97	97
		Okanran Meji	6	6
		Okanran Irosun	98	98
		Okanran Owonrin	99	99
		Okanran Ogunda	100	101
		Okanran Osa	101	102
		Okanran Irete	102	103
		Okanran Otura	103	104
		Okanran Oturupon	104	105
		Okanran Ika	105	106
		Okanran Oshe	106	107
		Okanran Ofun	107	99

			Simple RANK	Complex RANK
		Irosun Ogbe	108	108
		Irosun Oyeku	109	109
		Irosun Iwori	110	110
		Irosun Odi	111	111
		Irosun Obara	112	112
		Irosun Okanran	113	113
		Irosun Meji	7	7
		Irosun Owonrin	114	114
		Irosun Ogunda	115	116
		Irosun Osa	116	117
		Irosun Irete	117	118
		Irosun Otura	118	119
		Irosun Oturupon	119	120
		Irosun Ika	120	121
		Irosun Oshe	121	122
		Irosun Ofun	122	114

		Simple RANK	Complex RANK
Owonrin Ogbe		123	123
Owonrin Oyeku		124	124
Owonrin Iwori		125	125
Owonrin Odi		126	126
Owonrin Obara		127	127
Owonrin Okanran		128	128
Owonrin Irosun		129	129
Owonrin Meji		8	8
Owonrin Ogunda		130	130
Owonrin Osa		131	131
Owonrin Irete		132	132
Owonrin Otura		133	133
Owonrin Oturupon		134	134
Owonrin Ika		135	135
Owonrin Oshe		136	136
Owonrin Ofun		137	137

		Simple RANK	Complex RANK
Ogunda Ogbe		138	138
Ogunda Oyeku		139	139
Ogunda Iwori		140	140
Ogunda Odi		141	141
Ogunda Obara		142	142
Ogunda Okanran		143	143
Ogunda Irosun		144	144
Ogunda Owonrin		145	145
Ogunda Meji		9	10
Ogunda Osa		146	147
Ogunda Irete		147	148
Ogunda Otura		148	149
Ogunda Oturupon		149	150
Ogunda Ika		150	151
Ogunda Oshe		151	152
Ogunda Ofun		152	145

Appendix B

	Simple RANK	Complex RANK
Osa Ogbe	153	153
Osa Oyeku	154	154
Osa Iwori	155	155
Osa Odi	156	156
Osa Obara	157	157
Osa Okanran	158	158
Osa Irosun	159	159
Osa Owonrin	160	160
Osa Ogunda	161	162
Osa Meji	10	11
Osa Irete	162	163
Osa Otura	163	164
Osa Oturupon	164	165
Osa Ika	165	166
Osa Oshe	166	167
Osa Ofun	167	160

			Simple RANK	Complex RANK
		Irete Ogbe	168	168
		Irete Oyeku	169	169
		Irete Iwori	170	170
		Irete Odi	171	171
		Irete Obara	172	172
		Irete Okanran	173	173
		Irete Irosun	174	174
		Irete Owonrin	175	175
		Irete Ogunda	176	177
		Irete Osa	177	178
		Irete Meji	11	12
		Irete Otura	178	179
		Irete Oturupon	179	180
		Irete Ika	180	181
		Irete Oshe	181	182
		Irete Ofun	182	175

			Simple RANK	Complex RANK
		Otura Ogbe	183	183
		Otura Oyeku	184	184
		Otura Iwori	185	185
		Otura Odi	186	186
		Otura Obara	187	187
		Otura Okanran	188	188
		Otura Irosun	189	189
		Otura Owonrin	190	190
		Otura Ogunda	191	192
		Otura Osa	192	193
		Otura Irete	193	194
		Otura Meji	12	13
		Otura Oturupon	194	195
		Otura Ika	195	196
		Otura Oshe	196	197
		Otura Ofun	197	190

			Simple RANK	Complex RANK
		Oturupon Ogbe	198	198
		Oturupon Oyeku	199	199
		Oturupon Iwori	200	200
		Oturupon Odi	201	201
		Oturupon Obara	202	202
		Oturupon Okanran	203	203
		Oturupon Irosun	204	204
		Oturupon Owonrin	205	205
		Oturupon Ogunda	206	207
		Oturupon Osa	207	208
		Oturupon Irete	208	209
		Oturupon Otura	209	210
		Oturupon Meji	13	14
		Oturupon Ika	210	211
		Oturupon Oshe	211	212
		Oturupon Ofun	212	205

Appendix B

		Simple RANK	Complex RANK
Ika Ogbe		213	213
Ika Oyeku		214	214
Ika Iwori		215	215
Ika Odi		216	216
Ika Obara		217	217
Ika Okanran		218	218
Ika Irosun		219	219
Ika Owonrin		220	220
Ika Ogunda		221	222
Ika Osa		222	223
Ika Irete		223	224
Ika Otura		224	225
Ika Oturupon		225	226
Ika Meji		14	15
Ika Oshe		226	227
Ika Ofun		227	220

		Simple RANK	Complex RANK
Oshe Ogbe		228	228
Oshe Oyeku		229	229
Oshe Iwori		230	230
Oshe Odi		231	231
Oshe Obara		232	232
Oshe Okanran		233	233
Oshe Irosun		234	234
Oshe Owonrin		235	235
Oshe Ogunda		236	237
Oshe Osa		237	238
Oshe Irete		238	239
Oshe Otura		17	17
Oshe Oturupon		239	240
Oshe Ika		240	241
Oshe Meji		15	16
Oshe Ofun		241	235

			Simple RANK	Complex RANK
		Ofun Ogbe	242	242
		Ofun Oyeku	243	243
		Ofun Iwori	244	244
		Ofun Odi	245	245
		Ofun Obara	246	246
		Ofun Okanran	247	247
		Ofun Irosun	248	248
		Ofun Owonrin	249	137
		Ofun Ogunda	250	250
		Ofun Osa	251	251
		Ofun Irete	252	252
		Ofun Otura	253	253
		Ofun Oturupon	254	254
		Ofun Ika	255	255
		Ofun Oshe	256	256
		Ofun Meji	16	8

Selected Bibliography

A great many reference materials were used as background in the writing of this book. The ones I found most useful were . . .

Primary Sources

William Bascom, *Ifa Divination—Communication between Gods and Men in West Africa*, Bloomington, IN: Indiana University Press, 1969, 1991.

William Bascom, *16 Cowries—Yoruba Divination from Africa to the New World*, Bloomington, IN: Indiana University Press, 1980, 1993.

Awo Fa'lokun Fatunmbi (Donald G. Wilson), *Ifa and the Theology of Orisha Divination* (1992), and *Iwa-Pele—Ifa Quest, The Search for the Source of Santeria and Lucumi* (1991), Bronx, NY: Original Publications.

Judith Gleason, *A Recitation of Ifa, Oracle of the Yoruba*, New York: Grossman Publishers, 1973. (I also recommend Judith Gleason's *Leaf and Bone—African Praise Poems*, Penguin Books, 1994.)

Migene González Wippler, *Introduction to Seashell Divination* (1992), and *Rituals and Spells of Santeria* (1984), Bronx, NY: Original Publications.

Secondary Sources

Michael Loewe and Carmen Blacker, editors, *Oracles and Divination*, Boulder, CO: Shambhala Press, 1981.

Joseph M. Murphy, *Santeria—An African Religion in America*, Boston: Beacon Press, 1988.

Philip John Neimark, *The Way of the Orisa—Empowering Your Life Through the Ancient African Religion of Ifa*, Harper San Francisco: 1993.

Selected Bibliography

Philip M. Peek, editor, *African Divination Systems—Ways of Knowing*, Bloomington, IN: Indiana University Press, 1991.

Stephen Skinner, *Terrestrial Astrology—Divination by Geomancy*, London: Routledge & Kegan Paul, 1980.

Useful Background Materials

Donald Attwater, *Dictionary of Saints*, New York: Penguin Books, 1965, 1983.

Sandra T. Barnes, editor, *Africa's Ogun—Old World and New*, Bloomington, IN: Indiana University Press, 1989.

Jack Berry and Richard Spears, editors, *West African Folk Tales*, Evanstan, IL: Northwestern University Press, 1991.

Alison Jones, *Saints*, Endinburgh: W. & R. Chambers, Ltd., 1992.

Alvin M. Josephy, Jr., editor, *The Horizon History of Africa*, New York: American Heritage Publishing Co., 1971.

John S. Mbiti, *African Religions and Philosophy*, Garden City, NY: Anchor Books, 1970.

John E. Eberegbulam Njoku, *A Dictionary of Igbo Names, Culture, and Proverbs*, Washington, DC: University Press of America, 1978.

Kalu Ogbaa, *Gods, Oracles and Divination*, Trenton, NJ: African World Press, 1992.

Julia Stewart, *African Names*, New York: Citadel Press, 1993.

Claudia Zaslavsky, *Africa Counts—Number and Pattern in African Culture*, Chicago: Lawrence Hill Books, 1979, 1990.

Tangential Sources

C. G. Berger, M.D., *Our Phallic Heritage*, New York: Greenwich Book Publishers, Inc., 1966.

Hy Freedman, *Sex Link, The Three-Billion-Year-Old Urge and What the Animals Do About It*, New York: M. Evans & Co., 1977.

Richard Payne Knight and Thomas Wright, *Sexual Symbolism—A History of Phallic Worship*, including "A Discourse on the Worship of

Priapus" and "The Worship of the Generative Powers," New York: The Julian Press, 1957 (originally published in 1781).

Franz Steiner, *Taboo*, New York: Philosophical Library, 1956.

Lee Alexander Stone, M.D., *The Story of Phallicism*, Chicago: Pascal Covici Publishers, 1927.

Hutton Webster, Ph.D., *Primitive Secret Societies—A Study in Early Politics and Religion*, New York: The Macmillan Company, 1908.

Hutton Webster, *Taboo—A Sociological Study*, New York: Octagon Books, 1973.

Bernard Weiner, *Boy into Man—A Father's Guide to Initiation of Teenage Sons*, San Francisco: Transformation Press, 1992.

Some Other African Divination Systems to Try

Raymond Buckland and Kathleen Binger, *The Book of African Divination—Interpreting the Forces of Destiny with Techniques from Venda, Zulu, and Yoruba*, Rochester, VT: Destiny Books, 1992.

Ulufudu, *The Zulu Bone Oracle*, Berkeley, CA: Wingbow Press, 1989.

Index

ALL THE QUESTIONS YOU CAN ASK
(And Everything You Can Do)

Once you have mastered the basic techniques described in the Readings, you are welcome to use this Index of questions to help you focus in on topics and specific Readings you want to do tonight. For easier look-up and in order to give you a sense of what each Reading covers, I've arranged the listings in Reading-number order (like an outline). This side-by-side comparison of equivalent Readings from Part I and Part II of the book will also help you compare how the two parts of the book differ, if you're trying to decide down which path to head. Or you might also consider it as a framework for using both parts of the book together.

The Index to the Methods, which follows this topical outline, will point you to the place in the book where key concepts and techniques are introduced. It will also help you find tables and other useful reference material that you might want to refer to later.

425

Overview of Part I

Reading #2

What is my destiny?
Where does this road lead me?
What is my horoscope?
What is my sign?
What do I need to know?
In general? Right now?
What is my African spirit?

Reading #3

How is my love life?
**How is my relationship going
with _____?**
How can we make things go
better?
**Is there any future in this love
affair?**
If we go through with it, what
then?
What is <u>our</u> destiny?
**What was the meaning of my
relationship with
_____?**

Reading #4

How can I get ahead?
Financially? Job-wise?
**How will my money go this
year?**
**How can I get myself out of
the red?**
A better job?
**What will happen if I take this
offer?** Position? Risk?
**Did I make the right financial
decision?**

Overview of Part II

Reading #12

True? or False?
How must I refrain?
What is my taboo?

Reading #13

What animal am I?
What is my mascot?
Who is my mentor?
My hero? My role model?
**Who will lead me through this
part of the book?**
Who is my spirit guide?

Reading #14

What must I prove?
What challenge must I face?
What hurdles must I leap?
What bridges must I cross?
How can I improve myself?
What weakness should I focus
on?
What goal should I set?
How can I be a better man?
How can I become the person I
was born to be?

Index

Overview of Part I

Reading #5

What should I do?
How can I get what I want?
  Out of life? In this lifetime?
**What will make things work
out for me?**
What should my plan be?
  My strategy?
**How can I resolve the problem
that I face?**

Reading #6

What are my blessings?
  How will I be blessed?
**What blessing is coming my
way?** Next week? This year?
**What do I need to watch out
for?** In love? In general?
How am I cursed? What's my
problem?

Reading #7

What must I give? To assure
success? To gain love? To
have more money?
What should I give up? To
assure long life? Feel personal
pride?
What is my sacrifice?
What must I stay away from?
What is my taboo?
What should I never do?

Overview of Part II

Reading #15

What's in it for me? What will
I get out of working at this
place?
**What will I get if I take this
new job?** The big
promotion? The step down?
What if I quit tomorrow?
What do I have coming to me?
As a result of the long hours I
have put in? For my loyalty?
**Will there be anything extra in
my pay?** Anytime soon?

Reading #16

Who are my enemies?
  In the workplace?
  On the street? In this
  endeavor?
Who are my rivals?
  My competitors? My
  challengers?
**How can I overcome my
enemies?**

Reading #17

What are my alternatives?

427

Overview of Part I

Reading #8

What will make me feel better?
About myself? My situation?
The one I love?
How can I purify myself? Pamper myself? Prepare myself?
What will soothe my spirit? Relieve my tensions? Dispel my worries? Pain? Grief? Anguish? Anxiety? Whatever?
What is the cure for that which ails me? Bugs me? Fails me?
What do you prescribe?

Reading #9

What should I do about ____?
Why do I feel ____?
How should I proceed with ____?
How will ____ turn out?
What prevents me from ____?

Overview of Part II

Reading #18

How far can I go?
In my chosen line of work?
In my present job? in love?
At life in general?
How far can I get?
In my relationship with X?
In my dealings with Z?
In learning this oracle?
In discovering myself?

Reading #19

What can I do about ____?
How can I get ____?
What will result from ____?
How will ____ turn out?
What is the point of doing ____?
How can I overcome ____?

INDEX TO THE METHODS

Part I
Erindinlogun (seashell divination)

* Extra Credit section
** Extra, Extra Credit section

PART II
Ifa (palm-nut divination)

* Extra Credit section
** Extra, Extra Credit section

Index

* Extra Credit section
** Extra, Extra Credit section

Acknowledgments

There was a particular set of songs that I listened to while I worked on the White Cotton Road (the first part of this book). I'd like to acknowledge the artists listed here for their part in providing me with the backdrop music for seashell divination. Since all of the songs featured such great beats, thanks especially to the drummers.

Genesis, *Genesis Live: The Way We Walk*, Vol. 2: The Longs, Atlantic Records, 1992: "Driving the Last Spike" and "Home by the Sea."

Midnight Oil, *Earth and Sun and Moon*, Columbia, 1993: "The Drums of Heaven."

Tina Turner, *Private Dancer*, Capitol Records, 1984: "I Can't Stand the Rain" and "Show Some Respect."

Yothu Yindi, *Tribal Voice*, Mushroom Records, 1992: "Tribal Voice" and "Treaty."

Jon Secada, *Jon Secada*, EMI Records, 1992: "Do You Believe in Us" and "I'm Free."

Jimi Hendrix, *The Ultimate Experience*, MCA Records, 1993: "Red House" and "Purple Haze."

Tracy Chapman, *Matters of the Heart*, Electra Records, 1992: "I Used to Be a Sailor" and "Dreaming on a World."

Arrested Development, *3 Years, 5 Months, and 2 Days in the Life*, Chrysalis Records, 1992: "Washed Away" and "Mr. Wendel."

- **Janet Jackson,** *Rhythm Nation—1814,* A&M Records, 1989: "Rhythm Nation" and "Escapade."

- **Brent Lewis,** *Earth Tribe Rhythms,* Ikauma Records, 1990: "Bone to Bone" and "Tribal Consciousness."

Elton John, *Duets,* MCA Records, 1993: (with k.d. lang) "Teardrops" and (with RuPaul) "Don't Go Breaking My Heart."

- **Sade,** *Love Deluxe,* Epic Records, 1992: "No Ordinary Love" and "Cherish the Day."

- **Michael Jackson,** *Dangerous,* Epic Records, 1991: "In the Closet" and "Black or White."

- **Diana Ross,** *25 #1 Hits from 25 Years,* Vol. 1 and Vol 2., Motown Records, 1985: (with Lionel Richie) "Endless Love" and (with The Supremes) "You Can't Hurry Love."

- **Prince,** *Graffiti Bridge,* Warner Bros., 1990: "Graffiti Bridge" and "Can't Stop This Feeling I Got."

- **The Neville Brothers,** *Live on Planet Earth,* A&M Records, 1994: "Sands of Time" and "Congo Square."

- **Kwamé & a New Beginning,** *Nastee,* Atlantic Records, 1992: "These Wordz" and (with Tasha Lambert) "Without You."

- **A Tribe Called Quest,** *Midnight Marauders,* Zamba Records, 1993: "Sucka Nigga" and "Oh, My God."

- **Da Lench Mob,** *Guerillas in Tha Mist,* Atlantic Records, 1992: "Buck the Devil" and "Guerillas in tha Mist."

Genesis, *Genesis Live: The Way We Walk,* Vol. 1: The Shorts, Atlantic Records, 1992: "Jesus He Knows Me."

In writing the male part of the book, an expanded soundtrack—sharing many songs with the first, but in a different order—proved equally inspirational. I would like to thank everyone who contributed to the audio portion of this endeavor to understand Ifa.

Midnight Oil, *Earth and Sun and Moon*, Columbia, 1993: "Feeding Frenzy," "My Country," "Bushfire," and "The Drums of Heaven."

Brent Lewis, *Earth Tribe Rhythms*, Ikauma Records, 1990: "Tribal Consciousness," "Voodoo You're Mine," "Doom Tac A Doom," and "Bone to Bone."

Yothu Yindi, *Tribal Voice*, Mushroom Records, 1992: "Gapu," "Treaty," "Dhum Dhum," and "Tribal Voice."

Prince, *Graffiti Bridge*, Warner Bros., 1990: "Can't Stop this Feeling I Got," "New Power Generation," "Tick, Tick, Bang," "Thieves in the Temple," and "Graffiti Bridge."

Janet Jackson, *Rhythm Nation—1814*, A&M Records, 1989: "Interlude: Livin' in Complete Darkness," "Interlude: Let's Dance," "Miss You Much," "Escapade," "Someday Is Tonight," and "Rhythm Nation."

Toto, *Toto 4*, CBS Records, 1982: "Make Believe," "Good for You," "Afraid of Love," and "Africa."

Arrested Development, *3 Years, 5 Months, and 2 Days in the Life*, Chrysalis Records, 1992: "Eve of Reality," "Man's Final Frontier," "Mr. Wendel," "Fishin' for Religion," and "Washed Away."

Tina Turner, *Private Dancer*, Capitol Records, 1984: "I Can't Stand the Rain," "What's Love Got to Do With It," "Steel Claw," and "Show Some Respect."

Jimi Hendrix, *The Ultimate Experience*, MCA Records, 1993: "Fire," "Purple Haze," "Manic Depression," and "Red House."

Diana Ross, *25 #1 Hits from 25 Years*, Vol. 1 and Vol 2., Motown Records, 1985: "You Can't Hurry Love," "Baby Love"

Acknowledgments

"Ain't No Mountain High Enough," and (with Lionel Richie) "Endless Love."

Elton John, *Duets*, MCA Records, 1993: (with RuPaul) "Don't Go Breaking My Heart," (with k.d. lang) "Teardrops," and (with Marcella Detroit) "Ain't Nothing Like the Real Thing."

Jon Secada, *Jon Secada*, EMI Records, 1992: "I'm Free," "Just Another Day," "Angel," and "Do You Believe in Us."

Sade, *Love Deluxe*, Epic Records, 1992: "No Ordinary Love," "Cherish the Day," "Bullet Proof Soul," and "Feel No Pain."

Ace of Base, *The Sign*, Arista Records, 1993: "Voulex-Vous Danser," "All That She Wants," "The Sign," and "Happy Nation."

Da Lench Mob, *Guerillas in Tha Mist*, Atlantic Records, 1992: "Buck the Devil," "Lord Have Mercy," "All On My Nut Sac," and "Guerillas in tha Mist."

A Tribe Called Quest, *Midnight Marauders*, Zamba Records, 1993: "A Million Stories," "Sucka Nigga," "Oh, My God," "Keep it Rollin'," and "The Chase, Part II."

Kwamé & a New Beginning, *Nastee*, Atlantic Records, 1992: "Nastee," "Don'tmatta," "Don't Wanna B Your Love Thang," (with Tasha Lambert) "Without U," and "U Got It."

The Neville Brothers, *Live on Planet Earth*, A&M Records, 1994: "Congo Square," "Her African Eyes," "Sands of Time," "Voodoo," and "Yellow Moon."

Tracy Chapman, *Matters of the Heart*, Electra Records, 1992: "Matters of the Heart," "I Used to Be a Sailor," "Dreaming on a World," "Woman's Work," and "Open Arms."

Michael Jackson, *Dangerous*, Epic Records, 1991: "In the Closet," "She Drives Me Wild," "Black or White," and "Keep the Faith."

Otis Redding, *The Dock of the Bay,* Atlantic Records, 1968: "(Sittin' on) The Dock of the Bay."

Genesis, *Genesis Live: The Way We Walk,* Vols. 1 and 2, Atlantic Records, 1992, 1993: "Land of Confusion," "Jesus He Knows Me," "Home by the Sea," "Driving the Last Spike," and "Drum Duet."

This book was written entirely on location, at The Claremont Apartments, 10th and Clinton Streets, Philadelphia, PA. Thanks to: Logan's restaurant for keeping me in black coffee; The Foodery for the candles, Marlboros, and headset batteries at all hours; and Michael Singer Realtors for keeping the heat cranked up so high, I was forced to write *African Oracles* in the nude—that is, of course, when I was not dancing. What can I say? It worked for me. I hope it works for you. *Ma re-wa,* my friend. Hello. Good-bye. And come back soon. Greetings.

It won't be long, it's not far away
You will see Orisha make it come true like a dream.

—Nigerian Diviner Maranoro Salako,
William Bascom translation

FASCINATING BOOKS
OF SPIRITUALITY
AND PSYCHIC DIVINATION

CLOUD NINE: A DREAMER'S DICTIONARY
by Sandra A. Thomson
77384-8/$6.99 US/$7.99 Can

SECRETS OF SHAMANISM:
TAPPING THE SPIRIT POWER
WITHIN YOU
by Jose Stevens, Ph.D. and Lena S. Stevens
75607-2/$5.99 US/$6.99 Can

TAROT IN TEN MINUTES
by R.T. Kaser
76689-2/$11.00 US/$15.00 Can

THE LOVERS' TAROT
*by Robert Mueller, Ph.D., and Signe E. Echols, M.S.,
with Sandra A. Thomson*
76886-0/$11.00 US/$13.00 Can

SEXUAL ASTROLOGY
by Marlene Masini Rathgeb
76888-7/$11.00 US/$15.00 Can